Fundame1 in Mathematics Education

Fundamental Constructs in Mathematics Education is a unique sourcebook crafted from classic texts, research papers and books in mathematics education. Linked together by the editors' narrative, the book provides a fascinating examination of, and insight into, key constructs in mathematics education and how they link together. The choice of constructs is based on (some of) the many constructs which have proved fruitful in research and which have informed choices made by teachers.

This book is divided into two parts: learning and teaching.

The first part includes views about how people learn from Plato to Dewey, as well as constructivism, activity theory and French didactiques. The second part includes extracts concerned with initiating, sustaining and bringing to a conclusion learners' work on mathematical tasks.

Fundamental Constructs in Mathematics Education provides access to a wide range of constructs in mathematics education, and will orient the reader towards important original sources. It is a valuable resource for anyone reading literature related to learning mathematics be they lecturer, teacher, adviser or higher degree student.

John Mason is Professor of Mathematics Education at The Open University.
Sue Johnston-Wilder is a Senior Lecturer at The Open University.

Companion Volumes

The companion volumes in this series are:

Mathematics Education: exploring the culture of learning
Edited by: Barbara Allen and Sue Johnston-Wilder

Researching Your Own Practice: the discipline of noticing
Author: John Mason

All of these books are part of a course: *Researching Mathematics Learning*, that is itself part of The Open University MA programme and part of the *Postgraduate Diploma in Mathematics Education* programme.

The Open University MA in Education

The Open University MA in Education is now firmly established as the most popular post-graduate degree for education professionals in Europe, with over 3,500 students registering each year. The MA in Education is designed particularly for those with experience of teaching, the advisory service, educational administration or allied fields.

Structure of the MA

The MA is a modular degree and students are therefore free to select from a range of options in the programme which best fits in with their interests and professional goals. Specialist lines in management and primary education and lifelong learning are also available. Study in The Open University's Advanced Diploma can also be counted towards the MA and successful study in the MA programme entitles students to apply for entry into The Open University Doctorate in Education programme.

OU Supported Open Learning

The MA in Education programme provides great flexibility. Students study at their own pace, in their own time, anywhere in the European Union. They receive specially prepared study materials supported by tutorials, thus offering the chance to work with other students.

The Graduate Diploma in Mathematics Education

The Graduate Diploma is a new modular diploma designed to meet the needs of graduates who wish to develop their understanding of teaching and learning mathematics. It is aimed at professionals in education who have an interest in mathematics including primary and secondary teachers, classroom assistants and parents who are providing home education. The aims of the Graduate Diploma are to:

- develop the mathematical thinking of students;
- raise students' awareness of ways people learn mathematics;
- provide experience of different teaching approaches and the learning opportunities they afford;
- develop students' awareness of, and facility with, ICT in the learning and teaching of mathematics; and
- develop students' knowledge and understanding of the mathematics which under-pins school mathematics

How to apply

If you would like to register for one of these programmes, or simply to find out more information about available courses, please request the *Professional Development in Education* prospectus by writing to the Course Reservations Centre, PO Box 724, The Open University, Walton Hall, Milton Keynes, MK7 6ZW, UK or by phoning 0870 900 0304 (from the UK) or +44 870 900 0304 (from outside the UK). Details can also be viewed on our web page www.open.ac.uk.

Fundamental Constructs in Mathematics Education

Edited by John Mason and Sue Johnston-Wilder

 RoutledgeFalmer
Taylor & Francis Group

LONDON AND NEW YORK

 The Open University

First published in 2004
by RoutledgeFalmer
2 Park Square, Milton Park, Abingdon, Oxon, OX14 4RN

Simultaneously published in the USA and Canada
by RoutledgeFalmer
270 Madison Ave, New York, NY 10016

Reprinted 2005

Transferred to Digital Printing 2008

RoutledgeFalmer is an imprint of the Taylor & Francis Group, an informa business

© 2004 Compilation, original and editorial material, The Open University

Typeset in Garamond by
Bookcraft Ltd, Stroud, Gloucestershire
Printed and bound in Great Britain by
TJI Digital, Padstow, Cornwall

British Library Cataloguing in Publication Data
A catalogue record for this book is available from the British Library

Library of Congress Cataloging in Publication Data
Fundamental constructs in mathematics education / edited by John Mason
and Sue Johnston-Wilder
        p. cm.
    Includes bibliographical references and index.
    1. Mathematics--Study and teaching (Elementary)–Handbooks, manuals, etc.
    2. Mathematics--Study and teaching (Secondary)–Handbooks, manuals, etc.
    I. Mason, John, 1944– II. Johnston-Wilder, Sue

    QA11.2.F86 2004
    510'.7'1--dc22   2003016652

ISBN 10: 0-415-32697-4 (hardback : alk. paper)
ISBN 10: 0-415-32698-2 (paperback : alk. paper)

ISBN 13: 978-0-415-32697-1 (hardback : alk. paper)
ISBN 13: 978-0-415-32698-8 (paperback : alk. paper)

Contents

Sources

The authors and the publishers wish to thank the following for allowing their work to be reproduced in the book.

Extracts reprinted by permission of the publisher from *Toward A Theory of Instruction* by Jerome S. Bruner, pp. 160, 161, 163, 44-5, 10, 12, 14 Cambridge, Mass.: The Belknap Press of Harvard University Press, copyright © 1966 by the President and Fellows of Harvard College.

Hewitt, D., 'Arbitrary and Necessary, Part 1: A Way of Viewing the Mathematics Curriculum', *For the Learning of Mathematics*. Extracts reprinted with permission of the publisher, FLM Publishing Association.

Marton, F. and Booth, S., *Learning and Awareness*, Erlbaum Mahwah, 1997. Extracts reprinted by permission of the publisher Lawrence Erlbaum Associates.

Hughes, M., *Children and Number: Difficulties in Learning Mathematics*, Blackwell, Oxford, 1986. Reprinted by permission of the Blackwell Publishing Limited.

Extracts from *The Psychology of Learning Mathematics* by Richard R. Skemp Penguin Books, 1971, copyright © Richard Skemp, 1971. Reproduced by permission of Penguin Books Ltd.

Extracts from *A Boolean Anthology: Selected Writings of Mary Boole on Mathematical Education*, D. Tahta, Derby, 1972. Reprinted by permission of The Association of Teachers of Mathematics.

Extracts from *What We Owe Children: The Subordination of Teaching to Learning* by Caleb Gattegno, Routledge & Kegan Paul, London, 1970. Reprinted by permission of Taylor & Francis Books Ltd.

Extracts reprinted with the permission of Scribner, an imprint of Simon & Schuster Adult Publishing Group, and with the permission of Cambridge University Press from *The Aims of Education and Other Essays* by Alfred North Whitehead. Copyright © 1929 by The Macmillan Company; copyright renewed © 1957 by Evelyn Whitehead.

Wheeler, D., 'Teaching for Understanding', *Mathematics Teaching* **33**, pp.45–7, 1965, Association of Teachers of Mathematics, Derby. Extracts reprinted by permission of The Association of Teachers of Mathematics.

Dewey, J., *The Child and the Curriculum & The School and Society*, University of Chicago Press, 1902. Copyright © J. Dewey, 1902. Extracts reprinted with permission of the University of Chicago Press.

Dewey, J., *How We Think: A Restatement of the Relation of Reflective Thinking to the Educative Process*, © 1933 by D. C. Heath & Company. Adapted with permission of Houghton Mifflin Company.

Teplow, D., 'Fresh Approaches: Promoting Teaching Excellence', www.acme-assn.org/almanac/jan97.htm. Extracts reprinted with permission of the Alliance for CME.

Table from 'Personal Theories of Teaching' by D. Fox, Studies in *Higher Education*, (1983) **8** (2), reprinted with permission of Taylor & Francis Journals, www.tandf.co.uk.

Figure from Pirie, S. and Kieren, T. (1989), 'A recursive theory of mathematical understanding', *For the Learning of Mathematics*, **9** (3). Reprinted by permission of FLM Publishing Association.

Two figures taken from 'A Study of Proof Conceptions in Algebra' by L. Healey & L. Hoyles in *The Journal for Research in Mathematics*, July 2000 (Figure 1, p. 400 and Figure 5, p. 404) Reprinted with permission from the *Journal for Research in Mathematics*, copyright © 2000 by the National Council for Teachers of Mathematics. All rights reserved.

Figure 'Interconnections' taken from *Thinking Mathematically* by Mason, Burton & Stacey © Addison Wesley Publishers Limited 1982, reprinted by permission of Pearson Education Limited.

Kluwer Academic Publishers for permission to use extracts from the following:

Bell, A. 'Principles for the Design of Teaching', *Education Studies in Mathematics*, Kluwer Academic Publishers, 1993.

Christiansen, B. and Walther, G., 'Task and Activity' in B. Christiansen, G. Howson and M. Otte, *Perspectives in Mathematics Education*, Dordrecht, Reidel, 1986 (Kluwer).

Fischbein, E., *Intuition in Science and Mathematics: An Educational Approach*, Reidel, Dordrecht 1987 (Kluwer).

Freudenthal, H., *Revisiting Mathematics Education: China Lectures*, Kluwer, Dordrecht, 1991.

Every attempt was made to contact the copyright holders of third party material. The publishers apologise for any omissions and will be happy to hear from anyone who has been missed.

Introduction

John Mason and Sue Johnston-Wilder

This book is part of a long-term project called *Meaning Enquiry in Mathematics Education* whose aim is to draw together in an accessible form the many distinctions, constructs, and strategies that inform and constitute the practice of teachers and educators, often without our being aware of it. This book concentrates on constructs.

Structure of the book

The first chapter is a collection of classic tasks that have been used repeatedly in the mathematics education literature. It provides readers with access to the original (or close to original) description of the task so that they can both try it out for themselves, and be knowledgeable when they encounter references to it in other writings.

The structure of the remainder of the book consists of relatively short extracts (from a few lines to several paragraphs) from the original authors who introduced or developed the particular construct, linked together by a commentary. The aim is to make the whole informative, and yet to provide access to the original voices, and to create a valuable reference for researchers and teachers. Sometimes a comment has been inserted into an extract to guide you or to refer you to related extracts. For added interest, we have taken the unusual step of including the author's birthplace.

The more we read earlier authors, the more connections we find between what different people have said in different ways. The result is that it is very difficult to find a coherent linear path through the vast range of observations and distinctions. You may wish to read the chapters in this book in order or you may wish to dip in and out of the book, for example, to follow a particular line of enquiry. To facilitate the latter, at various points in the text we have included references that point forwards and backwards to related topics set in italics. In addition, separate author and subject indexes are provided so extracts can be found easily.

Choices

Our interest is in locating and drawing attention to important and informative distinctions made by authors as a result of their research. In undertaking to extract passages from the lengthy and considered works of authors who have significantly influenced the development of mathematics education as a disciplined domain of enquiry, choices inevitably have to be made. We were somewhat surprised to find that it was often remarkably difficult to locate a clear but succinct statement of many of the constructs that we have found useful and that we wanted to include. There are also many more constructs that we would have liked to include but space has not permitted.

Recognising a tendency to alight on passages which resonate or challenge our experience, we realise that the passages chosen tell you as much about us as they do about mathematics education. Nevertheless, it is our hope that this collection will enable colleagues to experience some of the pleasure we have had in rediscovering the considered thoughts of earlier authors, and that this will stimulate colleagues to return to some of the original works from which these extracts have been drawn.

What is a construct?

Phenomena

In the context of mathematics education, a *phenomenon* is something that is distinguished from the flow of events and recognised as having happened previously: recognising it involves discerning some feature or aspect as (relatively) invariant in the midst of other things changing. For example:

- A child is seen using a physical object in order to help her think about a question.
- A teacher asks a class a question and pauses, waiting for learners to think about the question, then invites them to talk with a neighbour about the question before expecting them to contribute to the whole-class discussion. When one participant suddenly sees a way through and expresses excitement, others pick up the idea and elaborate on it.

In the first example, you might recognise that 'using a physical object to help you think' is something that people do naturally, and that teachers could encourage. In the second example, you might recognise that how long a teacher waits after asking a question is something that could serve as an indicator of teacher–learner interaction. Researchers then label the phenomenon in some way for easy reference: in the first case, perhaps *use of apparatus* or *use of manipulables*, and in the second case, *wait-time*. The label brings the phenomenon into existence as an object of thought, that can be discussed and negotiated between colleagues, and studied by individuals. Researchers then enquire into what is involved in the phenomenon, what makes the phenomenon effective, what effectiveness might mean, what learners experience, links to other aspects of teaching and learning, and so on.

Constructs

Enquiry and study lead to the formulation of *constructs* both to describe a phenomenon in a recognisable form (thus *apparatus* and *wait-time* become things) and to account for the phenomenon or to place it in some broader or more general context. Thus apparatus becomes an *enactive mode of interaction* involving a *representation*, and wait-time leads to *talking-in-pairs* as a pedagogic strategy to be employed and studied. *Class discussion* is identified as a social phenomenon to study; the mechanism of *infectious ideas* (a metaphor for ideas quickly spreading through a class) and a teacher belief or principle of *trying to do for the learners only what they cannot yet do for themselves* are identified. A great deal can come from noticing similarities in several observations!

A construct is experienced as an awareness. It is signified by a label for a distinction that has been and can be made. It is an abstraction from experience of a phenomenon. It may be a label for the phenomenon itself, or for something that explains or accounts for the phenomenon. It is usually associated with some action that has physical (a classroom practice), mental (recognition, theorising) and emotional (stimulation, judgement) components. With use the label comes to be the construct, so it is necessary from time to time to experience again the underlying awareness.

Frameworks

Constructs enable practitioners to function. A *framework* is a label or a set of labels for a collection of constructs. Labels act as triggers so that, in the midst of a situation, some possibility comes to mind associated with one or more constructs. Thus *enactive mode of interaction*, when combined with mental (iconic) and verbal–symbolic modes, becomes a framework: Jerome Bruner's *Enactive–Iconic–Symbolic* framework, which can come to inform teaching through acting as a reminder that learners need to be weaned from physical manipulation of apparatus through the use of mental images and memories of that enaction, to manipulating symbols which stand for or are exemplified by those images.

Use of frameworks of constructs

Since many constructs are implicit and are below the surface of immediate awareness, bringing them into awareness opens them up for validation, modification, and even replacement. Becoming aware of, adopting, and adapting effective frameworks enables teachers to discern phenomena more closely, to distinguish phenomena more sensitively, to notice more than they would be able to without the framework labels.

Constructs require rich personal experience if they are to be internalised and if they are to inform practice. Frameworks as collections of labels for constructs are only useful and effective when the label is founded on rich personal experience and associated with action. Consequently, it is important to exemplify the constructs and to base them in significant experience. One way to do this is to begin with a collection of *classic research tasks* which have entered the mathematics education literature and been taken up by numerous authors. Readers can then imagine or actually try them out for themselves, as well as use the constructs to think about the tasks and what they found, and employ the research findings to enrich their sense of the constructs.

Section 1

Activating and analysing learning

This is the first of the two sections making up the body of the text. It consists of extracts from a wide range of authors, addressing questions such as 'What does it mean to learn mathematics?' and 'What is actually learned?' It is followed by a section on guiding and directing learning.

This section begins with a collection of some of the classic tasks used by researchers to 'probe' learners' understanding. You are encouraged to try these with the learners with whom you work.

The section continues from Chapter 2 with a variety of constructs used in descriptions of what constitutes learning and of conditions which seem to foster and sustain learning. The extracts reveal an ongoing struggle to reach satisfactory definitions of learning, while illustrating a number of different approaches and analyses. The consensus is that learners need to be encouraged and supported in actively taking initiative in their learning. This raises the complex matter of motivation and affect, which attracts researchers to use a wide range of subtly different constructs. If learning involves action, then what learners bring to class to enable them to take initiative and to participate in those actions are natural powers of sense-making. What is learned is the use and extension of those powers applied to mathematical topics. The section ends with constructs which offer a means to expose underlying structure in any mathematical topic.

1 Probing thinking

Introduction

In this chapter we have brought together extracts which include brief descriptions of research tasks which have been designed to probe thinking and which have been taken up in the mathematics education literature and referred to by other workers over the years. The intention of this chapter is to give enough description that the interested reader can try these 'probes' with learners of mathematics.

The probes are arranged broadly in order of age of the learners:

- early years (including lower primary);
- middle years;
- later years (secondary and tertiary).

However, many of them are accessible to learners across a wide range of year groups.

Early years

Children's invention of written arithmetic

I decided to devise a game in which the children's written representations would serve a clear communicative purpose. The idea for this game arose fairly naturally from my earlier work with boxes and bricks. Young children seemed to be attracted by a closed box containing a number of bricks, and I thought they might be intrigued by the idea of putting a written message on the lid of a box to show how many bricks were inside.

The game centred on four identical tobacco tins, containing different numbers of bricks: usually there were three, two, one and no bricks inside each tin. After letting the child see inside the tins, I shuffled them around, and asked the child to pick out 'the tin with two bricks in', 'the tin with no bricks in' and so on. At this stage the child had no alternative but to guess. After a few guesses, I interrupted the game with 'an idea which might help'. I attached a piece of paper to the lid of each tin, gave the child a pen, and suggested that they 'put something on the paper' so that they would know how many bricks were inside. The children dealt with each tin in turn, its lid being removed so that they could see inside. When they had finished, the tins were shuffled around again, and the children were asked once more to identify particular tins and see whether their representations had 'helped them play the game'. The Tins game thus provided not only a clear rationale for making written representations, but also an opportunity to discover what children understood about what they had done.

I carried out a study in which I played the Tins game with twenty-five children, aged 3 years 1 month to 5 years 10 months. Fifteen of the children were in the nursery class and ten children in class 1 of a predominantly middle-class school. Each child was seen individually in a small room away from the classroom ... .

There was little doubt about the popularity of the game. The children found the initial guessing-game intriguing and were excited by the idea of making representations with paper and pencil. Several of their comments showed that they were very aware of how this could help them, such as: 'It's easy now coz I've done some writing.'

There was also little doubt that their representations did in fact help them play the game. Before they made their representations their ability to recognise each tin was at chance level, but afterwards their performance was significantly higher: over two-thirds of the pre-school group and every child in class 1 was able to identify the tins from their representations.

(Hughes, 1986, pp. 64–5)

I was impressed by the children's ability to recognise their representations, and was curious whether they would still be able to recognise them if some time had elapsed. I therefore returned to the school about a week later and showed each child the tins bearing the representations they had made the previous week. As before, I shuffled the tins, and the children had to guess which tin contained which number of bricks.

The results were striking: the children were just as good at recognising their representations a week later as they had been at the time. Those children ... who had made idiosyncratic representations and had been unable to recognise them during the first session, were also unable to recognise them a week later. On the other hand, both Richard and Paul were still able to recognise their idiosyncratic representations a week later, with Richard again spontaneously referring to the 'tail' on his representation of zero.

I also used this second visit to the school to find out whether those children who had initially produced any unrecognisable idiosyncratic representations would benefit from the chance to have another go. These children – there were seven, all in the pre-school group – were first asked: 'Would you like to try it again?' Most of the children simply responded by saying they couldn't or wouldn't think of another way to do it, while those who did try again were no more successful than before. I then suggested the idea of one-to-one correspondence by saying, for example, 'Why don't you make two marks on the tin with two bricks in?' The response to this was immediate. Five of the seven adopted the iconic strategy at once from a single example, generalising without further suggestions to the remaining tins. ... The other two children required further examples, but they too eventually adopted the rule. All these children were then able to identify their responses correctly. Thus, by the end of the study, all twenty-five children had produced recognisable sets of responses, with or without prompting.

(ibid., pp. 70–2)

Recognising shapes

For this activity, you need a collection of solid shapes (two copies of each). They might be made up from Multilink cubes, or come from a set of prisms and pyramids, they might be packages, etc.

Recognising 3-D shapes: Display one copy of each object, and place the second copy of one of them in a bag or *Feely box* [so that everyone except the 'player' can see]. Now get someone to feel the object and describe what features they are using to identify which of the visible shapes it is.

This is an example of becoming aware of what you are stressing in order to identify something.

Recognising 2-D shapes: Make up a collection of shapes, or a pack of cards with shape drawings ... on them, and sort them into groups. Provide a name for each group. Then look at how other people have sorted them, and try to work out the basis of their sorting, providing names for their groups. Then compare notes.

[...]

Revealing shapes: Construct a screen so that you can gradually reveal a large cardboard two-dimensional shape from behind it. Every so often, pause to get learners to discuss all the possible shapes it could be, to make a conjecture, and to say why they think that conjecture might be right.

(Mason, 1990, pp. 9–10)

Covered counting

A collection of objects (bottle tops, cubes, beans, ...) are counted by each and every learner present, and agreement reached as to the number of them (say 12). Eyes are closed, and some of the objects are hidden under a cloth. The remaining objects are clearly visible.

> The task is to figure out how many are hidden when there are seven visible and 12 in all. ... The child who needs to 'count all', and needs perceptual materials, is unable to solve this task as posed. Another child may be able to count on, saying, 'seven ... eight, nine, ten, eleven, twelve', while putting up one finger with each number word, beginning at eight. She may then notice that five fingers are up and report five as the answer. Another child may proceed in almost the same way but may need to count the fingers that are up to know that five have been counted. Yet another child might say, 'I know that 8 + 4 is 12 so 7 + 5 must be 12. So there are five hiding.' This child is using a thinking strategy approach.
>
> (Cobb and Merkel, 1989, quoted in Yackel, 2001, p. 19)

(See Floyd *et al.*, 1982, Block 2 for an equivalent alternative.)

Children making sense

Listening to children, and following their line of thought can be most rewarding. It can also provide insight into the delicate and lengthy process of making sense through acting according to current conjectures and then modifying those conjectures as a result of feedback. In the following extract, a mother and her young child were having lunch when the window cleaner appeared in the garden. The mother went out to the kitchen to get him some water. While she was there she called out to a neighbour, Pamela.

> *Child:*   What did Pamela say?
> *Mother:*   She's having to pay everybody else's bills for the window-cleaner, 'cause they're all out.
> *Child:*   Why [are] they all out?
> *Mother:*   'Cause they're working or something.
> *Child:*   Aren't they silly!
> *Mother:*   Well, you have to work to earn money, don't you?
>
> (Tizard and Hughes, 1984, p. 120)

After an interlude for pudding, the child reverted to the conversation:

> 3 *Child:*   Umm ... she can't pay everybody's, er ... all the bills to the window cleaner, can she?

 4 *Mother:* No, she can't pay everybody's bills ... she sometimes pays mine if I'm out.
 5 *Child:* 'Cause it's fair.
 6 *Mother:* Mm, it is.
 7 *Child:* Umm, but where does she leave the money?
 8 *Mother:* She doesn't leave it anywhere, she hands it to the window cleaner, after he's finished.
 9 *Child:* And then she gives it to us?
10 *Mother:* No, no, she doesn't have to pay us.
11 *Child:* Then the window cleaner gives it to us.
12 *Mother:* No, we give the window cleaner money, he does work for us and we have to give him money.
13 *Child:* Why?
14 *Mother:* Well, because he's been working for us cleaning our windows. He doesn't do it for nothing.
15 *Child:* Why do you have money if you have ... if people clean your windows?
16 *Mother:* Well, the window cleaner needs money doesn't he?
17 *Child:* Why?
18 *Mother:* To buy clothes for his children and food for them to eat.
19 *Child:* Well, sometimes window cleaners don't have children.
20 *Mother:* Quite often they do.
21 *Child:* And something on his own to eat, and for curtains?
22 *Mother:* And for paying his gas bills and electricity bill. And for paying for his petrol for his car. All sorts of things you have to pay for, you see. You have to earn money somehow, and he earns it by cleaning other people's windows, and big shop windows and things.
23 *Child:* And then the person who got the money gives it to people ...

It seems until turn 11 the child was under the impression that the window-cleaner pays the housewives, and not the other way round. In the course of the conversation the relationship between work, money and goods is slowly outlined for her, but it is still unclear from her last remark whether she has really grasped all that has been said.

(ibid., pp. 120–1)

The authors concluded that the conversation of which this extract is part 'reveals something which is characteristic of the slow and gradual way in which a child's understanding of an abstract or complex topic is built up' (ibid., p. 122). It would seem that the child is aware that she has not grasped the full picture and she returns to the conversation repeatedly. In the end the adult closes it down, apparently before the child has fully resolved it to her satisfaction.

Knowing in action, knowing in words

> … in the case of a sling made of a ball attached to a string which the child whirls around and then throws into a box, it has been found that the action is performed successfully at age four to five after several tries, but its description is systematically distorted. The action itself is successful: the child releases the ball sideways, its trajectory tangential to the circumference of the circle described while being whirled. But he maintains that he released the ball either in front of the box or at the point of the circumference nearest to it, or even in front of himself, as if the ball pursued a straight line from himself to the box, first passing through the diameter of the circle described by his arm.
>
> The reason is first of all that in his eyes the action consists of two separate actions: whirling, then throwing (and not throwing alone). Second, it is usual to throw a ball into a box in a straight line perpendicular to the box. What is particularly curious is that although the action can be successfully executed at age four to five, a good description of it cannot usually be given before age nine to eleven. The object and the action itself (hence awareness of the latter) are doubtless perceived but are, as it were, 'repressed' because they contradict the child's preconceived ideas.
>
> (Piaget, 1973, p. 25)

Children invent subtraction

> Mark Davies is seven years two months old … . From a very early age he has displayed clear, mathematical talent and a capacity for abstract, logical thinking.
>
> In order to appreciate the significance of Mark's discovery, it is necessary to recall an occasion in his mathematical development. Once, when he was five, he asked me, "What is 1 take away 3?"
>
> Somewhat taken by surprise, I replied, "3 take away 1 is 2, agreed?"
>
> He agreed impatiently.
>
> "Well," I continued, "1 take away 3 is minus 2." (I realise that I may be reproached for using the term 'minus 2' and not the more fashionable term 'negative 2'.)
>
> I went on to say that it was rather like climbing up and down on the rungs of a ladder, and then attempted, in simple language, an explanation, using the ladder application approach, of what amounted to the addition and subtraction of integers. Mark was fascinated by my answer.
>
> It became apparent over the subsequent months that Mark could work out mentally problems similar to the one that he had posed, though I made no attempt to consolidate or develop his thinking about negative integers.
>
> A few days ago I asked Mark, "What is 16 take away 9?"

He gave the correct answer.

"How did you get the answer?" I enquired.

"Well," he replied, "6 take away 9 is minus 3, and 10 take away 3 is 7."

I was intrigued. Immediately I asked, "How would you take 29 from 47?"

His reply was, "7 take away 9 is minus 2, 40 take away 20 is 20, and 20 take away 2 is 18."

I asked him whether he could get the answer using a different method. His reply was, "Yes; 7 take away 9 is minus 2, 40 take away 2 is 38, and 38 take away 20 is 18."

(Davies, 1978, pp. 15–16)

The children were subtracting from 50 using dice and Dienes blocks. They were trying to get to 0. They wrote down 50 and subtracted the number shown on the die, using Dienes blocks as a check on their mental calculation. Jenny had 3 left and shook 5. She said: 'I can't take this away. I would owe two.' She tried this on a calculator and said: 'It is take away two.' She later tried to make other negative numbers, and she could do this. When given the problem 'The answer is –1. What is the question?', she produced a pattern of questions:

1 – 2

2 – 3

3 – 4

...

...

When asked what needed to be taken away from 100 to give –1, she said: 'Easy ... 101.' She said she always made the second number one bigger. She could use this method when the answer was –2, but not for –3.

(Shuard *et al.*, 1991, p. 16)

Concept learning from instances

Let us set before a subject all of the instances representing the various combinations of four attributes, each with three values ... an array of 81 cards, each varying in shape of figure, the number of figures, color of figure, and number of borders. We explain to the subject what is meant by a conjunctive concept – a set of the cards that share a certain set of attributes values, such as 'all red cards', or 'all cards containing red squares and two borders' – and for practice ask the subjects to show us all the exemplars of one sample concept. The subject is then told that we have a concept in mind and that certain cards before him illustrate it, others do not, and that it is his task to determine what this concept is. We will always begin by showing him a card or instance that is illustrative of the concept, a positive instance. His task is to choose cards for testing, one at a time, and after each choice we will tell him whether the card is positive or negative. He may hazard an hypothesis after any choice of a card, but he may not offer more than one hypothesis after any particular choice. If he does not wish to offer an hypothesis, he need not do so. He is asked to arrive at the concept as efficiently as possible. He may select the cards in any order he chooses. That, in essence, is the experimental procedure.

(Bruner *et al.*, 1956, p. 83)

The authors found four strategies being used in this task: testing one hypothesis at a time on each instance; trying to test all hypotheses simultaneously on each instance; imagining altering one attribute at a time of a positive instance to see if it remains a positive instance; and changing more than one attribute at once.

Recipes

You need $\frac{3}{8}$ cup of flour to make one muffin. You have 35 cups of flour. If you make all the muffins you can make with this flour, how much flour will you have left?

(Nunes, webref)

Such questions get low correct responses even from teachers! The lectures on the website includes other examples of probes used.

Conservation and invariance

... take the five-year-old, faced with two equal beakers, each filled to the same level with water. He will say that they are equal. Now pour the contents of one of the beakers into another that is taller and thinner and ask whether there is the same amount to drink in both. The child will deny it, pointing out that one of them has more because the water is higher. This incapacity to recognize invariance of magnitude across transformations in the appearance of things is one of the most striking aspects of this stage.

(Bruner, 1966, p. 13)

Horizontal and vertical arithmetic

This work began in the mid-1980s when Cobb first conducted a number of individual interviews with American first and second grade pupils designed to gain an understanding of their concepts of number, including numerical operations. Subsequently, such interviews became an integral part of our classroom-based research and were conducted by various members of the research team.

One question that was posed in a number of interviews is the following: 'Do you have a way to figure out how much is 16 + 9?' The problem was presented in horizontal format using plastic numerals. Students used a variety of methods, including counting methods. No matter which method the students used, virtually all of them answered with 25. Later in the same interview the pupils were presented with what appeared to be a typical school workbook page. One item the pupils were asked to answer was 16 + 9, this time written in vertical format.

Interestingly, for a number of pupils, the problem written in this format was a completely different task from the task they had completed earlier. This time a number of students attempted to use algorithmic procedures they had been taught in school. While some children obtained the correct answer of 25, other children answered with 15, still others with 115. What was most disturbing were the responses these children gave when asked about the discrepancy between these answers and their former answers of 25. For example, Cobb (1991) describes an episode with one girl who answered 15. He pointed out that she had obtained 25 when solving the problem presented in horizontal format. He had asked her if both answers could be right and if one answer was better. She responded that, if you were counting cookies, 25 would be right but that in school 15 was always right.

(Yackel, 2001, pp. 17–18)

L'âge du capitaine

This task gained such notoriety that it has been used and written about in many different countries, and generated an entire book on the way learners try to make sense of tasks they are given.

> Sur un bateau, il y a 26 moutons et 10 chèvres. Quel est l'âge du capitaine?
> [On a boat there are 26 sheep and 10 goats. What is the age of the captain?]
> (Baruk, 1985, p. 23)

All over the world (see, for example, Merseth, 1993, webref) teachers find that, whereas over the space of several years learners become proficient at adding two-digit numbers, a surprisingly high proportion of the responders to the captain's age problem (and others like it) continue to add the numbers in the question. Learners are not used to being asked questions you cannot do, and if they can see something obvious to do with the numbers, they often do it without thinking.

Variants used by Baruk (1985) included:

1   J'ai 4 sucettes dans ma poche droite et 9 caramels dans ma poche gauche. Quel est l'âge de mon papa? [I have 4 lollipops in my right pocket and 9 toffees in my left. How old is my father?]

2   Dans un bergerie il y a 125 moutons et 10 chiens. Quel est l'âge du berger? [There are 125 sheep and 10 dogs on a farm. How old is the shepherd?]

[…]

4   Dans une classe, il y a 12 filles et 13 garçons. Quel est l'âge de la maîtresse? [There are 12 girls and 13 boys in a class. How old is the teacher?]

5   Dans un bateau, il y a 36 moutons. 10 tombent à l'eau. Quel est l'âge du capitaine? [There are 36 sheep on a boat, but 10 fall in the water. How old is the captain?]

6   Il y a 7 rangées de 4 tables dans la classe. Quel est l'âge de la maîtresse? [There are 7 rows of 4 tables each in a classroom. How old is the teacher?]

(Baruk, 1985, p. 25)

There are close similarities with a study by Christine Shiu (1978) in which learners with no knowledge of Chinese were given problems presented in Chinese and in English (all numbers were in numerals). They scored higher on the Chinese than on the English problems!

Good conjecture, bad data

'Oh point five times oh point five is oh point twenty-five'
'Oh point four times oh point four is oh point sixteen'
'What is 0.3×0.3?'

On this experience, it is a good conjecture that the answer to the first question must be 'oh point nine'; however, the conjecture is based on 'bad data', for it is unwise to read decimals using 'teens'.

Middle years

Street arithmetic

Researchers observed and interviewed children selling things on the streets in Brazil, and contrasted their arithmetical competence on the street with their performance in school.

The children were approached by the interviewers on street corners or at markets where they worked alone or with their families. Interviewers chose subjects who seemed to be within the desired age range – schoolchildren or young adolescents – and obtained information about their age and level of schooling along with information on the prices of their merchandise. Test items in this situation were presented in the course of a normal sales transaction in which the researcher posed as a customer. Purchases were sometimes carried out. In other cases the 'customer' asked the vendor to perform calculations on possible purchases. At the end of the informal test, the children were asked to take part in a formal test, which was given on a separate occasion no more than a week later, and by the same interviewer. Subjects answered a total of 99 questions on the formal test and 63 questions on the informal test. Since the items in the formal test were based upon questions in the informal test, the order of testing was fixed for all subjects.

The informal test was carried out in Portuguese in the subject's natural working situation, that is, at street corners or an open market. Testers posed successive questions about potential or actual purchases and obtained verbal responses. Responses were either tape-recorded or written down by an observer, along with comments. After obtaining an answer for the item, testers questioned the subject about his or her method for solving the problem.

[…]

After subjects were interviewed in the natural situation, they were asked to participate in the formal part of the study, and a second inter-view was scheduled at the same place or at the subject's house. …

From all the mathematical problems successfully solved by each subject (regardless of whether they constituted a test item or not), a sample was chosen for inclusion in the subject's formal test. This sample was presented in the formal test either as a mathematical operation dictated to the subject (e.g., 105 + 105) or as a word problem (e.g., Mary bought *x* bananas; each banana cost *y*; how much did she pay alto-gether?). In either case, each subject solved problems employing the same numbers involved in his or her own informal test. Thus, quantities used varied from one subject to another.

[…]

In order to make the formal test situation more similar to the school setting, subjects were given paper and pencil and were encouraged to use them. When problems were nonetheless solved without recourse to writing, subjects were asked to write down their answers. Only one subject refused to do so, claiming that he did not know how to write. …

[…]

Problems presented in the streets were much more easily solved than ones presented in school-like fashion. We adjusted all scores to a 10-point scale for purposes of comparability. The overall percentage of correct responses in the informal test was 98.2 (in 63 problems solved by the 5 children). In the formal-test word problems (which provide some descriptive context for the subject), the rate of correct responses was 73.7%, which should be contrasted with a 36.8% rate of correct responses for the arithmetic operations.

(Nunes *et al.*, 1993, pp. 18–21)

Sharing

> During the course of their work on fractions [the teacher] asked the children to collect any examples they found at home where fractions were useful. And so the 'interest table' in the class grew as the children produced their examples. One of them involved sharing two [identical] chocolate biscuits between three children. [Another involved] sharing eight [identical] sausages between five people, and ... eight marbles among five children wanting to play.
>
> (Floyd *et al.*, 1982, pp. 73–4)

> '3 spoonfuls of coffee in a 4-cup machine' and '4 spoonfuls for 6 cups'; which coffee will be stronger?
>
> (Streefland, 1991, p. 50)

> When Anja and Monica Fractured come home from school they may have an apple each.
>   But what do you make of the difference in size [in the pictured apples, in which one is large and the other small]?
>
> (ibid., p. 63)

Sorting

Many researchers have used sorting tasks as a means of finding out what learners consider to be 'the same' and 'different', and so revealing what particular attributes the learners are attending to.

For example, sort the following statements (each presented on its own card):

If 3 boxes of sugar cost £1.95, what does one box cost?	If one box of sugar costs 65 pence, what do 3 boxes cost?
If 3 bags of sugar cost £1.95, what does one bag cost?	If one bag of sugar costs 65 pence, what do 3 bags cost?
If 3 boxes of flour cost £1.95, what does one box cost?	If one box of flour costs 65 pence, what do 3 boxes cost?
If 3 bags of flour cost £1.95, what does one bag cost?	If one bag of flour costs 65 pence, what do 3 bags cost?

Getting several people to sort, and then go round and try to express in words how other people have sorted, often opens up fresh ways of seeing.

Using symbols

Children's responses (14-year-olds)

6(i) (Level 1)	11(i) (Level 2)	11(ii) (Level 2)	14 (Level 3)
What can you say about a if $a + 5 = 8$?	What can you say about u if $u = v + 3$ and $v = 1$?	What can you say about m if $m = 3n + 1$ and $n = 4$?	What can you say about r if $r = s + t$ and $r + s + t = 30$?
$a = 3$ 92%	u = 4 61%	$m = 13$ 62%	$r = 15$ 35%
			$r = 30 - s - t$ 6%
	$u = 2$ 14%	other values 14%	$r = 10$ 21%

(Küchemann, 1981, p. 105)

Algebra perimeter task

Write down an expression for the perimeter of each shape:

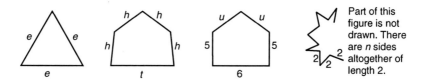

Correct responses amongst nearly 1000 14-year-olds are given in the table.

94%	68%	64%	38%
3e	4h + t	2u + 16	2n
	4h + 1t	u + u + 16	n2
		2u + 25 + 16	

(Küchemann, 1981, p. 102)

The book from which these Küchemann extracts come is *Children's Under-standing of Mathematics: 11–16* (Hart *et al.*, 1981). This book was one outcome of the Concepts in Secondary Mathematics and Science (CSMS) project which is still the most comprehensive survey of learners' responses ever made in the UK.

Snowflakes

As a preliminary investigation, nine children of varying abilities aged 11 to 15 years were individually interviewed and given the question shown in Figure [1]. Typical answers drawn by children were as follows:

The roof of a small garden shed has 16 square tiles as in the picture. It begins to snow. After a while a total of 16 snowflakes have fluttered down onto the roof. Put a cross X for each snowflake to show where you think they would land on the roof. Explain your answer.

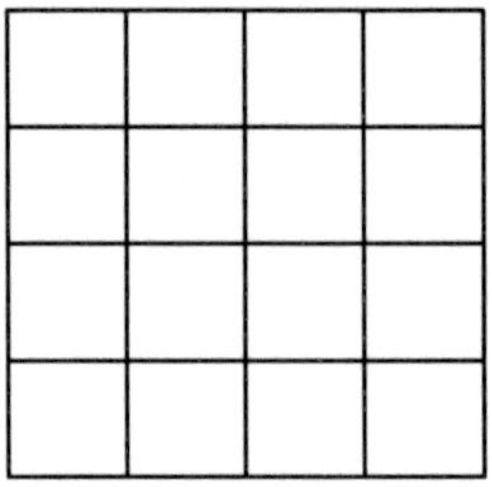

Figure 1 Pilot test: snowflakes drawing question

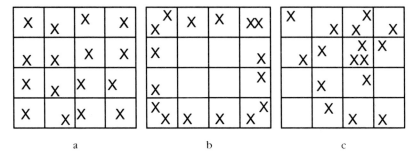

Figure 2 Pilot test: typical children's drawings of snowflake distribution

One per square (Figure 2a): Andrew (11, very able); Maria (13, above average).

All round the edge (Figure 2b): Dawn (12, low ability).

Random distribution (Figure 2c): Wendy (11, very able).

Of the nine, only two produced a random pattern. It was apparent that most of them felt compelled to put the snowflakes neatly one per square but, possibly, this was influenced by their being asked to *draw* the distribution. Therefore, as a follow-up, the question was changed to a multiple-choice format so that just recognizing the most appropriate distribution was required.

(Green, 1989, p. 29)

Relative reasoning

Harry is taller than Tom.
Harry is smaller than Dick.
Who is tallest: Tom, Dick, or Harry?
[...]
Harry is 5 foot tall.
Harry is 2 inches taller than Tom.
Harry is 6 inches taller than Dick.
What are the heights of Dick and Tom?
[...]

There are many other possible variables, for instance:

   (i) whether it is stated at any point in the problem ... that there are three
       terms involved ... ;
  (ii) whether the terms are named in any introductory statement, such as:
       'There are three boys called Tom, Dick, and Harry'; and, if so,
       whether the names appear in an order corresponding to that of the
       correct solution;
 (iii) whether the link is actually named twice, or whether it is referred to
       pronominally in respect of the second relation in which it figures –
       for example, one might say 'Dick is taller than Harry, who is taller
       than Tom'; or, 'Dick, who is taller than Harry, is smaller than Tom'.

                                                       (Donaldson, 1963, pp. 83–6)

and also

> We want to find out the ages of two girls called Jean and May. We know
> that a third girl, Betty, is 15, and that she is 3 years older than one of the
> two girls and 5 years older than the other. If we had one more piece of
> information we could calculate the ages of Jean and May. What is that
> piece of information?

                                                              (ibid., p. 87)

Mr Short and Mr Tall

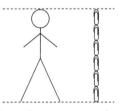

You can see the height of Mr. Short measured with paper clips. Mr. Short
has a friend Mr. Tall. When we measure their height with matchsticks:

Mr. Short's height is four matchsticks
Mr. Tall's height is six matchsticks
How many paperclips are needed for Mr. Tall's height?

   The incorrect strategy in which the child concentrated on the difference $a - b$ rather than a/b would result in:

Mr. Short needs two more paperclips than matchsticks so Mr. Tall needs
   two more paperclips than matchsticks, so the answer is eight.

The use of this 'addition' strategy occurred at the 25–50 per cent level on four of the most difficult items on the ratio test.

[...]

... asked to enlarge a rectangle [3 cm by 5 cm] so that the new base was 12, the height using the addition strategy would be 10 cm. This amount makes the figure look like a square, and so produced an obvious distortion. Some children, aware that it was two large, fell back on the method, 'take two 3 cm pieces and the extra two, answer 8 cm'.

(Hart *et al.*, 1981, pp. 94–5)

Student–teacher ratios

In a certain college there are six times as many students as professors. Using S for the number of students and P for the number of professors, write down an expression.

... when students incorrectly translate 'There are six times as many students as professors' as $6S = P$, the equation is perceived not as symbolizing a sequence of words ('six', ['times'], 'students', 'professors') but instead as representing a group of six students associated with one professor. Under this interpretation, the equals sign denotes correspondence or association rather than equality, and the letters S and P are labels for students and professors. With a cognitive science perspective, Davis (1984) attributed the reversal error to a difficulty in selecting between two frames: (a) the labels frame, dealing with labels or units (e.g., 1 m = 100 cm); and (b) the numerical-variables equation frame, dealing with relations between numbers (e.g., $x = 100y$).

(MacGregor and Stacey, 1993, p. 219)

The original study of this problem appears to be in Rosnick and Clement (1980), but it has been widely used and reported on with various explanations offered. See MacGregor (1991) for a summary of this and related probes including additive ones.

Which angles are bigger?

Each learner is given two copies of the same shape triangle, one small but large enough to measure the angles, and one relatively large. Each learner is asked to predict the relative sizes of the angles in the two copies (to expose conjectures that the angle size depends on the size of the angle arms) and the sum of the angles in each copy. Measurements are made, and the class results are plotted on a histogram, leading to discussion about the merits of measurement and about the sizes of the angles in the two copies of the triangle (based on Balacheff (1990), see also p. 83).

Next the learners form teams of three or four. Each team has two copies of each of three triangles: one copy is quite small, and one copy is quite large. Again predictions of the angle sum are followed by measurements and the class results are plotted.

Subsequent discussion is likely to confront individuals with the fact that the angle sum appears to be constant (within measurement error) and independent of triangle size. The discussion may also lead to the conjecture that there must be some way to see why the angle sum is always constant.

Warehouse

> In a warehouse you obtain 20% discount but you must pay a 15% sales tax. Which would you prefer to have calculated first, discount or tax?
>
> (Mason, Burton and Stacey, 1982, p. 1)

The task can be extended: you could change the numbers; or ask what difference it makes to the management, or how the government requires the tax to be calculated in a sale.

Proof task

Learners can be asked questions like 'what convinces you?' and 'what do you think will convince a teacher?' in the context of both familiar and unfamiliar conjectures. For example, a *familiar* conjecture to be proved might be

> A4: Prove that *when you add any 2 odd numbers, your answer is always even*. (Write down your answer in the way that would get you the best mark you can.)
>
> (Healy and Hoyles, 2000, p. 404)

An *unfamiliar* conjecture to be proved might be

> A7: Prove that if *p and q are any two odd numbers*, $(p + q) \times (p - q)$ *is always a multiple of 4*. (Write down your answer in the way that would get you the best mark you can.)
>
> (ibid., p. 404)

Overleaf is a typical layout for the probes:

A1: Arthur, Bonnie, Ceri, Duncan, Eric and Yvonne were trying to prove whether the following statement is true or false:
When you add any 2 even numbers, your answer is always even.

Arthur's answer	Bonnie's answer
a is any whole number	$2 + 2 = 4$ $4 + 2 = 6$
b is any whole number	$2 + 4 = 6$ $4 + 4 = 8$
2*a* and 2*b* are any two even numbers	$2 + 6 = 8$ $4 + 6 = 10$
	So Bonnie says it is true.
$2a + 2b = 2(a + b)$	
So Arthur says it is true.	
Ceri's answer	Duncan's answer
Even numbers are numbers that can be divided by 2. When you add numbers with a common factor, 2 in this case, the answer will have the same common factor.	Even numbers end in 0, 2, 4, 6, or 8. When you add any two of these, the answer will still end in 0, 2, 4, 6, or 8.
So Ceri says it is true.	*So Duncan says it is true.*
Eric's answer	Yvonne's answer
Let x = any whole number	
y = any whole number	
$x + y = z$	
$z - x = y$	
$z - y = x$	
$z + z - (x + y) = x + y = 2z$	*So Yvonne says it is true.*
So Eric says it is true.	

From the above answers, choose the *one* that would be closest to what you would do if you were asked to answer the question.

From the above answers, choose the *one* to which you think your teacher would give the best mark.

(ibid., p. 400)

Evens and vowels

You are presented with four cards showing, respectively, 'A', 'D', '4', '7', and you know from previous experience that every card, of which these are a subset, has a letter on one side and a number on the other side. You are then given this rule about the four cards in front of you: 'If a card has a vowel on one side, then it has an even number on the other side'.

Next you are told: 'Your task is to say which of the cards you need to turn over in order to find out whether the rule is true or false [for these cards]'.

(Johnson-Laird and Wason, 1977, p. 143)

Originated by Peter Wason in 1966, this task has been used extensively with many variations of context and subjects from school children to medical doctors. Most find it surprisingly difficult at first. The article goes on to observe that most people say 'A' or 'A and 4', both of which are incorrect!

Later years

Encountering obstacles

Reasoning is not always convincing enough to overcome deeply held intuitions:

> A group of 17-year-old humanities students were shown, on examples, how to convert periodic decimal expansions of numbers into ordinary fractions (Sierpinska, 1987).

> $x = 0.1234123412341234\ ...$

> Multiply both sides by 10000: $10000x = 1234.123412341234\ ...$

> Subtract the first equality from the second: $9999x = 1234$

> Divide by 9999: $x = 1234/9999$

> The students were accepting the arguments for expansions like the one above (0.989898 ... , 0.121121 ... , etc.) but refused to believe that 0.999 ... = 1 even though it was obtained in an analogous way.
> At first the students refused both the reasoning and the conclusion, but later, their attitudes started to differentiate. One student, Ewa, began to accept the proof as mathematically valid, and the conclusion as mathematically correct, but refused to accept it as true 'in reality'.
> (Sierpinska, 1994, pp. 78–9)

Birthday

> A certain town is served by two hospitals. In the larger hospital about 45 babies are born each day, and in the smaller hospital about 15 babies are born each day. As you know, about 50 percent of all babies are boys. However, the exact percentage varies from day to day. Sometimes it may be higher than 50 percent, sometimes lower.
> For a period of 1 year, each hospital recorded the days on which more than 60 percent of the babies born were boys. Which hospital do you think recorded more such days?

- The larger hospital (21)
- The smaller hospital (21)
- About the same (that is, within 5 percent of each other) (53)

The values in parentheses are the number of undergraduate students who chose each answer.

Most subjects judged the probability of obtaining more than 60 percent boys to be the same in the small and in the large hospital, presumably because these events are described by the same statistic and are therefore equally representative of the general population. In contrast, sampling theory entails that the expected number of days on which more than 60 percent of the babies are boys is much greater in the small hospital than in the large one, because a large sample is less likely to stray from 50 percent. This fundamental notion of statistics is evidently not part of people's repertoire of intuitions.

(Tversky and Kahneman, 1982, p. 6)

Knowing and not knowing

I asked the students to solve [the following problem].

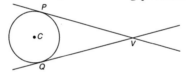

In the figure, the circle with center *C* is tangent to the top and bottom lines at the points *P* and *Q* respectively. (a) Prove that *PV* = *QV*. (b) Prove that the line segment *CV* bisects angle *PVQ*.

The students, working as a group, generated a correct proof. I wrote the proof on the board [which made use of the figure shown below].

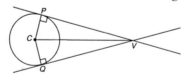

A few minutes later I gave the students [the following problem].

You are given two intersecting straight lines and a point *P* marked on one of them, as in the figure [below] .... Show how to construct, using straightedge and compass, a circle that is tangent[ial] to both lines and that has the point *P* as its point of tangency to the top line.

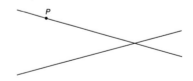

Students came to the board and made the following conjectures, in order:

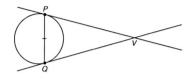

(a) Let Q be the point on the bottom line such that $QV = PV$. The center of the desired circle is the midpoint of line segment PQ.

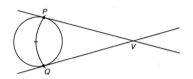

(b) Let A be the segment of the arc with vertex V, passing through P, and bounded by the two lines. The center of the described circle is the midpoint of the arc A.

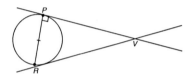

(c) Let R be the point on the bottom line that intersects the line segment perpendicular to the top line at P. The center of the desired circle is the midpoint of line segment PR.

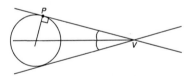

(d) Let L_1 be the line segment perpendicular to the top line at P, and L_2 the bisector of the angle at V. The center of the desired circle is the point of intersection of L_1 and L_2.

The proof that the students had generated – which both provides the answer and rules out conjectures a, b, and c – was still on the board. Despite this, they argued for more than ten minutes about which construction was right. The argument was on purely empirical grounds (that is, on the grounds of which construction looked right), and it was not resolved. How could they have this argument, with the proof still on the board? I believe that this scene could only take place if the students simply didn't see the proof problem as being relevant to the construction problem.

(Schoenfeld, 1985, pp. 35–6)

Problem solving

Painters are at work, painting and decorating the inner walls of a church. Somewhat above the altar there is a circular window. For a decoration, the painters have been asked to draw two vertical lines at a tangent to the circle, and of the same height as the circular window; they were then [told] to add half circles above and below, closing the figure. This area between the lines and the window is to be covered with gold. For every square inch, so and so much gold is needed. How much gold will be needed to cover this space (given the diameter of the circle); or, what is the area between the circle and the lines?

(Wertheimer, 1961, p. 266)

Probability

All families of six children in a city were surveyed. In 72 families the *exact order* of births of boys and girls was G B G B B G.

What is your estimate of the number of families surveyed in which the *exact order* of births was B G B B B B?

The two birth sequences are about equally likely, but most people will surely agree that they are not equally representative. The sequence with five boys and one girl fails to reflect the proportion of boys and girls in the population. Indeed, 75 of 92 [subjects] judged this sequence to be less likely than the standard sequence ($p < .01$ by a sign test). The median estimate was 30.

(Kahneman and Tversky, 1982, p. 34)

First impressions

A number of years ago, I deliberately put the problem

$$\int \frac{x\,dx}{(x^2 - 9)}$$

as the first problem on a test, to give my students a boost as they began the exam. After all, a quick look at the fraction suggests the substitution $u = x^2 - 9$, and this substitution knocks the problem off in just a few seconds. 178 students took the exam. About half used the right substitution and got off to a good start, as I intended. However, 44 of the students, noticing the factorable denominator in the integrand, used partial fractions to express $x / x^2 - 9$ in the form $A / (x - 3) + B / (x + 3)$. Correct but quite time-consuming. They didn't do too well on the exam.

And 17 students, noting the $(u^2 - a^2)$ form of the denominator, worked the problem using the substitution $x = 3 \sin \theta$. This too yields the right answer – but it was even more time-consuming, and the students wound up so far behind that they bombed the exam.

Doing well, then, is based on more than 'knowing the subject matter'; it's based on knowing which techniques to use and when. If your strategy choice isn't good, you're in trouble.

(Schoenfeld, 1987, p. 32)

2 Conditions for learning

Introduction

Philosophers, authors, and teachers have tried to describe and define what they have understood by *learning*. That learning is important to us as organisms, and particularly as human beings, is not in doubt. But what exactly is it, how can it be recognised, and how can it be fostered and sustained? These are difficult questions.

There are marked differences in how teachers and educators from different cultures approach teaching for learning. For example, Margaret Brown (2001) has suggested there is a tendency in France to want to clarify and expose underlying theories on which to base the development of practice, and a tendency in America to want everything based logically and explicitly on research that demonstrates what works and what does not. In contrast, Anglo-Saxon pragmatic empiricism leads to trying things out and only later (often much later!) locating, articulating, and clarifying the underlying theories. An observer can often discern consistencies which seem to act as theories or assumptions about teaching, about learning, about the people being taught, about the school as institution, and so on.

The purpose of this chapter is to act as reminder that current issues in mathematics education stretch back a long way, and that current practices have deep historical roots.

Assumptions and theories

As a teacher, it is easy to dismiss theories as irrelevant to practice, but many different doers and thinkers have come to the conclusion that every practice is based on theories, even if these theories are implicit and hidden.

Practice and theory: Leonardo da Vinci

Leonardo da Vinci (1452–1519), famous as artist, scientist, draftsman, engineer, inventor and anatomist, wrote that: 'He who loves practice without theory is like the sailor who boards ship without a rudder and compass and never knows where he may cast' (da Vinci, webref).

Some practices are handed on from generation to generation, as when young children 'play school' by standing up and telling their dolls what they should know. Still, there are theories underlying these behaviours which have deep roots. By probing the depths to locate these deeply embedded theories and by trying to make them explicit, it is possible to bring them to the surface so as to examine them carefully, to challenge and perhaps to modify them. Otherwise they remain a dominant force inaccessibly hidden behind behaviour (see also p. 48).

Observation

Frederick Bartlett (b. Gloucestershire, 1886–1969) pioneered the modern application of psychology to educational issues. His principal focus was on the functioning of memory. He observed that:

> ... our memories are constantly mingled with our constructions, are perhaps themselves to be treated as constructive in character.
>
> (Bartlett, 1932, p. 16)

> ... the name, as soon as it is assigned, immediately shapes both what is seen and what is recalled.
>
> (ibid., p. 20)

This is both an echo and a development of a suggestion by Michel de Montaigne (1533–1592) who as a French Seigneur was perhaps the first person to publish a large collection of essays based on his observations of himself and the world around him: Montaigne said, 'Human eyes can only perceive things in accordance with such Forms as they [already] know' (de Montaigne, 1588, p. 600).

Another way of saying this is that all observation is actually theory-based, and Norwood Hanson (1924–1967), an English philosopher of science, generalised this to: 'there is a sense ... in which seeing is a 'theory-laden' undertaking' (Hanson, 1958, p. 19).

This is mirrored by an observation of Louis Pasteur (1822–1895), the French scientist who discovered pasteurisation among many other things: *'Dans les champs de l'observation le hazard ne favorise que les esprits préparés'* ('Where observation is concerned, chance favours only the prepared mind') (Pasteur in *Oxford Dictionary of Quotations*).

Nelson Goodman (b. Massachusetts, 1902–1998) was a philosopher with a wide range of interests whose work influenced social scientists and educators concerning the nature of observation. He took Hanson's idea one stage further by suggesting that '[facts] are as theory-laden as we hope our theories are fact-laden' (Goodman, 1978, pp. 96–7).

Kurt Lewin (b. Prussia, 1890–1947) eventually moved to the USA. He is often referred to as the 'father of social psychology'. He was a pioneer of what came to be called *action research*. He is much quoted as saying that 'theory without practice is sterile; practice without theory is blind' and 'nothing is so practical as a good theory'.

Alfred Orage (b. Yorkshire, 1873–1934) was an influential magazine editor in both England and New York who prompted the study of psychoanalysis and psychosynthesis. He wrote 'The observation of others is coloured by our inability to observe ourselves impartially. We can never be impartial about anything until we can be impartial about our own organism' (Orage, 1966, p. 58). This parallels observations attributed to Montaigne: 'When most people speak about themselves they are not speaking about something they actually know'.

Here then is support for the contention that in order to be sensitive to learners' experience, and hence effective in interactions with them, it is vital to work on sensitising oneself through observation of one's own experience. 'There is no higher or lower knowledge, but one only, flowing out of experimentation' (attributed to da Vinci). Da Vinci advised: 'Avoid the teachings of speculators whose judgments are not confirmed by experience' (da Vinci, quoted in Zammatio *et al.*, 1980, p. 133).

This book is intended to inform experimentation. Extracts have been chosen which are, on the whole, brief and succinct, and therefore also dense. The challenge for the reader is to look for examples of incidents that illustrate the constructs and theories presented in the extracts, by examining past experience, and also by experimenting in the future. It is to be expected that some of these constructs will fit with past experience and inform future choices, while others may not do so at first or, indeed, ever.

Human psychology

The term *psyche* refers to inner experiences and functioning, often equated with the mind, but also encompassing emotions and behaviour. From ancient times people have found it useful to discern structure in inner life, and to seek links and evidence in outer behaviour.

Human psyche: The Upanishads

In the ancient Hindu scriptures, a person is likened to two birds.

> Two birds
> Close yoked companions,
> Both share the self-same tree.
> One eats of the sweet fruit;
> The other looks on, without eating.
> (Rig Veda)

The image of two birds, one eating and the other watching pervades Eastern and Western art. There are multiple interpretations (indeed an image is considered powerful only when there are several contrasting, even contra-dictory interpretations). The single image serves to hold all of these interpretations together. An educational interpretation is that the two birds are forms of attention, and the tree represents the material world of sensation. The eater is the part of us that gets caught up in doing, while the watcher is an internal monitor–witness that observes without judging. The watcher has been likened to conscience, which needs to be awakened and developed. The overall purpose of education is to awaken and make use of the second bird, the 'inner watcher'. When applied to specific techniques, the notion of the inner watcher means having a part of you that is separate from the execution of the technique in order to guide activity, remember goals, and so on. When applied to teaching, it means having a part of you separately witnessing the lesson, able to observe and to suggest alternative actions.

In another part of the scriptures, a person is likened to a horse, chariot, and driver. Later versions change the chariot into a carriage, and then a hansom cab, as appropriate to the times. The owner (originally a charioteer) hires a driver, who has responsibility for maintaining the chariot fabric and tackle, and for looking after the horses. If the chariot body is allowed to decay, if the reins and harness go mouldy or stiff, if the horses become hungry or mangy, or if the driver becomes dissolute, then the chariot cannot be used properly. If the horses are not guided, they will be thrown off course by each sudden movement, and graze at every opportunity. If the carriage is not maintained, it will creak and crack under stress. If the driver is not paying attention to where the chariot is headed, then the route will be missed, and there may be crashes.

The Katha Upanishad (III, v3–4) offers one reading:

> Know thou the atman (self) as the owner of a chariot,
> The chariot as the body,
> Know thou the buddhi (intellect) as the chariot driver,
> And mind as the reins.
> The senses, they say, are the horses;
> The objects of sense, what they range over.
> What then is experience?
> 'Self, sense and mind conjoined,' the sage replies.
>   (adapted from Zaehner, 1966, p. 176)

Reins and harness (mental imagery) enable the driver to guide and direct the horses (emotions, senses), while the shafts enable the horse's energy to pull the chariot. The particular version shown here has five horses for the five senses.

The image of the chariot can be useful when preparing lessons and when teaching by acting as a reminder that behaviour (chariot) is driven by emotion (horses) and guided by intellect (driver by means of the reins and harness (mental imagery).

Complaints about education

Education: Plato

Plato (c.428BC–c.348BC) was an aristocrat. He was a student of Socrates and a teacher of Aristotle (who himself taught Alexander the Great). Plato set down accounts of Socrates' dialogues with different students. He also constructed his own philosophy, which was so influential that it has been said that western philosophy is no more than a series of footnotes to Plato. Here Plato praises the way the Egyptians teach their children arithmetic, implying criticism of Greek education.

> *Athenian*: ... I maintain that freeborn men should learn ... as much as in Egypt is taught to vast numbers of children along with their letters. To begin with, lessons have been devised there in cyphering for the veriest children which they can learn with a good deal of fun and amusement, problems about the distribution of the fixed total number of apples or

garlands among larger and smaller groups, and the arranging of the successive series of 'byes' and 'pairs' between boxers and wrestlers as the nature of such contests requires. More than this, the teachers have a game in which they distribute mixed sets of saucers of gold, silver, copper, and similar materials or, in other cases, whole sets of one material.

(Plato, Laws VII, paras 819b to c,
in Hamilton and Cairns, 1961, pp. 1388–9)

Failings of current education: Herbert Spencer

It is much easier to see what is wrong about current education than it is to do something about it. People have complained about perceived deficiencies from earliest recorded discussions of education. Herbert Spencer (b. Derbyshire, 1820–1903) had a lot to say on the subject and he is known as the 'father of British sociology'. Lawrence Cremin (b. New York, 1925–1990), himself a distinguished historian of American education, cited Spencer as chief inspiration for people such as John Dewey and Edward Thorndike to consider learning from the perspective of the learner (see Cremin, 1961). According to Spencer:

> Nearly every subject dealt with is arranged in abnormal order: defini-
> tions and rules and principles being put first, instead of being disclosed,
> as they are in the order of nature, through the study of cases. And then,
> pervading the whole, is the vicious system of rote learning – a system
> sacrificing the spirit to the letter. See the results. What with perceptions
> unnaturally dulled by early thwarting, and a coerced attention to books –
> what with the mental confusion produced by teaching subjects before
> they can be understood, and in each of them giving generalizations
> before the facts of which they are generalizations – what with making
> the pupil a mere passive recipient of others' ideas, and not in the least
> leading him to be an active inquirer or self-instructor – and what with
> taxing the faculties to excess; there are very few minds that become as
> efficient as they might be. Examinations being once passed, books are
> laid aside; the greater part of what has been acquired, being unorga-
> nized, soon drops out of recollection; what remains is mostly inert – the
> art of applying knowledge not having been cultivated; and there is but
> little power either of accurate observation or independent thinking.
>
> (Spencer, 1878, p. 28)

To *tell* a child this and to *show* it the other, is not to teach it how to observe, but to make it the mere recipient of another's observations: a proceeding which weakens rather than strengthens its powers of self-instruction – which deprives it of the pleasures resulting from successful activity – which presents this all-attractive knowledge under the aspect of formal tuition – and which thus generates that indifference and even disgust not unfrequently felt … .

(ibid., 1878, p. 79)

After his diatribe against contemporary educational practices, which valued language (Latin, Greek, English) and arts over science, Spencer argued that language involves memory (meanings of words), but science (including mathematics) involves both memory and understanding using reason.

Dangers of rote learning: Augustus de Morgan

Augustus de Morgan (b. India, 1806–1871) became the first professor of mathematics in the University of London, where he collaborated with George Boole (b. Lincolnshire, 1815–1864) on the development of symbolic logic (see also p. 119). He wrote extensively about the nature of mathematics and how teaching could be improved.

> Mathematics is becoming too much of a machinery; and this is more especially the case with reference to the elementary students. They put the data of the problems into a mill and expect the result to come out ready ground at the other end. An operation which bears a close resemblance to that of putting in hemp seed at one end of a machine and taking out ruffled shirts ready for use at the other end. This mode is undoubtedly exceedingly effective in producing results, but it is certainly not soaked in teaching the mind and in exercising thought.
>
> (de Morgan, 1865)

His voice was not alone.

> If children fail in other subjects they fail more often here (in arithmetic). It is a subject which seems beyond the comprehension of the rural mind.
>   In arithmetic, I regret to say worse results than ever before have been obtained – this is partly attributable, no doubt, to my having so framed my sums as to require rather more intelligence than before: the failures are almost invariably traceable to radically imperfect teaching.
>   (Stafford and Darby, HMI, 1876; quoted in McIntosh, 1977, pp. 92–3; reprinted in Floyd, 1981, pp. 6–11)

Note that these extracts, along with all the extracts in this book from a wide range of authors, could be seen as presenting principles without experiences from which to draw generalisations. However, it is assumed that you, the reader, have a great deal of experience on which to draw; the extracts will either resonate with, or contradict, either your espoused or your enacted perspective, thus promoting further investigation and probing on your part.

Principles and theories

Recitation as learning: Ignatius Loyola

Ignatius Loyola (b. Basque country, 1491–1556) founded the Jesuits in 1540, though the constitution and detailed structure of the Jesuit teaching methods were not perfected until after his death. One feature of Jesuit instruction was oral contact between teacher and student. The teacher initiated lessons with a modified form of lecture, the *prelection*. First, the general meaning of the entire passage was described; then the meaning and construction of each clause was thoroughly explained; then, under the term *erudition*, historical, geographical, archaeological, scientific and mathematical and other information was provided concerning the passage; this was followed by explanation of the rhetorical and poetical forms and their rules by which the passage was constructed; then the Latin in the passage was compared with other passages written at other times; finally, moral lessons were drawn.

Each day's work consisted of a review of the previous day's passage, followed by in-depth study of the current day's passage, with opportunities to recite to each other and to the whole class, and to discuss with each other rhetorical, grammatical, historical and scientific points of the lesson (called *concertations*). Each week's work was reviewed, and the entire year's work was also reviewed, with those destined for the Jesuit order undertaking a review by teaching all the material (based on Monroe, 1909, p. 427).

The notion of *recitation* of lessons remained a cornerstone of education for centuries, surviving into the nineteenth century in American universities, where students were called upon to recite portions of the previous day's lecture. Even today the tutorial sessions, which run in parallel with lectures, are called *recitations* in some countries. The idea that discussion helps to crystallise learning can trace its roots back at least to the Jesuits, if not to Plato's academy. Likewise, the view that constant repetition and review of material enhances learning has ancient roots.

Principles of learning: John Comenius

John Comenius (b. near Prague, 1592–1670) was a highly influential educator who championed the use of the vernacular for education. However, his influence was largely indirect, his writings disappearing for two centuries before surfacing again in the nineteenth century. He participated in and propounded the *pansophic* movement, which attempted to capture and organise all knowledge. He wanted to give 'an accurate anatomy of the universe, dissecting the veins and limbs of all things in such a way that there shall be nothing that is not seen, and that each part shall appear in its proper place and without confusion' (quoted in Monroe, 1909, pp. 483–484).

To this end, Comenius developed a successful method of teaching both the vernacular and Latin by displaying pictures (the closest a text author could get to displaying the things themselves) with labels. Each label was used once within a sentence. This was in reaction to the textbooks of the time which were entirely in Latin and in which the words were merely treated as words with rules of grammar and form, not words used to express ideas. In 1641, he was summoned by the English Parliament with a view to setting up a model school, but the 'Irish Rebellion' intervened and nothing came of it. Although his general methods of teaching ('according to nature') did not bear fruit beyond the teaching of language, he put forward a number of principles, which are recognisable even today, even if you do not agree with them all.

1   Whatever is to be known must be taught (that is, by presenting the object or idea directly to the child, not merely through form or symbol).
2   Whatever is taught should be taught as being of practical application in everyday life and of some definite use.
3   Whatever is taught should be taught straightforwardly, and not in a complicated manner.
4   Whatever is taught must be taught with reference to its true nature and its origin; that is to say, through its causes.
5   If anything is to be learned, its general principles must first be explained. Its details may then be considered, and not till then.
6   All parts of an object (or subject), even the smallest, without a single exception, must be learned with reference to their order, their position, and their connection with one another.
7   All things must be taught in due succession, and not more than one thing should be taught at one time.
8   We should not leave any subject until it is thoroughly understood.
9   Stress should be laid on the differences which exist between things, in order that what knowledge of them is acquired may be clear and distinct.

(Monroe, 1909, pp. 488–9)

Exercising faculties: John Locke

John Locke (b. Somerset, 1632–1704) was a philosopher concerned with the nature of human knowledge and understanding. He was a major force behind the notion that education is a discipline, concerned with training the faculties of the mind rather like muscles are trained through disciplined exercise. He and others of his time promoted the view that the process of learning, rather than the thing being learned, is the important and determining feature of education (based on Monroe, 1909, p. 508).

The business of education is not to make the young person perfect in any one of the sciences, but so to open and dispose their minds as may

best make them capable of any [science], when they shall apply themselves to it. ... [not to gain a] stock of knowledge but a variety and
freedom of thinking; as an increase of the powers and activities of the
mind, not as an enlargement of its possessions.

[...]

... mathematics, which therefore I think should be taught all those
who have the time and opportunity, *not so much to make them mathematicians, as to make them reasonable creatures* ...

(Locke, 1693; quoted in Monroe, 1909, pp. 518–19)

Locke seemed not to notice that as with any subject, learning can be superficial and *rote* (see p. 151), or deep and *relational* (see p. 295). Nevertheless,
he introduced a fundamental conundrum of education which several shifts
in discourse and perspective have failed to elucidate in the intervening
centuries, namely, the issue of transfer: how is it that something learned in
one situation can come to mind to be used in some fresh situation? Education
proceeds largely by isolating and teaching skills that have proved useful, in
the expectation that learners will then be able to use those skills wherever
they are relevant. If only it were that easy!

Natural development of faculties: Johann Pestalozzi

Some of Herbert Spencer's ideas (see p. 35 and p. 116) were based on those
of Johann Pestalozzi (b. Switzerland, 1746–1827), who was one of the first to
advocate education for all, including the poor. According to Spencer,
Pestalozzi advocated that:

... education must conform to the natural process of evolution – that
there is a certain sequence in which the faculties spontaneously
develop, and a certain kind of knowledge which each requires during its
development; and that it is for us to ascertain this sequence, and supply
this knowledge.

(Spencer, 1911, p. 61)

Spencer was not overly impressed with the way that this was carried out in
practice, but he acknowledged that teachers had not fully taken the ideas on
board. Indeed, Jean Piaget's researches (see p. 92) can be seen in this light as
elucidating the natural development of human faculties.

Three laws: Edward Thorndike

Edward Thorndike (b. Massachusetts, 1874–1949) was a behavioural psychologist, and one of the first American researchers to use developments in
psychology to formulate research programmes in education. His view of
learning involved the making of connections between stimulus and response.

From this perspective, he initiated *educational psychology* as a particular branch of psychology. He proposed that 'almost everything in arithmetic should be taught as a habit that has connections with habits already acquired' (Thorndike, 1922, p. 194), a theme that recurs in other authors (see *practice makes perfect*, p. 176).

Thorndike derived three laws of learning from his studies:

1   Exercise and repetition: the more often a skill is repeated, the longer it will be retained.
2   Effect: responses associated with satisfaction are strengthened, while those associated with pain are weakened.
3   Readiness: a series of responses can be chained together to satisfy some goal which will result in annoyance if blocked.

(based on Thorndike, 1914)

Thorndike's perspective arose from and supported a fragmentation of content into components that can be mastered in a relatively short period of time through training behaviour. The possibility of meaning was ignored on the grounds that it was not observable as or in behaviour.

Teaching as a cultural activity: James Stigler and James Hiebert

James Stigler and James Hiebert are American educators who played a leading role in the Third International Mathematics and Science Study (TIMSS) of mathematics proficiency in many different countries.

> Teaching is a complex system created by the interactions of the teacher, the students, the curriculum, the local setting, and other factors that influence what happens in the classroom. The way one component works – say the curriculum – depends on the other components in the system, such as the teaching methods being used. To say that teaching is a cultural activity reveals an additional truth: Cultural activities, such as teaching, do not appear full-blown but rather evolve over long periods of time in ways that are consistent with the stable web of beliefs and assumptions that are part of the culture. The scripts for teaching in each country appear to rest on a relatively small and tacit set of core beliefs about the nature of the subject, how students learn, and the role that a teacher should play in the classroom. These beliefs, often implicit, serve to maintain the stability of cultural systems over time. Just as features of teaching need to be understood in terms of the underlying systems in which they are embedded, so too these systems of teaching, because they are cultural, must be understood in relation to the cultural beliefs rapidly becoming a cultural activity. Children, for example, learn naturally, by hanging around computers. But there still are those for whom learning about computers has the

distinctly non-cultural trait of intentionally and deliberately and self-consciously working through the activity.

(Stigler and Hiebert, 1998, pp. 4–11)

Types of knowledge: Lee Shulman

Lee Shulman (b. Illinois, USA, 1938–) follows in the footsteps of John Dewey, building particularly on the notion of *psychologising the subject matter* in order to afford learners access (see p. 45). Here he distinguishes between content knowledge and pedagogical content knowledge, and adds a few more distinctions between the different kinds of knowledge necessary to teach effectively, which have been much quoted (and challenged, see for example, Elbaz, 1983).

A teacher knows something not understood by others, presumably the students. The teacher can transform understanding, performance skills, or desired attitudes or values into pedagogical representations and actions. These are ways of talking, showing, enacting, or otherwise representing ideas so that the unknowing can come to know, those without understanding can comprehend and discern, and the unskilled can become adept. Thus, teaching necessarily begins with a teacher's understanding of what is to be learned and how it is to be taught. It proceeds through a series of activities during which the students are provided specific instructions and opportunities for learning, though the learning itself remains the responsibility of the students. ... Although this is certainly a core conception of teaching, it is also an incomplete conception. Teaching must properly be understood to be more than the enhancement of understanding; but if it is not even that, then questions regarding performance of its other functions remain moot. ...

[To teach effectively the teacher needs:

- teacher knowledge;]
- content knowledge;
- general pedagogical knowledge, with special reference to those broad principles and strategies of classroom management and organization that appear to transcend subject matter;
- curriculum knowledge, with particular grasp of the materials and programs that serve as 'tools of the trade' for teachers;
- pedagogical content knowledge, that special amalgam of content and pedagogy that is uniquely the province of teachers, their own special form of professional understanding;
[...]
- knowledge of educational contexts, ranging from the workings of the group or class, the governance and financing of school districts, to the character of communities and cultures;

- knowledge of educational ends, purposes, and values, and their philosophical and historical grounds.

(Shulman, 1987, pp. 3–4)

See Shulman (webref) for a short clip of him explaining what he means by 'the scholarship of teaching'.

Metaphors for teaching: Dennis Fox

Often it may seem difficult to speak directly about teaching and learning. Rather, everything is spoken about indirectly, in terms of something else. For example, teachers are sheepdogs and learners are skittish sheep, or teachers deliver skills to waiting learners. When people say 'teaching is guiding', for example, they are using a metaphor, in which one thing (teaching) is said to be something else (guiding). Sometimes this is given as a simile (teaching is like guiding), or even as an analogy (teaching is like guiding, and learners are like skittish sheep) in which relationships are carried across from one context to another more familiar one. Some metaphors are so deeply ingrained that they are almost impossible to avoid, so habitual have they become. These are called frozen metaphors (Lakoff and Johnson, 1980)

Dennis Fox (1983) identified four underlying metaphors – transfer, shaping, travelling and growing – and some of the words that contribute to them.

	Transfer theory	*Shaping theory*	*Travelling theory*	*Growing theory*
Verbs commonly used	Convey, impart, implant, imbue, give, expound, transmit, put over, get across, tell, ...	Develop, mould, demonstrate, produce, instruct, condition, prepare, direct, [...]	Lead, guide, direct, help, show, [...]	Cultivate, encourage, nurture, develop, foster, enable, bring out, ...
Content	Commodity to be transferred, to fill a container.	Shaping tools, pattern, blueprint.	Terrain, vantage point, [perspective]	Experiences ...
Learner	Container to be filled.	[Matter] (clay, wood, metal) to be shaped.	Explorer, [trouper, prisoner].	[Plant]
Teacher	Pump attendant, food processor, [delivery agent].	Skilled craftsman ...	Guide ...	Gardener, [cultivator, pruner, fertiliser]

	Transfer theory	Shaping theory	Travelling theory	Growing theory
Standard teaching methods	Lectures, reading lists, duplicated notes.	Laboratory, workshop, practical instructions, recipes. Exercises with predictable outcomes.	Simulations, projects, etc. Exercises with unpredictable outcomes. Discussions; independent learning.	Experiential methods, similar to travelling theory but less structured and more spontaneous.
Monitoring progress	Measuring and sampling contents of vessel.	Checking size and shape of product.	Comparing notes with travelling companion.	Listening to reflections on personal development.
Explanation of failure – teacher's view	Leaky vessels, small container.	[Flawed, faulty raw material]	Blinkered vision; lack of stamina. Unadventurous, lethargic.	Poor start; inadequately prepared; no will to develop.
Explaination of failure – student's view	Poor transfer skills, poor aim.	Poor guides; poor equipment; too many restrictions on route.	Poor guides; poor equipment; too many restrictions on route.	Restricted diet; unsuitable food; incompetent gardener.

(Fox, 1983, p. 163)

It can be informative to notice which kinds of words you find yourself using predominantly and whether they are consistent with your overall perspective.

Educational beliefs: John Dewey

John Dewey (b. Vermont, USA, 1859–1952) was a pragmatic philosopher and educator who undertook to reform the American education system. He set up an experimental school attached to the University of Chicago where he developed an approach to learning that was based on the experience of the learner, and on learners actively making use of their own *powers* (p. 115) to explore and make sense of the world. The much maligned 'discovery learning' and 'child-centred education' were derived from his approach, but being overly simplified, soon turned into the opposite of what Dewey intended (see *integrated teaching*, p. 224). The John Dewey Society continues his work, promoting educational practices consonant with his original ideas and modern versions of them.

Here are brief extracts from the first of five parts of Dewey's 'creed', published in 1897. Its value today lies perhaps most strongly in how we choose to stress differently in some places, and similarly in others. It is an excellent but difficult exercise to try to write your own *creed*.

Article I. What Education Is

I believe that all education proceeds by the participation of the individual in the social consciousness of the race. This process begins unconsciously almost at birth, and is continually shaping the individual's powers, saturating his consciousness, forming his habits, training his ideas, and arousing his feelings and emotions. ...

I believe that the only true education comes through the stimulation of the child's powers by the demands of the social situations in which he finds himself. Through these demands he is stimulated to act as a member of a unity, to emerge from his original narrowness of action and feeling and to conceive of himself from the standpoint of the welfare of the group to which he belongs. Through the responses which others make to his own activities he comes to know what these mean in social terms. ...

I believe that this educational process has two sides – one psychological and one sociological; and that neither can be subordinated to the other or neglected without evil results following. Of these two sides, the psychological is the basis. The child's own instincts and powers furnish the material and give the starting point for all education. Save as the efforts of the educator connect with some activity which the child is carrying on his own initiative independent of the educator, education becomes reduced to a pressure from without. It may, indeed, give certain external results but cannot truly be called educative. Without insight into the psychological structure and activities of the individual, the educative process will, therefore, be haphazard and arbitrary. If it chances to coincide with the child's activity, it will get a leverage; if it does not, it will result in friction, or disintegration, or arrest of the child's nature.

[...]

I believe that the psychological and social sides are organically related and that education cannot be regarded as a compromise between the two, or a superimposition of one upon the other.

[...]

... In order to know what a power really is we must know what its end, use, or function is; and this we cannot know save as we conceive of the individual as active in social relationships. But, on the other hand, the only possible adjustment which we can give to the child under existing conditions, is that which arises through putting him in complete possession of all his powers. ... it is impossible to prepare the child for any precise set of conditions. To prepare him for the future life means to give him command of himself; ...

In sum, I believe that the individual who is to be educated is a social individual and that society is an organic union of individuals. ...

(Dewey, webref)

Study: John Dewey

Dewey suggests that 'the interest in ... the successful carrying on of an activity, should be gradually transferred to the *study* of objects – their properties, consequences, structures, causes and effects.' In the next extract, he discusses the possibilities afforded by education in childhood.

> The outcome, the *abstract* to which education is to proceed, is an interest in intellectual matters for their own sake, a delight in thinking for the sake of thinking. It is an old story that acts and processes that at the outset are incidental to something else develop and maintain an absorbing value of their own. So it is with thinking and with knowledge; at first incidental to results and adjustments beyond themselves, they attract more and more attention to themselves till they become ends, not means. Children engage, unconstrainedly and continually, in reflective inspection and testing for the sake of what they are interested in doing. Habits of thinking thus generated may increase in amount till they become of importance on their own account. It is part of the business of the teacher to lead students to extricate and to dwell upon the distinctively intellectual side of what they do until there develops a spontaneous interest in ideas and their relations with one another – that is, the genuine power of abstraction, of rising from engrossment in the present to the plane of ideas.

(Dewey, 1933, p. 226)

Psychologising the subject matter: John Dewey

Dewey considered that the role of the teacher was not to try to impart knowledge or instruct directly, but rather to establish and maintain conditions that support and focus learning. He developed the notion of *psychologising the subject matter*, by which he meant locating problems and situations that would lead learners naturally to confront, resolve, and learn important ideas and techniques, thus underlining his basic approach of starting with the experiences (past and present) of learners. Dewey invented the notion of *psychologising the subject matter* to mean transforming the subject matter into a form that matches the learner (see p. 228). He wrote at one point that the purpose of education is to organise problem-solving and then teach it to students (Dewey, 1933).

One consequence of Dewey's approach is that teaching a topic is not a matter of sorting it out clearly in your own mind and then expounding it to learners, but of making contact with learner experience and interest, and devising new experiences that will prompt learners to confront and resolve important and relevant problems.

Much of Dewey's thinking (and that of most other modern authors) can be traced back to the German philosopher Immanuel Kant (b. Prussia, 1724–1804) who did for modern philosophy what Plato did for ancient philosophy: he organised it, delineated problems, considered various stances and put forward a consistent and reasoned position. This has allowed subsequent authors to compare and contrast their own positions with those of Kant. Put another way, Kant said much of what had previously been said, and much of what has since been said, about the way in which people come to know things they did not know before. According to Kant, ' ... all human cognition begins with intuitions, proceeds from thence to conceptions, and ends with ideas' (Kant, 1781, p. 429, quoted in Polya, 1962, p. 99). Fischbein and colleagues (see p. 63) have developed the role of intuition in learning science and mathematics.

It was Kant who also said, though not in so many words, that a succession of perceptions does not necessarily add up to a perception of succession. In other words, a learner can go through a succession of activities but not end up with any sense of it as anything more than a succession, even a smorgasbord, of activities. If the second bird (see p. 32) is not awake, then a sequence of experiences remains just that, a sequence of experiences.

Rhythms of education: Alfred North Whitehead

Alfred North Whitehead (b. Kent, 1861–1947) was a mathematician and philosopher, fellow of the Royal Society, and colleague of Bertrand Russell (1872–1970). He was deeply concerned about education and was concerned to locate the unity in various approaches. He is perhaps best known in mathematics for his attempt, with Bertrand Russell, to place mathematics on firm axiomatic foundations through deriving the axioms from logic.

Whitehead, in common with many thinkers and researchers, endeavoured to find some structure in the experience of learning. Here he draws attention to how energy ebbs and flows, and how people go through different phases in their perspectives on life and hence on learning. He identifies three principal, interacting phases or rhythms of learning.

> Life is essentially periodic. It comprises daily periods, with their alternations of work and play, of activity and of sleep, and seasonal periods, which dictate our terms and our holidays; and also it is composed of well-marked yearly periods. These are the gross obvious periods which no one can overlook. There are also subtler periods of mental growth, with their cyclic recurrences, yet always different as we pass from cycle to cycle, though the subordinate stages are reproduced each cycle. That is why I have chosen the term 'rhythmic', as meaning essentially the conveyance of difference within a framework of repetition. Lack of

attention to the rhythm and character of mental growth is the main source of wooden futility in education. ... In relation to intellectual progress [there is] the stage of romance, the stage of precision, and the stage of generalisation.

The stage of romance is the stage of first apprehension. The subject-matter has the vividness of novelty; it holds within itself unexplored connexions with possibilities half-disclosed by glimpses and half-concealed by the wealth of material. ... We are in the presence of immediate cognisance of fact, only intermittently subjecting fact to systematic dissection. Romantic emotion is essentially the excitement consequent on the transition from the bare facts to the first realisations of the import of their unexplored relationships. ...

In [the stage of precision], width of relationship is subordinated to exactness of formulation. ... It proceeds by forcing on the students' acceptance a given way of analysing the facts, bit by bit. New facts are added, but they are the facts which fit into the analysis.

[...]

The final stage of generalisation ... is a return to romanticism with added advantage of classified ideas and relevant technique. It is the fruition which has been the goal of the precise training. It is the final success. ...

Education should consist in a continual repetition of such cycles. Each lesson in its minor way should form an eddy cycle issuing in its own subordinate process. Longer periods should issue in definite attainments, which then form the starting-grounds for fresh cycles. ... The pupils must be continually enjoying some fruition and starting afresh – if the teacher is stimulating in exact proportion to his success in satisfying the rhythmic cravings of his pupils.

(Whitehead, 1932, pp. 27–31)

... [I] ask you not to exaggerate into sharpness the distinction between the three stages of a cycle. ... Of course, throughout a distinction of emphasis, of pervasive quality – romance, precision, generalisation, are all present throughout. But there is an alternation of dominance, and it is this alternation which constitutes the cycles.

(ibid., p. 44)

There are some similarities between Whitehead's rhythms and the van Hiele *phases* (see p. 63), and the *structure of attention* (see p. 60). There are also resonances with other three-fold frameworks that have been devised to inform teaching preparation and the design and use of tasks (see p. 263). Whitehead also wrote, amongst other things, about the need to develop 'mental habits' so they become 'the way in which the mind reacts to the appropriate stimulus ... ' (ibid., p. 42).

Education: Jerome Bruner

Jerome Bruner (b. New York, 1915–) is a psychologist who promulgated the notion of spiral learning, claiming that you can teach any topic to any person by adapting and pitching the ideas appropriately. He also supported the much misunderstood and maligned concept of 'discovery learning' (see also *integrated teaching*, p. 224). He was one of the people who helped introduce Vygotsky's ideas to the west, particularly the notion of *scaffolding* (see p. 266), and *zone of proximal development* (see p. 88). As one of the leaders of the 'cognitive revolution' and of cultural psychology, Bruner studied how people's personal 'stories' influence who they are and how they act.

In the following passage, Bruner provides a reason for attending to theories, because teaching and learner development are both intimately tied up with views about how knowledge is gained, created, and communicated, as well as what knowledge is.

> ... the heart of the educational process consists of providing aids and dialogues for translating experience into more powerful systems of notation and ordering. And it is for this reason that I think a theory of development must be linked both to a theory of knowledge and to a theory of instruction, or be doomed to triviality.
>
> (Bruner, 1966, p. 21)

Bruner also supports the view that education is about bringing processes to the surface and expressing them, often in succinct ways, in order to build on them.

Conditions for learning: Robert Gagné

Robert Gagné (b. Massachusetts, 1916–) is an experimental psychologist who applies theories to learning. He began by studying military training. Gagné suggested that learning tasks for intellectual skills can be organised in a hierarchy according to complexity: stimulus recognition, response generation, procedure following, use of terminology, discriminations, concept formation, rule application, and problem solving. The primary significance of the hierarchy is to identify the prerequisites to facilitate learning at each level. Prerequisites are identified by doing a task analysis of a learning/ training task. Learning hierarchies provide a basis for the sequencing of instruction.

In addition, Gagné's theory outlines nine instructional events and corresponding cognitive processes:

1   gaining attention (reception);
2   informing learners of the objective (expectancy);

3 stimulating recall of prior learning (retrieval);
4 presenting the stimulus (selective perception);
5 providing learning guidance (semantic encoding);
6 eliciting performance (responding);
7 providing feedback (reinforcement);
8 assessing performance (retrieval);
9 enhancing retention and transfer (generalisation).

(Based on Gagné *et al.*, 1992.)

Learning: John Holt

John Holt (b. New York, 1923–1985) was a classroom teacher who paid close attention to learners and pondered deeply his own observations of children in his classrooms. He spearheaded a revival of child-sensitive teaching, but became disappointed with the impossibility of transforming ordinary schools. He turned to the home-schooling movement that he helped found. His many books are as inspiring as they are crystal clear, based on vivid accounts of incidents that altered his awareness. He enquired openly about learners' experience with a view to improving his own teaching. He was also influenced by Caleb Gattegno, and by visits to classes in Leicestershire, England, in the 1960s. He was the inspiration for the *Education Otherwise* movement of home education. Here he suggests that education which is completely teacher and system directed is at best inefficient and at worst damaging.

> … I believe that we learn best when we, not others, are deciding what we are going to try to learn, and when, and how, and for what reasons or purposes; when we, not others, are in the end choosing the people, materials, and experiences from which and with which we will be learning; when we, not others, are judging how easily or quickly or well we are learning, and when we have learned enough; and above all when we feel the wholeness and openness of the world around us, and our own freedom and power and competence in it. What then do we do about it? How can we create or help create these conditions for learning?
>
> (Holt, 1970, p. 95)

As usual, Holt is very demanding in this passage. How can classes of 30, or in many countries, 50 or more, enable or even permit such learner-centred education? Can learners really pick and choose and decide for themselves? Perhaps that is what they are doing anyway, which is why they often do not appear to learn what teachers are trying to teach them.

Learning: Hans Freudenthal

Hans Freudenthal (b. Germany, 1905–1990) spent most of his influential career in the Netherlands. As a mathematician turned educator he worked with Jean Piaget and with Caleb Gattegno as co-founder of a research society that still runs biannual conferences (AEIEM). He founded an institute in Utrecht, now known as the Freudenthal Institute, and established the approach known as *realistic mathematics*. His weighty tome *Didactical Phenomenology of Mathematical Structures* analyses how to *psychologise the subject matter* (see p. 45 and p. 230) of mathematics by finding the basis for each school topic in learners' experiences of phenomena. He believed that the problem should grow out of the situation, and also that the child should recognise the problem in the situation.

> Mathematical concepts, structures, and ideas serve to organise phenomena
> – phenomena from the concrete world as well as from mathematics.
> [...]
> Phenomenology of a mathematical concept, a mathematical structure, or a mathematical idea means, in my terminology, describing [a] *nooumenon* [thought object] in relation to the *phainomena* [original Latin spelling] of which it is the means of organising, indicating which phenomena it is created to organise, and to which it can be extended, how it acts upon these phenomena as a means of organising, and with what power over these phenomena it endows us. If in this relation of *nooumenon* and *phainomenon* I stress the didactical element, that is, if I pay attention to how the relation is acquired in the learning–teaching process, I speak of *didactical* phenomenology of this *nooumenon*.
>
> (Freudenthal, 1983, pp. 28–9)

Freudenthal prefers to see the development of concepts as the constitution of mental objects through experience of phenomena rather than through concrete embodiments (see p. 203 and p. 249).

Philosophical perspectives: Philip Ballard

Different philosophical perspectives or stances might be thought to be luxuries decorating the surface of education, but, in fact, educational principles are considered to drive behaviour, even when those principles are hidden beneath the surface. For example, Philip Ballard (b. Wales, 1865–1950) was the author of many textbooks in the 1920s on mathematics education, especially concerning early years, which were popular enough to go into several editions. Here Ballard comments on the very different approaches to teaching arithmetic to be found in England and the United States in the 1920s, but he shows that the roots of these approaches go very deep into Greek schools of philosophy:

[England:] … follow tradition in stressing the rational side of arithmetic. After making a few concessions to the immature mind, which may be allowed to gain its first notions of number from bricks or beans, they hasten to apply general principles to particular instances. They proceed deductively. Every step at every stage has to be reasoned out. No unexplained process is allowed to be taken on trust and used on the sole ground that the process works. No lumps of knowledge, however useful they may be as they are, are allowed, even for a while, to escape the grinding of the logical machine. And arithmetic is almost made to appear as a mere branch of deductive logic.

[America:] … arithmetic is presented as an inductive science. Reasoning starts with the concrete fact and ends with the concrete fact. Children learn arithmetic by working sums. The justification for the mode of procedure is that the answer is right. The ground for believing the answer to be right is the word of the teacher, or the result got by reversing the process, or, in the last resort, the irrefutable evidence afforded by counting. The child does a thing first and understands it after. Doing is the important thing; and practice in doing – the practice that, 'line upon line, here a little and there a little', fixes deeper and deeper a series of habits. Arithmetic is in fact not so much an application of broad general principles as an organisation of habits.

Thus we have on the one hand the English view that arithmetic is logic, and the American view that it is habit. The contrast is interesting and significant; but it is not new. It resembles, in fact, the antithesis between the Platonic and the Aristotelian views of virtue. To Plato virtue is knowledge; to Aristotle it is habit. To Plato it is an intellectual grasp of the consequences of our acts; to Aristotle it is the practice of choosing the mean between two extremes.

These differences in emphasis and outlook are not of mere theoretical import: they vitally affect practice. They prescribe what we shall teach, how we shall teach it, and how we shall test it.

(Ballard, 1928, pp. xi–xii)

The American approach developed over some 100 years as American arithmetic textbook authors imported ideas based on Pestalozzi (see below) and developed what they first called the *inductive system* of teaching, later renamed as *synthetic* (in contrast to *analytic* or *deductive*). Of course within a generation even newer textbooks were advocating a fusion of the *analytic* and *synthetic* methods (Nietz, 1966).

For a comprehensive selection of extended extracts from three thousand years of educational writing, see Ulich (1999).

Distinguishing cognition (awareness), affect (emotion) and enaction (behaviour) is supposed to make it easier to make sure that all three are involved, in order to make learning effective.

Reflection is best stimulated by awakening an internal monitor which watches and questions what we are doing while we are doing it.

Every generation, every educator tries to articulate their sense of what learning is, and how it can best be supported and made efficient and effective. There are deep roots for even the most modern and radical of proposals.

There are fundamental obstacles to learning; learners need help in overcoming these through psychologising of the subject matter.

What is learning?

Once you start to enquire into the nature of learning, it is amazing how hard it is to pin down what you mean. In every generation, authors have tried because in order to develop effective teaching, it is necessary to be able to identify and verify learning. The extracts in the rest of this chapter begin with education in general, and then move on to focus on aspects with more specific relevance to mathematics.

Education in general

Education: Alfred North Whitehead

Whitehead was concerned not only with learning, but also with teaching. Here he coins the expression *inert knowledge* (see also p. 288):

> I appeal to you, as practical teachers. With good discipline, it is always possible to pump into the mind of a class a certain quantity of inert knowledge. You take a text-book and make them learn it. So far, so good. ... But what is the point of teaching a child to solve a quadratic equation? There is a traditional answer to this question. It runs thus: The mind is an instrument, you first sharpen it, and then use it; the acquisition of the power of solving a quadratic equation is part of the process of sharpening the mind. Now there is just enough truth in this answer to have made it live through the ages. But for all its half-truth, it embodies a radical error which bids fair to stifle the genius of the modern world. ... The mind is never passive; it is a perpetual activity, delicate, receptive, responsive to stimulus. You cannot postpone its life until you have sharpened it. Whatever interest attaches to your subject-matter must be evoked here and now; whatever powers you are strengthening in the pupil, must be exercised here and now; whatever possibilities of mental life your

teaching should impart, must be exhibited here and now. That is the golden rule of education, and a very difficult rule to follow.

The difficulty is just this: the apprehension of general ideas, intellectual habits of mind, and pleasurable interest in mental achievement can be evoked by no form of words, however accurately adjusted. All practical teachers know that education is the patient process of the mastery of details, minute by minute, hour by hour, day by day. There is no royal road to learning through an airy path of brilliant generalisations. There is a proverb about the difficulty of seeing the wood because of the trees. That difficulty is exactly the point which I am enforcing. The problem of education is to make the pupil see the wood by means of the trees.

(Whitehead, 1932, pp. 8–10)

Note the resonances between attributes you wish to evoke in the minds of children and Dewey's notion of *psychologising the subject matter* (see p. 45 and p. 203), Freudenthal's *didactical phenomenology* (see p. 202), and Gattegno's *educating awareness* (see p. 61 and 204) among others. Whitehead here also seems to be referring to a form of the *transposition didactique* (see p. 83).

Learning in general

What does it mean to know?: Gianbattista Vico

Gianbattista Vico (b. Naples, 1668–1744) was a philosopher scientist who probed what it means 'to know'. His ideas have only relatively recently been taken up and developed. He concluded that people can only know for certain what they have made: other kinds of knowing are not certain in the same way. When people make things with their hands they have objects that they can show to others to say 'This is what I know.' However, when people make mental objects it is not so easy to offer them to others to check out or to use. Vico's refrain was *Verum ipsum factum*: 'the truth is the same as the made'; this can be expanded to ' ... human truth is what man comes to know as he builds it, shaping it by his actions' (Vico, quoted in von Glasersfeld, 1984, p. 27).

The aim of learning is to construct meaning for ourselves, not to attain external, pre-existent meanings. At the same time, we need to conform to agreed social practices. In education, this belief was most notably taken up by Dewey (see p. 45) who said that education should involve the use and development of what learners bring with them to their learning, thus drawing a picture of active learners taking some kind of personal roles in their construction of meaning.

Vico's ideas were brought to the attention of the mathematics education community largely through the writing and scholarship of Ernst von

Glasersfeld who was seeking the roots of Piaget's notion of the learner as constructer of knowledge (*genetic epistemology*, p. 148).

Constructivism: Ernst von Glasersfeld

Ernst von Glasersfeld (b. Munich, 1917–) was at various times a student of mathematics, journalist, and farmer before emigrating to the United States where he established a reputation amongst educationalists for his challenging position as a *radical constructivist* (see p. 93), and as a philosopher and cybernetician. Building on both Piaget and Vico, von Glasersfeld extended and sharpened Piaget's own form of constructivism, *genetic epistemology* (see p. 148). His fluency in German, Italian and French led him to criticise most translations of Piaget for their inaccuracy and misleading nature. Here he summarises key aspects of his *radical constructivism* in relation to Piaget and Vico.

> From an explorer who is condemned to seek 'structural properties' of an inaccessible reality, the experiencing organism now turns into a builder of cognitive structures intended to solve such problems as the organism perceives or conceives. ... Piaget (1937) characterized this scenario as neatly as one could wish: 'intelligence organizes the world by organizing itself'. What determines the value of the conceptual structures is their experiential adequacy, their goodness of *fit* with experience, their *viability* as means for solving of problems, among which is, of course, the never-ending problem of consistent organization that we call *understanding*.
>   The world we live in, from the vantage point of this new perspective, is always and necessarily the world as we conceptualize it. 'Facts', as Vico saw long ago, are *made* by us and our way of experiencing, rather than *given* by an independently existing objective world.
>
> (von Glasersfeld, 1983, pp. 50–1)

There are similarities with Bartlett, Hanson and Goodman (see p. 31). While Dewey and many others had stressed the need for learners to be active, Piaget was claiming that learners are necessarily active, even if they are not actively making the sense that the teacher expects or intends them to make. Von Glasersfeld pushed that further to suggest that there is no way in which the existence of an objective external reality can be affirmed. Rather, all observers have to go on is their sense of 'fit' between what they conjecture and what they construe from their sense impressions. For example, once a lesson is finished, a teacher cannot say that there was a single lesson, but rather the lesson-event consists of the stories told by each participant in thinking back over it.

Learning as making distinctions

We turn now to more specific and mathematically pertinent views of learning. The root awareness, which all babies have even before they are born, is the awareness of distinction making, for example, distinguising the sound of mother's voice from other noises. Distinction making is perhaps the most fundamental power possessed by all sensate beings (including all animals and plants). Differences between organisms arise in the difference (there it is again: making distinctions) between the range and refinement of distinctions made. Distinction-making often creates tension, which is a form of disturbance, prompting further exploration of relationships, properties and so on, all in an attempt to re-integrate the distinguished and appreciate the whole.

Discernment: Ference Marton

Ference Marton (b. Hungary, 1939–) moved eventually to Sweden where he has led a long programme of research at all levels and in all subjects. He and his colleagues also developed the approach to research known as *phenomenography* (Marton, 1981), which charts (-graphy) the variations in lived experience (phenomena) of learners as opposed to phenomenology, which is a well-established philosophical movement.

> … learning takes place, knowledge is born, by a change in something in the world as experienced by a person. The new way of experiencing something is constituted in the person–world relationships and involves both. … Person and world, the inner and outer are not separated. We do not have to account for how knowledge travels from one to the other. Instead of trying to account for how the person–world relationship is established, we posit this relationship and study how it changes as time passes.
>
> (Marton and Booth, 1997, p. 139)

> … teachers mold experiences for their students with the aim of bringing about learning, and the essential feature is that the *teacher takes the part of the learner*, sees the experience through the learner's eyes, becomes aware of the experience throughout the learner's awareness. If we … consider the learner to be internally related to the object of learning, and if we consider the teacher to be internally related to the same object of learning, we can see the two, learner and teacher, meet through a shared object of learning. In addition to this, the teacher makes the learner's experience of the object of learning into an object of her own focal awareness: the teacher focuses on the learner's experience of the object of learning.
>
> (ibid., p. 179)

In the next extracts, Marton and Booth focus on the fundamental act of discerning foreground from background, and emphasise that making distinctions is the basis of learning. What you cannot discern, you cannot see.

> In order to experience something *as* something we must be able to discern it from and relate it to a context, and be able to discern its parts and relate them to each other and to the whole. But we discern wholes, parts, and relationships in terms of aspects that define the wholes, the parts, and the relationships. To discern the spatial arrangement of the landscape we have to experience the spatial arrangement as *a* spatial arrangement (among other conceivable spatial arrangements).
>
> (ibid., p. 108)

> ... the act of gaining knowledge about the world involves qualitative differences ... in the way things are experienced (understood, conceptualized, apprehended, etc.) – as phenomena, situations, or learning itself. The question that now becomes interesting is that of what it means and what it takes to experience something in a particular way ...
>
> (ibid., p. 86)

> The aspects of the phenomenon and the relationships between them that are discerned and simultaneously present in the individual's focal awareness define the individual's way of experiencing the phenomenon. Being focally aware of the weight of the body immersed in some fluid as compared to its weight when not immersed, of the fact that a certain volume of the fluid is displaced by the act of immersion, of the weight of the fluid displaced – all at the same time – amounts to what it takes to discover, or to understand, Archimedes' principle. The key feature of the structural aspect of a way of experiencing something (and thereby also of the referential aspect with which the structural aspect is intertwined) is the set of different aspects of the phenomena as experienced that are simultaneously present in focal awareness.
>
> (ibid., p. 101)

For example, discerning the vertices and edges of a figure instead of just the overall shape, and discerning the positions of digits in a numeral as representing powers of ten and not just a string of numerals, alter how you see, what you can do, and the choices available to you.

Dimensions-of-variation: Ference Marton and Shirley Booth

Marton and Booth considered what learners are learning to discern in a typical lesson. They were thinking in terms of concepts, and the use and meaning of technical terms.

To experience a particular situation in terms of the general aspects, we have to experience the general aspects. These aspects correspond to *dimensions of variation*. That which we observe in a specific situation we tacitly experience as *values* in those dimensions. A certain way of experiencing something can at best be understood in terms of the dimensions of variation that are discerned and are simultaneously focal in awareness, and in terms of the relationships between the different dimensions of variation.

(Marton and Booth, 1997, p. 108)

If we notice that something *is the case* (e.g., there are 7 marbles hidden in one box), the variation is implicit; there is an implication that there could have been 6 or 8 or some other number of marbles, but we do not focus on it. The dimensions are discerned in relation to the thematic field against the background of which the phenomenon, and the situation in which it is embedded, is seen.

(ibid., p. 101)

Learning is seen as learning to discern, which requires simultaneity–discernment–variation. See also Marion Walter's work on 'what-if' questions (Brown and Walter, 1993).

Dimensions-of-possible-variation: Anne Watson and John Mason

Anne Watson (1948–) has taught in secondary schools in England, been head of department, and been a teacher educator at both primary and secondary level. Her focus is always on mathematics, and she works to promote inclusive mathematics learning and teaching. With Ference Marton, together with his student Ulla Runesson and John Mason, Anne has extended the notion of *dimension-of-variation* to recognise that within any one dimension-of-possible-variation different people might be aware of different permissible choices. For example, in an identity such as $(x-1)(x+1)$, some people, aware that x can take 'any' value, might be thinking only in terms of x as an integer, or as a rational number, or as a real number, or as a complex number, or as a square matrix, or as a differential operator … . Another dimension-of-possible-variation is the exponent 2, leading to factoring of $x^n - 1$, and again people may be aware of different ranges of permissible change for n (see also Stein, p. 177). A third dimension-of-possible-variation is the constant term 1 with a range-of-permissible-change being the nth power of some term. Thus tasks that reveal the *dimensions-of-possible-variation*, and the corresponding *range-of-permissible-change* in each dimension of which learners are aware, are pedagogically useful. They indicate where further work may be required. See Watson and Mason (in press).

A single exercise or problem is an example of a task. Asking yourself what could be changed, while using the same approach or technique, opens up dimensions-of-possible-variation; asking what sorts of change can be made in any one such dimension opens up range-of-permissible-change, leading to the notion of variable and parameter. Together these two ideas transform a set of exercises from a sequence of tasks for learners to work through piecemeal, into a domain of generality – a technique in the full sense of the word.

Whenever learners see through a particular mathematical object to a more general class of objects, or through a particular or mathematical exercise to a class of problems, they are demonstrating awareness of a dimension-of-possible-variation. There are similarities with Whitehead on *generalising* (see p. 132) and also with the van Hiele *phases* (see p. 59) and the *structure of attention* (see p. 60).

Learning as structuring attention

The terms *attention* and *awareness* are used differently by different authors, often even interchangeably. We start with Marton and Booth who use *awareness* in much the way that others use *attention*.

Structuring awareness: Ference Marton and Shirley Booth

In Marton and Booth's work on the anatomy of awareness (Marton and Booth, 1997), it is posited that a person's way of experiencing something is related to how their awareness is structured. There is both a 'what' aspect, which corresponds to the object of the experience, and a 'how' aspect, which relates to the act of experiencing. The way of experiencing can be couched in terms of a dynamic relationship between the two aspects of the phenomenon, the structural aspect and the referential (or meaning) aspect.

> If we consider an individual at any instant, he or she is aware of certain things or certain aspects of reality focally while other things have receded to the background. But we are aware of everything all the time, even if not in the same way all the time. The structure of an individual's awareness keeps changing all the time, and that totality of experience is what we call the individual's awareness. An experience is an internal relationship between the person experiencing and the phenomenon experienced: it reflects the latter as much as the former. If awareness is the totality of all experience, then awareness is as descriptive of the world as it is of the person. A person's awareness is the world as experienced by the person.
>
> (Marton and Booth, 1997, p. 108)

There are similarities with *stressing and ignoring* (p. 127).

Structuring attention: Van Hiele and Van Hiele

Dina and Pierre van Hiele (b. The Netherlands) studied the development of geometrical thinking, particularly in school. Dina was an experienced teacher of mathematics who was notable (see p. 163) for studying her own teaching, but died tragically young; Pierre is the theorist who then extended their work beyond geometry.

The clearest exposition of the different types of thinking that the van Hieles discerned can be found in later authors (for example, Burger and Shaughnessy, 1986) who tried to develop tests to distinguish the different 'levels' of thinking. However, the van Hiele 'levels' were intended to describe thinking in the moment, not to categorise learners. At any given moment a person can be looking at one aspect holistically but without discerning features, while being aware of other properties and reasoning quite formally with still others. The following descriptions of the van Hiele levels have been modified by replacing 'a student at this level' (which implies that people can be classified as at certain levels) by 'functioning at this level' (which implies that at different times people may function differently).

- Level 1 (*Visualisation*) Functioning at this level involves reasoning about basic geometric concepts, such as simple shapes, primarily by means of visual considerations of the concept as a whole without explicit regard to the properties of its components. One 'sees', for example, that two triangles are similar, without recourse to reasons or aspects (see also van Hiele, 1986, p. 83).
- Level 2 (*Analysis, description using language developed at previous level*) Functioning at this level involves reasoning about geometric concepts by means of an informal analysis of component parts and attributes. Necessary parts of the concept are established. For instance, similar triangles can be recognised and justified in terms of possession of properties (see also van Hiele, 1986, pp. 83–4).
- Level 3 (*Abstraction, using language for distinctions developed at previous level*) Functioning at this level involves thinking of, say, a rectangle as a collection of properties that it must have (necessary conditions). When asked why a figure is a rectangle, the response would be a litany of properties: 'Opposite sides are parallel, opposite sides are congruent, opposite angles are equal, you have four right angles … '. Likewise, similar triangles can be located and justified by recourse to necessary conditions, using an argument involving statements following from or depending on each other in sequence (see also van Hiele, 1986, p. 84).
- Level 4 (*Informal deduction*) Functioning at this level means selecting sufficient conditions from the 'litany' described in Level 3 to determine a rectangle. Properties are ordered logically and the role of general

definitions is appreciated. Simple inferences can be made, and class inclusions are recognised (for example, squares are rectangles).

- Level 5 (*Rigour, Formal deduction*) Functioning at this level means comparing systems based on different axioms, and studying various geometries in the absence of concrete models.

(adapted from Burger and Shaughnessy (1986))

In van Hiele terms, Level 3 awareness of a geometric figure means awareness of a variety of properties, each of which constitutes a relationship that holds between perceived details of the figure. However, connections between these properties are at best dimly sensed, and the properties are seen as pertaining to the particular geometrical object rather than independent of it. Thus, angles, edge-lengths, triangles and circles may be discerned, but not the necessary links between them. The notion that some properties are sufficient to force a figure to have a certain quality such as being a square or a parallelogram is part of the fourth level awareness. Recognising equality of angles as implying similarity and so being led to look at ratios of corresponding lengths shows logical organisation of properties, hence level five awareness.

The SOLO taxonomy (see p. 309) has some similarities with van Hiele phases, as does Alan Bell's *principles of task design,* and also the onion model of understanding (see p. 298).

There is a slightly different way of thinking about phases, which corresponds closely to that of van Hiele but which was derived quite independently from ancient sources (Bennett, 1956–1966; 1993). It focuses on what learners are attending to at any moment, and describes this in terms of *the structure of attention*:

- attention on the whole, the global;
- attention on distinctions, distinguishing and discerning aspects, detailed features and attributes;
- attention on relationships between parts or between part and whole, among aspects, features and attributes discerned;
- attention on relationships as properties that objects like the one being considered can have, leading to generalisation;
- attention on properties as abstracted from, formalised and stated independently of any particular objects, forming axioms from which deductions can be made.

There are also important shifts from seeing something in its particularity to seeing it as representative of a general class.

For distinction-making as a natural human *power*, see p. 124; for its biological basis see later in this section (p. 70).

Experiencing the world: Ingrid Pramling

Ingrid Pramling (b. Sweden, 1946–) was a research student of Ference Marton. Here she describes in the abstract of her thesis the approach that she takes to working with young learners:

> How children conceptualise, experience, discern, see, understand the world around them is the ground from which their skills and knowledge originate. This implies that early childhood education should primarily focus on the different ways children are capable of being aware of the various phenomena in the world around them. Above all, we should find out the critical, and usually taken for granted, aspects of our ways of experiencing the world around us on which our capabilities for dealing with the world rest. Learning from this perspective is learning to experience the world in particular ways.
>
> (Pramling, 1994)

Pramling has developed this view into the importance of *reflection* (see p. 286).

Learning as educating awareness

Educating awareness: Caleb Gattegno

Caleb Gattegno (1911–1988) grew up in Alexandria. His lifelong concern was to develop a systematic enquiry into human learning. He moved to England where he was involved in teacher education, founding what later became the Association of Teachers of Mathematics and co-founding the International Commission for the Study and Improvement of Mathematics Teaching (CIEAEM), an international body, which has an annual conference in Europe. He discovered Cuisenaire's 'rods', which he developed and promulgated around the world, making films of demonstration lessons and publishing books about their use. He then moved into teaching foreign languages, using what he called *The Silent Way* based on the use of colours to represent sounds. Gattegno went on to articulate a *science of education* based on close analysis and study of the universe of babies and how learning takes place in the first few years.

> Observation of very young babies yields evidence that in crying, for instance, there is the presence of consciousness and that crying is not only the use of reflex mechanisms but also reveals the presence of the crier in the cries. Only the presence of consciousness explains the reason these cries can be made louder, more prolonged, and can be structured at will to express small things the baby knows intimately from inside. At four weeks, for example, a baby may find in his or her cry sounds which have attributes that can be extracted from the whole, singled out for special attention and examined per se before the baby

returns to crying and the purpose for which the crying was started and is being continued.

Perhaps one must have encountered a phenomenon like this to allow oneself to entertain as an instrument of study the multiple dialogues the self has with itself, even from conception.

(Gattegno, 1987, p. 7)

When someone becomes aware that they can establish a one-to-one correspondence between marks on wood and sheep, say, then the act of counting becomes available for study, whereas previously it had only been an action to undertake. This for Gattegno is the source of all disciplines: people becoming aware of the actions they perform and turning these into an object of study: aware of their awareness.

Further levels are generated as people move into teaching, and then into teacher education (see Mason, 1998). There are similarities with *theorems-in-action* (see p. 63), and with *enactivism* (see p. 70).

Gattegno's notion of teaching as arranging for learners to *educate their awareness* is extended to include *training in behaviour* through *harnessing of emotions* (see p. 204).

Awareness-in-action

As has already been pointed out, there are things that people are not aware of but which are vital to how they function, and things that they have been aware of but no longer need to be. The latter can be referred to as awareness-in-action. For example, people can count without being aware of one-to-one correspondence, and people can add, subtract, multiply, and divide, without being explicitly aware of their awarenesses-in-action of numerals, place-value, routines, the role of order, and so on, which makes that arithmetic possible. People can form and detect patterns and locate formulae that generalise specific cases without being explicitly aware of their awarenesses-in-action of same and different, relatedness, induction, stressing and ignoring. People can combine fractions according to rules, without being aware of how fractions relate to decimals and to integers, and how they generalise number, without being aware of the slide between operator and object and without relating them to a number-line.

Awareness therefore has different forms, here exemplified by the notion of *angle*:

- *awarenesses-in-action*: things you can do with an angle, but cannot articulate or even be consciously aware of (but which are consonant with what later become theorems);
- *awarenesses of sense*: things which are pre-articulate, yet somehow present in consciousness and informing action: a sense of big angles and of rotation;

- *awarenesses in articulation*: things you can say about angles, not just do with them, and even things you know but find hard to do physically.

Vergnaud (1981) referred to *awarenesses-in-action* as *theorems-in-action*, while *awarenesses-in-articulation* are conscious *theorems*.

Awareness is not everything though. Awareness is based on actions, and leads to further actions. Behaviour, whether physical, mental, symbolic or virtual develops as a result of becoming aware of existing awarenesses. Awareness alone is like knowledge without skill: nothing actually happens. Learning involves both educating awareness and using that awareness to direct behaviour, which can be trained by developing habits.

Awareness and behaviour together are not sufficient to characterise learning, because something is needed to produce action – to make things happen. The source of energy lies in the emotions. Emotions are what have to be harnessed in order to engage in activities through which learning can take place. This view is captured in the image of the human psyche as a *chariot* or *carriage* (see p. 33). The notions of discipline, of being systematic, of concentrating and persisting, all depend on emotional energy. If you are feeling unconfident or if you feel unvalued, then attention and desire can be greatly attenuated. Emotions come into play when people become aware of a *disturbance* (see p. 55 and p. 101).

Learning as developing intuition

Awareness and intuition are closely related though not identical.

Intuition: Efraim Fischbein

Efraim Fischbein (b. Romania, 1920–1998) was an Israeli mathematics educator and researcher. He was the founding president of the international group Psychology of Mathematics Education (PME), which runs an annual international conference. As a researcher he was particularly interested in the role that intuition plays, both in problem solving and in learning new concepts, and he is best known for his seminal work on intuition in science and mathematics. More recently he studied the role of diagrams in teaching.

Intuition needs to be set against formal deduction, which so many people believe characterises mathematics, even though mathematicians themselves see deductive proof as merely the final step, the wrapping up in order to convince others. The creative aspects of mathematics lie in bringing to expression nascent and developing intuitions.

> There is today much evidence – both experimental and descriptive – that no productive mathematical reasoning is possible by resorting only to formal means. One may possess all the formal knowledge relevant to a mathematical topic (definitions, axioms, theorems, proofs, etc.) and yet

the system does not work by itself in a productive manner (for *solving* problems, *producing* theorems and proofs, etc.).

(Fischbein, 1987, p. 16)

Our theory is that mental behavior (reasoning, solving, understanding, predicting, interpreting) including mathematical activity, is subjected to the same fundamental constraints. *The mental 'objects' (concepts, operations, statements) must get a kind of intrinsic consistency and direct evidence similar to those of real, external, material objects and events, if the reasoning process is to be a genuinely productive activity.*

(ibid., p. 20)

Here Fischbein considers how mathematics relates to the material world and the world of symbols. His views are challenged by those who see mathematics as necessarily fallible and social.

This world of constructs – the world of mathematics – seems to mirror all the features which enable the known real world to function. To be sure, it mirrors them on its own terms, but all the ingredients seem to exist for conferring credibility, consistency, coherence, on this world of mentally produced abstractions.

In other words, the human mind seems to have learned from the basic general properties of empirical reality how to build an imaginary, structured world, similarly governed by rules and similarly capable of consistency and credibility. The fundamental difference is that in the empirical world the constraints (invariant properties and relationships) are implicitly given, while in the formal world every property and every relationship is stated and justified explicitly. The history of mathematics is the history of the human endeavor for shaping a new type of certitude dealing with explicitly postulated entities governed by explicitly, formally-stated rules.

… the ideal aim of this endeavor has been, and still is, the creation of a world of concepts which may function coherently in an absolutely autarchic way. This was the dream of the modern, axiomatic approach.

(ibid., p. 16)

Mathematics is perhaps unique in formalising concepts in succinctly manipulable symbols that stand for mathematical objects (see *reification*, p. 167). This leads to problems of how to explain the effective interaction between these three worlds – the worlds of concepts, symbols and objects. How can ideas influence the material world? How is it that the symbols and equations of mathematics so effectively enable the prediction of events in the material world when many of those ideas go well beyond anything that can be found in the material world (for example, infinite decimals, complex numbers, and so on). This 'unreasonable effectiveness' was marvelled at by Eugene Wigner (see p. 194).

An intuition is, then, an *idea* which possesses the two fundamental properties of a concrete, objectively-given reality; *immediacy* – that is to say intrinsic *evidence* – and *certitude* (not formal conventional certitude, but practically meaningful, immanent certitude).

(Fischbein, 1987, p. 21)

We consider that the emergence of apparently self-evident, self-consistent cognitions – generally termed intuitions – is a fundamental condition of a normal, fluent, productive reasoning activity. An intuition is a complex cognitive structure the role of which is to organize the available information (even incomplete) into apparently coherent, internally consistent, self-evident, practically meaningful representations.

(ibid., p. 211)

In the last extract, one might wish to replace 'certitude' with 'strong conjecture'!

The notion of where and whether mathematical objects and intuitions 'exist' has haunted mathematical philosophers ever since Plato decided that they belong to an independent world of forms, accessed through mental imagery. Fischbein was not so concerned about where mental objects exist:

Mathematical entities such as numbers and geometrical figures do not have an external, independent existence as the objects of the empirical sciences do. In mathematics, we deal with entities whose properties are completely fixed by axioms and definitions. Dealing with such entities requires a mental attitude which is fundamentally different from that required by empirical, materially existing realities.

(ibid., p. 206)

In terms of van Hiele *levels* (see p. 59), Fischbein is looking at the need to become aware of properties independent of particular objects, and how deductions can be made from those properties alone on the basis of conjectures arising from familiarity with one or more examples. This leads to didactical challenges:

An essential recommendation is to create didactical situations which can help the student to become aware of ... conflicts. However, rendering manifest the latent conflicts does not solve the problem by itself. This procedure has to be associated with the already mentioned activity of analyzing explicitly the properties – as stated by definitions – of the mathematical entities considered (in contrast with the intuitive interpretations).

[...]

... initial intuitive interpretations become very strongly attached to the respective concepts and, consequently, it becomes very difficult to escape their impact. Yet it is impossible to avoid using intuitive means initially when introducing new mathematical concepts. While there is no general recipe for solving the dilemma, this is what we recommend. One has to start, as early as possible, preparing the child for understanding the formal meaning and the formal content of the concepts taught. This may be done, first of all, by revealing the relationships between concepts and operations and by rendering explicit the underlying common structures of different concepts and operations. Multiplication and division, for instance, are inverse aspects of multiplicative structures which, in turn, are related to proportional reasoning.

[...]

... it is important to develop in students the conviction that: (a) one possesses also correct, useful intuitions and (b) that we may become able to control our intuitions by assimilating adequate formal structures.

[...]

When referring to the development of intuitions one has to consider also anticipatory intuitions. Though mathematics is a deductive system of knowledge, the creative activity in mathematics is a constructive process in which inductive procedures, analogies and plausible guesses play a fundamental role. The effect is very often crystallized in anticipatory intuitions. Much more attention should be given, in our opinion, to educating students' sensibility for similarities, the ability to identify ... and describe, structures.

(ibid., pp. 208–10)

Compare the first paragraph in the extract above with the role of *disturbance*, surprise and Festinger's *cognitive dissonance* (see p. 69). There are similarities with *didactic phenomenology* (p. 202) and *awareness of awareness* (p. 186 and p. 189).

The issue of intuition, as opposed to deductive rigour, and of objective existence of mathematical objects in some 'world', leads to the need to distinguish between what is arbitrary (decided by *convention*) and what is necessary (see Hewitt, p. 159).

Beyond practically defined circumstances [the concept of a straight line] is a *convention* defined in the frame of a certain group of axioms, *which may be changed*. But via extrapolation (from a behavioral meaning contextually dependent on an absolute universal concept), *one tends to believe in the absoluteness of the concept, one tends to confer on this notion, based on conventions, the absoluteness of a given, objectively existing fact*. In our terminology, this means conferring *intuitivity* on the concept, or, in other words, the concept of a straight line gets an intuitive meaning for the individual.

(ibid., p. 21)

Intuitivity is closely related to *reification* (see p. 167). Fischbein concludes with:

> It is important to emphasize that new, correct intuitions do not simply replace primitive, incorrect ones. Primary intuitions are usually so resistant that they may coexist with new, superior, scientifically acceptable ones. That situation very often generates inconsistencies in the student's reactions depending on the nature of the problem.
>
> [...]
>
> In order to cope successfully with the instructional problems, one has first to have a good, serious understanding of the psychological aspects of the concepts involved. Much more research is needed in this respect. We have to know what are the tacit interpretations the student attaches to these concepts, what are the intuitive reactions, the intuitive models he produces, the impact they may have on the acquisition of the new concepts. On the other hand, one has to evaluate the effect of the various didactical means on the complex and labile relationships between the intuitive loading of the concepts taught and their formal structure. An inadequate strategy may destroy the productive interaction of these two components.
>
> (ibid., pp. 213–14)

Fischbein taught that incomplete or inappropriate intuitions are always present, but hopefully overlaid with educated intuitions. Also that through an appropriate classroom atmosphere and ethos, learners can develop intuitions concerning gaps in arguments, dissonances between different ways of thinking about or describing situations, and so on.

Note the similarities between Fischbein's reflections and Tall and Vinner's notion of *concept-image* (see p. 200).

Learning as response to disturbance

Virtually every educational theory acknowledges that organisms (incuding humans) respond to disturbances from their environment. Some theories make more of this than do others.

Discrepancies lead to discovery: Theodoret Cook

This extract is taken from the preface of Cook's book *The Curves of Life* (Cook, 1979) in response to heavy criticism of his conjectural notebooks in which he had used mathematical ideas to model pure form from which manifestations in nature seemed to deviate.

> It is largely by noting approximations ... and then investigating the deviations that 'knowledge grows from more to more'. Discrepancies lead to

> Discovery. ... deviations are one cause of beauty and one manifestation
> of life; and this is why the study of exceptions is the road to progress.
>
> (Cook, 1979, preface)

Attending to what learners are struggling to express, and interacting with
them on that basis, can lead to more open and less limiting forms of questioning. However, attending to deviation from an ideal is at the heart of the
language of learners' *errors and misconceptions* (see p. 212), and leads
naturally to forms of questioning that are limiting, and even to *funnelling*
(see p. 274).

Disturbance: Jerome Bruner

Bruner proposed that human beings are essentially narrative animals, telling
stories to themselves and others as a way of making sense of the world. Here
he is analysing the components of a narrative, and discovers that at the heart
of a good narrative is some sort of disturbance.

> At a minimum, a 'story' (fictional or actual) involves an Agent who Acts
> to achieve a Goal in a recognizable Setting by the use of certain Means.
> What drives the story, what makes it worth telling, is Trouble: some
> misfit between Agents, Acts, Goals, Settings, and Means. Why is Trouble
> the license for telling a story? Narrative begins with an explicit or implicit
> prologue establishing the ordinariness or legitimacy of its initial circum-
> stances – "I was walking down the street minding my own business
> when ... ". The action then unfolds leading to a breach, a violation of
> legitimate expectancy. What follows is either a restitution of initial legiti-
> macy or a revolutionary change of affairs with a new order of legitimacy.
> Narratives (truth or fiction) end with a coda, restoring teller and listener
> to the here and now, usually with a hint of evaluation of what has
> transpired.
>
> (Bruner, 1996, pp. 94–5)

Note the parallels with *assimilation* and *accommodation* (see p. 149), recast
here as the basis for the construction of narrative. People 'wake up' when
there is some sort of disturbance from the expected flow; the same applies to
learners' experiences in lessons. There is more likely to be some meaning-
making through the construction of personal narratives based on shared
classroom and peer group narratives if there is something that surprises or
disturbs, something that catches attention.

Learner narratives include *purposes* for specific activities and for school
itself, as well as for how a technique is used, and why.

> ... what *is* [important] is the procedure of the inquiry, of mind using,
> which is central to the maintenance of an interpretive community and a

democratic culture. One step is to choose the crucial problems, particularly the problems that are prompting change within our culture. Let those problems and our procedures for thinking about them be part of what school and classwork are about. This does not mean that school becomes a rallying place for discussion of the culture's failures. ... Trouble is the engine of narrative and the justification for going public with the story. It is the whiff of trouble that leads us to search out the relevant or responsible constituents in the narrative, in order to convert the raw Trouble into a manageable Problem that can be handled with procedural muscle.

(ibid., pp. 98–9)

Choosing fundamental problems for learners to work on over a period of time is one common approach to curriculum development (see also *investigative teaching*, p. 225).

Cognitive dissonance: Leon Festinger

Leon Festinger (b. New York, 1919–1989) was a social psychologist interested in human learning. He is best known for his *theory of cognitive dissonance*, which can be used to account for certain observations that most teachers will have experienced, if not marked and remarked upon for themselves: it requires some sort of a disturbance, some sort of surprise or broken expectation to capture attention and initiate enquiry.

1   The existence of dissonance, being psychologically uncomfortable, will motivate the person to try to reduce the dissonance and achieve consonance.
2   When dissonance is present, in addition to trying to reduce it, the person will actively avoid situations and information which would likely increase the dissonance.
   [...]
   ... dissonance, that is, the existence of nonfitting relations among cognitions, is a motivating factor in its own right. ... Cognitive dissonance can be seen as an antecedent condition which leads to activity oriented toward dissonance reduction just as hunger leads to activity oriented toward hunger reduction.

(Festinger, 1957, p. 3)

Festinger suggested a number of different sources for dissonance, including: local and global inconsistencies; cultural mores; past experience; rewards or threats for behaviour at variance with personal opinion; and, after a decision, when positive features of the rejected alternative, and negative features of the chosen one, become salient.

Festinger went on to make conjectures about the effects of differing magnitudes of dissonance and consonance. Alan Bell's *diagnostic teaching*

(p. 233) is particularly notable for making use of the role of cognitive dissonance as disturbance in the design of teaching.

Disturbance is often experienced as *surprise* (see Moshovits-Hadar, p. 101),
and this is a component that is central component to *motivation* and the
harnessing of emotions (see p. 55 and p. 204). When an organism responds
to disturbance in its environment, the disturbance leads to action, and action
produces learning.

Learning as action

Enactivism: Humberto Maturana and Francisco Varela

A rather different perspective on learning arises from the writings of
Humberto Maturana (1928–), who principally researches the biological bases
of communication, extending his research into many different domains. He
takes a view referred to as *enactivism* in which 'action is knowledge and
knowledge is action'.

There are similarities with Piaget's remark 'intelligence organises the world
by organising itself' (see p. 94).

> An observer is a human being, a person, a living system who can make
> distinctions and specify that which he or she distinguishes as a unity, as
> an entity different from himself or herself that can be used for manipula-
> tions or descriptions in interactions with other observers. An observer
> can make distinctions in actions and thoughts, recursively, and is able to
> operate as if he or she were external to (distinct from) the circumstances
> in which the observer finds himself or herself. Everything said is said by
> an observer to another observer, who can be himself or herself.
>
> (Maturana, 1978, p. 31)

The last statement may seem rather obvious at first, but it has profound
implications, for it asserts that any form of speech is second order: it is not
direct experience but experience recast into language, as if from an observer.
There are significant implications for this perspective. For example:

> An explanation is always a proposition that reformulates or recreates the
> observations of a phenomenon in a system of concepts acceptable to a
> group of people who share a criterion of validation.
>
> (Maturana and Varela, 1988, p. 28)

This fits well with conclusions drawn by Hanson and by Goodman among
many others (see p. 31), underlying the *discipline of noticing* (Mason,
2002c), about the intricate intertwining of observation and validity, and the
view that there are no objective criteria for 'truth'.

Maturana goes on to elaborate:

> ... we can distinguish four conditions essential to proposing a scientific explanation. They do not necessarily fall in sequential order but do overlap in some way. They are:
>
> a describing the phenomenon (or phenomena) to be explained in a way acceptable to a body of observers;
> b proposing a conceptual system capable of generating the phenomenon to be explained in a way acceptable to a body of observers (explanatory hypothesis);
> c obtaining from (b) other phenomena not explicitly considered in that proposition, as also describing its conditions for observation by a body of observers;
> d observing these other phenomena obtained from (b).
>
> (Maturana and Varela, 1988, p. 28)

Maturana's writing slides quickly from the pragmatic to the ethereal. Here he and his colleague Francisco Varela (b. Chile, 1946–2001) reject some of the distinctions others make, say, between different worlds (see p. 73), and then address the issue of 'observation' from a researcher's or a teacher's point of view: what can we see when we observe?

> ... our experience is moored to our structure in a binding way. We do not see the 'space' of the world; we live in our field of vision. We do not see the 'colors' of the world; we live our chromatic space. Doubtless ... we are experiencing a world. But when we examine more closely how we get to know this world, we invariably find that we cannot separate our history of actions – biological and social – from how this world appears to us. It is so obvious and close that it is hard to see.
>
> (ibid., p. 23)

This is entirely compatible with von Glasersfeld's *radical constructivism* (see p. 93), and with Goodman's and Hanson's views (see p. 31).

> ... underlying everything we say is this constant awareness that the phenomenon of knowing cannot be taken as though there were 'facts' or objects out there that we grasp and store in our head. The experience of anything out there is validated in a special way by the human structure, which makes possible 'the thing' that arises in the description.
>
> This circularity, this connection between action and experience, this inseparability between a particular way of being and how the world appears to us, tells us that *every act of knowing brings forth a world.* ... *All doing is knowing, and all knowing is doing.*
>
> (ibid., p. 25–6)

The notion of 'bringing forth a world' aptly describes experience as someone launches into speech and others try to make sense of what is said. This applies specifically to mathematics, where a teacher is comfortably navigating a world brought forth by some stimulus, but learners bring forth only the worlds available to them.

Several authors have taken up the enactivist view. For example, there is a close agreement with Greeno's *environment view* of mathematical learning, and with Cobb, Yackel and Wood's enriched constructive view of classroom life that may help situate them:

> In the environmental view, knowing a set of concepts is not equivalent to having representations of the concepts but rather involves abilities to find and use the concepts in constructive processes of reasoning. ... The person's knowledge ... is in his or her ability to find and use the resources, not in having mental versions of maps and instructions as the basis for all reasoning and action.
>
> (Greeno, 1991, p. 175)

> We emphasize that mathematics is both a collective human activity ... and an individual constructive activity.
>
> (Cobb *et al.*, 1992, p. 17)

Enactivism: Sen Campbell and Sandy Dawson

Sandy Dawson (b. Alberta, 1940–) is a teacher and teacher educator inspired by Caleb Gattegno and by Humberto Maturana. Sen Campbell (b. Alberta, 1952–) is also a strong advocate of enactivism. Both Dawson and Campbell see the classroom in terms of stressing and ignoring, whether by the learner or by the environment:

> ... the learner chooses to stress certain aspects of the activities and to ignore others. It is not just a one-way street, however, with the learner being the predominant force. The environment exerts itself by putting limits on what pathways the learner is able to pursue. Learning occurs at the interstices where the learner meets the environment, stresses particularities within that environment, and generates a response whose viability in the environment is then determined. However, the realm of the possible must intersect with the predilection of the learner to take notice of it. The particular pathway mutually determined by the learner and the environment is rarely unique. Other pathways are possible. The one selected is but one of many ways of satisfying the demands of the interaction as seen by the learner and permitted by the environment.
>
> (Campbell and Dawson, 1995, p. 244)

There is similarity with *affordances* (p. 246).

... the learning which teachers hope will occur does not happen simply as the result of engaging learners in particular activities, whether those activities are, for example, a teacher talking to/with learners, learners watching a film, or learners using a computer ... . however, if learners *don't get it*, (whatever *it* might be), it doesn't follow that there is something wrong with the learners, or that the learners weren't listening, or weren't paying attention. It is just that the learners were at that point in time *stressing* things other than those which the teacher might have anticipated, or that environment and those learners – given their particular history of structural coupling – did not opt for the pathway expected by the teacher. It is evident, then, that teaching is not telling.

(ibid., p. 245)

See also *epistemological obstacles* (p. 303).

Radical enactivism: Brent Davis, Dennis Summara and Tom Kieren

A more radical perspective on *enactivism* sees learning and action as one and the same (see also Maturana, p. 70):

Learning should not be understood in terms of a sequence of actions, but in terms of an ongoing *structural dance* – a complex choreography – of events which, even in retrospect, cannot be fully disentangled and understood, let alone reproduced.

(Davis, Summara and Kieren, 1996, p. 153)

Three worlds (material, imagined, symbolic): Jerome Bruner

Where do the actions take place that are so strongly espoused as the essence of learning? Immersed as we are in the material world, philosophers from Plato and before were aware that human beings, at least, occupy themselves with an inner world of mental images, ideas, and concepts, and a mediating world of symbols that afford access to images and that express images.

... a view of human beings who have developed three parallel systems for processing information and for representing it – one through manipulation and action, one through perceptual organization and imagery, and one through symbolic apparatus. It is not that these are 'stages' in any sense; they are rather emphases in development. You must get the perceptual field organized around your own person as center before you can impose other, less egocentric axes upon it, for example. In the end, the mature organism seems to have gone through a process of elaborating three systems of skills that correspond to the three major tool systems to which he must link himself for full expression of his capacities – tools for the hand, for the distance receptors, and for the process of reflection.

(Bruner, 1966, p. 28)

The fundamental triad: Anna Sierpinska

Anna Sierpinska (b. Poland, 1947–) moved to Canada where she is a leading researcher and mathematics educator.

> [Hall (1981)] speaks of the 'fundamental triad': three levels of experiencing the world by man, three ways of transmission of this experience to children, three types of consciousness, three types of emotional relations to things: the 'formal', the 'informal', the 'technical'.
>
> The 'formal' level is the level of traditions, conventions, unquestioned opinions, sanctioned customs and rites that do not call for justification. The transmission of this level of culture is based on direct admonition, explicit correction of errors without explanation. ... Built up over generations, the formal systems are normally very coherent. ...
>
> The 'informal' level is the level of the often unarticulated schemes of behaviour and thinking. Our knowledge of typing, or skiing, or biking belongs to this level of culture if we do not happen to be instructors of these skills. This level of culture is acquired through imitation, practice and participation in a culture, and not by following a set of instructions. Very often neither the imitated nor the imitating know that some teaching–learning process is taking place.
>
> At the 'technical level', knowledge is explicitly formulated. This knowledge is analytical, aimed to be logically coherent and rationally justified.
>
> ... technical education starts with errors and correction of errors, but a different tone is used here and the student is being explained his error (Hall, 1981).

(Sierpinska, 1994, pp. 161–2)

The three levels are the basis for a description of mathematical modelling as a process (see p. 190).

One person's useful distinctions (for example, 'three worlds') is another person's artificial and unhelpful separation. Some stances are based around achieving unity rather than distinction, but then make their own distinctions in other ways. For instance, an enactivist stance (see Maturana, p. 70), a social interactionist stance, and a social constructivist stance might question the notion of worlds, claiming that there is only the world of experience of the individual, or the world of social interactions!

Learning is not a single event but a continual adjustment (assimilation–accommodation) to impacts from the environment (physical and social, imagined, symbolic), and learning is partly about gaining flexibility in moving between these three worlds in which we all participate.

Learning as social interaction

Learning as participation in practices: Jean Lave and Etienne Wenger

Lave is a social anthropologist interested in learning as a social practice. She was inspired by the findings of Terezinha Nunes and colleagues (p. 17 and p. 78), and discovered immense differences between people's competence in arithmetic when in a practical situation such as outside a supermarket, and in an educational setting. This prompted her to consider traditional forms of learning such as apprenticeships that still function in the Middle and Far East. Etienne Wenger (1952–) was a student and is now a colleague of Jean Lave. They teach that:

> … all learning is situated in practice and represents a progression from legitimate peripheral participation to more central, expert participation in that practice; learning can be seen as a form of apprenticeship.
>
> (adapted from Lave and Wenger, 1991)

Learning as social: Etienne Wenger

Wenger collaborated with Lave in the development of an influential social perspective on learning.

> Our institutions are largely based on the mistaken assumption that learning is an individual process, that it is best separated from the rest of our activities, and that teaching is required for learning to occur.
>
> (Wenger in Teplow, webref)

Wenger offers seven principles of learning:

1. Learning is inherent in human nature. Learning happens all the time regardless of intention, design, or expectation. What is learned may not reflect what is taught nor is it necessarily good for us or our organization.
2. Learning is fundamentally social. The opportunity for social participation drives learning and makes it meaningful. Our thoughts, works, concepts, images and symbols reflect our social participation. Therefore, learning is most effective when it occurs within the context of social participation.
3. Learning changes who we are because it transforms our relationships with the world and our identities as social beings.

4 Learning is a matter of engagement in practice. Learning enables us to engage in the world in certain ways, participate in socially-defined activities and contribute to a community and its enterprise. The engagement in practice determines what we learn and our ability to contribute to the community.

5 Learning reflects participation in communities of practice. Shared enterprise promotes the development of a common practice, shared ways of doing things and relating to each other that enable individuals to achieve shared and individual objectives. Over time, recognizable bonds are forged among members who share a common practice and a community of practice forms. Communities of practice are infinitely varied: formal or informal, enduring over centuries or over the course of a single project, productive and harmonious or destructive and adversarial. Learning is both the vehicle and the result of participation in a community of practice. Finally, communities of practice provide deep knowledge established over time and with the potential to create new knowledge.

6 Learning means dealing with boundaries. Communities of practice, by definition, create boundaries between participants and non-participants. Learning is the recognition and reconciliation of these boundaries. In successful learning organizations, boundaries of practice can be leveraged by promoting interaction and innovation.

7 Learning is an interplay between the local and the global. Multiple communities of practice usually exist within an organization, creating constellations of interrelated communities of practice. Local communities of practice are the locus of work that reflects and affects broader organizational issues and relationships. Whereas the relationship between an individual and the organization may be obscure, participation in local communities of practice provides the link. It is where learning takes place and where the meaning of belonging to the organization is forged and experienced.

(ibid.)

Interactionism: Heinrich Bauersfeld

Heinrich Bauersfeld (b. Germany, 1926–) is a philosophical mathematics educator with deep concern for the social interactions that form the core of teaching and learning. Here he contrasts his stance with individualistic and collectivist perspectives:

Individualistic perspectives: learning is the individual change, according to steps of cognitive development and to context. Prototype: cognitive psychology.

Collectivist perspectives: learning is enculturation into pre-existing societal structures, supported by mediator means or adequate representations. Prototype: activity theory.

Interactionist perspectives: teacher and students interactively constitute the culture of the classroom, conventions both for subject matter and social regulations emerge, communication lives from negotiation and taken-as-shared meanings. Prototypes: ethnomethodology, symbolic interactionism, discourse analysis.

(Bauersfeld, 1993, p. 137)

[The core convictions of our interactionist position are, in brief, as follows:]

1 *Learning* is a process of personal life formating, a process of an interactive adapting to a culture through active participation (which in parallel also produces and develops the culture itself) rather than a transmission of norms, knowledge, and objectified items.

2 *Meaning* lies with the use of words, sentences, or signs and symbols rather than in the related sounds, signs, or pictures ...

3 *Languaging* ... is a social practice, serving in communication for pointing at shared experiences and for orientation in the same culture, rather than an instrument for the direct transportation of sense or as a carrier of attached meanings.

4 *Knowing* or *remembering something* denotes an actual activation of options from experienced actions [in their totality] rather than a storable, [deliberately] treatable, and retrievable object-like item, called *knowledge*, from a loft, called *memory*.

5 *Mathematising* is a practice based on social conventions rather than the applying of a universally applicable set of the eternal truths ... .

6 (Internal) *Representations* are individual constructs, emerging through social interaction as a viable balance between the person's actual interests and her realised constraints, rather than an internal one-to-one mapping of something pre-given or a fitting reconstruction of 'the' world.

7 Using *visualisations* and *embodiments* with the related intention of using them as didactical means depends on taken-as-shared social conventions [...] rather than on a plain reading or the discovering of inherent or inbuilt mathematical structures and meanings.

8 *Teaching* describes the attempt to organise an interactive and reflective process, with the teacher engaging in a constantly continuing and mutual[ly] differentiating and actualising of activities with the students, and thus the establishing and maintaining of a classroom 'culture', rather than the transmission, introduction, or even rediscovery of pre-given and objectively codified knowledge.

(Bauersfeld, 1992, pp. 20–1)

Learning as engaging in cultural practices: Terezinha Nunes

Terezinha Nunes (b. Brazil, 1947–) is a psychologist who concentrates on mathematical learning. She studied street children in Brazil, before moving to England. She is well known for designing clever experiments to test theories. Her research interests include the learning of number by deaf children. Here she summarises an article in which she takes the view that mathematics is a cultural practice.

> This article offers an integrated theoretical perspective of work where mathematics is defined as a cultural practice. The implication of this definition is that to learn mathematics is to become socialized into the ways of knowing used in the community of mathematicians and mathematics teachers. Four aspects of the process of socialization are discussed: the redescription of meanings to fit with the systems of signs learned in mathematics, the influence of the connections created by teachers in the classroom between the new concepts and the old meanings, the consequences of using particular systems of signs as mediators in reasoning, and the development of social representations of what mathematics is (and the associated process of valorization of particular methods) that takes place in the classroom. Implications for multicultural classrooms are briefly discussed.
>
> (Nunes, 1999, p. 33)

Learning has been described as being about making distinctions, restructuring attention, educating awareness, developing intuitions, responding to disturbance, taking action and engaging in social interaction. Effective learning of mathematics depends on, even lies in, the nature of social interactions. Effective teaching draws on prior experiences rather than trying to displace them.

3   Analysis of learning for informing teaching

Introduction

Implications for teaching of the theories put forward in the previous chapter are many and varied depending on which aspects are stressed and which are relatively ignored. In this chapter the influential approach to learning and to designing teaching led by Guy Brousseau in France is developed and explored. Conditions for effective learning are very complex and intertwined. In addition to the sorts of assumptions and theories described in the previous chapter there are more detailed tensions and issues to be examined and closely probed.

Theory of didactic situations

Guy Brousseau (b. Morocco, 1933) is a leading researcher and theorist in France. He has built a substantial theory and practice based on observations, on some earlier constructs such as *epistemological obstacles* (p. 303) and *transformation didactique* (p. 83), making use of Vygotsky's stress on the social aspects of classrooms (see p. 86). The theory leads to systematic research into and development of teaching materials, in a process called *didactic engineering* (see Laborde, 1989; Artigue, 1993).

Didactic contract: Guy Brousseau and Michel Otte

The *situation didactique* identified by Guy Brousseau consists of the learners, the teacher, the mathematical content and the classroom ethos, as well as the social and institutional forces acting upon that situation, including government directives such as a National Curriculum statement, inspection and testing regimes, parental and community pressures and so on. Within the *situation didactique*, Brousseau identified an implicit contract (*contrat didactique*) between teacher and learners, together with some concomitant forces, pressures and tensions.

The didactic contract is that 'the teacher is obliged to teach and the pupil to learn' (Brousseau and Otte, 1991, p. 18), or at least to pass the assessment.

The teacher sets tasks, the learners carry them out; the contract is that by doing the tasks the learners will do enough to pass.

> The contract must be honored at all costs, for otherwise there will be no education. Yet to be obeyed, the contract must be broken, because knowledge cannot be transmitted ready-made and hence nobody – neither the teacher nor the pupil – can be really in command.
>
> (Brousseau and Otte, 1991, p. 180)

Situation didactique: Colette Laborde

Colette Laborde (b. France, 1946–) is a leading French educator and researcher. Here she traces the origins of a collective stance towards educational research.

> … One of the concerns widely shared within the French community is that of setting up an original theoretical framework developing its own concepts and methods and satisfying three criteria: relevance in relation to observable phenomena, exhaustivity in relation to all relevant phenomena, consistency of the concepts developed within the theoretical framework (Brousseau, 1986). …
>
> What we call *didactique des mathématiques* in France covers the study of the relationships between teaching and learning in those aspects which are specific to mathematics. One widespread ideology presupposes a connection of simple transfer from teaching towards learning: the pupil records what is communicated by teaching with perhaps some loss of information. Numerous studies conducted within PME [an annual international conference] have shown clearly how mistaken this point of view is by highlighting in particular the characteristics of the concepts constructed by pupils concerning arithmetic, algebraic or geometric notions which are not contained in the teaching discourse: these concepts are local, partial and even false. These observations forewarn us of the complexity of the links between teaching and learning. *This complexity is the origin and at the core of our research.*
>
> [...]
>
> French research in didactics has shown a desire to apprehend teaching situations globally, to develop a modelization which encompasses their epistemological, social, and cognitive dimensions and which attempts to take into account the complexity of the interactions between knowledge, pupils and teachers within the context of a particular class, or more generally of an educational group. …
>
> One of the axes of research in didactics consists in extracting the constraints which influence the didactic system and analyzing how they function. The most important of these constraints are:

1 the characteristics of the knowledge to be taught, in particular the dependence between the mathematical objects which must be taken into account in the creation of the coherence in the content to be taught;

2 the social and cultural constraints which act within the educational project to determine the teaching content;

3 the temporal characteristics of teaching fixed by the syllabi, in particular its linearity;

4 the pupils' concepts, their modes of cognitive development which condition access to new knowledge;

5 the teacher–learner asymmetry in relation to the knowledge embedded in teaching situations (*didactic contract*) [see p. 79];

6 the teachers' knowledge, their ideas and beliefs about mathematics, teaching, learning, and their own profession.

These constraints act together and have only been separated in order to be exposed. They do not all occur at the same levels of the teaching process; constraints 1, 2, 3 and 4 particularly affect the determination of the knowledge to be taught (*didactic transposition* [see p. 83]) in the upper part of the teaching process, whereas constraints 4, 5, and 6 operate more especially in the lower part, where the teaching is carried out.

[...]

Three types of choice are fundamental, those relative to

- the choice of content to be taught;
- the planning of interactions between learners and the knowledge to be learnt;
- the interventions and role of the teacher in a class situation.

The choice of teaching content and its organization is based on epistemological-type hypotheses and learning hypotheses... .

In the practice of teaching there is generally a process of contextualization of the knowledge taught – that is to say, the organization of a context which *situates* this knowledge, in which the activity of the pupils can operate. The interactions between knowledge and pupils operate through the context, the *milieu* (Brousseau, 1986). The anticipated interactions can arise from different choices.

(Laborde, 1989, pp. 31–3)

See also *using situations* (p. 249).

Of central importance are the questions to which the learners actually reply (not necessarily the one asked by the teacher) and the ways in which the situation itself offers learners opportunities to check and modify their thinking. Consequently, *problems* (see p. 45 and p. 303) play a central role in the research, with learners expected to be *active* (see p. 53).

Didactic tension

Next comes a paradox of learner–teacher interaction and task setting:

> … the 'paradox of the didactic contract' between teacher and learner. If both the problem and the information about its solution are communicated by the teacher this deprives the pupil of the conditions necessary for learning and understanding. The pupil will only be able to reproduce the method of handling and solving the problem communicated to her. … mathematics is not just a method. We do know, on the other hand, that isolated problem situations do not of themselves produce means for their analysis or solution. And, in addition to that: what would be the relevance of the specific application of knowledge or of the solving of a particular problem?
>
> (Brousseau and Otte, 1991, p. 121)

The paradox, inescapably present in any classroom or teaching situation, can usefully be thought of as an endemic didactic tension:

> Everything he does to make the pupil produce the behaviour he expects tends to deprive the pupil of the conditions necessary for understanding and learning the notion concerned. If the teacher says what he wants, he can no longer obtain it.
>
> (Brousseau, 1984, p. 110)

> … most of the time the pupil does not act as a theoretician, but as a practical man. His job is to give a solution to the problem the teacher has given to him, a solution that will be acceptable in the classroom situation. In such a context the most important thing is to be effective. The problem of a practical man is to be efficient, not to be rigorous. It is to produce a solution, not to produce knowledge.
>
> (Balacheff, 1986, quoted in Sierpinska, 1994, p. 19)

> The *more* explicit I am about the behaviour I wish my pupils to display, the more likely it is that they will display that behaviour without recourse to the understanding which the behaviour is meant to indicate; that is, the more they will take the *form* for the substance.
> The *less* explicit I am about my aims and expectations about the behaviour I wish my pupils to display, the less likely they are to notice what is (or might be) going on, the less likely they are to see the point, to encounter what was intended, or to realise what it was all about.
>
> (Mason, 1988, p. 33)

The didactic tension creates a dilemma for teachers. If you think that learners ultimately have to reconstruct ideas for themselves, how do you arrange for learners to reconstruct accurately and appropriately without 'telling them'? If you think that it is through being immersed in practices that learners adopt the language and habits of experts and so learn to become relatively expert themselves, then what sorts of practices are effective, and what has to happen during the 'immersion'? If you think that it is possible to prepare learners to be in a position to hear what the teacher-expert has to say, what advice they have to give, then although it seems possible to achieve learning through direct instruction, what do you do when learners misconstrue, or construct meanings and approaches and ways of thinking different to those of the teacher?

Problématique: Nicolas Balacheff

Nicolas Balacheff (b. Germany, 1947–) is a leading researcher in mathematics education in France. He helped to expose to the English speaking research community various constructs and approaches coming from colleagues such as Guy Brousseau (*situation didactique*, see p. 79), Yves Chevellard (*tranposition didactique* the expert awareness is transposed into instruction in behaviour) and Gaston Bachelard (*obstacles*, see p. 303). Balacheff also pioneered a constructivist perspective, both psychological and social, in the analysis of classroom teaching.

> A *problématique* is a set of research questions related to a specific theoretical framework. It refers to the criteria we use to assert that these research questions are to be considered and to the way we formulate them. It is not sufficient that the subject matter being studied is mathematics for one to assert that such a study is research on mathematics teaching. A problem belongs to a *problématique* of research on mathematics teaching if it is specifically related to the mathematical meaning of pupils' behavior in the mathematics classroom. ...
>
> Our theoretical framework is grounded on two hypotheses: the *constructivist hypothesis* and the *epistemological hypothesis*.
>
> The constructivist hypothesis is that pupils construct their own knowledge, their own meaning. The fact that previous knowledge is questioned, the disequilibration in the Piagetian sense, results in the construction of new knowledge as a necessary response to the pupils' environment.
>
> The epistemological hypothesis (Vergnaud, 1982) is that problems are the source of the meaning of mathematical knowledge, but also intellectual productions turn into knowledge only if they prove to be efficient and reliable in solving problems that have been identified as being important practically (they need to be solved frequently and thus economically) or theoretically (their solution allows a new understanding of the related conceptual domain).
>
> (Balacheff, 1990, pp. 258–9)

There are similarities with *disturbance* (see p. 55) and *surprise* (see p. 101).

> We consider the aim of teaching to be carrying pupils from their initial conceptions related to a given item of mathematical knowledge to resultant conceptions through what we call a *didactical process*. The control and design of this didactical process constitutes the heart of our approach.
>
> ... the fundamental means to initiate this process are mathematical problems. Mathematical problems are fundamental insofar as they constitute means to challenge the pupils' initial conceptions and to initiate their evolution. Also, they are fundamental because they convey the meaning of the mathematical content to be taught mainly by making explicit the epistemological obstacles [see p. 303] that must be overcome for the construction of that meaning.
>
> Pupils' behaviors in the context of a classroom situation cannot be understood only through an analysis of the mathematical content involved or its related psychological complexity. The problems offered to pupils in a didactical situation are set in a social context dominated by both explicit and implicit rules that permit it to function but also that give meaning to pupils' behaviors. ... The rules of social interaction in the mathematics classroom include such issues as the legitimacy of the problem, its connection with the current classroom activity, and responsibilities of both the teacher and pupils with respect to what constitutes a solution or to what is true. We call this set of rules a *didactical contract*. A rule belongs to the set, if it plays a role in the pupils' understanding of the related problem and thus in the constitution of the knowledge they construct.
>
> (ibid., p. 260)

A useful history and background for French *didactiques* can be found in Laborde (1989) and in Caillot (2002). A similar Italian approach is described in Bussi (webref).

In designing tasks, it is important to bear in mind the didactic transposition by constructing tasks which provoke the learner to reconstruct distinctions, relationships, properties, etc..

Over time, the force is for learners to work out what behaviour is required and to produce that, while the teacher is looking for that behaviour to be generated or constructed by the learners (didactic tension).

Activity theory

Lev Vygotsky (b. Belarus, 1896–1934) was a psychologist who developed an approach that has come to be known as *activity theory*. Vygotsky's ideas were brought to the west by Jerome Bruner and by James Wertsch (1991) and developed by many mathematics teacher-educators and reseachers, including Steve Lerman from whose writing the following extract is taken.

Activity theory: Lev Vygotsky

Lerman extracts from Vygotsky's work four key elements as a mechanism for learning: the priority of the inter-subjective; internalisation; mediation; and the zone of proximal development:

- Every function in the child's cultural development appears twice: first, on the social level, and later, on the individual level; first *between* people (*interpsychological*), and then *inside* (*intrapsychological*). ... All the higher functions originate as actual relations between human individuals.

    (Vygotsky, 1978, p. 57, quoted in Lerman, 2000, p. 34)

- ...the process of internalization is not the transferral of an external [activity] to a pre-existing, internal 'plane of consciousness'; it is the process in which this internal plane is formed.

    (Leont'ev, 1979, p. 57, quoted in Lerman, 2000, p. 34)

- Human action typically employs 'mediational means' such as tools and language, and that these mediational means shape the actions in essential ways ... the relationship between action and mediational means is so fundamental that it is more appropriate, when referring to the agent involved, to speak of 'individual(s) acting with mediational means' than to speak simply of 'individual(s)'.

    (Wertsch, 1991, p. 12, quoted in Lerman, 2000, p. 34)

- We propose that an essential feature of learning is that it creates the zone of proximal development; that is, learning awakens a variety of developmental processes that are able to interact only when the child is interacting with people in his environment and in cooperation with his peers.

    (Vygotsky, 1978, p. 90, quoted in Lerman, 2000, p. 34)

Activity theory: Aleksej Leont'ev

Leont'ev was a colleague of Vygotsky and principal theorist of activity theory. Wertsch (1991, p. 255, pp. 86–7, and pp. 264–5), describes Leont'ev as defining three levels of activity: energised or motivated activity, action defined by a goal, and operational. Operational activity is unaware of goals or subgoals, and energised or motivated activity may not have conscious goals.

For Leont'ev, sense designates personal intent, as opposed to meaning, which is public, explicit, and literal. Sense derives from the relations of actions and goals to motivated (higher order) activities of which they are a particular realisation. Zinchenko showed that 'material that is the immediate goal of an action is remembered concretely, accurately, more effectively, more durably. When related to the means of an action (to operations) the same material is remembered in a generalized way, schematically, less effectively, and less durably' (ibid., p. 317). Activity theory influenced those who developed the notion of situated cognition (cognition is always limited by the situation in which it occurs: see p. 292), and there are similarities with *theorem-in-action* (see p. 63), which could be seen as undifferentiated wholistic behaviour in which the actor is unaware of the principles by or through which they are acting.

In the next extract Leont'ev compares experiences of others with inner experiences in order to support the view that everything is first experienced socially before being internalised.

> ... Vygotsky laid the foundations, in his early works, for analyzing activity as a method of scientific psychology. He introduced the concepts of the tool, tool ('instrumental') operations, the goal, and – later – the motive ('the motivational sphere of consciousness'). ...
>
> [...]
>
> ... we always deal with *specific* activities. Each of these activities answers to a specific need of the active agent. It moves toward the object of this need, and it terminates when it satisfies it. Also, it may be reproduced under completely different circumstances. Various concrete activities can be classified according to whatever features are convenient, such as form, means of execution, emotional level, temporal and spatial characteristics, physiological mechanisms, etc.. However, the main feature that distinguishes one activity from another is its object. After all, it is precisely an activity's object that gives it a specific direction. ... an activity's object is its real motive. ...
>
> (Leont'ev, 1979, p. 59)

There are similarities with *purpose* (see p. 42) and *motivation* (see p. 99).

> The basic 'components' of various human activities are the *actions* that translate them into reality. We call a process an action when it is subordinated to the idea of achieving a result, i.e., a process that is subordinated to a conscious *goal*. Just as the notion of a motive is tied to an activity, so the notion of a goal is connected with the notion of an action. The emergence in activity of goal-directed processes or actions was historically the consequence of the transition of humans to life in society.
>
> (ibid., pp. 59–60)

Higher and lower psychological processes: Lev Vygotsky and
Heinrich Bauersfeld

Bauersfeld succinctly compares lower and higher psychological processes:

> In a transient phase of this thinking about 1930, Vygotsky discriminated
> higher from lower mental functions through their genesis. The lower
> mental functions follow stimulus–response constellations; they develop
> through maturation. In contrast, higher mental functions are mediated
> through the use of tools and signs, and are open to conscious and delib-
> erate training. The higher functions develop only within societal rela-
> tions, 'through the internalisation of self-regulatory pattern pre-given in
> society'... .
>
> (Bauersfeld, 1993, p. 134)

An important feature of learning for Vygotsky was the role of relative experts
in displaying *higher psychological processes* to be picked up and internalised
by novices, during which they are generalised, verbalised, abbreviated and
so afford the possibility of further development. Higher psychological
processes include the use of tools (physical and virtual) including most
importantly speech and signs, but also things like tables for laying out data,
formats for doing arithmetical calculations, use of diagrams to depict and
display, and so on.

> ... higher psychological processes unique to humans can be acquired
> only through interaction with others, that is, through *interpsychological*
> processes that only later will begin to be carried out independently by
> the individual. When this happens, some of these processes lose their
> initial, external form and are converted into intrapsychological
> processes.
> ... the process of interiorization is not the *transferal* of an external
> activity to a pre-existing, internal 'plane of consciousness': it is the
> process in which this internal plane is formed.
>
> (Leont'ev, 1979, pp. 56–7)

> ... the general genetic law of cultural development... : Any function in
> the child's cultural development appears twice, or on two planes. First it
> appears on the social plane, and then on the psychological plane. First it
> appears between people as an interpsychological category, and then
> within the child as an intrapsychologicial category. This is equally true
> with regard to voluntary attention, logical memory, the formation of
> concepts, and the development of volition. ... Social relations or rela-
> tions among people genetically underlie all higher functions and their
> relationships.
>
> (Vygotsky, 1979, p. 163)

Zone of proximal development: Lev Vygotsky

Bruner used Vygotsky's ideas as the basis of his research on the role of a tutor (see p. 89). Here is Vygotsky:

> ... consciousness and control appear only at a late stage in the development of a function, after it has been used and practised unconsciously and spontaneously. In order to subject a function to intellectual ... control, we must first possess it.
>
> (Vygotsky, 1962, p. 90)

Compare this with 'teaching for *understanding*' (see p. 293) and educating *awareness* (see p. 61 and p. 204).

Bruner translates the previous Vygotsky extract into more accessible language, and explains what Vygotsky meant by the *zone of proximal development*.

> ... prior to the development of self-directed, conscious control, action is, so to speak, a more direct or less mediated response to the world. Consciousness or *reflection* is a way of keeping mind from (if the mixed metaphor will be permitted) shooting from the hip. That much is familiar enough as a form of conscious inhibition. But what of the instruments by means of which mind now grapples itself to 'higher ground'?
>
> This is the heart of the matter, the point at which Vygotsky brings to bear his fresh ideas about the now famous Zone of Proximal Development (the ZPD hereafter). It is an account of how the more competent assist the young and the less competent to reach that higher ground, ground from which to reflect more abstractly about the nature of things. To use his words, 'the ZPD is the distance between the actual developmental level as determined by independent problem-solving and the level of potential development as determined through problem-solving under adult guidance or in collaboration with more capable peers.' (Vygotsky, 1978, p. 86). 'Human learning' he says, 'presupposes a specific social nature and a process by which children grow into the intellectual life of those around them' (Vygotsky, 1978, p. 88). ... 'Thus the notion of a zone of proximal development enables us to propound a new formula, namely that the only 'good learning' is that which is in advance of development' (Vygotsky, 1978, p. 89).
>
> (quoted in Bruner, 1986, p. 73)

Consciousness for two: Jerome Bruner

Bruner comments that nowhere in Vygotsky's writing could he find specific descriptions of how a tutor could scaffold the learner's experience in order

that consciousness and control can arise after the function is well and spontaneously mastered.

> The tutor, Dr Ross, was not only knowledgeable about children but genu-
> inely interested in what they were doing and how they could be helped.
> ... she turned the task into play and caught it in a narrative that gave it
> continuity.
>   What emerged was, I suppose, obvious enough. She was indeed 'con-
> sciousness for two' for the three- and five-year-olds she tutored, and in
> many ways. To begin with, it was she who controlled the focus of attention.
> It was she who, by slow and often dramatized presentation, demonstrated
> the task to be possible. She was the one with the monopoly on foresight.
> She kept the segments of the task on which the child worked to a size and
> complexity appropriate to the child's powers. She set things up in such a
> way that the child could *recognize* a solution and perform it later even
> though the child could neither do it on his own nor follow the solution
> when it was simply *told* to him. In this respect, she made capital out of the
> 'zone' that exists between what people can recognize or comprehend
> when present before them, and what they can generate on their own – and
> that is the Zone of Proximal Development, or the ZPD. In general, what the
> tutor *did* was what the child could *not* do. For the rest, she made things
> such that the child could do *with* her what he plainly could not do *without*
> her. And as the tutoring proceeded, the child took over from her parts of
> the task that he was not able to do at first but, with mastery, became
> consciously able to do under his own control. And she gladly handed those
> over. (Interestingly, when the observations were repeated years later using
> young children as tutors for younger children, they were not as different as
> expected, save in one crucial respect: the young tutors would not hand
> over parts of the task as the younger child achieved mastery.)
>   (Bruner, 1986, pp. 75–6)

Note the importance for Bruner of *narrative* (see p. 68).

Realm of developmental possibilities: Paul Cobb

Paul Cobb (b. Hertfordshire, 1953–) moved to the USA as a researcher and has
led the shift to focus more strongly on the role of the social and cultural in
learning mathematics in classrooms as the basis for current thinking.

> During the analysis of the interviews, frequent reference is made to the
> conceptual interpretations that the children seemed to make, and to the
> arithmetical objects they are inferred to have constructed. This way of
> talking is a shorthand used for ease of explication. The intended
> meaning in each case is that, in the course of his or her participation in
> the interview, the child acted in ways that justify making particular

cognitive attributions. The situated nature of these inferences is particularly apparent in those instances in which the researcher attempted to
support the child's mathematical activity. In several of these instances,
children did in fact seem to make conceptual advances that they would
not, in all probability, have made on their own.

(Cobb, 1995, p. 29)

Note the care in not over-reaching what can be said about what learners are
observed doing.

One standard way of accounting for these advances is to use Vygotsky's
construct of the 'zone of proximal development'. However, this notion
elevates interpersonal social processes above intrapersonal cognitive
processes (Cole, 1985). Thus, analyses that use this construct typically
focus on the adult's role in scaffolding the child's activity. As a consequence, the treatment of both the child's interpretations and his or her
contributions to interactions is relatively limited. The zone of proximal
development was therefore replaced by a construct that is more relevant
to the purposes of the investigation, that of the 'realm of developmental
possibilities'. This construct delineates the situated conceptual advances
the child makes while participating in an interaction such as that in which
an adult intervenes to support his or her mathematical activity. The zone
of proximal development is concerned with what the child can do with
adult support, whereas the realm of developmental possibilities addresses
the way in which the child's conceptions and interpretations evolve as he
or she interacts with the adult. The latter construct, therefore, brings the
cognitive perspective more to the fore and, thus, complements sociological analysis of the situations in which that development occurs.

(ibid., p. 29)

Attention: Lev Vygotsky

Vygotsky notes the importance of learning to direct attention.

Attention should be given first place among the major functions in the
psychological structure underlying the use of tools. ... scholars have
noted that the ability or inability to direct one's attention is an essential
determinant of the success or failure of any practical operation.
However, the difference between the practical intelligence of children
and animals is that children are capable of reconstructing their perception and thus freeing themselves from the given structure of the field.
With the help of the indicative function of words, the child begins to
master his attention, creating new structural centers in the perceived
situation. ... the child is able to determine for herself the 'center of gravity' of her perceptual field; her behavior is not regulated solely by the

salience of individual elements within it. The child evaluates the relative importance of these elements, singling out new 'figures' from the background and thus widening the possibilities for controlling her activities.

In addition to reorganizing the visual–spatial field, the child, with the help of speech, creates a time field that is just as perceptible and real to him as the visual one. The speaking child has the ability to direct his attention in a dynamic way. He can view changes in his immediate situation from the point of view of past activities, and he can act in the present from the viewpoint of the future.

(Vygotsky, 1978, pp. 35–6)

There are similarities with *three worlds* (see p. 73) and *proximal relevance* (see p. 110).

Labelling and distinctions: Lev Vygotsky

Note in this extract the role of labelling in assisting and preserving distinctions discerned.

> A series of related observations revealed that labeling is the primary function of speech used by young children. Labeling enables the child to choose a specific object, to single it out from the entire situation he is perceiving. Simultaneously, however, the child embellishes his first words with very expressive gestures, which compensate for his difficulties in communicating meaningfully through language. By means of words children single out separate elements, thereby overcoming the natural structure of the sensory field and forming new (artificially introduced and dynamic) structural centers. The child begins to perceive the world not only through his eyes but also through his speech. As a result, the immediacy of 'natural' perception is supplanted by a complex mediated process; as such, speech becomes an essential part of the child's cognitive development.
>
> [...]
>
> The role of language in perception is striking because of the opposing tendencies implicit in the nature of visual perception and language. The independent elements in a visual field are simultaneously perceived; in this sense, *visual perception is integral.* Speech, on the other hand, requires sequential processing. Each element is separately labeled and then connected in a sentence structure, *making speech essentially analytical.*
>
> Our research has shown that even at very early stages of development, language and perception are linked. In the solution of nonverbal tasks, even if a problem is solved without a sound been uttered, language plays a role in the outcome.
>
> (Vygotsky, 1978, pp. 32–3)

> Learners need not just to be 'active', but to be in the presence of others who display the 'higher psychological functioning' before they can be expected to internalise it for themselves.
>
> Labelling distinctions in language enables distinctions to be made in the future, and this applies to identifying relationships, properties and so on.

Constructivisms

Piaget's notion of *genetic epistemology* came to be referred to as *constructivism*, with roots in Vico (see p. 53) and other earlier writers. The version that was taken up in education was rather simplified, so Ernst von Glasersfeld introduced *radical constructivism* to stress the less comfortable aspects. However, many felt that the individual was overemphasised at the expense of the social, so *social constructivism* redressed this, but in many cases was taken to an extreme as *radical social constructivism*. Meanwhile in the context of robots and computers the notion of *constructionism* emphasised physical construction of objects.

Constructivism: Jean Piaget

Jean Piaget (b. Switzerland, 1896–1980) was a biologist turned philospher concerned with how organisms, especially humans, learn. He was head of a Montessori school before becoming a researcher. In collaboration with many colleagues over the years, Piaget devised numerous probes for revealing the development of children's thinking, and these investigations continue at the Piaget Institute in Geneva. His experiments and conclusions profoundly influenced Western education.

Piaget formulated the notion of *genetic epistemology* to capture his sense of children being genetically prepared to construct knowledge of the world for themselves, with, of course, the support and under the influence of their social and cultural environment. This includes direct instruction they receive from teachers (including parents) as well as the myriad of implicit forces and practices in which they are imbedded. Primary among these is language, for it is through language that we express ourselves to others, and show that we can participate socially. Various forms of constructivism have been proposed and advocated as 'telling the best story' about what learners do.

The various constructivisms are a response to the challenge to explain how learners construct the mathematical ways of knowing as they interact with others in the course of their mathematical acculturation (Cobb, Yackel and Wood, 1992, p. 17).

Radical constructivism: Ernst von Glasersfeld

The basic principle of the constructivist theory is that cognitive organisms act and operate in order to create and maintain their equilibrium in the face of perturbations generated by conflicts or unexpected novelties arising either from their pursuit of goals in a constraining environment or from the incompatibility of conceptual structures with a more or less established organization of experience. The urge to know thus becomes the urge to *fit;* on the sensory-motor level as well as in the conceptual domain, and learning and adaptation are seen as complementary phenomena.

If one accepts this principle, one can no longer maintain the traditional idea of knowledge as representing an 'external' reality supposed to be independent of the knower. The concept of knowledge has to be dismantled and reconstructed differently. This is a shocking suggestion, and I have elsewhere laid out the reasons for such a radical step (von Glasersfeld, 1985). I have called my position *radical* constructivism to accentuate the changed concept of knowledge and to differentiate myself from those who speak of the construction of knowledge in the framework of a traditional epistemology. ... It is intended to be used as a working hypothesis whose value can lie only in its usefulness.

(von Glasersfeld, 1996, pp. 24–5)

1 Training aims at the ability to repeat the performance of a given activity and it must be distinguished from teaching. What we want to call *teaching* aims at enabling students to generate activities out of the understanding *why* they should be performed and, ultimately, also how one can explain that they lead to the desired result.

2 Knowledge has to be built up by each individual learner, it cannot be packaged and transferred from one person to another.

3 Language is not a conveyor belt or means of transport. The meaning of words, sentences and texts is always a subjective construction based on the individual's experience. Though language cannot 'convey' the desired constructs to students, it has two important functions: it enables the teacher to orient the students' conceptual construction by means of appropriate constraints; and when students talk to the teacher or among themselves in groups, they are forced to reflect upon what they are thinking and doing.

4 Students' answers and their solutions of problems should always be taken seriously. At the moment they are produced, they mostly make sense to the student even if they are wrong from the teacher's point of view. Ask students how they arrived at their answer. This helps to separate answers given to please the teacher from those that are the results of understanding or misunderstandings.

5   Only a problem the student sees as his or her own problem can focus the student's attention and energy on a genuine search for a solution.
6   Rewards (i.e., the behaviorists' external reinforcements), be they material or social, foster repetition, not understanding.

(ibid., pp. 25–6)

There are similarities with Spencer's observations (see p. 35).

7   Intellectual motivation is generated by overcoming an obstacle, by eliminating a contradiction, or by developing principles that are both abstract and applicable. Only if students have themselves built up a conceptual model that provides an explanation of a problematic situation or process, can they develop the desire to try their hand at further problems; only success in these attempts can make them aware of their power to shape the world of their experience in a meaningful way.

(ibid., p. 26)

Note the use of learners' *powers* (see p. 115 and p. 233).

Radical constructivism, thus, is *radical* because it breaks with convention and develops a theory of knowledge in which knowledge does not reflect an 'objective' ontological reality, but exclusively an ordering and organization of a world constituted by our experience. The radical constructivist has relinquished 'metaphysical realism' once and for all and finds himself in full agreement with Piaget, who says: 'Intelligence organizes the world by organizing itself'.

(von Glasersfeld, 1984, p. 24)

Constructionism: Seymour Papert

Seymour Papert (b. South Africa, 1928–) started working life as a mathematician. He worked with Piaget before moving to the USA where he became a leader in the development of the field of artificial intelligence. In his groundbreaking book (Papert, 1980), which promulgated the use of LOGO as a computer program accessible to children, he maintained that learning is most effective when learners are constructing things through actions they perform, although his focus is largely on computers and computer-driven robots.

Constructionism is built on the assumption that children will do best by finding ('fishing') for themselves the specific knowledge they need. Organized or informal education can help most by making sure they are supported morally, psychologically, materially, and intellectually in their efforts. … the goal is to teach in such a way as to produce the most learning for the least teaching.

(Papert, 1993, p. 139)

Social constructivism

In addition to the classic triad of subject matter, learner and teacher, there is the environment within which all the interactions take place, the *milieu* as Brousseau calls it (p. 91). Stressing the milieu is one way of describing a complex and multifaceted perspective often referred to as social constructivism. An early advocate was Kurt Lewin who coined a number of pithy sayings that are still much quoted today such as 'If you want truly to understand something, try to change it' (see also p. 161), but who is also famous for framing behaviour as both individual and social: '*behaviour is a function both of the person and of the environment*'. In the twenty-first century this seems self-evident to us perhaps, but it was an attempt to reconcile two competing strains of psychology, which continue to vie with each other for ascendancy. Stressing the person leads to emphasis on psychology, and often specifically on cognition, on thinking, and on behaviour. Stressing the environment leads to emphasis on the social and on the role of language in its most general sense as the medium in which, and by means of which, we take up and use social practices of various kinds, and also through which we are used by our culture. Stressing individuals as sense-makers leads to *psychological constructivism*, whereas stressing the social leads to *social constructivism* and stressing the individual–environment pair leads to *enactivism* (p. 70).

Community of practice: Jean Lave

Lave and Wenger developed the notion of a *community of practice* in which people experience the behaviour of relative experts.

A *practice* is any behaviour, including mental actions, which are typical of a group of people (the community). As a member of a school there are certain things you do, ways you dress, things you say; as a participant in a lesson about mathematics there are typical things you learn to say and do. These are all *practices*. Practices are picked up from others in the community.

This conforms with Vygotsky's notion that what he called *higher psychological processes* are first experienced in the behaviour of others, and only later internalised into learners' practices. As these ideas developed some people put forward the 'radical' notion that knowledge is not something possessed or accessed by individuals, but rather resides in the social practices of different communities. A simple social perspective holds that discussion and peripheral participation is a valuable component of learning; a radical perspective holds that learning consists in becoming adept at carrying out the practices (speaking and acting in recognised and established ways).

> ... a decentred view of the locus and meaning of learning, in which learning is recognized as a social phenomenon constituted in the experienced, lived-in world, through legitimate peripheral participation in

ongoing social practice; the process of changing knowledgeable skill is subsumed in processes of changing identity in and through membership in a community of practitioners; and mastery is an organizational, relational characteristic of communities of practice.

(Lave, 1993a, p. 64, also quoted in Boaler, 2000, p. 5)

Constructivist positions summarised

For an admirable summary of various constructivist positions linked together from a single perspective see (Confrey, 1990; 1991; 1994; 1994a; 1994b; 1995). A useful source of writings on various forms of constructivism can be found at Selden and Selden (webref), in Steffe and Gale (1995) and on mathematics education, specifically in Steffe *et al.* (1996).

A teaching dilemma: Paul Cobb

Cobb drew attention to an ever-present and apparently inescapable dilemma. As a teacher convinced that learners have to make sense, have to construct and reconstruct meaning for themselves, how is it possible for a teacher to arrange that learners construct what experts have constructed and not something that is fallacious or confused? Is it possible to ensure that they construct appropriate meanings and interpretations, construct useful models and ways of perceiving, notice what experts consider worthy of notice?

Furthermore, on the whole, meanings do seem to be shared, or at least, as Paul Cobb, Erna Yackel, and Teri Wood (1992, p. 8) put it, are 'taken as shared', perfectly effectively for the most part. Yet if learners are making sense, are reconstructing meaning, are interpreting for themselves, how can the considerable agreement that is achieved be accounted for?

Cobb looked initially for a resolution of this apparent paradox by placing confidence in learners to adjust and accommodate over the long term.

> Our approach is ... that activities are provided for the teachers who implement them very much in a problem centred way. They are under no obligation to ensure that all children come up with a certain idea on a particular day. The meanings emerge over a long period of time in the course of discussions. ... The actual specifics of how do I get all these children to see the relationship between these numbers does not arise for our teachers.
>
> (Cobb, Open University interview, July 1988)

Dissatisfied with this, he went on to stress social aspects, and to go so far as to place knowledge in the language and practices of the community rather than in the individual. Thus the learner adopts practices and ways of speaking. But this may overlook the experience that when something is being articulated, being expressed in some way (through diagrams and pictures, through movement, sculpting and so on, and through words and symbols), there is something of or about the individual that is being expressed and that is not entirely social.

Instead of going to an extreme social-constructivist position, it is tenable to remain with the observation that it is in the nature of evolving responsive organisms to adjust to the environment, whether in the sense of *fitting* used by von Glasersfeld (see p. 93), through *assimilating* or *accommodating* (Piaget, p. 149) or in not seeing any distinction between the organism and its environment, as in *enactivism* (see p. 70).

The dilemma is not confined to a constructivist perspective. It faces every teacher no matter what their perspective, for learners will make sense in whatever way they find they can. Telling learners something is sometimes effective, though often not very effective (see p. 73, p. 116 and p. 229). But even where learners are told, if they are going to do more than recite it back again from memory, if they are to integrate it into their awareness, then some change, some transformation, some alteration in how they perceive, what they notice and how they act, and how they account to themselves for what they perceive and notice comes about.

Cobb's response is that when tasks are sufficiently carefully designed, with attention paid to various principles described in these pages, and when suitable conditions are established, learners will in fact come to similar conclusions about mathematical facts and theorems.

There is a mathematical version of the surprising agreement in meaning, which has exercised mathematicians: how can one account for the 'unreasonable effectiveness of mathematics' (Wigner, 1960 webref) for modelling, predicting, and controlling the material world, if mathematics is a construction of the human mind?

See Hamming (1980; webref) for one reply, and Newman (1956) for others.

Teaching dilemma: Derek Edwards and Neil Mercer

Derek Edwards (b. Liverpool, 1948–) and Neil Mercer (b. Northamptonshire, 1948–) together tackled the dilemma in the context of teaching generally, with some special attention to science and mathematics. They were shocked to find little discussion and social negotiation of meaning in the classrooms they observed.

> ... The teacher's dilemma is to have to inculcate knowledge while apparently eliciting it. This gives rise to a general ground-rule of classroom discourse, in which the pupils' task is to come up with the correct solutions to problems seemingly spontaneously, while all the time trying to discern in the teacher's clues, cues, questions and presuppositions what that required solution actually is.
>
> (Edwards and Mercer, 1987, p. 126)

These tensions cannot be resolved. Being endemic means that energy is stored in them. Instead of trying to avoid the tension, the fact of the tension can serve as a constant reminder that learning and hence teaching are dynamically varying processes, which are never completed and which rapidly change their nature over short and long periods of time. Attention therefore usefully moves to considering the actions that learners can undertake in order to learn, and from that, specific suggestions arise for teaching.

Ultimately, it is learners who make sense of the world through reconstructing ideas for themselves (psychological constructivism). It is when learners are actively involved, and ideally literally as well as metaphorically building something, that learning is most efficient (constructionism). The practices, especially use of language and ways of behaving picked up from others, are for some the principal source from which meaning is constructed (social constructivism) and, for some, knowledge resides in the community and not in the individual as such (strong social constructivism).

4 Affect in learning mathematics

Introduction

Many factors affect what a learner learns from an educational activity. The motivations of learners and the intentions of teachers inevitably differ. Other factors relate to the context within which activity takes place and the authenticity of the activity as experienced by the learner. When teachers, influenced by their own desires, interact with learners, they may influence the learner's motivation and self-esteem. These issues are the subject of this chapter.

Motivation, intention and desire

Motivation is a complex matter. It is a word used to describe, literally, what moves learners. Teachers, and the school ethos and setting, play a significant role, both in motivating and in demotivating. Both of these can be through subtle, covert features of ways of working and interacting with learners, and overtly through the provision of examples and contexts to which learners can readily relate.

Philosophers have long felt that mathematics provides an ideal context in which to encounter pleasure in the use of human powers. For example, Plato extols pure arithmetic:

> ... they must carry on the study until they see the nature of numbers in the mind only ...
> [...]
> ... pursued in the spirit of a philosopher and not of the shopkeeper!
> [...]
> ... arithmetic has a very great and elevating effect, compelling the soul to reason about abstract number, and if visible or tangible objects are obtruding upon the argument, refusing to be satisfied.
> (Plato: The Republic VII, p. 525, Jowett, 1871, p. 360)

Not all learners aspire to such dizzy heights! The presence of unmotivated and unappreciative learners is no new phenomenon. The Hadow Report of

1931 found the need to 'emphasise the principle that no good can come from teaching children things that have no immediate use for them, however highly their potential or prospective value may be estimated.' It stated that the curriculum should be thought of not as knowledge and facts but as activity and experience (Hadow Report, 1931, p. 73; quoted in McIntosh, 1977, p. 94; reprinted in Floyd, 1981, p. 9.)

Motivating: Lancelot Hogben

Lancelot Hogben (b. Hampshire, 1895–1975) was an eminent zoologist who became an expositor of science and mathematics 'for the millions'. Just like Robert Recorde (b. Wales, 1510–1558) who wrote the first arithmetic and algebra books in English, Hogben wanted to provide everyone with access to the important and powerful ideas of science and mathematics. In a talk he gave in England in 1938 he formulated conclusions about the role of the mathematics teacher. There are similarities with *psychologising the subject matter* (see p. 45 and p. 203) and use of learners' *powers* (p. 115 and 233).

> The primary task of an educationalist is to establish a personal relationship by enlisting the personal interest of individual pupils in the exercise of their reasoning powers. Thus the problem of the mathematics teacher is not a problem of mathematics as such. The recipe for good mathematics teaching is to put into the teaching of mathematics something which does not belong to the subject-matter of mathematics as such. There are obviously many levels at which this can be done. ... The aesthetic, which, at its most primitive level, is the play motive, is one which an enthusiastic and efficient teacher will not neglect, though I do not think it carries us very far by itself.
>
> [...]
>
> ... let me urge that we should resist the temptation to make the examination system an excuse for lack of enterprise in education.
>
> ... I believe that the teacher who ... takes the trouble to stimulate his pupils by devoting a substantial part of his time to topics which lie quite outside the syllabus will get better examination results than the teacher who keeps one eye glued on the syllabus.
>
> (Hogben, 1938, pp. 111–3)

Motivation: Richard Skemp

Richard Skemp (b. Avon, 1919–1995) took both a mathematics degree and then a psychology degree, and pioneered the use of psychology within mathematics education in the UK. In addition to curriculum development, he developed a sophisticated model of intelligence, which integrates cognitive and emotional dimensions. One component is the notion of *goal-states* (to be sought) and *anti-goal-states* (to be avoided). One person may wish to avoid challenge (see Dweck, p. 112) while another relishes it; one may avoid conflict with teachers, and another may seek it out as a means of getting attention from adults and/or from peers. Skemp points out (1979, p. 15) that where there is no novelty in a situation, there is likely to be a low level of consciousness; where there is excessive novelty, the learner may not be able to cope and so blocks off inputs; where there is some novelty but not excessive amounts, consciousness is likely to be at a maximum and so the learner is in the best position to learn.

> Can one person motivate another?
> [...]
> The general sense in which 'A motivates B' is used means, roughly, that A gets B to do something that A wants B to do, and which B would not otherwise have done. With this is an implication that the action by A is intentional, and unilateral. ...
> What can A do whereby to bring about the action which he wants B to do? A can command or threaten, strongly or mildly, explicitly or implicitly. He can request or persuade, again strongly or mildly, explicitly or implicitly. These appear as direct approaches. He can change B's environment in a way that will bring about the desired action by B. This appears to be indirect. But in fact, all are indirect. A has no direct access to any of B's director systems. A can only get B to do something by making a change in B's environment which sets in action one or more of B's director systems.
>
> (Skemp, 1979, pp. 107–8)

Skemp goes on to point out that when motivation is seen in terms of what A does to B, it misses the complexity of B as a human being with will and desires, and propensities to conform or to rebel. He claims that 'a person who is unaware that he has a choice, effectively has not (ibid., p. 110).

This applies as well to teachers and researchers as to learners.

Surprise and disturbance as motivation

Surprise: Nitsa Movshovits-Hadar

Nitsa Movshovits-Hadar (b. Israel, 1941–) is an educator and researcher. Here she expresses clearly and cogently a sentiment, which many teachers have experienced: the facts and relationships that make up mathematics are full of potential surprise and delight and thus a positive form of disturbance (see p. 55, p. 101 and p. 161) motivating learning.

> Intellectual surprise usually gives us a sense of fulfillment, an appreciation of some wisdom, a joy from its wittiness, and a drive to find some more. *Making mathematical findings appear unexpected, or even as contra-*

expected, is the secret of teaching mathematics the surprise-way. Such a way of teaching is not an end in itself, of course. It is however quite a promising means for achieving students' interest, which has for long been known to be positively correlated with successful learning.

[...]

Every single theorem can be turned into a surprise by considering the unexpected matter which that theorem claims to be true. Sometimes the theorem is so well known that it is hard to see the point. For example what is so exciting about the claim that the sum of the interior angles of a triangle is 180 degrees?

To reach the surprise potential of a theorem it is usually helpful to assume we do not know it. Suppose we do not know that the sum of the interior angles of a triangle is 180 degrees. Would it be reasonable to suspect that *all* triangles, of *any* shape and size – equilateral, isosceles, scalene, acute-angled, right-angled, obtuse-angled, very large (in area) and very small, narrow and wide – must all have the *same* sum for their interior angles? Would it not take a novice by surprise to discover that the sum of the interior angles of triangles of various kinds is a constant?

(Movshovits-Hadar, 1988, pp. 34–5)

Other examples she offers include Pythagoras' theorem: if you did not know it, what a challenge to find such a triangle; could there be a right-angled triangle that did not satisfy the theorem? What relationships between squares of sides characterises obtuse-angled and acute-angled triangles? What happens if you replace 'squares' on the sides by another shape, using the area of similar shapes on the sides of the triangle? Notice the implicit use of *dimensions-of-possible-variation* applied to Pythagoras' theorem.

It is the mathematics teacher's responsibility to recover the surprise embedded in each theorem and to convey it to the students. The method is simple: just imagine you do not know this fact. This is where you meet your students. Let them examine their expectations, and make them realize that they get new and very unusual results in every theorem.

(Movshovits-Hadar, 1988, p. 39)

Natural, conflicting and alien: Janet Duffin and Adrian Simpson

In an extension of Piaget's notions of *assimilation* and *accommodation* (see p. 149), Festinger's notion of *cognitive dissonance* (see p. 69), and of the role of *disturbance* and *surprise*, two university teacher-researchers, Janet Duffin, who also evaluated the Calculator Aware Number Project (Duffin, 1996) and Adrian Simpson (b. Lincolnshire 1967–) suggested that examples and concepts provided by teachers can be classified into three groups, according to the responses of learners:

Our theory postulates that learners encounter three kinds of experience, which we have come to call natural, conflicting, and alien, to which they respond by modifying their internal mental structures in different ways. We define a natural experience as one that fits the learner's current mental structures and as one to which they respond by strengthening the structure. A conflict is an experience which jars with the existing structures, either by showing that the way of working associated with the structure cannot cope in the way expected or by showing that two or more – previously dissociated – mental structures can be brought to bear on the same situation. We conjecture that learners respond to such conflicts by weakening or destroying the structure, by limiting the domain of experiences with which the structure is expected to cope, or by constructing links between previously separate structures. In contrast, an alien experience is one that has no fit with the existing mental structures at all: it neither fits nor causes conflict. In response, a learner may ignore or avoid the experience or may absorb it as a new, separate structure that then becomes liable to modification through later natural, conflicting, and alien experiences.

(Duffin and Simpson, 1999, p. 416)

There are similarities with *assimilating* and *accommodating* (see p. 149) and *equilibration* (see p. 148). See also p. 301 where Duffin and Simpson go on to explore what it means to understand in mathematics. Note resonances with Festinger's *cognitive dissonance* (p. 69) and the role that such dissonance plays in motivating learners to learn, and with the notion of *fit* at the heart of radical constructivism (see p. 93).

Ruptures and surprise: Alain Bouvier

Alain Bouvier (b. France, 1943–) is a mathematician and educator who produced a French dictionary of mathematics. In this extract he identifies disturbances or *ruptures* as crucial for development of mathematical ideas, both historically, and for learners.

It is possible to find [ruptures in mathematical thought] although its occurrences are not as well known as in the other disciplines.

- The most frequently mentioned rupture in mathematics concerns the discovery of irrational numbers and the proof, by Pythagoras, of the irrationality of $\sqrt{2}$. Mathematics suddenly shifted from the idea that 'every number is a ratio of two whole numbers' (as we may express it in modern terms) to the conception of two categories of numbers: rational and irrational.

[…]

- Another famous rupture concerns the foundations of geometry. After trying to prove Euclid's fifth postulate, notably by developing the consequences of various forms of its negation in the hope that a contradiction would appear, and after hiding these results from the scientific community, it eventually became necessary for mathematicians to cross the Rubicon and allow new iconoclastic geometries to stand beside Euclidean geometry. The old framework suddenly exploded and within the framework of a plurality of geometries new problems arose, particularly the problem of classification.

- Without it ever having been made explicit, at the beginning of the nineteenth century it was understood that a continuous function was everywhere differentiable, save possibly at a few exceptional points. To imagine, as Weierstrass did, that functions could be found which are everywhere continuous but nowhere differentiable, was an enormous jump! Hermite refused to take any interest in these mathematical objects, which he termed *monsters*. ...

(Bouvier, 1987, pp. 18–19)

Surprise, disturbance, ruptures, are all manifested by the phrase 'I have a problem ... ', for the recognition of having a problem is evidence of awareness of something having altered without the possibility of a smooth *equilibration* (to use the biological metaphor used by Piaget: see p. 148). But being aware of 'having a problem' is a far cry from a list of questions or exercises or 'problems' in a textbook.

Hidden curriculum

Doing the tasks set by the teacher does not necessarily lead to success. More is expected, and more is required.

A template can be used mechanically to the extent of not learning from the experience, of not making a meta-cognitive shift to make sense of the process and to see it as a process that can be repeated in other contexts. In the context of worked examples, the more comprehensive the worked examples provided for the learners, the easier it is for learners to find a matching template, but the more likely they are to miss the intention, that is, of internalising the templates. In the context of example construction, if all the requisite examples have been provided, learners have only a task of searching for the appropriate one.

Hidden curriculum: Benson Snyder

In a famous work which introduced the notion of a *hidden curriculum* (see p. 104). Benson Snyder, an American sociologist of education, observed that learners 'played the game, read the cues, adapted to their immediate educational circumstances' (Snyder, 1971, p. xii).

[Students almost always translate what the faculty says they expect from students] into a series of discrete, more or less manageable tasks which they infer is the actual basis for the grade their professors will give them.

... tasks then lead students to a set of tactics or maneuvers. One student budgeted his time and commitment in a math course by doing the last problem in the nightly homework set of six. He assumed it contained all the necessary principles. Only if he had difficulty would he then do the fifth, fourth, etc.. He saw the course as consisting of these 'hurdles' drawn up by the professor. He said this 'exercise' would prepare him well enough for the ultimate race – the examination. ...

In effect, [students] are constantly asking questions about the differences between the formal and hidden curriculum: What are the actual hurdles one must jump? ... , and how is this reflected in the formal rules and explicit descriptions? The answer to these and many similar questions form the syllabus of the hidden curriculum. For most students, it is more important than the visible curriculum ...

(Snyder, 1971, pp. 6–7)

... To finish all the tasks of the formal curriculum would require far more time than is available. In a typical coping pattern the student finds he must neglect, selectively, certain aspects of the formal curriculum. He must learn what he can avoid doing, knowing where the risks are minimal and the cost is modest. The message is unstated, but it is as clear to the student as an item of information in the college catalogue.

(ibid., p. 12)

We have found repeatedly ... that when the student's sense of his worth is based principally on those narrow ranges of criteria of performance that are used by the institution, two things follow. First, the student's adaptation appears to be less likely to change, even in the face of new and different environmental pressures. Second, the student also appears to be less aware of the consequences of having adjusted than are his classmates. To fit the real diversity of students we may not need to teach them differently, we may just need to grade them differently.

(ibid., p. 159)

There are interesting resonances with the *didactic contract* and the *didactic tension* (see p. 79). There are also close similarities with the notion of *didactic transposition* (p. 83), with Dweck's findings concerning *self-esteem*, and with a social perspective on learning (see Maturana, p. 70). Calling features *hidden* suggests intention, and leads some authors to want to make everything explicit to learners. However there are substantial, not to say insurmountable difficulties (see *inner and outer aspects*, p. 241).

Intended curriculum: The BACOMET group

BACOMET is an international group of mathematics educators that carries out research on basic and fundamental topics of mathematics education. The composition of the BACOMET group changes between projects but its membership remains at around 20 from about ten different countries. In the first project, *Perspectives in Mathematics Education* (1980) members of BACOMET introduced ideas based on those of Vygotsky and colleagues set in the context of European mathematics education. Bent Christiansen (b. Denmark, 1921–1996) was an internationally respected researcher and organiser who was influenced by Georges Papy (see p. 108) among others. Here he and his teacher colleague, G. Walther, start by talking about motivation, and the difference between the intended and the actualised curriculum.

> Students are motivated and initiated into activities by deliberate steps taken by the teacher. These educational steps are planned in the perspective of educational purposes and intentions which more or less explicitly concern the learner's acquisition of specified knowledge and know-how *shared* with others, in short *social* knowledge and know-how. This *intended learning* is not limited to acquisition of closed end-products but should comprise process and product as complementary aspects. It should contain learning of different types and at different cognitive levels, and it should benefit from high priority on actions directed by the specific goal to *learn*.
>
> ... the problem is to identify means by which the teacher may promote a *unified conception* – within the learner – *of the role of task-and-activity, of learning, of mathematics, and of his personal, conscious control of his own learning process.*
>
> (Christiansen and Walther, 1986, p. 264)

There are similarities with the *teaching dilemma* (see p. 96).

> ... learning cannot take place through activity performed by an individual in isolation, but must unfold in relation to activity mediated by other persons – the teacher, the parents, the peer group, etc. – and often through activity performed by a group including the individual in question.
>
> (ibid., p. 267)

We list ... five questions, offer brief comments, and ask the reader to take these questions a starting points for his own reflections.

The context of the task? Is the task concerned with internal mathematical relationships? Or is it an application of a pro-forma type, such as the traditional 'word-problems'? Will the task fit properly into the teaching/ learning process which is in progress in the class? And will it be of appropriate interest and relevance for the students?

The complexity of the task? Will the solution of the task be established by means of a few rather obvious steps? Or will the performance call for several *series of actions?* And must these series be performed by the student in some definite order (to be identified, perhaps, by himself in the course of the activity on the task)? Is the demand for a *logical* analysis of the task?

The degree of openness? Is the task described in an open form as in *How much does it cost to keep a dog?*, or is a high degree of guidance inherent in the textual formulation ... ? Are the objects to be worked upon given clearly and explicitly? Are some of the possibilities to be investigated mentioned in the text? Are opening examples provided? Is an appropriate context set for *further* independent decisions and activity?

The form and appearance of the task? This question is about the form and effect of the technical presentation of the task. Thus our interest lies at this stage on an analysis of the ways in which the 'task as text' presents itself to the student. ...

Another important aspect is to what extent the text contains incitement to and starting points for reflection – or even for a dialogue between the reader and the text or 'within' the reader. And a third aspect for analysis is, whether the text is challenging to an appropriate degree.

(ibid., pp. 276–7)

Christiansen and Walther go on to consider the task as a component of a larger 'system':

The structure of human activity is determined by a complex system of mutually related factors: (1) the object for the activity and the inherent conditions; (2) the motive of the activity and the goals of the actions by which it proceeds; (3) the internal conditions and resources of the acting subject; and (4) the external frames of the activity. ...

As regards (1), the object (the task) is only to some extent directly available for the student. It must be created for him or mediated to him and this brings about an initial state of affairs which differs from that of 'natural' human activity.

As regards (2), needs, motive, and object are connected closely in genuine human activity. Whereas, in the case of an educational task, questions arise about the extent to which the motive for the envisaged activity is inherent in the task.

Finally, in relation to (3) and (4), the task *as presented* serves to initiate different students in varying degrees and extents to the development of actions which are potentially inherent in the envisaged activity.

[...]

When task-and-activity is taken as the basic vehicle for learning, the following three factors assume high importance: (i) the student's conception of tasks in school as tools for his own learning; (ii) the student's performance of actions 'inherent in the task' as needed for intended learning; (iii) the student's personal control and evaluation of learning.

(ibid., pp. 290–1)

... three stages of interaction between teacher and learners in relation to a task selected or constructed by the teacher: (1) a stage of *presentation*; (2) a stage of *independent activity* individually or in groups; and (3) a stage of *concluding reflection*. The activity of the students on the task proceeds (in different forms) through these three stages. And the *teacher* performs in each of these many different functions, although certain roles and functions have priority in each of the stages ... .

(ibid., p. 293)

Authentic activity

Many authors have decried the artificiality of classroom activities. There are sharp contrasts between what children do in one context (for example, selling things on the streets in Brazil) and in school (see Nunes, p. 17; Lave, p. 75; Spencer, p. 115). This led to the notion of *authentic activity* as a motivational contribution: asking learners to engage in activities that mirror activities carried out by adults in non-school contexts.

Personalising the curriculum: Jerome Bruner

Let me turn now to ... the personalization of knowledge, getting to the child's feeling, fantasies, and values with one's lessons. A generation ago, the progressive movement urged that knowledge be related to a child's own experience and brought out of the realm of empty abstractions. A good idea was translated into banalities about the home, then the friendly postman and trashman, then the community, and so on. It is a poor way to compete with the child's own dramas and mysteries.

[...]

... to personalize knowledge one does not simply link it to the familiar. Rather one makes the familiar an instance of a more general case and thereby produces awareness of it.

(Bruner, 1966, pp. 160–1)

There are similarities with Dewey's notion of *psychologising the subject matter* (p. 45 and p. 203)

Authentic activity: Georges Papy

Georges Papy (b. Belgium, 1920–), was a teacher, educator and founder of the Belgian Centre of Mathematical Pedagogy. He promoted the use of the language of sets for unifying mathematics, at the very youngest ages in school. Much maligned in the 1960s because curriculum innovators were unable to communicate the force and insight of Papy and others, his aims were much the same as those advocating *authentic tasks*, though completely differently expressed and manifested.

From the foreword, by Howard Fehr, of Papy's book, *Modern Mathematics*:

> All of the concepts begin in everyday situations familiar to all students. If we are to teach more mathematics of the modern variety, to more students, and we are to promote the desire of our education system to serve as a stairway to fulfilling the needs and dreams of men, then surely it will be necessary to cultivate in some manner a genuinely modern global instruction in mathematics. This book serves as a great step forward in this direction.
>
> Today, in our schools we are under great pressure to teach more mathematics to students at an earlier age because of the steady growth in the applications of mathematics. At the same time, we are more sensitive to the psychology of learning as related to mathematics, about which, however, our knowledge is limited. These factors make the problem of creating a unified modern syllabus a very complex one. On the other hand today we have a greater understanding and deeper insight into the concepts and theories of contemporary mathematics. It is this knowledge which places us in a good position to produce a unified syllabus. As one looks at the structures of mathematics, it is clearly seen that the subject has acquired a unity, largely through the use of set theory. No longer do we think of mathematics as a collection of disjoint branches – arithmetic, algebra, geometry, analysis – having no inner relations to each other. We think of it as a set of structures, all intimately related, and all applicable to many diverse situations.
>
> (Papy, 1963, pp. v–vii)

And from Papy himself:

> Mathematics, which at the beginning of the century had few applications outside physics and engineering, has become a fundamental element of contemporary life and an indispensable tool in most spheres of thought, including science and technology. It has therefore become necessary to teach the basic elements of modern mathematics to all secondary school pupils, since any one of them may find himself in need of it.
>
> Happily the development of mathematics and the variety of its applications have profoundly modified the science and given it a more humane appearance.
>
> The advances made during the last hundred years have completely transformed mathematics so that it now appears more familiar, more intelligible, more precise, more accessible and more interesting.
>
> Previously, elementary mathematics teaching could only deal with

artificial situations in which pieces of technical work were mixed in with vague (and usually not explicit) appeals to intuition.

Today a quite different approach is possible, in which the student is encouraged to take an active part in the building of the mathematical edifice starting from simple, familiar situations.

Such is the object of this book, which is aimed at all those who wish to be initiated into the mathematics of today, whatever their age and whatever their previous development.

(ibid., preface p. ix)

Authenticity and the zone of proximal relevance

While some teachers focus on setting tasks in *authentic* contexts (Brown *et al.*, 1989), some in contexts that enable direct action (Frankenstein, 1989; Mellin-Olsen, 1987), some in contexts that fit with learners' immediate experience, and others are content to work on abstracted mathematical objects removed from contexts until the techniques are mastered, a middle ground is looking for settings and contexts that can 'become real' for learners. The Dutch Realistic Mathematics project (see Gravemeijer, 1994) is not centrally concerned with what learners are specifically interested in, but rather with what they might become interested in if their attention is suitably directed. Thus every learner has the power to imagine, and through exercise of their mental imagery can become interested and intrigued in questions that are not immediately practical. The term *zone of proximal relevance* is useful in order to refer to settings and tasks that, although not already of immediate relevance to learners as they see things, can become 'real' for them through the use of their power to imagine.

Teacher desire

Concern about learner motivation leads teachers to exercise their own desires that learners actually learn something. Learners can be motivated by teachers who display a love of and enthusiasm for their subject. Learners can also be turned off by a teacher who cannot resist probing, and explaining, not letting learners internalise ideas for themselves.

Teacher lusts: Mary Boole

Finding it hard to wait for learners to think about and respond to questions is one version of what Mary Boole called *teacher lusts*, a strong term, but often appropriate. Desire to explain, and desire that learners enjoy their mathematics and appreciate what the teacher has appreciated serve as barriers rather than supports for teaching.

The teacher (whether school-teacher, minister of religion, political leader, or head of a family) has a desire to make those under him conform themselves to his ideals. Nations could not be built up, nor children preserved from ruin, if some such desire did not exist and exert itself in some degree. But it has its gamut of lusts, very similar to those run down by the other faculties. First, the teacher wants to regulate the actions, conduct, and thoughts of other people in a way that does no obvious harm but is quite in excess both of normal rights and of practical necessity. Next, he wants to proselytise, convince, control, to arrest the spontaneous action of other minds, to an extent which ultimately defeats its own ends by making the pupils too feeble and automatic to carry on his teaching into the future with any vigour. Lastly, he acquires a sheer automatic lust for telling other people 'to don't', for arresting spontaneous action in others in a way that destroys their power even to learn at the time what he is trying to teach them. What is wanted is that we should pull these three series tight so as to see their parallelism, and not go on fogging ourselves with any such foolish notion as that sex-passion is the lust of the flesh and teacher-lust a thing in itself pure and good, which may legitimately be indulged in to the uttermost.

(Tahta, 1972, p. 11)

Explaining: John Holt

Explanations: We teachers – perhaps all human beings – are in the grip of an astonishing delusion. We think that we can take a picture, a structure, a working model of something, constructed in our minds out of long experience and familiarity, and by turning that model into a string of words, transplant it whole into the mind of someone else. Perhaps once in a thousand times, when the explanation is extraordinarily good, and the listener extraordinarily experienced and skillful at turning word strings into non-verbal reality, and when explainer and listener share in common many of the experiences being talked about, the process may work; and some real meaning may be communicated. Most of the time explaining does not increase understanding, and may even lessen it.

(Holt, 1967, p. 178)

Alertness and passivity: Mary Boole

Suppose I'm teaching, say, the process of multiplication. There are two things which the pupils can get out of my instruction: (A) skill in performing the operation of multiplication itself; and (B) a little of the power to find out for themselves how to do other arithmetical operations. Every process that I teach ought to be so taught as to add something to the pupil's chance of someday making out a rule for himself without the aid of a teacher.

If we add together all the As of a child's arithmetical career, they constitute ... the *body* of his arithmetical knowledge; if we sum up the

Bs, they constitute what is called its *life*. The sum of the combined A elements constitutes the ability to reckon the bulk or number of dead material and to keep accounts according to any system chosen by an employer. The sum of the B elements gives the extra power of bringing one's knowledge to bear in forming a sound judgment on problems connected with living forces … .

Now the A element in any mathematical lesson can be imparted while the class is alert and eager; the B element cannot be imparted except under the peculiar condition called by some mystic writers 'Silence in the soul' awaiting further Light.

The two states, the alert and the passive, alternate in any good educational *regime*; the alert phases being very much the longest, the passively recipient ones short but quite undisturbed.

But under stress of competition the passive mystic phases of study are being crowded out. The reason is that England is so saturated with the spirit of advertisement that, in any given committee, the majority are almost sure to be against the teaching of anything for which there is nothing to show at the *next forthcoming* examination.

(Tahta, 1972, p. 22)

Learner self-esteem

Not all activity produces learning. In the context of the *didactic contract* (see p. 79), Guy Brousseau and Michael Otte identify some learner responses to challenges intended to motivate learners to understand more deeply. They observe that some learners take on challenges but become immersed in details of the challenge; others prefer to avoid challenge altogether wherever possible.

Altogether, one may in fact observe the inclination of certain pupils to take on willingly the first moment, namely the questions and problems, the uncertainty and openness, the complexity and the playing on the verge of knowledge. But they cannot quit or leave this gambling, autotelic, unrewarded behaviour and cannot get involved in a really responsible manner … .

For others, it is impossible to accept the first moment. Problems and open questions are not tolerable for them. … A question without an immediately conceivable answer causes anguish for them. They obsessionally ask the teacher for answers, for decision procedures to reach an answer, for algorithms.

(Brousseau and Otte, 1991, pp. 33–4)

Learner theories: Carol Dweck

Carol Dweck (b. New York, 1946–) is an American psychologist who has focused on the issue of self-esteem in learners. In Dweck (1999) she summarises for teachers a lifetime of work with numerous colleagues, making specific suggestions for working with learners with low self-esteem. Here she distinguishes two theories learners have about themselves, and their implications for learning.

> Some people believe their intelligence is a fixed trait. They have a certain amount of it and that's that. ...
>
> This view has repercussions for students. It can make students worry about how much of this fixed intelligence they have. ... They must look smart and, at all costs, not look dumb.
>
> [To feel smart they need] easy, low-effort successes, and outperforming other students. Effort, difficulty, setbacks, or higher-performing peers call their intelligence into question ... .
>
> Challenges are a threat to self esteem. ...
>
> [Lavish well-meaning praise for very little fosters] an over concern for looking smart, a distaste for challenge, and a decreased ability to cope with set-backs.
>
> [Other people believe intelligence is] ... something they can cultivate through learning. ... [Everyone], with effort and guidance, can increase their intellectual abilities. ...
>
> It makes them want to learn ... Why waste time worrying about whether you look smart or dumb, when you could be becoming smarter? ...
>
> [...]
>
> Self-esteem ... is a positive way of experiencing yourself when you are fully engaged and are using your abilities to the utmost in pursuit of something you value.
>
> (Dweck, 1999, pp. 2–4)

For learners with low self-esteem convinced that their intelligence is limited and fixed ('I can't so I won't'), it is natural to try to persuade the teacher to give them less challenging 'easier' work 'to ease them along'. This minimises the possibility of being brought to the edge of understanding, and so to revealing how little they feel they know. Learners identified as 'low-attaining' and put together in a group are well aware that they are being given 'simpler tasks'.

The teacher, meanwhile, is eager to develop learners' self-esteem and so simplifies the tasks in order to find a level at which the learners can operate successfully. The aim is to convert them to an inner language of 'I can', with their intelligence something that grows in response to challenge, and so gradually to restore the challenge level of the work. Unfortunately, this idealised process usually stalls, as it is in the learners' short-term interests to keep the work as simple as possible without it becoming overtly 'baby-ish'.

Note the parallels with *funnelling* (see p. 274): there the questions are made simpler until the learner feels safe in answering. Here the tasks are made simpler until the learners finally engage. Dweck suggests converting 'I can't so I won't' into 'I can and I will' by replacing 'I'm at my limits' by 'I can try harder'. This proves to be a useful contribution to the perhaps inevitable simplifying of tasks, and a powerful device for re-invigorating depressed learners. The teacher's art is in simplifying or altering just enough so that learners can feel success and can experience improving their thinking, so as to reactivate their motivational desires and interest hand in hand with conversion to 'I can and I will'. Notice also the similarity with the *didactic contract* (see p. 79).

Learners can all too easily develop a habit of mind that they do not understand, even when they palpably respond appropriately. Some people seek support by justifying tasks through authentic contexts and authentic tasks, or through real problem-solving. But by the time learners have reached the point where they are convinced that they will not succeed, that they 'can't do maths', contexts are merely a diversion.

Experiences can be natural, conflicting or alien. There is widespread agreement that appropriate disturbance, disruption of expectation, is what initiates and motivates acting in such a way as to make sense, and to learn.

Learners need encouragement and personal control over the amount of choice and freedom being dealt with at any one time. Some learners are motivated more by effectiveness and success in the material world (authenticity of activity), some are motivated more by aesthetics of patterns and structures.

Teachers' excessive desire that their learners learn and develop may in some cases be part of the barrier to that learning; teachers' low expectation may similarly blunt learners' motivation.

---

5   Learners' powers

Introduction

In this chapter, the extracts relate to the notion that learners make use of their natural powers to make sense of the world in general, and that these are a resource to be developed by the teacher of mathematics. The chapter starts with a collection of extracts about these natural powers in general and subsequent extracts look at particular examples.

Natural powers

In his comprehensive advice to teachers, J. Calkin (1910) summed up from a Canadian perspective a sentiment which seems to have been pervasive in educational circles in many countries, even if not in practice in schools. ' ... the mind is a power to be developed rather than a receptacle to be filled is a sound maxim in education' (Calkin, 1910, p. 18).

Herbert Spencer observed what parents and teachers have always observed:

> ... 'that children in the household, the streets and the fields' (Spencer, 1911, p. 24) learn all kinds of things effortlessly, with eager pleasure, yet these same children often have great difficulty learning quite elementary things in formal educational settings.
>
> (Egan, webref a)

There are interesting connections with the work of Nunes and colleagues (1993) on the facility of young children selling things in the streets in contrast to their performance in a school setting. This theme was taken up by Lave (1988) and then by Seeley Brown and colleagues (1989) who developed the notions of *authentic mathematics* (see p. 108) and learning through *apprenticeship* (see p. 75).

Powers: Herbert Spencer

Spencer proposed that children are naturally inquiring, constructing, and active beings, so the developing powers of children provide the basis for his educational philosophy (see also p. 35).

> Who, indeed, can watch the ceaseless observation and inquiry and inference going on in a child's mind, or listen to its acute remarks on matters within the range of its faculties, without perceiving that these powers it manifests, if brought to bear systematically upon studies *within the same range*, would readily master them without help? This need for perpetual telling results from our stupidity, not the child's. We drag it away from the facts in which it is interested, and which it is actively assimilating of itself. ...
>
> (Spencer, 1878, p. 72)

Kieran Egan (b. Ireland, 1942–) is now a Canadian researcher with an unusual perspective on education. He accuses Spencer of a negative influence on modern education:

> In this paper I will argue that the conception of education that continues to shape our schools, and influences what we do to children in its name, was given its modern sense as a result of ideas that were largely formulated in the 1850s. I will try to show the source of many of our present most generally held beliefs about learning, development, and the curriculum, and show that they were based on ideas that were, simply, wrong. These ideas continue to be the source of catastrophic damage and waste of life, and are responsible for the general ineffectiveness of schooling.
>   In describing a catastrophe one needs an appropriate villain, and the best villain of modern education is Herbert Spencer. ... his educational ideas, based on general principles shown to be false, became the rarely-questioned basis of modern education.
>
> (Egan, webref a)

Egan points out that Spencer coined the expression 'evolution', which was snappier than Darwin's original 'descent with modifications' or 'natural selection'. Spencer also coined the term 'survival of the fittest' which Darwin later took up in a limited fashion, while Spencer applied it to all and everything.

Powers: Bertrand Russell

Bertrand Russell (b. Wales, 1872–1970) was a mathematician and philosopher. As mathematician he worked with Whitehead to try to place mathematics on a firm foundation of logic; as a philosopher he promoted sensitivity to feelings as well as rational and deductive thinking. Here he summarises a long description of how early education was based on the widespread practice of trying to force learners to learn through corporal punishment.

> The spontaneous wish to learn, which every normal child possesses, as shown in efforts to walk and talk, should be the driving-force in education. The substitution of this driving-force for the rod is one of the great advances of our time.
>
> (Russell, 1926, p. 25)

Discovery: Alfred North Whitehead

Here Whitehead encompasses issues which are still with us, including utility (see *authenticity*, p. 108).

> Let the main ideas which are introduced into a child's education be few and important, and let them be thrown into every combination possible. The child should make them his own, and should understand their application here and now in the circumstances of his actual life. From the very beginning of his education, the child should experience the joy of discovery. The discovery he has to make, is that general ideas give an understanding of that stream of events which pours through his life, which is his life.
>
> (Whitehead, 1932, p. 3)

> Whatever interest attaches to your subject matter must be evoked here and now; whatever powers you are strengthening in the pupil, must be exercised here and now; whatever possibilities of mental life your teaching should impart, must be exhibited here and now. That is the golden rule of education, and a very difficult rule to follow.
>
> (ibid., p. 9)

Thinking: Max Wertheimer

Max Wertheimer (b. Prague, 1880–1943) was one of the major thinkers and forces behind the elucidation of gestalt psychology in Germany. He left for the USA in 1933 where he was professor of psychology and philosophy in the New School for Social Research in New York. Writing in the 1930s, Wertheimer is describing the components of thinking, first from what we would call an experiential or phenomenological point of view, and then, extracted here, from a behavioural point of view.

Thinking consists in

- envisaging, realizing structural features and structural requirements; proceeding in accordance with, and determined by, these requirements;

and thereby changing the situation in the direction of structural improve-
ments, which involves:

- that gaps, trouble-regions, disturbances, superficialities, etc., be viewed
  and dealt with structurally;
- that inner structural relations – fitting or not fitting – be sought among
  such disturbances and the given situation as a whole and among its
  various parts;
- that there be operations of structural grouping and segregation, of
  centering, etc.;
- that operations be viewed and treated in their structural place, role,
  dynamic meaning, including realization of the changes which this
  involves.

(Wertheimer, 1961, pp. 235–6)

Note that Wertheimer makes use of the notion of *disturbance* (see p. 55) as
underlying or producing learner action. Although he expresses himself in
terms of thinking actions, it is clear that he thinks people have the requisite
powers to act in these ways.

- realizing structural transposability, structural hierarchy, and sepa-
  rating structurally peripheral from fundamental features – a special
  case of grouping;
- looking for structural rather than piecemeal truth.

In human terms there is at bottom the desire, the craving to face the true
issue, the structural core, the radix of the situation; to go from an
unclear, inadequate relation to a clear, transparent direct confrontation –
straight from the heart of the thinker to the heart of his object, of his
problem. All the items hold also for real attitudes and for action, just as
they do for thinking processes.

(ibid., p. 236)

Wertheimer then suggests that it is perfectly possible to rephrase these
observations in terms descriptive of what behaviour an observer might
notice, contrasting superficial and structural awareness, in terms of: *compar-
ison* and *discrimination* (identification of similarities and differences); *analysis* (looking at parts); *induction* (generalisation, both empricial and
structural); *experience* (gathering facts or vividly grasping structure); *experimentation* (seeking to decide between possible hypotheses); expressing
'*one variable is a function of another variable*'; *associating* (items together
and recognising structural relationships); *repeating*; *trial and error*; and
learning on the basis of success (with or without appreciating structural
significance) (based on Wertheimer, 1961, pp. 248–51).

Powers: Mary Boole

Mary Boole (b. England, 1832–1916) was brought up in France before returning to England. She edited the books and papers of her husband (George Boole, creator of Boolean Algebra) until his death. Mary then taught mathematics and wrote extensively about teaching, as well as pursuing her interests in Eastern religious thought.

Some extracts from her extensive educational writings can be found in a collection made by Dick Tahta (1972, see also p. 110).

> My husband told me that when he was a lad of seventeen a thought struck him suddenly, which became the foundation all his future discoveries. It was a flash of psychological insight into the conditions under which a mind most readily accumulates knowledge. Many young people have similar flashes of revelation as to the nature of their mental powers; those to whom they occur often become distinguished in some branch of learning; but to no one individual does the revelation comes with sufficient clearness to enable him to explain to others the true secret of his success.
>
> (Boole, 1901, p. 951 (from a letter written in 1901))

Powers: Vadim Krutetskii

Krutetskii was a Soviet psychologist, deputy director of the research Institute of General and Educational Psychology at the USSR Academy of Pedagogical Sciences, and head of the section on abilities of the Vygotsky school. His monumental study of mathematical ability has influenced generations of researchers. Here he traces some of the background to his own work and that of his colleagues (see *activity theory*, p. 84).

> Soviet psychology resolves, from a Marxist position, one of the most complicated issues in the psychology of ability: the relationship between the innate and the acquired in ability. A basic tenet of Soviet psychology on this issue is the thesis that social factors have a decisive value in the development of abilities; that the leading role is played by man's social experience – by the conditions of his life and activity. Mental traits cannot be inborn. This can be said of abilities as well. Abilities are always the result of development. They are formed and developed in life, during activity, instruction, and training.
>
> … Man is endowed at birth with only one ability: the ability to form specifically human abilities. …
>
> […]
>
> Abilities cannot be inborn; only inclinations for abilities – certain anatomical and physiological features of the brain and nervous system – are present at birth.
>
> (Krutetskii, 1976, pp. 60–1)

Krutetskii isolates seven assumptions underlying his research; here are four of them:

- Abilities are always *abilities for a definite kind of activity*; they exist only in a person's specific activity. Therefore they can show up only on the basis of an analysis of a specific activity. Accordingly, a mathematical ability exists only in a mathematical activity and should be manifested in it.
- Ability is a dynamic concept. It not only shows up and exists in an activity but is created and even developed in it. Accordingly, mathematical abilities exist only in a dynamic state, in development; they are formed and developed in mathematical activity.
- At certain periods in a person's development, the most favorable conditions arise for forming and developing individual types of ability, and some of these abilities are provisional or transitory. ...
- Progress in a mathematical activity depends not on an ability taken separately, but on a complex of abilities.

(ibid., pp. 66–7)

Powers: Maria Montessori

Maria Montessori (b. Italy, 1870–1952) was the first female medical graduate from the University of Rome. Frustrated by failings of the education system and deeply concerned about the poverty she saw around her, she was convinced that children could learn to read and write if only they were put in an environment in which it was useful to them to learn. Her methods involving learners taking responsibility for choosing, using, and putting away structured apparatus has influenced primary education everywhere. She advocated observing children in order to learn how to improve teaching: she herself called 'the discovery of the child' her greatest contribution.

> According to Maria Montessori, 'A child's work is to create the person she will become'. To carry out this self-construction, children have innate mental powers, but they must be free to use these powers. For this reason, a Montessori classroom provides freedom while maintaining an environment that encourages a sense of order and self-discipline. 'Freedom in a structured environment' is the Montessori dictum that names this arrangement.
>
> Like all thinkers in the Aristotelian tradition, Montessori recognized that the senses must be educated first in the development of the intellect. Consequently, she created a vast array of special learning materials from which concepts could be abstracted and through which they could be concretized. In recognition of the independent nature of the developing intellect, these materials are self-correcting – that is, from their use, the child discovers for himself whether he has the right answer. This feature

of her materials encourages the child to be concerned with facts and truth, rather than with what adults say is right or wrong.

Also basic to Montessori's philosophy is her belief in the 'sensitive periods' of a child's development: periods when the child seeks certain stimuli with immense intensity, and, consequently, can most easily master a particular learning skill. The teacher's role is to recognize the sensitive periods in individual children and put the children in touch with the appropriate materials.

[…]

… Dewey's concern was with fostering the imagination and the development of social relationships. He believed in developing the intellect late in childhood, for fear that it might stifle other aspects of development. By contrast, Montessori believed that development of the intellect was the only means by which the imagination and proper social relationships could arise. Her method focused on the early stimulation and sharpening of the senses, the development of independence in motor tasks and the care of the self, and the child's naturally high motivation to learn about the world as a means of gaining mastery over himself and his environment.

(Enright and Cox, webref)

The focus on self-realization through independent activity, the concern with attitude, and the focus on the educator as the keeper of the environment (and making use of their scientific powers of observation and reflection) – all have some echo in the work of informal educators. However, it is Maria Montessori's notion of the Children's House as a stimulating environment in which participants can learn to take responsibility that has a particular resonance.

(Smith, M., 1997)

Powers: Caleb Gattegno

In the postscript to one of his less philosophical books, Gattegno summarises his thinking about learners' powers. The development of children's powers and making use of them in teaching formed the backbone of all Gattegno's investigations, so it is a theme which he returns to again and again.

What is it, then, that will allow us to teach mathematics to anyone with a functioning mind and an inclination to learn? Simply, finding a way to make the learner aware of the powers of his mind – the powers he uses every day, those which allowed him to learn his native language and to use imagery and symbolism. This means that the job of teaching is one of bringing about self-awareness in learners through whatever means are available in the environment: words, actions, perceptions of transformations, one's fingers, one's language, one's memory, one's games,

one's symbolisms, one's inner and outer wealth of perceived relationships, and so on.

> (Gattegno, 1974, p. 111, postscript)

Young children are continually investigating their powers of perception
and action; they use these powers spontaneously – without having to be
taught – in order to elaborate their experience of themselves and of the
world. … this can become part and parcel of mathematical education.

> (Gattegno, 1988, p. 165)

Teachers of children will say that the greatest power of the mind is the
capacity to transform. Anyone who speaks and speaks properly – as
many two year-olds can do very easily – can transform according to his
perception of the situation and according to the criteria that he has
mastered and understood.

> (Gattegno, 1970, p. 23)

Powers: Dick Tahta, Bill Brookes and David Wheeler

Brookes, Tahta and Wheeler were early members of what became the Association of Teachers of Mathematics which was initiated by Gattegno. They
met regularly to observe lessons together and discuss what they saw.

> If in our enthusiasm for providing active experience for young children
> we do no more than provide the springs and balances, the sand and
> water, with requests for recording of what happens in certain selected
> situations, then we run the danger of abdicating from mathematics alto-
> gether. We certainly encourage the same abdications if we think in terms
> of children 'discovering' relations in certain external situations. Some of
> the most important mathematics relations stem from the earliest mental
> and emotional activity of the infant. We make sense of our environment
> by imposing these relations upon it. In developing our understanding
> and control of these relations in this way we further provide the possi-
> bility of a control of the environment. In order to develop the fullest
> resources of the human mind, it may be more important to think of
> creating mathematics rather than discovering it. In the creation of likes
> and unlikes we detect 'the mind at work creating works of the mind'.
> And this is mathematics.
>
> (Tahta and Brookes, 1966, p. 8)

There are similarities in their concern with a dilemma raised by Ainley (see
p. 250).

Powers: Colin Banwell, Dick Tahta and Ken Saunders

Banwell, Tahta, and Saunders were teachers and teacher educators in Devon when they wrote an immensely practical book which inspired generations of teachers to move towards teaching investigatively, engaging learners in thinking and exploring mathematically. This brief extract is taken from their summary.

> In developing and using the powers that he already has there is no other feedback than his own judgement and descision, though these may be affected by the conventions of social agreement.
>
> (Banwell *et al.*, 1972, p. 61)

They also wrote 'Everyone is a mathematician though he may not know this. The mind knows more than it knows it knows.' (Banwell *et al.*, 1972 (updated 1986), p. 61.) We suggest that no better summary of the power of human minds can be given.

Powers: Richard Skemp

Skemp was similarly impressed with what very young children achieve.

> An infant aged twelve months, having finished sucking his bottle, crawled across the floor of the living room to where two empty wine bottles were standing and stood his own empty feeding bottle neatly along side them. A two-year-old, seeing a baby on the floor, reacted to it as he usually did to dogs, patting it on the head and stroking its back. (He had seen plenty of dogs, but had never before seen another baby crawling.)
>
> In both these cases the behaviour of the children concerned implies: … some kind of classification of their previous experience; [and] the fitting of their present experience into one of these classes.
>
> We all [behave like this] all the time; it is thus that we bring to bear our past experience on the present situation. The activity is so continuous and automatic that it requires some slightly unexpected outcome thereof, such as the above, to call it to our attention.
>
> At a lower level, we classify every time we recognize an object as one which we have seen before. On no two occasions are the incoming sense data likely to be exactly the same, since we see objects at different distances and angles, and also in varying lights. From these varying inputs we abstract certain *in*variant properties, and these properties persist in memory longer than the memory of any particular presentation of the object.
>
> (Skemp, 1971, pp. 19–20)

Note the passing reference to *disturbance* (see p. 55) and particularly the use of *imagery* (see p. 129).

Powers: John Mason

John Mason (b. Ontario, 1944–) was profoundly influenced in his teaching by seeing a film in 1967 of George Polya teaching some undergraduates, by year-long contact with the mathematician and teacher J. G. Bennett (1897–1974), and by contact with Gattegno. This book arose from his growing awareness that themes he had been promoting had actually been propounded in earlier generations. Here he advocates thinking in terms of learners' powers.

> Every child that gets to school has already exhibited amazing powers. They have decoded the sounds that adults make, and learned to fashion sounds that others make sense of. They have learned to coordinate gross and fine muscles in order to move about, to pick things up and put them down. They have worked out that unsupported things fall, that some things are heavy and others light, with some even rising all by themselves unless held down. They have worked out that there are patterns to light and dark, to adults' presence and absence. They have learned to recognise people despite changes in hair shape and colour, clothes, glasses, etc.. Indeed, an amazing intelligence has been displayed. They have nascent theories about people (and when people are happy, sad, irritated, angry, etc.).
>
> Then they come to school. We try to formalise some of what they can do intuitively (speech becomes print, ordering and counting become numbers, talk becomes writing). In the process we do not always manage to draw upon those existing powers as fully as we might, with the result that many children act as if they believe those powers are not actually wanted in the classroom.
>
> (Mason, 2001a)

Every learner comes to school having already demonstrated tremendous powers of sense-making. Specific powers are described in the following sections.

> Learners have natural powers with which they make sense of the world in general. These are a valuable resource to be developed by the teacher of mathematics.

Discerning similarities and differences

The power to distinguish, to discern, to make distinctions is of course central to education. However, authors who draw attention to it imply that learners are not always encouraged to use this power for themselves.

Discernment: Thyra Smith

Many authors have marvelled at the powers of young babies to make sense of the world in which they suddenly 'discover themselves'. Smith became an Her Majesty's Inspector of Schools (HMI) and received an OBE for her services to education. Her short but immensely practical book begins with observations of a baby. She goes on through the book to describe the child's various powers and how they develop through experience of the world.

> A young baby can suck and grasp and move; but he does not appear at first to know what he grasps or sucks or moves. At a very early stage however he knows whether what he sucks is satisfying or otherwise; this is probably the beginning of discrimination.
>
> During the first months his waking periods are occupied in fairly continuous motion; but his movements appear random. They bring him in contact with things that are grasped or sucked or pushed away and rolled about in a fashion that suggests that he is aware of their presence but not of their nature.
>
> (Smith, 1954, p. 1)

> Perhaps it is useful to summarize very generally what arithmetical and mathematical conceptions are gained by the young child in a natural and practical way.
>
> He is aware of self, and not-self, that is of 'I' and of other things that have a life of their own. He is aware of 'some' and 'a lot' and 'none'. The last named is possibly mere absence or lack which is expressed either by hunting to find things or by making requests to be supplied. 'Bigness' and 'Littleness' are known as are 'High' and 'Low'. None of these terms may be used spontaneously, though they are evidently understood. Parts of the body are known and the difference between unity and plurality is appreciated practically and intuitively. ...
>
> Ideas of differences in shape are shown in reactions to balls that will roll, bricks that can be pushed together or placed on one another, boxes that open and shut and so forth.
>
> [...]
>
> Power of discrimination is shown by preferences shown for particular toys. Things are hustled together or pushed apart to make groups of varying sizes without any consideration for the 'size' aspect of the matter

except that obviously he differentiates between what is enough to be satisfying or too few to be interesting.

[...]

Knowledge at this stage is 'sensed' intuitively and we are aware of its existence through observation and interpretation of the child's actions. Much repetition and continued use will establish greater sureness and when the time is ripe the child will show that he is aware – that he knows what he knows. But thus far his basis is firmly set on concrete things; ...

(ibid., pp. 9–10)

Note the similarity with *theorems-in-action* (see p. 63). Note also the influence of Piaget's research in describing different ways in which children encounter and engage with the world (see p. 92), and similarities with *structure of attention* (see p. 60), and the role of *practice* (see p. 174).

Discernment: Caleb Gattegno

Another attribute a child brings with him is the ability to notice differences and assimilate similarities. What does this mean? Aristotle put the ability to perform this operation at the foundation of basic logic and every child owns it: he brings it with him. Every child knows that the basis of living is to recognize differences and similarities.

Of two cups of the same make, we can hold one cup with the handle in front, the other so that the handle is at the back. One may be pink, the other white. We still say both are cups, not two distinct kinds of objects, a pink object without a handle, a white object with a handle – but cups and that there are two of them.

We would say otherwise if we could not ignore differences and find the attributes that bring them together, as well as see the attributes that separate them.

(Gattegno, 1970, pp. 25–6)

Distinction making is the first thing we need to do as organisms, even before we are born. Distinction making then develops into more sophisticated ways of making sense of the world. See van Hiele (p. 59 and p. 163) and Maturana (p. 70) for example.

Stressing and ignoring: Caleb Gattegno

The very act of discerning involves stressing some sense impressions, or more generally, some features, and ignoring others. As Gattegno says 'To isolate the mental activity called mathematics is as easy as to merge it with any other, for *it is a property of the mind to isolate and merge, to stress and ignore*' (Gattegno, 1970a, p. 136). He recognised that this fundamental action which leads to discernment, to distinction making, and hence to classification, is the very basis for abstraction and generalisation.

Stressing and ignoring: John Dewey

Of course, once alerted to a distinction, it is possible to find it in earlier writers. Here is John Dewey on stressing and ignoring, which he calls *selective emphasis*.

> The favoring of cognitive objects and their characteristics at the expense of traits that excite desire, command action and produce passion, is a special instance of the principle of selective emphasis which introduces partiality and partisanship into philosophy. Selective emphasis, with accompanying omission and rejection, is the heart-beat of mental life. To object to the operation is to discard all thinking. But in ordinary matters and in scientific inquiries, we always retain the sense that the material chosen is selected for a purpose; [but] there is no idea of denying what is left out, for what is omitted is merely that which is not relevant to the particular problem and purpose in hand.
>
> (Dewey, 1938, pp. 24–5)

Dewey also points to the related concept of *invariance in the midst of change* (see p. 129) as lying at the heart of scientific enquiry.

> [A scientist] seizes upon whatever is so uniform as to make the changes of nature rhythmic, and hence predictable. But the contingencies of nature make discovery of these uniformities with a view to prediction needed and possible. Without the uniformities, science would be impossible. But if they alone existed, thought and knowledge would be impossible and meaningless. The incomplete and uncertain gives point and application to ascertainment of regular relations and orders. These relations in themselves are hypothetical, and when isolated from application are subject-matter of mathematics (in a non-existential sense). Hence the *ultimate* objects of science are *guided* processes of change.
>
> (ibid., p. 160)

John Dewey spoke elsewhere in terms of how experience of a 'thing' already involves selection of certain attributes to attend to, with others being ignored, and that this is how 'things' come into existence for learners as 'things in themselves'. (See *reification*, p. 167).

> Ideas ... are *suggestions*. Nothing in experience is absolutely simple, single, and isolated. Everything experienced comes to us along with some other object, quality, or event. Some object is focal and most distinct, but it shades off into other things. A child may be absorbed in watching a bird; for the bright center of his consciousness there is nothing but the bird

there. But of course it is somewhere – on the ground, in a tree. And the actual experience includes much more. The bird also is doing something – flying, pecking, feeding, singing, etc.. And the experience of the bird is itself complex, not a single sensation; there are numbers of related qualities included within it. This highly elementary illustration indicates why it is that the next time a child sees a bird, he will 'think' of something else that is not then present. That is to say, a portion of his present experience which is like that of prior experience will call up or *suggest* some thing or quality connected with it which was present in the total previous experience; that thing or quality in turn may suggest something connected with itself; it not only *may* do so, but it *will* do so unless some new object of perception starts another train of suggestions going. In this primary sense, then, the having of ideas is not so much something we do, as it is something that happens to us. Just as, when we open our eyes, we see what is there; so, when suggestions occur to us, they come to us as functions of our past experience and not of our present will and intention. So far as thoughts in this particular meaning are concerned, it is true to say "it thinks" (as we say "it rains"), rather than "I think". Only when a person tries to get control of the *conditions* that determine the occurrence of a suggestion, and only when he accepts responsibility for using the suggestion to see what follows from it, is it significant to introduce the 'I' as the agent and source of thought.

(Dewey, 1933, pp. 41–2)

Dewey is referring to what Skemp called *resonance* as the mechanism whereby stimuli of the senses produces complex experiences which include 'thinking of something that is not then present'. The observation that 'it thinks' is more accurate than 'I think' has far reaching implications in the development of useful habits, and working against obstructive habits.

Same and different: Dick Tahta and Bill Brookes

Asking learners to look out for what is the same and what differs between two or more objects, situations or phenomena proves remarkably fruitful at invoking learners' powers to stress and ignore, which lies behind the mathematical theme of *invariance in the midst of change* (see p. 193).

It is in these choices [of uses of words such as 'same'] that the essence of mathematics resides.
   If certain choices about the use of the word 'same' lie at the heart of mathematical activity then mathematics starts in the cradle, for a sense of one's own identity from one moment to the next is one of the first lessons to be learnt. Mummy is quickly felt to be the same person when she comes and goes; it takes much longer for Daddy to acquire the same invariance. The rattle is seen from different positions and felt in different

ways. Each perception is different but as it is explored helps to build up the idea of something permanent, something that is always the same. Later on it becomes more and more difficult to recapture the differences between our perceptions. We very rarely see a circle when we look at a penny, but that is the shape we say that we see when we are asked. In an agreed sense, a circle remains the same wherever we perceive it from; in another agreed sense it does not. In one case a circle and an ellipse are the same but in the other they are different.

[...]

It is significant that the use of the word 'same' reveals an incredibly complicated sequence of changes of view-points during the time that it is being used. To recognise that a child uses this word in this manner is to recognise some of the capabilities for abstraction which he is often denied.

(Tahta and Brookes, 1966, pp. 4–5)

One of the principal themes of mathematics is *invariance in the midst of change* (see p. 193). The device of asking learners 'what is the same and what is different' and then negotiating what is worth attending to, has been extensively exploited and researched by the team of Alf Coles (b. London, 1970–) and Laurinda Brown (b. Yorkshire, 1952–). They found it to be extremely effective in promoting active learners of mathematics (Brown and Coles, 1999; 2000; Coles and Brown, 1999).

Distinguishing things on the basis of stressing some features as being different, while treating others as 'being the same' is the basis of *classification* (see p. 135), as Skemp has already suggested. Putting things in order, comparing and contrasting, can be seen in the play of very young children, in the organisation of collecting as adolescents, and in the structure of mathematics. We succeed as organisms because we can classify, that is, we can discriminate and recognise similarities and differences, which we do by stressing some features and ignoring others. This ability to stress-and-ignore at the same time lies behind the various powers mentioned here: it is the basis for specialising and generalising, for imagining and expressing, and for ordering and classifying.

> Stressing and ignoring produces discrimination, leading to classification and recognition. Using 'what is the same and what different about ... ' as a pedagogical device makes use of these powers.

Mental imagery and imagination

It is through the power of mental imagery that we are able to be simultaneously present and yet 'somewhere else'; that we are able to enter the world of mathematical images, and through that, the world signified by symbols. It is the means by which we identify 'things' as 'things' that Dewey mentioned in the previous extract.

Imagery: Caleb Gattegno

Every one of us knows of the fantastic things that can happen in our dreams and nightmares. Looking both at the dynamics of imagery and at how it affects the content of our dreams, we can learn a great deal about what children bring with them to their mathematics studies.

The type of transformation met in this context, when the teacher calls upon mental evocations to advance mathematical understanding, is one that remains in contact with mental energy, keeps some continuity between the initial and the final forms of the images (which are dynamic, as in dreams), and produces effects that display the algebras applied to them. When concentrating on imagery, one is more aware of content than of transformation and stresses images per se all through the process.

By asking students to shut their eyes and to respond with mental images to verbal statements enunciated by the teacher, one makes them aware:

- that in their mind imagery is connected with the rest of their experience, and
- that in itself is a power.

Indeed this type of relationship between teacher and students can be used to generate whole chapters of mathematics. The key here is the dynamic attribute of imagery, which can be seen as being equivalent to certain mathematical properties.

(Gattegno, 1970, pp. 26–7)

An excellent source of specific and practical tasks for this purpose can be found in Leapfrogs (1982). 'Leapfrogs' is the name for a group which met regularly to develop resources for mathematics classrooms designed to maximise the potential for their use in different situations and for different purposes.

Here Gattegno is referring to the use of mathematical animations and then links algebra and imagery:

Because images are dependent on our will, once we begin deliberately to employ them, we can very soon obtain an awareness that indeed imagery is a power of the mind, and it can yield in a short time vast amounts of insights into fields that become almost sterile when the dynamics are removed from them … .

Algebra is present in all mathematics because it is an attribute of the functioning mind. Imagery is present at will and can remain present while the mind is at work on it or on some elements within it.

Who can doubt that many more children will be at home with mathematics when features of it are presented to them as the recognition of what one can contemplate within one's mind when it is responding to mental stimuli.

(ibid., pp. 27–8)

Imagination: Kieran Egan

Egan views teaching as a form of story telling (see also Bruner, p. 68), and points to the importance of imagination, even if it is difficult to get hold of.

> A continuing theme of this book (Egan, 1986) is that children's imaginations are the most powerful and energetic learning tools. Our most influential learning theories have been formed from research programs that have very largely focused on a limited range of children's logical thinking skills. That research has largely neglected imagination, because imagination is, after all, difficult stuff to get any clear hold on. Consequently the dominant learning theories that have profoundly influenced education, helping to form the dominant model and principles mentioned above, have taken little account of imagination.
>
> (Egan, webref)

Imagery: Grayson Wheatley

Grayson Wheatley (b. USA) is a mathematician and mathematics educator who has focused particularly on the role of mental imagery in teaching and learning mathematics.

> All meaningful mathematics learning is imaged-based. While there may be certain forms of mathematical reasoning that seem not to use imagery, most mathematical activity has a spatial component. If school mathematics is procedural, students may fail to develop their capacity to form mental images of mathematical patterns and relationships. It is well documented that students who reason from images tend to be powerful mathematics students. Further, we know that the ability to use images effectively in doing mathematics can be developed. When students are encouraged to develop mental images and use those images in mathematics, they show surprising growth. All students can learn to use images effectively. Thus, developing spatial sense should be a priority in school mathematics.
>
> (Wheatley, webref)

Wheatley advocates use of tasks such as *Quick Draw* in which a geometrical figure is displayed for a few seconds and the learners are challenged to try to make a quick drawing.

Every child has the power to imagine what is not physically present, and to manipulate those images mentally. They also have the power to express those images (though it takes some time before they realise that those images are not shared with the people to whom they are talking). Expression takes the form of verbal language (demands, wishes, instructions, descriptions, chat), but also drawings, movement etc.. There is a real tension between inviting self-expression, and controlling the expressions of thirty or more children in a confined space.

Generalising and abstracting

The young child quickly associates different voice tones with the same adult. This is an example of generalisation. So is language. Nouns are labels for classes of objects, rarely for specific objects (personal names and names for pets and toys being an exception). Thus chair, cup and spoon refer not to specifics but to general classes. The notion of a noun is both a generalisation and an abstraction.

While people deal with generalities and abstractions all the time, generalisations play a central role in mathematics, where they are expressed in a succinct notation which is manipulated so as to draw out further conclusions which may be particular or general. Mathematics deals with relationships per se, and so context is of the least importance; hence the prevalence of abstractions in mathematics.

Generalisation: Alfred North Whitehead

As mathematician and philosopher, Whitehead was very concerned about education, taking the view that:

> ... The progress of science consists in observing ... interconnexions and in showing with a patient ingenuity that the events of this ever-shifting world are but examples of a few general connexions or relations called laws. To see what is general in what is particular and what is permanent in what is transitory is the aim of scientific thought. ...
>
> Now let us think of the sort of laws which we want in order completely to realize this scientific ideal. Our knowledge of the particular facts of the world around us is gained from our sensations.
>
> [...]
>
> ... when we have put aside our immediate sensations, the most serviceable part – from its clearness, definiteness, and universality – of what is left is composed of our general ideas of the abstract formal properties of things; in fact, ... abstract mathematical ideas ... . Thus mathematical ideas, because they are abstract, supply just what is wanted for a scientific description of the course of events.
>
> (Whitehead, 1911, pp. 4–5)

> ... what the mathematician is seeking is Generality. ... Any limitation whatsoever on the generality of theorems, or of proofs, or of interpretation is abhorrent to the mathematical instinct.
>
> (ibid., p. 57)

A related and extended version is 'seeing the general through the particular, and the particular in the general' (see p. 138). Generalisation is certainly present when through examination of a number of cases, often sequential in some manner, a common pattern is detected, as in recognising the sequence of odd numbers, or two more than a perfect square. But generalisation often takes place on the contemplation of a single example, as David Hilbert demonstrates.

Generalisation: David Hilbert

David Hilbert (b. Prussia, 1862–1943) was one of the leading mathematicians at the end of the nineteenth century, making contributions to a wide range of mathematical topics. His list of 23 problems posed to mathematicians at the beginning of the twentieth century directed mathematical development for several generations of mathematicians. He was associated with a *formalist* view of mathematics in which mathematics is seen as the manipulation of formal symbols according to specified rules. Here is a report from a colleague of his in Göttingen, Richard Courant (1888–1972), who moved to the USA and founded what is now known as the Courant Institute of Mathematical Sciences.

> He [Hilbert] was a most concrete, intuitive mathematician who invented, and very consciously used, a principle; namely, if you want to solve a problem first strip the problem of everything that is not essential. Simplify it, specialize it as much as you can without sacrificing its core. Thus it becomes simple, as simple as can be made, without losing any of its punch, and then you solve it. The generalization is a triviality which you don't have to pay much attention to. This principle of Hilbert's proved extremely useful for him and also for others who learned it from him. Unfortunately, it has been forgotten.
>
> (Courant, 1981, p. 161)

Both approaches to generalisation, which are sometimes distinguished as *empirical* and *structural* or as *empirical* and *generic* (see Bills and Rowland, 1999) are directed towards detecting and expressing underlying structure. See Krutetskii (p. 139) for further types of generalisation.

For some people, abstraction and generalisation are barely distinguishable, if at all, while for others, abstraction and generalisation are quite different. While both involve stressing some features and so ignoring (hence removing) other features, which become mere context, generalisation expresses structure, while abstraction is the process of taking that structure as the object of study axiomatically (see van Hiele *phases*, p. 59 and *structure of attention*, p. 63). Thus 'the sum of two odd numbers is even, of two evens is even, and of one odd and one even is odd' expresses a generality within numbers, whereas the structure of 'the sum of two of one type is of the second type, two of the second type is of the second type, and of one of each type is of the first type' abstracts the structure. An alternative view is to see this as further generalisation by ignoring the context of odd and even numbers.

Abstraction: Caleb Gattegno

Gattegno sees abstraction as essential, and algebra as vital to human functioning:

> Nobody has ever been able to reach the concrete. The concrete is so 'abstract' that nobody can reach it. We can only function because of abstraction. Abstraction makes life easy, makes it possible. Words, language have been created by man, so that it does not matter what any reader evokes in his mind when he sees the word red, so long as when we are confronted with a situation we shall agree that we are using the same word even for different impressions. Language is conveniently vague so that the word car, for example, could cover all cars, not just one. So anyone who has learned to speak, demonstrates that he can use classes, concepts. *There are no words without concepts.* ...
>
> Therefore, how can we deny that children are already the masters of abstraction, specifically the algebra of classes, as soon as they use concepts, as soon as they use language, and that they of course bring this mastery and the algebra of classes with them when they come to school.
> [...]
> ... The essential point is this: the algebra is an attribute, a fundamental power, of the mind. Not of mathematics only.
>
> Without algebra we would be dead, or if we have survived so far, it is partly thanks to algebra – to our understanding of classes, transformations, and the rest. ...
>
> (Gattegno, 1970, pp. 23–5)

Abstraction: Richard Skemp

Skemp continues his previous extract (p. 123) on babies having the power to classify, to extend it into abstraction. There are similarities here with van Hiele *phases* (see p. 59) and *structure of attention* (see p. 60).

> ... [from] successive past experiences of the same object, say a particular chair ... we abstract certain common properties ... .
>
> We progress rapidly to further abstractions. From particular chairs ... we abstract further invariant properties, by which we recognize ... a new object seen for the first time ... as a member of this class. It is the second-order abstraction ... to which we give the name 'chair'. The invariant properties which characterize it are already becoming more functional and less perceptual – that is, less attached to the physical properties of [the object]. ...
>
> From the abstraction *chair*, together with other abstractions such as the *table, carpet, bureau*, a further abstraction, *furniture*, can be made, and so on. These classifications are by no means fixed. ...

Naming an object classifies it. This can be an advantage or a disadvantage. A very important kind of classification is by function; and once an object is thus classified, we know how to behave in relation to it. ... But once it is classified in a particular way, we are less open to other classifications.

(Skemp, 1971, pp. 20–1)

Generalisation: Augustus de Morgan

Here de Morgan ponders the need for individuals to participate in abstraction rather than being presented with predigested abstractions.

We now come to a rule which presents more peculiar difficulties in point of principle than any at which we have yet arrived. If we could at once take the most general view of numbers, and give the beginner the extended notions which he may afterwards attain, the mathematics would present comparatively few impediments. But the Constitution of our minds will not permit this. It is by collecting facts and principles, one by one, and thus only, that we arrive at what are called general notions; and we afterwards make comparisons of the facts which we have acquired and discover analogies and resemblances which, while they bind together the fabric of our knowledge, point out methods of increasing its extent and beauty. In the limited view which we first take of the operations which we are performing, the names which we give are necessarily confined and partial; but when, after additional study and reflection, we recur advice to our former notions, we soon discover processes so resembling one another, and different rules so linked together, that we feel it would destroy the symmetry of our language if we were to call them by different names. We are then induced to extend the meaning of our terms, so as to make two rules into one. Also, suppose that when we have discovered and applied a rule and given the process which it teaches a particular name, we find that this process is only a part of one more general, which applies to all cases contained in the first, and to others besides. We have all the alternative of inventing a new name, or extending the meaning of the former one so as to merge the particular process in the more general one of which is a part.

(de Morgan, 1898, pp. 33–4)

Note the importance placed on labels and on the accumulation of numerous examples: other authors recognise the need for *structural generalisation* (see p. 133 and p. 139).

Generalisation: Lev Vygotsky

Vygotsky emphasises, perhaps more clearly than most, that generalisation is not a one-off event but a constant and ongoing process:

At any age, a concept embodied in a word represents an act of generalization. But word meanings evolve. When a new word has been learned by the child, its development is barely starting; the word at first is a generalization of the most primitive type; as the child's intellect develops, it is replaced by generalizations of a higher and higher type – a process that leads in the end to the formation of true concepts.

(Vygotsky, 1965, p. 83)

Generalisation and symbols: Zoltan Dienes

Zoltan Dienes (b. Hungary, 1916–) went to school in Hungary and France before moving to England where as a teacher, he developed his notion that young children can be taught abstract mathematical structures through participation in games. He is best known for designing and using Multi-base Arithmetic Blocks, also known as Dienes Blocks, for teaching place-value addition and subtraction. Here he considers the introduction of symbols for generalisations:

The fundamental problem is whether generalization should take place simultaneously on a broad front, or on several narrow fronts followed by abstraction into a broader front later. Younger children seem to find generalizations on a narrow front, that is within certain well-defined fields, easier. This may be part of the developmental pattern. ...

One of the problems about using symbolism is how to find the best time for introducing it. If this is done too early, it tends to be an empty shell. Classroom work in mathematics can so easily degenerate into learning certain rules by which the signs can be manipulated, and studying situations in which they are applicable, each application being separately learned. This of course is necessary if the signs do not symbolize anything. On the other hand, it is possible to wait too long before introducing symbolism. When a child has become familiar with a mathematical structure he needs a language in which to talk about it, think about it, and eventually transform it. New constructions need new names, their properties must be described by new symbols if more of the detail of the structure is to be grasped at one time, and so reflected upon more effectively. ...

There is also the question of whether symbolism can be used as a tool for cutting through relevant noise during the abstraction process, or whether it can only be used to formulate what has already been abstracted. If the latter, then every learning situation will have a ceiling determined by (1) the amount of noise generated, (2) the amount of noise the learner is able to cut through. ...

(Dienes, 1963, pp. 160–1)

See also Bruner (p. 108) on the need for questioning to move beyond the asking of particulars about some generalization stated by the teacher.

Generalisation: Jerome Bruner

Generalisation (see p. 138), or 'seeing the general through the particular' is an example of classification, something that young children quickly learn to do, since it is the basis for language (use of an appropriate noun signals recognition of an appropriate classification of objects as judged by listeners). Involuntary classification can block as easily as facilitate; intentional classification can be questioned, interrogated, and the boundaries and uses explored.

Generalising: John Mason

> Generalization is the heartbeat of mathematics, and appears in many forms. If teachers are unaware of its presence, and are not in the habit of getting students to work at expressing their own generalizations, then mathematical thinking is not taking place.
>
> (Mason, 1996, p. 65)

> Generalising and abstraction are the foundations of language, and hence something learners have already demonstrated in using language effectively. A lesson without the opportunity for learners to generalise is not a mathematics lesson.

Generalising and specialising

Generalising is only one side of the coin. In order that language can function the power to *particularise*, also referred to as *specialising*, is vital. Whenever we encounter a generality, we check it against our experience, against particular cases with which we are familiar. The following extracts illustrate seeing the general through the particular.

Generalising through specialising: Paul Halmos

> Another ... idea ... is to concentrate attention on the definite, the concrete, the specific. ... We all seem to have an innate ability to generalize ... . The teacher's function is to call attention to a concrete special case that hides (and, we hope, ultimately reveals) the germ of the conceptual difficulty.
>
> (Halmos, 1994, p. 852)

There are similarities with *seeing the general through the particular* (see p. 132).

Specialising and generalising: John Mason

> Whenever I encounter a generality, I find myself testing it against partic-
> ular cases. If I am trying to decide *whether* the general assertion is true,
> or *when* it is true, I consider special, often extreme cases. The purpose of
> trying out particular cases is not just to seek a counter-example, but to
> attend to *how* the calculations are done, with an eye to seeing if they
> generalise. This is exactly what students are expected to do when
> learning a new technique: do some exercises *in order to see how the
> technique works* [in general] (not just to 'get the answers'). Specialising is
> an act I can perform in order to make sense of what *always* happens, in
> order to appreciate and reconstruct generality.
>
> [...]
>
> There are two important perceptions here:
>
> • seeing the *particular in the general* (seeing not just a general asser-
>   tion but the opportunity to try out specific particular cases and being
>   aware of what constitutes particular instances of the general);
> • seeing the *general through the particular* (seeing specific numbers
>   or other aspects as placeholders for other possibilities).
>
> When you find yourself 'doing an example' in front of students, you
> are probably seeing through the particular numbers, the particular
> computations, and are aware of generality. But some numbers may be
> structural rather than particular. What are you doing to draw students'
> attention to the difference?
>
> (Mason, 2002a, p. 108)

Learning is generalising and specialising: Zhoubi Suanjing

Evidence that generalising has been recognised and valued for a very long
time is provided by this quotation from the earliest known mathematics trea-
tise in Chinese, the Zhoubi Suanjing written possibly in the first century BC.
Here is the conclusion of a dialogue involving master Chén:

> ... 'man has a wisdom of analogy' that is to say, after understanding a
> particular line of argument one can infer various kinds of similar
> reasoning, or in other words, by asking one question one can reach ten
> thousand things. When one can draw inferences about other cases from
> one instance and one is able to generalize, then one can say that one
> really knows how to calculate. The method of calculation is therefore a
> sort of wisdom in learning ... The method of learning: after you have
> learnt something, beware that what you have learnt is not wide and after
> you have learnt widely, beware that you have not specialized enough.
> After specializing you should worry lest you do not have the ability to
> generalize. So by having people learn similar things and observe similar

situations one can find out who is intelligent and who is not. To be able to deduce and then to generalize, that is the mark of an intelligent man ... If you cannot generalize you have not learnt well enough. ...

(Li and Dù, 1987, p. 28)

Types of generalisation: Vadim Krutetskii

Krutetskii's research into mathematical ability led him to a large number of conclusions. At the core he identified the ability (as seen through Soviet psychology) to generalise, not just from several examples, but 'on the spot':

1   The method of gradual generalization is not the only way to a mastery of knowledge about mathematics; there is another way that differs from it in principle but that leads to the same result. Along with the method of gradual generalization of mathematical material on the basis of variations in a diversity of particular cases (the method for most pupils), there is another way, in which able pupils, without comparing the 'similar', without special exercises or hints from the teacher, independently generalize mathematical objects, relations, and operations 'on the spot', on the basis of an analysis of just *one* phenomenon, into a number of similar phenomena. They recognize every specific problem at once as the representative of a class of problems of a single type and solve it in a general form – that is, they work out a general method (an algorithm) for solving problems of the given type.
2   Capable pupils generalize mathematical material not only rapidly but broadly. They very easily find the essential and the general in the particular, the hidden generality in what seemed to be different mathematical expressions and problems.

(Krutetskii, 1976, p. 261–2)

Note the similarity with *same and different* (see p. 128), and with *structural generalisation* (see p. 133), and with Whitehead (*general in particular*, p. 132).

Conjecturing and convincing

Making an assertion about a pattern detected is one thing. Justifying it so that others are convinced is quite another. Learners learn to make distinctions, to discriminate in ways which adults find useful, and learn how to justify those distinctions and associated conjectures. Young children already display these powers in rudimentary forms. Various academic disciplines have more demanding requirements for justification and convincing, and these are experienced and developed in school.

Conjecturing: George Polya

George Polya (b. Hungary, 1887–1985) builds on specialising and generalising as an ascent and descent, in an ongoing process of conjecturing:

> ... [an inductive attitude] requires a ready ascent from observations to
> generalizations, and a ready descent from the highest generalizations to
> the most concrete observations. ...
>
> First, we should be ready to revise any one of our beliefs.
>
> Second, we should change a belief when there is a compelling reason
> to change it.
>
> Third, we should not change a belief wantonly, without some good
> reason.
>
> [...]
>
> The first point needs 'intellectual courage'. ...
>
> The second point needs 'intellectual honesty'. To stick to my conjec-
> ture that has been clearly contradicted by experience just because it is
> *my* conjecture would be dishonest.
>
> The third point needs 'wise restraint'. ... 'Do not believe anything, but
> question only what is worth questioning'.
>
> (Polya, 1954, pp. 7–8)

Conjecturing: Magdalene Lampert

Lampert is unusual in being a mathematics teacher who researches her own
practice and also educates teachers. Here her work is being described:

> ... Drawing particularly on Lakatos (1976) and Polya (1954), [Lampert,
> (1990)] argues that the discourse of mathematicians is characterized by a
> zig-zag from conjectures to an examination of premises through the use
> of counter-examples. One of her primary goals is to investigate whether
> it is possible for students to engage in mathematical activity congruent
> with this portrayal of disciplinary discourse. As a consequence, her focus
> is, for the most part, on how the teacher and students interact as they talk
> about and do mathematics. ...
>
> (quoted in Cobb, McClain and Whitenack, 1997, p. 273)

Conjecturing and intuition: Efriam Fischbein

Fischbein sees conjectures as expressions of intuitions:

> Anticipatory intuitions are conjectures associated with the feeling of total
> confidence. ... If the student finds that his conjectures may be
> misleading to such a high degree, he may not be willing to make any

more conjectures (at all) or at least to express them publicly (in the class-room). Such an effect would certainly block the student's solving capacity. The student has then to learn *to accept the risk* of erroneous guesses (even publicly). He should understand that this is the way in which *everybody* solves problems – not only the novice. Certainly we do not consider wild guesses, but only plausible conjectures based on serious preliminary analyses. On the other hand, one has to develop the student's capacity to analyze and check his findings, his anticipatory solutions, both formally and intuitively. Our belief is that it is possible to develop, through adequate training, the student's intuitive feelings of incongruences, of incompleteness of arguments, of flaws in the lines of thought. This together with the capacity to analyze formally and system-atically the preliminary solution (the anticipatory intuition) represents an essential condition of success in a problem solving endeavor.

(Fischbein, 1987, pp. 210–11; see also p. 63)

Conjecturing atmosphere: John Mason

Conjecturing provides the fodder for reasoning, for justifying conjectures. Once a conjecture is made, it needs to be challenged, tested, and possibly modified. Most powerful is to consider different possible conjectures at each stage (see also Crowley, 1987, p. 9). Often conjectures turn out to be false, so they need adjusting.

In a conjecturing atmosphere, everything that is said is said because by expressing it, by getting it outside of yourself, you make it possible to stand back from it and to test it and reason about it and with it. If you try to keep all your conjectures in your head, they will end up tumbling around like clothes in a dryer, getting tangled up. In a conjecturing atmosphere, other people invite you to modify your conjecture, or to consider a particular example that might challenge your conjecture. You do not declare someone else to be 'wrong'; you invite them to 'modify their conjecture'. In a conjecturing atmosphere you take opportunities to struggle to express when you are unsure, and you take opportunities to listen to others and to suggest modifications or amplifications or chal-lenging examples, when you are sure.

(Mason, 2002a, p. 109)

Mathematicians rarely solve the initial problems they set themselves. Most often they specialise, they conjecture, they modify and remodify until they find a problem they can do! When then they leave off work they note one or more conjectures and some supporting evidence. This is entirely respectable and sensible. It is much better to summarise work to date and then let go of it than simply to slink away with a feeling of failure.

Participating in a conjecturing atmosphere in which everyone is encouraged to construct extreme and paradigmatic examples, and to try to find counter-examples (through exploring previously unnoticed *dimensions-of-possible-variation*) involves learners in thinking and constructing actively. This involves learners in, for example, generalising and specialising.

6   Learning as action

Introduction

From the most ancient of recorded times, educators have stressed the importance of learners being active, as the extract from Plato on page 34 indicates. In the following extract the authors are concerned about the impact of lack of activity.

Enacting not receiving: Banwell, Tahta and Saunders

In general, mathematics cannot be received; it has to be enacted.

Commencing in the cradle, it is a symbolizing activity and carries an emotional charge that can easily explode.

It can become a mindless mind training and a refuge from reality or – unfortunately all too easily – a weapon of subjection and a focus for fear.

(Banwell *et al.*, 1972, p. 61)

Describing teaching: Hans Freudenthal

'Problem-Solving' and 'Discovery Learning' have become catchwords. I never liked them as mere slogans, and I like them even less since [the] first time I saw them exemplified. Problem solving: solving the teachers' or the textbook authors' or the researchers' problems according to methods they had in mind, rather than the learner himself grasping something as a problem. Discovery learning: i.e., uncovering what was covered up by someone else – hidden Easter eggs. ...

... mathematics in individual lives starts [as an activity]. But is the learner allowed to continue like this? Curious children will not ask for permission; indifferent and lazy ones prefer to be guided. So in order to explain how I imagined mathematics would be learned I long ago chose the term 'guided reinvention'. It didn't catch. Should I have done otherwise? Fortunately I did not.

(Freudenthal, 1991, pp. 45–6)

Types of actions: Eric Love and John Mason

The role of the teacher is to stimulate and prompt mathematically relevant actions by learners. In a monograph written for Open University students, Love and Mason began a discussion of modes of teacher interaction by listing a number of teacher actions designed to promote learner actions:

> Messages about mathematics, about its role and value in society and about how it is learned, are implicit in the ways that actions are carried out. And these are influenced by views of mathematics itself. Mathematics can be seen as a body of knowledge to be handed over to the next generation (from which comes the metaphor of *delivering the curriculum* (like some mail-order package) and it can be seen as a process of disciplined inquiry and analysis (from which comes the metaphor of *exploring and investigating*). Both views (and there are many variants) have an element of fit but when one view is elevated to *the* view of mathematics it leads to imbalance and impoverishment for pupils. Having an active, exploratory, investigative approach to mathematics does not guarantee that pupils will take pleasure in exploration and gain confidence with mathematics, just as an approach based on 'exposition-example-practice' does not guarantee that all pupils will succeed or even that all will struggle constructively.
>
> Mathematics teaching involves taking actions in classrooms in order to prompt pupils to act on:
>
> - physical objects by manipulating them (Dienes blocks, attribute blocks, Cuisenaire or colour factor rods, counters, shells and beads, compasses, protractors, rulers, calculators, and so on);
> - screen objects (images on computer screens, television, posters);
> - symbols (numerals, variables, labels, words);
> - mental objects (pictures-in-the-head, vague senses, intuitions).
>
> Often the action is precipitated by getting pupils to express their thinking to themselves, to other pupils, to the teacher, and to examiners, via talking, writing, drawing, computer programs, audio and videotapes, and drama.
>
> (Love and Mason, 1992, pp. 1–2)

If learners are to be encouraged to be active, it is important to work out in what way they can usefully be active. Doing lots of repetitive exercises is one form of being active, constructing mathematical objects meeting specified constraints is another, and there are many other possibilities. For example, Lichtenberg said 'What you have been obliged to discover by yourself leaves a path in your mind which you can use again when the need arises' (Lichtenberg: *Aphorismen*, quoted in Polya, 1962, p. 99).

On the basis of assumptions and theories, whether implicit or explicit, it is helpful to consider the types of actions which learners need to engage in, in order to learn efficiently and effectively.

No matter how tempting it is to blame learners, their conditions, or the teacher, for poor performance, many people have asserted that learners actually possess the requisite powers to think mathematically, as the next section shows.

Learner action

What is the basis and nature of learner actions in trying to learn, in trying to make sense? Are actions purely internal psychological processes? Are they an internalisation of something experienced in the social environment? Are they purely an external social act of adopting behavioural practices?

As a reminder that the issue of stimulating learners to be active has deep historical roots, the next extract is from 1840:

> If a child be requested to divide a number of apples among a certain number of persons, he will contrive a way to do it, and will tell how many each must have. The method which children take to do these things, though always correct, is not always the most expeditious ... To succeed it is necessary rather to furnish occasions for them to exercise their own skill in performing examples rather than to give them rules. They should be allowed to pursue their own method first, and then should be made to observe and explain it; and if it were not the best, some improvement should be suggested.
>
> Examples of any kind upon practical numbers are of very little use, until the learner has discovered the principle from practical examples. When the pupil learns by means of abstract examples, it very seldom happens that he understands a practical example the better for it; because he does not discover the connexion until he has performed several practical examples, and begins to generalise them. (*Intellectual Arithmetic* ... , 1840, p. iv)
>
> (McIntosh, 1977, p. 93–4 (reprinted in Floyd, 1981))

So the purpose of learners' actions is to internalise, comprehend, make sense of, reconstruct abstractions, in response to *disturbances* experienced (see p. 55, p. 101 and p. 161), through making use of their powers. What then would it mean for learners not to be active?

Learners always do something!: Margaret Brown

Margaret Brown (b. Merseyside, 1943–) has spent her career investigating learners' experience of mathematics classrooms, issues in teaching mathematics, and issues in supporting teachers. As a result of one of her many government funded projects, she commented:

One general point we noticed throughout the interviewing … was that almost all children could produce successful strategies for solving problems, even when they did not recognize the operations involved.

(Brown and Küchemann, 1976, p.16 (quoted in Floyd, 1981, p. 9))

(See also Brown and Küchemann, 1977, 1981.)

What they did not always do was communicate their method or their resolution effectively on tests. Learners always make sense of what is happening (see van Lehn, p. 210), even if that sense is 'I can't', or 'Mathematics isn't for me', or some other reinforcement of a personal narrative (see Bruner, p. 68 and Dweck, p. 112).

Van Lehn and Seeley Brown adopted the approach that learners make sense by adapting techniques in the face of difficulties, gluing together fragments of techniques to help them deal with awkward and unexpected situations (see p. 210).

Active learning principles: George Polya

As a highly respected and prolific mathematician, Polya was also highly respected as a teacher and as a teacher of teachers. His principal concern was to teach problem solving (see p. 187). Here he reflects on his teaching principles.

Any efficient teaching device must be correlated somehow with the nature of the learning process. We do not know too much about the learning process, but even a rough outline of some of its more obvious features may shed some welcome light upon the tricks of our trade. Let me state such a rough outline in the form of three 'principles' of learning. Their formulation and combination is of my choice, but the 'principles' themselves are by no means new; they have been stated and restated in various forms, they are derived from the experience of the ages, endorsed by the judgment of great men, and also suggested by the psychological study of learning.

[…]

1   *Active learning.* It is been said by many people in many ways that learning should be active, not merely passive or receptive; merely by reading books or listening to lectures or looking at moving pictures without adding some action of your own mind you can hardly learn anything and certainly you can not learn much.

[…]

2   *Best motivation.* Learning should be active, we have said. Yet the learner will not act if he has no motive to act. He must be induced to act by some stimulus, by the hope of some reward, for instance. The interest of the material to be learned should be the best stimulus to

learning and the pleasure of intensive mental activity should be the best reward for such activity. Yet, where we cannot obtain the best we should try to get the second best, or the third best, and less intrinsic motives for learning should not be forgotten.

For efficient learning, the learner should be interested in the material to be learned and find pleasure in the activity of learning. Yet, beside these best motives for learning, there are other motives too, some of them desirable. (Punishment for not learning may be the least desirable motive.)

Let us call this statement *the principle of best motivation.*

3   Consecutive phases. Let us start from an often quoted sentence of Kant: *Thus all human condition begins with intuitions, proceeds from thence to conceptions, and ends with ideas. ...*

[My version of what Kant was saying is] *learning begins with action and perception, proceeds from thence to words and concepts, and should end in desirable mental habits.*

To begin with, please, take the terms of this sentence in some sense that you can illustrate concretely on the basis of your own experience. (To induce you to think about your personal experience is one of the desired effects.) ...

[...]

A first *exploratory* phase is closer to action and perception and moves on a more intuitive, more heuristic level.

A second *formalizing* phase ascends to a more conceptual level, introducing terminology, definitions, proofs.

The phase of *assimilation* comes last: there should be an attempt to perceive the 'inner ground' of things, the material learned should be mentally digested, absorbed into the system of knowledge, into the whole mental outlook of the learner; this phase paves the way to applications on one hand, to higher generalizations on the other.

Let us summarize: *For efficient learning, an exploratory phase should precede the phase of verbalization and concept formation and, eventually, the material learned should be merged in, and contribute to, the integral mental attitude of the learner.*

This is the *principle of consecutive phases.*

(Polya, 1962, part II, pp. 102–4)

There are similarities with the See–Experience–Master framework (see p. 263).

Learner as active agent: Herbert Spencer

To *tell* a child this and to *show* it the other, is not to teach it how to observe, but to make it a mere recipient of another's observations: a proceeding which weakens rather than strengthens its powers of self-instruction – which deprives it of the pleasures resulting from successful activity – which presents this all-attractive knowledge under the aspect of formal tuition – and which thus generates that indifference and even disgust not unfrequently felt … .

(Spencer, 1878, p. 79)

Learner as active agent: Jerome Bruner

Bruner's views are summarised as:

To the extent that the materials of education are chosen for their amenableness to imaginative transformation and are presented in a light to invite negotiation and speculation, to that extent education becomes a part of … 'culture making'. The pupil, in effect, becomes a party to the negotiatory process by which facts are created and interpreted. He becomes at once an agent of knowledge making as well as a recipient of knowledge transmission.

(Bruner, 1986, p. 127)

This is the essence of what started out as *constructivism* (learners actively construct meaning) and which then diverged into psychological, radical and social constructivism, each with many variants. (See p. 92 for elaboration).

Biological bases

After Spencer, Piaget and Dewey had perhaps the greatest and most profound influence on education in the twentieth century. Piaget started as a biologist and became interested in epistemology: the study of how people learn. Since adults are relatively complex, he turned his attention to young children. He was for a time director of a Montessori school in Switzerland before establishing his highly productive and influential institute in Geneva.

Genetic epistemology: Jean Piaget

The fundamental core of Piaget's conclusions is that human beings actively construct meaning from the situations and environment in which they find themselves.

Equilibration: Jean Piaget

Piaget saw analogies between an organism responding to changes in its environment, and human beings responding to changes through what we call learning. A biological way of thinking of this is in terms of equilibration: the organism responds in such a way as to seek equilibrium, thus minimising disturbance.

... I was forced to the conclusion that [the] prime cause was a factor of gradual equilibration in the sense of auto-regulation. If equilibrium in action is defined as an active compensation set up by the subject against exterior disturbances, whether experienced or anticipated, this equilibration will explain, among other things, the more general character called logico-mathematical operations – that is, their reversibility (to every direction operation there corresponds an inverse one which cancels it out ...).

(Piaget, 1971, p. 12)

Assimilate–Accommodate: Jean Piaget

Biological equilibration involves assimilating some things and adjusting to accommodate others. Piaget suggested a cognitive version of these two interconnected processes.

... when an infant has formed the habit of making objects hung in front of it swing backward and forward (by pushing them without grasping them), and when it applies this behavior to some new object that it has not seen before, there has been assimilation of this new object or situation into the swinging schema.

(Piaget, 1971, p. 180)

The essential starting point here is the fact that no form of knowledge, not even perceptual knowledge, constitutes a simple copy of reality, because it always includes a process of assimilation to previous structures.

We use the term assimilation in the wide sense of integration into previous structures. ... without any break of continuity with the former state – that is, without being destroyed and simply by adapting ... to the new situation.

... when a baby pulls his blanket toward himself in order to reach some object that is on it but out of his reach, he is assimilating this situation into perceptual schemata (the connecting thought is 'on it') and active schemata (the behavior of the cover on which the object is lying). In short, any type of knowledge inevitably contains a fundamental factor of assimilation which alone gives significance to what is perceived or conceived.

(ibid., pp. 4–5)

This is the famous principle of *equilibration,* the resolving of *disturbance* (see p. 55). Piaget uses the example of a liquid in a container: as the container is tilted the liquid adapts to the shape of the bottle, but there is no lasting effect.

... adaptation [may be defined] as an equilibrium between assimilation and accommodation ... .

... assimilation and accommodation are not two separate functions but the two functional poles, set in opposition to each other, of any adaptation. ... There can be no assimilation of anything into the organism or its functioning without a corresponding accommodation and without such assimilations becoming part of an adaptation context.

... the basic functions of adaptation and assimilation [...] embodied in the most diverse structures, are to be found at every hierarchical level ... .

(ibid., p. 173)

Adaptation: Ernst von Glasersfeld

[Piaget saw that] the concept of adaptation could be incorporated in a theory of learning. In my view, this is the major contribution Jean Piaget has made to our understanding of cognition. Eventually this perspective led him to the conclusion that the function of intelligence was not, as traditional epistemology held, to provide cognitive organisms with 'true' representations of an objective environment. Rather, he began to see cognition as generator of intelligent tools that enable organisms to construct a relative *fit* with the world as they experience it.

Though the notion of 'fit' was borrowed from the biological concept of adaptation, it no longer contained the element of preformation or genetic determination in the cognitive domain. Here it was the product of intelligent construction, of the organism's own making, as the result of trial, error and the selection of what 'works'. ... Fit or viability in the cognitive domain is, of course, no longer directly tied to survival but rather to the attainment of goals and the mutual compatibility of constructs.

To make clear and emphasize the instrumental character of knowledge, be it on the level of sensory-motor activities or conceptual operations, I have always preferred the term *viability*. It seems more appropriate because, unlike 'fit', it does not suggest an approximation to the constraints.

During the last two decades of his life, when Piaget had realized that this theory had much in common with the principles formulated by cybernetics, he shifted his focus from the chronology of development in children to the more general question of the cognitive organism's generation and maintenance of *equilibrium*. In this regard, too, room was left for misunderstandings, because the term was not intended to have the same meaning on all levels of cognition. On the biological/physical level, an organism's equilibrium can be said to consist in its capability to resist and neutralize perturbations caused by the environment. On the conceptual level however, the term refers to the compatibility and non-contradictoriness of conceptual structures.

(von Glasersfeld, 1991, pp. 21–2)

Assimilate–Accommodate: Richard Skemp

Evidence of the widespread influence of Piaget's work is found in the use made of it by many authors, including Skemp, whose thesis was the first in mathematics education in the UK. His book *The Psychology of Learning Mathematics* (Skemp, 1971) was one of the first directed specifically to teachers and is still widely referred to. He developed a series of primary text-books based on extensive research and development, and his *Intelligence, Learning, and Action* (Skemp, 1979) describes his conclusions about the ways in which learning come about and can be initiated and supported.

> A concept can be described as a mental awareness of something in common among a certain class of experiences. A new concept cannot in general be communicated by a definition. A child needs to be given a carefully chosen collection of examples, from which he or she can make his own abstraction. These examples may themselves be other concepts, in which case careful planning is required to ensure these lower order concepts are available as necessary for the formation of a new one.
>
> The existing structure of knowledge (schema) is thus an essential tool for further learning. Fitting new ideas into an existing schema is called *assimilation*. Sometimes a new idea cannot be thus assimilated without a modification of the schema, and this is called *accommodation*. Both of these complementary processes are necessary for understanding, and failure of accommodation is a common cause of difficulty. ...
>
> In this context, problems can be seen as tasks which require accommo-dation of the pupil's existing schema, in greater or lesser degree. They can thus lead to progressive enlargement of the pupil schema. ... An under-standing of the process of schematic learning, with its related activities of assimilation and accommodation, will therefore be a considerable help to teachers who wish to make the best use of problems in their teaching.
>
> Mathematics is concerned with the manipulation of ideas, not of mate-rial objects. This ability to be aware of our own thoughts, and to manipu-late them in various ways, we as adults take for granted. But this ability is largely absent in young children, and only reaches its mature form during adolescence. It is therefore of great importance for the teaching of mathematics to take account of the various stages of development of this reflective use of intelligence, and to seek further knowledge of how we may help it grow.
>
> (Skemp, 1966, p. 76)

Note the indirect reference to *reflective abstraction* (see p. 151).

Meaningful learning

Meaningful learning is usually contrasted with rote or meaningless learning, though even if memorised as sounds there is still some meaning for the learner (sounds to be memorised in sequence for some purpose) even if it is not the meaning appreciated by the teacher (see also *understanding*, p. 293). Rote learning has been the *bête noire* of educators for generations.

Rote learning: Herbert Spencer

> The rote-system, like all other systems of its age, made more of the forms and symbols than of the things symbolized. To repeat the words correctly was everything; to understand their meaning, nothing; and thus the spirit was sacrificed to the letter. ... in proportion as there is attention to the signs, there must be inattention to the things signified ... .
>
> (Spencer, 1878, p. 56)

But rote learning is not by itself either harmful or unproductive. It all depends on whether the fact of having memorised is made further use of, or remains *inert* (see Whitehead, p. 288; Spencer, p. 35).

Rote learning: Ference Marton and Shirley Booth

Marton and Booth report on studies in Hong Kong with Chinese learners who are used to memorising:

> Asian learners, it was found, treated memorization as a step toward understanding, in that each repetition of a text or lesson give a new perspective on the content, and so an understanding was built up stage by stage. The parallel was drawn with Western actors learning their parts in a new play: Although rote memorization plays a large part in preparation, each repetition, recall, and rehearsal of the lines reveals a new layer of meaning in the part. An amateur actor who merely learns the lines of the part, maybe by mnemonic tricks, gives only a wooden representation of the character, whereas a professional who has made the lines his own by successive repetition and review has thereby extracted the necessary meaning from the lines and can bring the part to life.
>
> (Marton and Booth, 1997, p. 44)

Meaningful and rote learning: David Ausubel

David Ausubel (b. New York, 1918–) was influenced by Piaget. He adopted a strong position concerning the need for learners to have a sense of where they were being led, which became known as *advance organisers* (see p. 258). Here he probes the meaning of *rote* learning (see p. 35), which has bothered educationalists since the earliest recorded reflections on teaching and learning.

> ... the learner consciously acts upon this concept or [proposition] in an attempt to remember it so that it will be available at some future time. He may do this in either of two quite distinct ways. If the learner attempts to retain the idea by relating it to what he knows, and thereby 'make sense' out of it, then *meaningful learning* will result. On the other hand, if the learner merely attempts to memorize the idea, without relating it to his

existing knowledge, then *rote learning* is said to take place. ... any learning that occurs is not simply either meaningful or rote; it is, instead *more or less* meaningful or *more or less* a rote ... . thus *meaningful reception* learning will take place when the teacher presents the generalization in its final form, and the learner relates it to his existing ideas in some sensible fashion. On the other hand, *rote reception* learning would take place if the teacher presented the generalization, and the student merely memorized it. Again, *meaningful discovery* learning will occur if the student formulates meanings the generalization himself and subsequently relates it in a sensible way to his existing ideas. Finally *rote discovery* learning could occur if the learner, having arrived at the generalization himself (typically by trial and error), subsequently commit to memory without relating it to other relevant ideas in his cognitive structure.

(Ausubel and Robinson, 1969, pp. 44–5)

Actions

In order to avoid the merely *rote*, learners need to take action.

Actions: Jean Piaget

The foundation of Piaget's perspective is that human beings engage in actions in and on the material world, which he saw as a form of research initiated through 'natural seeking of meaning'. These actions influence and alter the organism, and mathematics is one means whereby we can study those actions.

> The importance of the concept of assimilation is twofold. On the one hand ... , it implies meaning, an essential notion because all knowledge has a bearing on meaning ... . On the other hand, this concept expresses the fundamental fact that any piece of knowledge is connected with an action and that to know an object or a happening is to make use of it by assimilation into an action schema.
>
> Knowing does not really imply making a copy of reality but, rather, reacting to it and transforming it (either apparently or effectively) in such a way as to include it functionally in the transformation systems with which these acts are linked.

(Piaget, 1971, pp. 5–6)

Mathematics functions for physicists as a language of description, but mathematics is much more than that, since it alone can enable us to reconstruct reality and to deduce what phenomena are, instead of merely recording them. To do this, mathematics uses operations and transformations which are still actions even though they are carried out mentally.

Mathematics [is], in fact, not simply a system of notations at the service of physical knowledge, but an instrument of structuralization, because it is of the nature of operations to produce transformations. The fact that the latter may be expressible in 'symbols' does not in any sense reduce their active and constructive nature: thus, the psycho-biological problem of the construction of mathematical entities cannot possibly be solved by linguistic considerations.

(Piaget, 1971, p. 47)

Mathematics consists not only of actual transformations but of all possible transformations. To speak of transformations is to speak of actions or operations, the latter being derived from the former, and to speak of the possible is to speak not simply of linguistic description of some ready-made immediate reality but of the assimilation of immediate reality into certain real or virtual actions.

(ibid., p. 6)

So learning is a description of how the organism and its environment influence and affect each other in a never ending dance, and in Piaget's view, this applies at the levels of biology and of the psyche: cognition, affect and behaviour.

Schema: Richard Skemp

Piaget introduced the notion of schema as the structures which people develop which constitute learning, and which direct action and response in the future. Here Skemp moves from powers to concepts to schemas.

It may be useful to relate some of the terms used so far. ... *Abstracting* is an activity by which we become aware of similarities (in the everyday, not the mathematical, sense) among our experiences. *Classifying* means collecting together our experiences on the basis of these similarities. An *abstraction* is some kind of lasting mental change, the result of abstracting, which enables us to recognize new experiences as having the similarities of an already formed class. Briefly, it is something learnt which enables us to classify; it is the defining property of a class. To distinguish between abstracting as an activity and an abstraction as its end-product, we shall hereafter call the latter a *concept*.

A concept therefore requires for its formation a number of experiences which have something in common. Once the concept is formed, we may (retrospectively and prospectively) talk about *examples* of the concept.

(Skemp, 1971, p. 22)

There are similarities with Freudenthal concerning *concepts* (see p. 50 and p. 136) and the process of *abstraction* (see p. 134).

... many people find it difficult to separate a concept from its name ... The distinction between a concept and its name is an essential one ... . A concept is an idea; the name of a concept is a sound, or a mark on paper, associated with it. ...

Naming can also play a useful, sometimes an essential, part in the formation of new concepts. Hearing the same name in connection with different experiences predisposes us to collect them together in our minds and also increases our chance of abstracting their intrinsic similarities (as distinct from the extrinsic one of being called by the same name). Experiment has also shown that associating different names with classes which are only slightly different in their characteristics helps to classify later examples correctly, even if the later examples are not named. The names help to separate the classes themselves.

(ibid., pp. 23–4)

The criterion for *having* a concept is not that of being able to say its name but that of behaving in a way indicative of classifying new data according to the similarities which go to form this concept. ...

[...]

... there are two ways of invoking a concept; that is, of causing it to start functioning. One is by encountering an example of the concept. The concept then comes into action as our way of classifying this example, and our subjective experience is that of *recognition*. The other is by hearing, reading or otherwise making conscious the name, or other symbol, for the concept. ... [To do the second requires] *the ability to isolate concepts from any of the examples which give rise to them.*

[...]

A concept is a way of processing data which enables the user to bring past experience usefully to bear on the present situation. Without language each individual has to form his own concepts direct from the environment. ... the concepts of the past, painstakingly abstracted and slowly accumulated by successive generations, become available to help each new individual form his own conceptual system.

(ibid., pp. 27–8)

Seeing language as enabling an action in which the past acts upon the present has similarities with comments about *observation* (see p. 31).

The actual construction of a conceptual system is something which each individual has to do for himself. But the process can be enormously speeded up if, so to speak, the materials are to hand. It is like the difference between building a boat from wood sawn to shape and having to start by walking to the forest, felling the trees, dragging them home, making planks – having first mined some iron ore and smelted it to make an axe and a saw!

(ibid., p. 29)

... when a number of suitable components are suitably connected, the resulting combination may have properties which it would have been difficult to predict from a knowledge of the properties of the individual components. ...

So it is with concepts and conceptual structures. ... a conceptual structure has its own name – *schema*. The term includes not only the complex conceptual structures of mathematics but also relatively simple structures which coordinate sensory-motor activity. ...

Among the new functions which a schema has, beyond the separate properties of its individual concepts, are the following: it integrates existing knowledge, it acts as a tool for future learning and it makes possible understanding.

When we recognize something as an example of a concept we become aware of it at two levels: as itself and as a member of this class. ... But this class-concept is linked by our mental schemas with a vast number of other concepts, which are available to help us behave adaptively with respect to the many different situations [we encounter].

(ibid., p. 37)

See also what makes an example *exemplary* (p. 173). Schemas are essential for perceiving and for learning, but may obstruct as well as facilitate.

... if a task is considered in isolation, schematic learning may take longer. For example, rules for solving a simple equation ... can be memorized in much less time than it takes to achieve understanding. So if all one wants to learn is how to do a particular job, memorizing a set of rules may be the quickest way. If, however, one wishes to progress, then the number of rules to be learnt becomes steadily more burdensome until eventually the task becomes excessive. A schema, even more than a concept, greatly reduces cognitive strain. Moreover, in most mathematical schemas, all the main contributory ideas are of very general application in mathematics. Time spent in acquiring them is not only of psychological value (meaning that present and future learning is easier and more lasting) but of mathematical value (meaning that the ideas are also of great importance mathematically). In the present context, good psychology is good mathematics.

The second disadvantage is more far-reaching. Since new experience which fits into an existing schema is so much better remembered, a schema has a highly selective effect on our experience. That which does *not* fit into it is largely not learnt at all, and what is learnt temporarily is soon forgotten. So, not only are unsuitable schemas a major handicap to our future learning: even schemas which have been of real value may cease to become so if new experience is encountered, new ideas need to be acquired, which cannot be fitted in to an existing schema. A schema can be as powerful a hindrance as help if it happens to be an unsuitable one.

... a strong tendency emerges towards the self-perpetuation of existing schemas. If situations are then encountered for which they are not adequate, this stability of the schemas becomes an obstacle to adaptability. What is then necessary is a change of structure in the schemas; they themselves must adapt. Instead of a stable, growing schema by means of which the individual organizes his past experience and *assimilates* new data to itself, [*reconstruction* is required before the new situation can be understood]. This may be difficult, and if it fails, the new experience can no longer be successfully interpreted and adaptive behaviour breaks down – the individual cannot cope.

[...]

... A schema is of such value to an individual that the resistance to changing it can be great, and circumstances or individuals imposing pressure to change may be experienced as threats – and responded to accordingly. Even if it is less than a threat, [reconstruction] can be difficult; whereas assimilation of [a new] experience to an existing schema gives a feeling of mastery and is usually enjoyed.

(ibid., pp. 43–5)

Piaget also took the line that when learners do not understand something, it is the lesson they fail to understand, not the subject matter. Lessons are ineffective when they attempt to force the learner to move too quickly from qualitative reasoning and appreciation to quantitative calculations (Piaget, 1973, p. 14). In a later chapter this is recast as taking time to move between *doing*, *talking* about what you are doing, and *recording* in pictures, words and symbols (see p. 262).

... active intention and consequent practical application of certain operations are one thing, and becoming conscious of them and thus obtaining reflexive and, above all, theoretical knowledge are another. Neither pupils nor teachers suspect that the instruction imparted could be supported by all manner of 'natural' structures. ... speaking to the child in his own language before imposing on him another ready-made and over-abstract one, and, above all, in inducing him to rediscover as much as he can rather than simply making him listen and repeat.

[...]

... the methods of the future will have to give more and more scope to the activity and the groupings of students as well as to the spontaneous handling of devices intended to confirm or refute the hypothesis they have formed to explain a given elementary phenomenon. In other words, if there is any area in which active methods will probably become imperative in the full sense of the term, it is that in which experimental procedures are learned, for an experiment not carried out by the individual himself with all freedom of initiative is by definition not an experiment but mere drill with no educational value: the details of the successive steps are not adequately understood.

(Piaget, 1973, pp. 18–20)

The same sentiment could be applied to any task which has pedagogic intentions. (See also *using situations*, p. 249 and p. 250.)

In short, the basic principle of active methods will have to draw its inspiration from the history of science and may be expressed as follows: to understand is to discover, or reconstruct by rediscovery, and such conditions must be complied with if in the future individuals are to be formed who are capable of production and creativity and not simply repetition.

(ibid., p. 20)

There are similarities with *discovery learning* (see p. 43 and p. 224).

... since so little learning is retained when it is learned on command, the extent of the program is less important than the quality of the work. A student who achieves a certain knowledge through free investigation and spontaneous effort will later be able to retain it; he will have acquired a methodology that can serve him for the rest of his life, which will stimulate his curiosity without the risk of exhausting it. At the very least, instead of having his memory take priority over his reasoning power, or subjugating his mind to exercises imposed from outside, he will learn to make his reason function by himself and will build his own ideas freely.

(ibid., p. 93)

See also *motivation* (p. 99).

... [operations] are not constructed nor do they acquire their full structures except through certain exercise that is not verbal alone, but, above all and basically, is related to action on objects and on experimentation; properly so called, an operation is an action, but interiorized and coordinated to other actions of the same type according to precise structures of composition. On the other hand, these operations are not the attribute of the individual alone, but necessarily require collaboration and exchange between people. Thus, is it enough for the student to listen for years to lessons, in the same manner as the adult listens to a lecturer, for logic to be created in the child and adolescent? Or does a real formation of the tools of the intellect require a collective atmosphere of active and experimental investigation as well as discussions in common?

(ibid., p. 95)

Note the emphasis on the *social* as well as on the *individual* (see *constructivism*, p. 54 and p. 92)

The principal action which learners perform, as emerged in the section on learners' powers (see p. 115) is to discern, to make distinctions, to stress something as foreground and consequently to ignore something else as background. As was previously mentioned, this is considerably developed and extended by Maturana (p. 70) and by the van Hieles (p. 59).

Arbitrary and necessary: Dave Hewitt

Born in England, Hewitt has been a secondary teacher, head of department, and teacher educator. Profoundly influenced by Gattegno, his focus is on learning (and hence teaching) economically, with a minimum of wasted energy and time. Here he distinguishes between things you have to be told as a learner, and things you could find out for yourself. One of the weaknesses of what came to be labelled *discovery methods* (see p. 43 and p. 224) was that this distinction was not made. Opponents of discovery recast it as meaning that children had to rediscover everything for themselves, which is patently impossible (some things you have to be told) and time-limited (how can you reconstruct everything developed over thousands of years?).

> I start with a proposition: If I'm having to remember … , then I'm not working on mathematics.
> […]
> … consider how you would respond before reading on.

Student:	How many sides has a square got?
Teacher:	Four.
Student:	Why?

The only reason why a square has four sides is that a decision was made a long time ago to call four-sided shapes with particular properties 'squares'. There is nothing about the shapes which means that they have to be called squares – indeed, in other languages, the same shapes are given different names. Looking at the shapes carefully is not going to help students to know what the name of the shapes is, just as looking at the person does not reveal what their name is. All names, within mathematics or elsewhere, are things which students need to be informed about, and part of a teacher's role is to inform students of such things.

Once students are informed, there is more work students still need to do. They have to memorise the word and associate the word with shapes with those particular properties. It is typical of the realm of memory that not only has a word, for example, to be memorised, but that word also has to be associated with the right things. Many times students successfully remember a word but may not have made the appropriate association. For example, a student may not call [a 'diamond' figure] a square, since the properties they associate with *square* do not include sides which are not horizontal or vertical.

(Hewitt, 1999, p. 2)

I describe something as *arbitrary* if someone could only come to know it to be true by being informed of it by some external means – whether by a teacher, a book, the Internet, etc.. If something is arbitrary, then it is arbitrary for all learners, and needs to be memorised to be known. ...

It is not only labels, symbols or names which are arbitrary. The mathematics curriculum is full of conventions, which are based on choices which have been made at some time in the past. For anyone learning those conventions today, they may seem arbitrary decisions. For example, why is the *x* coordinate first and *y* coordinate the second? ...

[...]

There are aspects of the mathematics curriculum where students do not need to be informed. These are things which students can work out for themselves and know to be correct. They are parts of the mathematics curriculum which are not social conventions but rather are properties which can be worked out from what somebody already knows. ... For example, if I turn a quarter turn and then a quarter turn again, I have made a half turn. It is possible to find out about other fractions of a whole turn without having to be informed. So, the mathematical content which is on a curriculum can be divided up into those things which are arbitrary and those things which are necessary.

(ibid., 1999, pp. 3–4)

If the teacher decides to inform students of some mathematics content which is necessary, then they are treating it as if it is arbitrary, as if it is something which needs to be told. For example, if a teacher stated that the angles inside a triangle add up to half a full turn rather than offering a task for students to become aware of this, then students are left with having to accept what the teacher says as true. In this case, it becomes just another 'fact' to be memorised. I call this *received wisdom*.

(ibid., p. 5)

... an awareness concerning properties can be based upon the adoption of a convention. For example, having adopted the convention that there are 360 degrees in a whole turn and that measurement of turn is based on a linear scale (both arbitrary), then I can use the awareness I have about linearity to say *if I halve this, then I halve that*. This leads me to be able to say definitely that there are 180 degrees in a half a full turn – the certainty worked out through awareness from the original adopted convention.

[...]

The necessary is about properties, and one possibility is for students to 'receive' properties through the teacher informing them just as for the arbitrary. However, this turns the necessary into received wisdom and students may well treat this as something else to be memorised. Indeed, they will have no other choice unless they are able and willing to do the work necessary to become aware of the necessity of this received wisdom. Some students may be able to do this work, in which case the received wisdom will become a derived certainty and be known through awareness rather than memory.

Another choice for a teacher is to provide a task which will make properties accessible through awareness. An appropriate task will help these properties to be more accessibly known through awareness than if the teacher informed students of them and left the students to their own devices to work out why they must be so.

A teacher taking a stance of deliberately not informing students of anything which is necessary is aware that developing as a mathematician is about educating awareness rather than collecting and retaining memories. Furthermore, this stance clarifies for the students the way of working which is appropriate for any particular aspect of the curriculum – the arbitrary has to be memorised, but what is necessary is about educating their awareness.

If I'm having to remember … , then I'm not working on mathematics.

(ibid., pp. 8–9)

Learning is an active process of exploring, formalising and assimilating. Learners participating in negotiation and creation enhance their learning. Some people see action and learning as the same thing.

Learners are constantly equilibrating disturbances perceived in the environment, adapting to their situation through accommodating and assimilating, that is, internalising, by adjusting old schema or constructing fresh ones. Arranging the environment so that it promotes useful, efficient and effective adaptation, challenging, but not excessively, is a fine art.

Learning is usefully seen as more-or-less meaningful and more-or-less rote, rather than simply one or the other. In fact both are tied up together.

The use of powers enables concepts to be formed through the creation and adaptation of schemas. Our ideas and awarenesses are linked together in schemas which are triggered by cues in new situations. Learners need to be told what is arbitrary convention, but to have their attention directed to what is necessary as a result of those arbitrary decisions.

Learning phases

Learning cycle: Kurt Lewin and David Kolb

Lewin is best known for his work in the field of organisation behaviour and the study of group dynamics. His research discovered that learning is best facilitated when there is a conflict between immediate concrete experience and detached analysis within the individual. His cycle of action, reflection, generalisation, and testing is characteristic of adult experiential learning (Kolb, 1984).

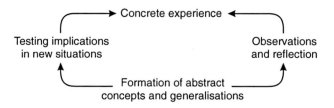

As long as this cycle is not followed algorithmically, it matches well with experience of conjecturing in mathematics (see p. 139). Atherton (webref) uses it to structure four aspects of learning styles, two ways of knowing, two ways of understanding through transforming knowledge, and four kinds of knowledge (see also p. 289 and p. 291).

When probed more deeply, learning seen as action and as reaction changes its nature over time. Various researchers have sought to capture phases or stages or levels of learning, but most of these have in the end caused as much confusion and heartache as insight. The problem is that when distinctions are made, they are interpreted as being clear and definite, rather than simply the result of a particular stressing and a particular ignoring. So the stages identified by Piagetian researchers must be considered cautiously, since behaviour corresponding to different stages can be witnessed in the behaviour of learners of very different ages.

Learning stages: Jean Piaget (summarised)

Piaget sought to characterise changes and development in the dominant behaviour of young learners.

- Sensory-motor attention: pre-verbal, pre-symbolic, spontaneous actions and reflexes based on acquired habits and acts of enquiry and exploration;
- Pre-operational: words used to denote things and actions; some manipulation of symbols or other representations;
- Concrete-operational: logical thought based on experience of physical manipulation;
- Formal-operational: hypothetical-deductive reasoning using ideas and symbols without need for physical manipulation.

Notice the parallels with the *structure of attention* (see p. 60).

Educators pushed Piagetian-based research into establishing age-bands in which these approaches to the world are supposed to be dominant, but even as adults it is possible to recognise each of these types of thinking in ourselves, depending on context and familiarity with a problematic situation. Sometimes we want things to manipulate, which may be labels, symbols, mental images, diagrams or physical objects; sometimes a spontaneous and intuitive act is difficult to articulate or to justify logically. By thinking of these as forms of attention, of different dispositions triggered in different contexts, it is possible to avoid the 'stage-age' mentality which constrained curriculum development for a generation or two.

There are strong overlaps with another approach to what came to be known as levels of learning, based originally on secondary school geometry.

Learning phases: van Hiele and van Hiele

Dina van Hiele-Geldof and her husband Pierre van Hiele were students of Freudenthal, who reported that Dina was able to observe more and more important details in lessons than he could.

> When the van Hieles started teaching they were just as unprepared as many other young teachers; nobody had told them how to do it. They had, of course, passively undergone teaching, and maybe even observed how their teachers performed, but this was not enough. As time went on, they had the opportunity to discuss their own teaching with each other and with others. They subjected their own actions to reflection. They observed themselves while teaching, recalled what they had done, and analysed it. Thinking is continued acting, indeed, but there are relative levels. The acting at the lower level becomes an object of analysis at the higher the level. This is what the van Hieles recognised as a remarkable feature of the learning process, namely in the learning process in which they learned teaching. They transferred this feature to the learning process that was the goal of their teaching, namely the learning processes of pupils who were learning mathematics. There they discovered similar levels. To me this seems an important discovery.
>
> (Freudenthal, 1991, p. 96)

Pierre van Hiele generalised the levels of geometric thinking which he and his wife identified (see p. 59), distinguishing five phases or stages of learning which correspond closely to the *structure of attention* (see p. 60):

1 In the first stage, that of *information*, pupils get acquainted with the working domain. [What Vergnaud calls the *conceptual field* (see p. 199).]
2 In the second stage, that of *guided orientation*, they are guided by tasks (given by the teacher or by themselves) with different relations of the network that has to be formed. [Vergnaud might describe this as developing *theorems-in-action*; Gattegno might describe this as using their *awarenesses* (see p. 61).]

3   In the third stage, that of *explicitation*, they become conscious of the relations, they try to express them in words, they learn the technical language accompanying the subject matter. [*Theorems-in-action* become explicit; learners become aware of some of their *awarenesses.*]

4   In the fourth stage, that of *free orientation*, they learn by general tasks to find their own way in the network of relations.

5   In the fifth stage, that of *integration*, they build an overview of all they have learned of the subject, of the newly formed network of relations now at their disposal. [Through what Piaget called *reflective abstraction* (see p. 171); Gattegno used *integration through subordination* (see p. 229).]

(van Hiele, 1986, pp. 53–4)

As long as van Hiele's stages are not seen as definitive of the individual or completely distinct, they can be useful. They can serve as a reminder to stimulate learners to use their powers. They can also serve as a reminder to allow learners sufficient time to lay an appropriate foundation so that their learning is efficient and effective, rather than rushing to formal records and algorithms before learners have assimilated and reconstructed the basic actions and processes. (See also *structure of attention*, p. 60.)

Prospective and retrospective learning: Hans Freudenthal

Freudenthal found it valuable to distinguish between prospective and retrospective learning:

- *Prospective learning*: taking advantage of predilections and natural tendencies and past experience; anticipatory or 'advance organisers'.
- *Retrospective learning*: recalling old ideas whenever it is apt, and reviewing from a higher stance or in a broader context and from a greater generality.

Intertwining learning strands: integration from past and future learning processes. ...

... learning should be organised in strands which are mutually intertwined as early, as long and as strongly as possible. When loose ends are inevitable, they're taken up at the first opportunity, where they can be connected to other ones in order to be continued. In a sense, examples of prospective and retrospective learning can also serve as such for intertwining learning strands, or at least for points where intertwining can start in order to be continued more consequently.

(Freudenthal, 1991, p. 118)

There are close similarities with *reflection* (see p. 280) and especially *reflective abstraction* (see p. 171).

Piagetian stages are most usefully identified as behaviour rather than as attributes of a an individual: sensory-motor attention; pre-operational; concrete-operational; formal-operational. Van Hiele phases involve thinking in terms of wholes through visualisation, analysis, abstraction, informal and formal deductions. Translated into structure of attention, it is possible to move rapidly between, or even to experience simultaneously, attention on wholes, on distinctions, on relationships, on properties and perceived objects, and on properties as independent of any particular instance.

Prospective learning through anticipation, and retrospective learning through recollection and reflection can be intertwined to produce effective learning.

Any one can be working at many of these at the same time, but apparent lack of competence may indicate some disruption, some as yet unintegrated distinction making, relationships, properties, etc..

Turning actions into objects

In the twentieth century, mathematics came to be seen as the study of transformations. To study an object you study various actions on that object. Once a transformation is identified, labelled and denoted by a symbol, it can become an object of study upon which to perform further transformations. Looking back over the school curriculum reveals this as an ongoing and continuing feature of learning and doing mathematics: processes become objects to be acted upon by further processes.

The important thing about the ways in which actions become objects is that the actions do not lose their action-quality. Rather a dual perception develops. Expressions such as $2 - (3 + 4)$ or $2x^2 - (3x + 4)$ or $y = 2x - (3x + 4)$ can be seen both as a process (a sequence of operations to be carried out) and as the result of carrying out those actions.

Being central to learning, the process of turning an action or a feeling into an object, has been studied by many researchers, each using their own vocabulary. Using the language of abstraction (see p. 59), Piaget suggested that:

Abstraction comes from action, rather than from the object acted upon.
(Piaget, 1972, p. 16)

Indeed, abstraction comes not just not from the action, or even from active engagement in that action, but from some sort of reflection on or integration of the experience as not just isolated and one-off, but recurring. Piaget coined the term *reflective abstraction*, and this was taken up by Dubinsky (see p. 171) in the context of teaching mathematics. Much of educational research is motivated by desire to learn how such a transformation comes about and how it can be fostered and exploited in the teaching of mathematics.

Compression: William Thurston

William Thurston (b. USA) is a highly productive and creative research mathematician.

> Mathematics is amazingly compressible: you may struggle a long time, step by step, to work through some process or idea from several approaches. But once you really understand it and have the mental perspective to see it as a whole, there is often a tremendous mental compression. You can file it away, recall it quickly and completely when you need it, and use it as just one step in some mental process. The insight that goes with this compression is one of the real joys of mathematics.
>
> (Thurston, 1990, pp. 846–7)

Procepts: Eddie Gray and David Tall

Gray is a mathematics educator who has concentrated on pupils in early years, while his colleague, Tall, has focused largely on learners at tertiary level. Nevertheless they find much in common, and in particular, how a procedure or action carried out can become an object of study, hence process-object becomes *procept*. For example, the symbol-expression $3x - 2$ can be seen both as specifying a calculation procedure given a value for x including an as-yet-unknown value, and also the answer to any such calculation, that is, the generality being expressed. Similarly, 2/3 is both a division operation and the answer to that operation being carried out.

> We do not consider that the ambiguity of a symbolism expressing the flexible duality of process and concept can be fully utilized if the distinction between process and concept is maintained at all times. ...
>
> An *elementary procept* is the amalgam of three components: a *process* that produces a mathematical *object*, and a *symbol* that represents either the process or the object.
>
> (Gray and Tall, 1994, p. 121)

Although their evidence draws only on early arithmetic, Gray and Tall indicate that the same proceptual thinking is required at all levels of mathematics. They go on to cite research showing that learners show evidence of qualitatively different approaches which can be accounted for in terms of procepts. They found that proceptual thinking is necessary to progress in mathematics, but that some learners find this move more difficult than others, creating a *proceptual divide*.

1   Procedural thinking is characterized by a focus on the procedure and the physical or quasi-physical aids that support it. The limiting aspect of such thinking is the more blinkered view that the child has of the symbolism: numbers are used only as concrete entities to be manipulated through a counting process. The emphasis on the procedure reduces the focus on the relationship between input and output, often leading to idiosyncratic extensions of the counting procedure that may not generalize.

2   Proceptual thinking is characterized by the ability to compress stages in symbol manipulation to the point where symbols are viewed as objects that can be decomposed and recomposed in flexible ways.

   [...]

   ... We therefore hypothesize that what might be a continuous spectrum of performance tends to become a dichotomy in which those who begin to fail are consigned to become procedural. We believe that this bifurcation of strategy – between flexible use of number as object or process and fixation on procedural counting – is one of the most significant factors in the difference between success and failure. We call it the *proceptual divide*.

(ibid., p. 132)

Once difficulties are encountered and processes remain as process (compare this with *theorems-in-action*, see p. 63), learners fall further and further behind. In their summing up, Gray and Tall call upon Thurston's use of *compression*.

... it is the compression of mathematical ideas that makes them so simple. As proceptual thinking grows in conceptual richness, procepts can be manipulated as simple symbols at a higher level or opened up to perform computations, to be decomposed and recomposed at will. Such forms of thinking become entirely unattainable for the procedural thinker who fails to develop a rich proceptual structure.

(ibid., p. 137)

Proceptual thinking is not a quality of a person, but of a person in a situation at a particular time regarding a particular concept. At any time and at any stage, learners can experience a topic 'running away from them' due to processes not becoming objects.

Reification: Anna Sfard

Anna Sfard (b. Poland) is an Israeli researcher and educator who uses the term *reification* for processes becoming objects. She distinguishes two kinds of definitions and concepts: *operational* and *structural*. Operational ones are specified in terms of actions, whereas structural ones are specified in the language of objects. She notes that similar distinctions have been made using the language of *conceptual entities* and *reasoning procedures* (Harel and Kaput, 1992), and *dynamic* and *static* interpretations (Goldenberg, Lewis and O'Keefe, 1992).

> [There is] a delicate distinction between the terms *object* and *entity* which seem to be used by other authors as synonymous. ...
>
> (Sfard, 1992, p.60)

Entity refers to an integrated whole while *object* conveys an assumption about existence.

> ... it is important to emphasize that the terms *process* and *object* are to be understood ... as *different facets of the same thing* rather than as totally distinct, separate components of the mathematical universe. In other words, the operational and structural modes of thinking, although ostensibly incompatible, are in fact complementary.
>
> [...]
>
> An important question ... concerns the origins of mathematical objects: where did these abstract entities come from, in both historical and psychological senses?
>
> (ibid., pp. 60–1)

Sfard (1991) tracks the development of the concept of function which she sees as a three-centuries long struggle for reification. She concludes from her historical and observational researches two principles:

> 1   New concepts should not be introduced in structural forms. ...
> 2   A structural conception should not be required as long as the student can do without it. ...
>
> (Sfard, 1992, p. 69)

These principles may be cast a little strongly, but they are consistent with Piaget's notion of action and knowing and learning coming about through action on familiar objects. There is no point in throwing learners objects as examples which are not already familiar and object-like for them. This principle is expressed slightly differently in the SEM and MGA frameworks (p. 263). Sfard identifies three stages of concept construction: *interiorisation*, *condensation* and *reification*.

> At the stage of *interiorisation* a learner gets acquainted with the processes which will eventually give rise to a new concept ... . These processes are operations performed on lower-level mathematical objects. Gradually, the learner becomes skilled at performing these processes. ... we would say that a process has been interiorised if it 'can be carried out through [mental] representations' (Piaget, 1970, p. 14),

and in order to be considered, analyzed and compared it needs no longer to be actually performed.

(Sfard, 1991, p. 18)

From an *activity theory* (see p. 84) perspective, interiorisation is only possible if the same process is encountered in the behaviour of relative experts.

> The phase of *condensation* is a period of 'squeezing' lengthy sequences of operations into more manageable units. At this stage a person becomes more and more capable of thinking about a given process as a whole, without feeling an urge to go into details. ... This is the point [when a name or label is attached] at which a new concept is 'officially born'. ... A progress in condensation would manifest itself also in growing easiness to alternate between different representations of the concept.
>   [...]
>   ... Only when a person becomes capable of conceiving the notion as a fully-fledged object, we shall say that the concept has been reified. *Reification,* therefore, is defined as an ontological shift – a sudden ability to see something familiar in a totally new light. Thus, whereas interiorisation and condensation are gradual, quantitative rather than qualitative changes, reification is an instantaneous quantum leap: a process solidifies into object, into a static structure. Various representations of the concept become semantically unified by this abstract, purely imaginary construct. The new entity is soon detached from the process which produced it and begins to draw its meaning from the fact of its being a member of a certain category. ... A person can investigate general properties of such [a] category and various relations between its representatives. He or she can solve problems involving finding instances of the category which fulfil a given condition.
>
> (ibid., pp. 19–20)

Objects: Willi Dörfler

Willi Dörfler is an Austrian mathematician, mathematics educator and researcher who combines practicality with philosophical analysis.

> ... at some point ... the learner has to make up his or her mind (a metaphoric expression) whether to consider 'this' (i.e., a matrix, a group, a graph, a term) as an object in its own right. This decision is combined with a change in point of view: Instead of regarding the various elements in their own right and with their individual properties and relations, they are viewed as forming a whole with distinct properties and relations. There is also a switch of focus of attention from the single elements to their totality and the emerging qualities of the new entity. ... Language supplies us with many means to realize linguistically this change of

perspective. It is a change in the way of speaking and thinking about the respective piece within our experience. Of course, there have to be reasons for adopting this new perspective.

... This object is kind of virtual, imagined, or assumed. Of course, after having made the decision for this change of perspective, nothing prevents one from considering the entity as a fully-fledged unit or object. This is supported by investigating the properties of the object as a whole and its behavior as an entity, which is categorically different from the properties of the constituting elements. Again, this is a way of describing the entity as an object and is formed during the process of describing its behavior. The object, so to speak, lives simply and exclusively in its descriptions and needs no other place to gain existence and relevance.

... Because the object was formed deliberately by an intentional act, it has no permanence beyond how and how long one wants to have it available as a unit. One can put it aside for some time and revive it if appropriate.

(Dörfler, 2002, pp. 342–3)

I do not claim that ... change of perspective to objects comes by itself or is always easy to make. ... The awareness that learning is partly an enculturation and an initiation into a way of speaking, of personally accepting specific decisions, attitudes, points of view, and conventions might change dramatically the overall attitude of students toward mathematics. If the so-called construction of mathematical objects is in fact interpreted as a decision to treat something as a unified or reified entity, then this decision has to be taken by each learner. The role of the teacher then would be to make this decision appear as sensible and plausible as possible. The new perspective for the students must be worth trying and they must feel empowered to enter into the proposed view. In principle, this essentially would also comprise the possibility of refusing the decision or adopting a new perspective only if it will prove successful and viable. I believe that mathematical constructions are not automatic for learners; rather, they have to agree to them, to accept them, and to decide to use them. That is, the learner has to want to treat something as a unit and an object. In the course of time, this decision for objectification then becomes a deliberate practice and a thinking strategy. The switch to an object view (or entity view, or unit view) can then be carried out at will as the need may arise, and, more important, can be reversed with the same ease even in hitherto unfamiliar situations. A model based on decision making better reflects the high degree of flexibility in handling mathematical objects (in creating and dissolving them), as shown by experienced students of mathematics.

(ibid., p. 346)

Notice how this extends the van Hiele phases (see p. 59) by suggesting movement in both directions among them.

Reflective abstraction: Ed Dubinsky

Ed Dubinsky (b. Pennsylvania, 1935–) is a mathematician who has worked hard to promote the cause of mathematics education at university level. He has developed software to enable undergraduates to manipulate concrete (virtual) objects in group theory, and following on from Piaget, has developed what he calls APOS theory as an approach to effective teaching (see below). Here he describes three forms of abstraction identified by Piaget:

> *Empirical abstraction* derives knowledge from the properties of objects (Beth and Piaget, 1966, pp. 188–189). We interpret this to mean that it has to do with experiences that appear to the subject to be external. The knowledge of these properties is, however, internal and is the result of constructions made internally by the subject. According to Piaget, this kind of abstraction leads to the extraction of common properties of objects and extensional generalizations, that is, the passage from 'some' to 'all', from the specific to the general (Piaget and Garcia, 1983, p. 299). ...
>
> *Pseudo-empirical abstraction* is intermediate between empirical and reflective abstraction and teases out properties that the actions of the subject have introduced into objects (Piaget, 1985, pp. 18–19). Consider, for example the observation of a 1–1 correspondence between two sets of objects which the subject has placed in alignment ... . Knowledge of this situation may be considered empirical because it has to do with the objects, but it is their configuration in space and relationships to which this leads that are of concern and these are due to the actions of the subject. Again, of course, understanding that there is a 1–1 relation between these two sets is the result of internal constructions made by the subject.
>
> Finally, *reflective abstraction* is drawn from what Piaget (1980, pp. 89–97) called *the general coordinations* of actions and, as such, its source is the subject and it is completely internal ... [for example] seriation, in which the child performs several individual actions of forming pairs, triples, etc., and then interiorizes and coordinates the actions to form a total ordering (Piaget, 1972, pp. 37–38). This kind of abstraction leads to a very different sort of generalization which is constructive and results in 'new syntheses in midst of which particular laws acquire new meaning' (Piaget and Garcia, 1983, p. 299).
>
> (Dubinsky, 1991, p. 97)

... when properly understood, reflective abstraction appears as a description of the mechanism of the development of intellectual thought. ...
[...]
According to Piaget, the first part of reflective abstraction consists of drawing properties from mental or physical actions at a particular level of thought. ... This involves, among other things, cognizance or

consciousness of the actions ... . Whatever is thus 'abstracted' is projected onto a higher plane of thought ... where other actions are present as well as more powerful modes of thought.

It is at this point that the real power of reflective abstraction comes in for, as Piaget observes, one must do more than dissociate properties from those which will be ignored or separate a form from its content ... . There is 'a process which will become increasingly evident over time: the construction of new combinations by a conjunction of abstractions' (Piaget, 1972, p. 23).

(ibid., p. 99)

APOS Theory: Ed Dubinsky

APOS is short for *actions, processes, objects, schemas* as a development when making sense of situations and solving problems:

> We begin with *objects*. These encompass the full range of mathematical objects: numbers, variables, functions, ... each of which must be constructed by an individual at some point in her or his mathematical development.
>
> At any point in time there are a number of *actions* that a subject can use for calculating with these objects. These actions go far beyond numerical calculation resulting in numerical answers. ...
>
> It is possible for a subject to work with actions in ways other than just applying them to objects. First, an action must be interiorized. ... this means that some internal construction is made relating to the action. An interiorized action is a *process*. Interiorization permits one to be conscious of an action, to reflect on it and to combine it with other actions. ...
>
> Interiorizing actions is one way of constructing processes. Another way is to work with existing processes to form new ones. This can be done, for example, by a reversal. ... If the process is interiorized, the student might be able to reverse it to solve problems. ...
>
> [...]
>
> In addition to using processes to construct new processes, it is also possible to reflect on a process and to convert it into an object. [This is encapsulation.]
>
> (Dubinsky, 1991, pp. 106–8)

See also Dubinsky (webref) and Davis, Tall and Thomas (webref). There are similarities with the *Manipulating–Getting-a-sense-of–Articulating* frame-work (see p. 264). *Transference* (see p. 291) is yet another description of how ideas and actions become objects, as is the transition of *theorems-in-action* into theorems (see p. 63).

Actions becoming objects of study with relationships, properties and even axioms (see *structure of attention*, p. 60) are hard enough to trap in yourself. Arranging conditions to foster the same transitions in learners is a challenge.

As soon as you try to 'make it happen', it becomes instruction rather than education; procedural content to be memorised rather than reconstructed and reconstructible experience of sense-making on the part of the learner. (See *didactic transposition*, p. 83 and the *constructivist dilemma*, p. 96.

Actions or processes becoming objects (reification, encapsulation, compression) can be thought of as precepts to reinforce their dual nature. One way to describe how this happens is as a sequence of interiorisation, condensation, and reification. Another description is in terms of empirical abstraction, pseudo-empirical abstraction and reflective abstraction. APOS 'theory' summarises this movement and has been used to inform teaching and curriculum development at tertiary level. Yet another description is in terms of educating awareness and shifts in the structure of attention.

Learning from examples

As Isaac Newton said so beautifully in his book on algebra:

> ... because craft skills are more easily learnt by example than by precept, it seems appropriate to adjoin the solutions of the following problems.
> (Whiteside, 1968, p. 429)

Examples are and always have been the mainstay of mathematics teaching. But what are learners supposed to do with examples? What actions do they need to perform so that what is exemplary to the teacher about an example, becomes exemplary for the learner? Put another way, if you do not appreciate what something is supposed to be an example of, how can it be an example of anything (relevant)? There is a growing literature on this question alone (see Anthony, 1994; Atkinson *et al.*, 2000; Benbachir and Zaki, 2001; Bills, 1996; Bills and Rowland, 1999; Chi and Bassok, 1989; Dahlberg and Housman, 1997).

When is an example exemplary: Anna Sierpinska

Anna Sierpinska raises the question of how something becomes exemplary:

> It is a pedagogical adage that 'we learn by examples'. Pedagogues, of course, think of paradigmatic examples in this case. They think of instances that can best explain a rule or a method, or a concept.
> The learner is also looking for such paradigmatic examples as he or she is learning something new. The problem is, however, that before you have a grasp of the whole domain of knowledge you are learning, you are unable to tell a paradigmatic example from a non-paradigmatic one. So you make mistakes, wrong choices, wrong generalizations (because, of course, you generalize from your examples). Moreover, as the example is normally represented in some medium (enactive, iconic

or symbolic) you may mistake the features of the representation for the features of the notion thus exemplified.

(Sierpinska, 1994, pp. 88–9)

It seems then that 'learning by examples' is a property of our minds that has little in common with the pedagogical expectations expressed in the adage. An example is always embedded in a rich situation that contains more elements, data, information than just those directly related to the object exemplified. The teacher cannot be sure that, from this sea, the students will fish only the bits strictly relevant for the formation of the concept. It is [not] hard, therefore, to understand the teacher's frustration, when, after having prepared the best examples, he or she finds that the students are still able to commit the most unbelievable mistakes and errors. The method of paradigmatic examples is not really a method of teaching. Rather, it is a way in which concepts are being formed: the examples cannot be transmitted from the teacher's mind to the learner's mind. The latter must construct or reconstruct examples that can be regarded as paradigmatic in some more objective sense. The teacher can only help the learner by organizing situations against which the consecutive tentative forms of these examples can be tested, in which they can be revealed, and in which a change can be discussed and negotiated, if necessary.

Examples are, in understanding abstract concepts, the indispensable prop and the necessary obstacle. It is on the basis of examples that we make our first guesses. When we start to probe our guesses, the fundamental role is slowly taken over by the definitions.

(ibid., p. 91)

There are similarities with van Hiele *phases* (see p. 59), and with Marton's notion of *dimensions-of-possible-variation* (see p. 56).

One of the questions to ask about examples is whether there are ambiguities between structural features (which are what make the thing an example) and special features which are particular to the example. For instance, a circle of radius 2 has a circumference of $2 \times \pi \times 2$ and an area of $\pi \times 2^2$. What is the difference between the various twos? Is it evident to learners?

What is exemplary for one person can be completely particular and isolated for someone else. Do learners appreciate what is exemplary: what can change and what has to remain invariant?

Practice and skills

Finally, we return to the issue of manipulative skill and facility with techniques which traditionally is seen as best learned through practice. Certainly prior to an examination, practice is valuable in getting up speed, which means reducing the amount of focused attention required to perform the technique so that you can be on the look out for slips and wrinkles, and maintain a direction towards the solution of the problems.

Practice: Mary Boole

Mary Boole uses the notion of 'fictions' for pedagogic devices, whether apparatus, images or symbols, mnemonics or other memory devices, which are introduced temporarily to aid comprehension but which ultimately have to be discarded or left behind if learners are to develop facility.

> ... Truth is never received into the human mind without an admixture of conventions, of what may be called fictions. These fictions have to be introduced, used, and then withdrawn. It would be impossible to teach even so straightforward a subject as mathematics without the temporary use of statements which are not true to the nature of things. The history of a child who is learning mathematics, like that of human thought, is very much a record of alternate introduction of convenient fictions and subsequent analysis of their true nature. A class, like the public, tends at times to become groovy and mechanical; to mistake the accidental for the essential; to treat necessary aids to learning is if they were actual truths; to lose sight of the relative importance of various kinds of information. A class in Botany tends to forget that classification and terminology are not so much part of the life of plants as circulation and fertilization; a class in analytical Geometry forgets that the coordinates are no part of a curve. ... A student tends to such forgetfulness in proportion as he becomes mechanical in his work; the genius of a teacher is very much shown by the manner in which he contrives to arouse the interest and correct the errors of a class which is becoming too mechanical.
>
> Theorists in education sometimes imagine that a good teacher should not allow the work of his class to become mechanical at all. A year or two of practical work in the school (especially with examinations looming ahead) cures one of all such delusions. Education involves not only teaching, but also training. Training implies that work should become mechanical; *teaching* involves preventing mechanicalness from reaching the degree fatal to progress. We must therefore allow much of the actual work to be done in a mechanical manner, without direct consciousness of its meaning; and intelligent teacher will occasionally rouse his pupils to full consciousness of what they are doing; and if he can do so without producing confusion, he may be complemented and his class congratulated.
>
> (Tahta, 1972, p. 15)

Note links with *awareness* (see p. 61) and *reflection* (see p. 280), with *pedagogic tools* and *cultural mediation* (see p. 85), and with *rote learning* (see p. 152).

Practice makes perfect: Shiqi Li

Shiqi Li writes from a culture in which memorisation is the foundation stone of learning. But care is needed when connecting with *learning by rote* as it is conceived in the West. For as Marton (Marton and Booth, 1997) has found, memorisation is only the starting point for achieving understanding over a period of time, just as people often value as adults having had to memorise good poems, speeches from Shakespeare, and the like, when they were young.

> 熟能生巧, corresponding to the English proverb *practice makes perfect*, is an ancient Chinese idiom. Many teachers in China as well as in East Asia believe it and consider it to be a general principle for all kinds of learning: through imitation and practice, again and again, people will become highly skilled. Is practice an effective way of teaching and learning, especially for mathematics education? In fact, I cannot answer simply 'yes' or 'no' to this question.
>
> (Li, 1999, p. 33)

Li neatly summarises much of the writing about how actions become 'learning'.

> It is now widely accepted that teaching mathematics means teaching through mathematical activities. Activity or action, in other words, involves thinking, doing and physical or mental manipulation. Why is activity necessary? Because the form of activity has profound implications and performs particular functions for cognition.
>
> First of all, mathematics learning involves (quasi-) empirical actions (Lakatos, 1976). Manipulative practice is a fundamental action for mathematics. No matter how students are to learn, whether in the traditional way with pencil and paper, or, in a more modern way, with the aid of a computer, mathematics is not learned by a wild flight of fancy. Although people sometimes may have a sudden inspiration in problem solving, it is still dependent on [ac]cumulating experience. Students, the same as mathematicians, will do mathematics themselves: knowledge is acquired through practical activities. In some aspects, the practicality of mathematics is not completely the same as that of experimental sciences such as physics, chemistry, etc.. However, behavioral or mental operation is still needed in mathematical activity.
>
> [...]
>
> Nevertheless, mathematical concepts do not come directly from fact. They are not abstracted from actual things, but are a product of coherent

actions on things. So a mathematical object is actually a particular object, a so-called mental object. For instance, the concept of addition is not produced from more marbles but from the process of adding or combining. ...

[...]

What psychological mechanism is needed by students in this course of concept formation? The basis of the organizing concept is provided by experience but the concept itself is not provided. To construct a concept, a more important thing is a leap in thinking, i.e. reflective abstraction (Piaget, 1970). ...

Without manipulation, the subsequent reflection cannot be put into effect. And if there were not a sufficiently strong background of manipulation, many contexts and properties would only be viewed as accidental phenomena that would not enable students to discover precise conclusions. Therefore students' manipulative practice in their learning will lay a foundation for their reflective abstraction. Moreover, these activities must be of their personal experience. Students should be involved in practical activities, organizing situations, sending messages and constructing their understanding. Even to see someone else's doing, s/he must perform it her/himself and make sense of her/his manipulation. Nothing can take the place of her/his own thinking. One of the functions of routine practice that we stress is to urge students to participate in their activities and let them learn swimming by swimming. In short, practice makes *perfect*; perfect will be formed on the solid basis of practice. If there were no fundamental activities, reflective abstraction would be a castle in the air.

(ibid., pp. 33–4)

Li quotes Freudenthal:

If a learning process is to be observed, the moments that count are its discontinuities, the jumps in the learning process (Freudenthal, 1978, p. 78).

(ibid., p. 35)

Algorithms drive out thought: Sherman Stein

Sherman Stein (b. California, 1930–) is a mathematician known particularly as a populariser of mathematics. Here he points out that 'teaching thinking' can ever so quickly become 'teaching how to solve classes of problems' which easily turns into teaching learners algorithms so they do not have to think. He recommends open-field tasks:

What is the point of [an] exercise? Is it to check a definition [is understood] or a theorem or the execution of an algorithm? ... Blinders are placed on the student to focus attention on particular facts or skills. For instance we may ask students to factor $x^4 - 1$.

An open-field exercise puts no blinders on the student. We might ask 'For which positive integers n does $x^2 - 1$ divide $x^n - 1$?' An open-field exercise may not connect with the section covered that day; it may not even be related to the course. Such an exercise may require the student to devise experiments, make a conjecture, and prove it. If it has all three parts, it is a 'triex', which is short for 'explore, extract, explain' or for 'try the unknown'.

[...]

... Prove that if 3 divides the sum of the digits of an integer, then 3 divides the integer. ...

... If 3 divides the sum of the digits of an integer, must it divide the integer? ...

... Let d be one of the integers 2 through 9. If d divides the sum of the digits of an integer, must it divide the integer? ...

(Stein, 1987, pp. 3–4)

What Stein is suggesting can be cast in terms of stimulating learners to experience *dimensions-of-possible-variation* (see p. 56), and in terms of *psychologising the subject matter* (see p. 45 and p. 203) in order to interest learners by getting them to use their natural *powers* (see p. 115 and p. 233).

Reversions: Bob Davis

Bob Davis (b. Maryland, 1926–1997) was a mathematics teacher and educator who was inspired by the teaching of Gattegno and other colleagues associated with the Association of Teachers of Mathematics in the UK, and who in turn inspired generations of teachers in the USA through his Madison Project. He fashioned and championed an approach to teaching which stimulated learners to reconstruct for themselves important mathematical properties, relationships and concepts. Here he reports a colleague noticing some classic errors: $4 \times 4 = 8$; $2^3 = 6$; $6 \div \frac{1}{2} = 3$.

... in every case, the student was *giving a correct answer* – but a correct answer *to a different question*. The student had not answered the original question ...

[Davis' colleague] proposed, and tested, a remediation procedure. He recommended that the teacher figure out the question ... that the student *had* answered; the teacher should then ask [that question]. [He] predicted that, in nearly every case, the student would not answer [that question] but would immediately correct the answer to [the original question]. ...

Teacher: how much is seven times seven?

Student (grade seven):   Fourteen.

Teacher: How much is seven plus seven?
Student: Oh! It should be forty-nine!

> The frequency of dialogues on this pattern suggests that there is some
> kind of echoic 'second hearing' or … 'instant replay capability'. … It
> reveals something interesting about the student's control structure, and
> about the student's understanding of the teacher's goals, that the student
> does NOT bother answering the second question, assuming (correctly)
> that what was really wanted was a correct answer to the original question.
>
> (Davis, 1984, pp. 100–1)

Until you actually notice a learner doing a *reversal*, it remains a 'theoretical
possibility'. A label such as *reversal* can help alert you to the phenomenon
when it happens, thus opening up the possibility of responding constructively.

Paradigm teaching strategy: Bob Davis

Davis describes his work on a task known as 'pebbles in a bag', in which a
bag with an unknown number of pebbles in it has known numbers of
pebbles added and removed, and learners are invited to develop a notation
to enable them to keep track of the number of pebbles in the bag relative to
the number at the start. Davis draws out principles for task design which he
calls *paradigm teaching strategy*:

> First, *it involves ideas for which virtually all students have powerful repre-*
> *sentations*. For example, nearly every student knows that if you have a
> bag that is partially filled with pebbles, and if you then put two pebbles
> into it, it will have *more* pebbles in it than it did before you did that.
>   Second, *it is a reliably accurate 'isomorphic image'* for all operations
> of the form $A + B$ and $A - B$, where A and B are positive integers … .
>   […]
> Finally, it is simple … .
>   […]
> … All important mathematics 'makes sense' – but more often than not
> one must have appropriate experiential background in order to under-
> stand the challenge that is being faced, and the nature of an effective
> response. Education must provide the experience, not assume it.
>
> (Davis, 1984, pp. 314–15)

Subordinating: Dave Hewitt

Inspired by Gattegno, Hewitt's focus is teaching and learning economically,
which means working with attention and awareness. In his thesis he
develops a number of themes, among which is the idea that if you want
someone to develop facility, then they need to integrate that functioning,

reducing the amount of attention which is required to act in the specified manner. To achieve this, you divert their attention, attracting them to place much of it in some higher-order task:

> Principle of economy: place attention in an activity which subordinates the desired learning. This means that something is practised whilst progress is made at a higher subordinate level (practice through progress).
>
> (Hewitt, 1994, p. 167)

In order to get learners to practise (integrate) a technique, Hewitt's practice is to offer learners a task which involves them in using that technique on examples which they construct in order to reach and check conjectures. Note resonances with Dewey (p. 127 and p. 233).

Practice which diverts attention away from the details of doing, so that the actions are integrated into automaticity, is helpful. Practice which means paying as little attention as possible but 'getting the answers' is not (compare with the didactic tension).

---

7 Learning what?

Introduction

Making lists of mathematical definitions, topics and techniques does not really answer the question of what it is that we want people to learn from years of school mathematics. Few of us solve quadratic equations or factorise quadratic expressions while shopping or otherwise going about our business, so what is actually essential? Is it simply facility with the four operations of arithmetic on small numbers? In this chapter we encounter sweeping visions of what learning and doing mathematics can offer young people in school: recognition and development of the learners' natural powers to make sense of the world, forms of mathematical thinking that enhance participation in society, and mathematical themes that pervade and link different mathematical topics. These global aims are consonant with the aims of education and the perspectives on learning displayed in earlier chapters.

Using powers

Whatever powers learners possess, they need to be invoked, honed and refined as part of their mathematical education.

Habits of mind: Al Cuoco, Paul Goldenberg and June Mark

Al Cuoco, Paul Goldenberg and June Mark have enormous experience in working with learners using computer software such as LOGO which offers learners the opportunity to construct mathematical objects for themselves. Here they advocate the sorts of 'habits of mind' that they would like learners to develop as a result of working on mathematics.

> ... Take [the word *should* in what follows] with a grain of salt. When we say students should do this or things like that, we mean that it would be wonderful if they did those things or thought in those ways, and that high school curricula should strive to develop these habits. We also realize that most students do not have these habits now, and that not

everything we say they should be able to do is appropriate for every situation. We are looking to develop a repertoire of useful habits; the most important of these is the understanding of when to use what.

(Cuoco, Goldenberg and Mark, 1996, p. 378)

There are similarities with *knowing-to* (see p. 289).

Students should be pattern sniffers: ... In the context of mathematics, we should foster within students a delight in finding hidden patterns in, for example, a table of the squares of the integers between 1 and 100. Students should always be on the lookout for short-cuts that arise from patterns in calculations ... . the search for regularity should extend to their daily lives and should also drive the kinds of problems students pose for themselves ... .

Students should be experimenters: Performing experiments is central in mathematical research, but experimenting is all too rare in mathematics classrooms. Simple ideas like recording results, keeping all but one variable fixed, trying very small or very large numbers, and varying parameters in regular ways are missing from the backgrounds of many high school students. When faced with a mathematical problem, a student should immediately start playing with it, using strategies that have proved successful in the past. Students should also be used to performing thought experiments ... [and] develop a healthy skepticism for experimental results.

Students should be describers: Give precise descriptions of the steps in a process. Describing what you do it is an important step in understanding it. ... One way for students to see the utility and elegance of traditional mathematical formalism is for them to struggle with the problem of describing phenomena for which ordinary language descriptions are much too cumbersome ... . Students should be able to convince their classmates that a particular result is true or plausible by giving precise descriptions of good evidence or (even better) by showing generic calculations that actually constitute proofs. ... Students should develop the habit of writing down their thoughts, results, conjectures, arguments, proofs, questions, and opinions about the mathematics they do, and they should be accustomed to polishing up these notes every now and then for presentation to others.

(ibid., pp. 378–9)

There are similarities with *Do–Talk–Record* (see p. 262).

Students should be tinkerers: ... Students should develop the habit of taking ideas apart and putting them back together. When they do this, they should want to see what happens if something is left out or if the pieces are put back in a different way.

Students should be inventors: Tinkering with existing machines leads to expertise at building new ones. Students should develop the habit of inventing mathematics both for utilitarian purposes and for fun. Their inventions might be rules for a game, algorithms for doing things, explanations of how things work, or even axioms for a mathematical structure.

Students should be visualizers: ... doing things in one's head that, in the right situation, *could* be done with one's eyes. ... constructing visual analogues to ideas or processes that are first encountered in nonvisual realms. ... visual accompaniments (not analogues, exactly) to totally non-visual processes.

Students should be conjecturers: The habit of making plausible conjectures takes time to develop, but it is central to the doing of mathematics.

Students should be guessers: Guessing is a wonderful research strategy. Starting at a possible solution to a problem and working backward (or simply checking your guesses) often helps you find a closer approximation to the desired result ... [and] find new insight, strategies, and approaches.

(ibid., pp. 379–84)

Powers: Caleb Gattegno

Gattegno's insights and suggestions were based on extensive observation and contemplation of the very young child's experiences, at an age when learning is at its most extensive and fastest.

> ... I know that children can do a great deal more with themselves than the most adventurous educator ever dreamed of.
>
> Children spontaneously stay with problems. And they stay for as long as is required. They consider abstraction (the simultaneous use of stressing and ignoring) naturally as their birthright. They give proof that they know many concepts but, more than that, that they know how to generate them in their awareness and how to recognise them as a representable by a word and as represented by an open class of elements to which new items can be added. Their mastery of the language of their environment in their tender years, whatever their language, tells us clearly that they can perceive mental structures as present in the mind, how the structures link to each other and how they affect each other.
>
> [...]
>
> Children spontaneously transform. They spontaneously know that everything is in flux and that a correct description of the world would be in dynamic terms. They know intimately that nothing is ever seen again in the same light, from the same distance and the same angle, and the objects are classes of impressions which are defined with respect to each other and by their overlapping parts. They know spontaneously that

conservation is not needed to make sense of a world in flux and systematically ignore it until there is a place for it in their perception of the world; for example, when quantity becomes an attribute of some qualities perceived within the field.

… The real structure behind equality and identity is … equivalence. Equivalence is the proper way of looking at the world because things are made to belong to each other (in a class of equivalence) when we stress one or more attributes and ignore others. It is the stressing that unifies, but since the ignoring is also present, it serves to reopen a question closed by the stressing.

(Gattegno, 1981, p. 6)

The teacher's challenge: John Mason

Children enter school already having displayed immense powers of imagining and expressing [describing what they see or imagine using language, displaying using their bodies, depicting], generalising and specialising (in picking up and using language), and conjecturing and reasoning (detecting patterns in language so as to be able to make up their own sentences to express themselves). Exercising, developing and extending one's powers is a source of pleasure and self-confidence. Failure to use those powers is at best throwing away an opportunity, and at worst, turns students off mathematics and off school.

So as a teacher I am faced with the question, 'Am I stimulating my students to use their powers, or am I trying to do the work for them?'.

(Mason, 2002a, p. 107)

> Becoming aware of your own powers and how you use them is an essential step towards planning lessons so that learners are stimulated to use their own powers.

Mathematical thinking

It is one thing to assert that what we really want is for learners to develop their mathematical thinking; it is quite another to be precise about just what that means. We may feel certain that learners who actively think about their mathematics, who develop mathematical 'habits of mind', who use their natural powers, will also do better on examinations and tests than those who are trained in a few techniques and typical problem types. There is even some evidence in favour of this view (Boaler, 1997; Watson, 2001; Houssart, 2001). But without some clarity about what we mean by mathematical thinking, aims expressed in terms of it are likely to prove as empty as most other general aims.

Mathematics is ... : Charles Saunders Peirce

Charles Saunders Peirce (b. Maryland, 1839–1914) was an influential American scientist, philosopher and logician. He formulated the school of pragmatism which he called *pragmaticism,* to distinguish it from the pragmatism of William James (1842–1910) and Dewey.

> It is difficult to decide between the two definitions of mathematics; the one by its method, that of drawing necessary conclusions; the other by its aim and subject matter, as the study of hypothetical states of things.
>
> (Peirce, 1902, p. 1779)

In fact it was his father, Benjamin Peirce, who in 1870 had first defined mathematics as 'the science of drawing necessary conclusions'. 'Another characteristic of mathematical thought is that it can have no success where it cannot generalize' (ibid., p. 1778).

Later mathematician-philosophers such as Imre Lakatos (1976) and Philip Kitcher (1983) proposed that mathematicians are often empirical, in the sense of detecting patterns on the basis of examples, and refining and altering conjectures and articulations of theorems many times before they settle down.

Mathematics is ... : Caleb Gattegno

> Man's mind is the generator of mathematics. Mathematics is a mental activity. Mathematical structures are mental structures.
>
> (Gattegno, 1981, p. 6)

This is quite a strong position, identifying doing mathematics with being aware of mental functioning. In another book, Gattegno expanded on this:

> [Mathematicians deal] with structures and relationships between structures, rather than with so-called 'mathematical objects'. In other words, mathematicians have become aware that the 'objects' of their science are particular mental constructs to which they apply their mental dynamism in order to make explicit the content involved in them by virtue of the imbedded structures.
>
> (Gattegno, 1963, pp. 39–40)

> My first discovery was that mathematicians are specialists who give themselves to becoming aware of relationships in themselves.
>
> ... The simplest illustration I know is the awareness I have of what I do when I climb steps. Everyone can recognise that the steps are of equal height, that they succeed each other, that they can be climbed up or down from beginning to end and that these are variable. As soon as I extract

these awarenesses, make a note of each of them and invent a shorthand way of referring to them, I can produce condensed virtual expressions of what I actually do in such activities. Such expressions looks strangely like the formulae found in chapters devoted to arithmetic progressions.

(Gattegno, 1983, p. 34)

Mathematics emerges as the expression and formalisation of awareness of awarenesses (such as climbing steps). The idea of making use of learner's experience in this way is also the core of Freudenthal's *didacical phenomenology* approach (see p. 202).

Gattegno suggested how 'mental objects' are formed:

Everyone knows how habits are acquired by repeated drill and increasingly frequent check[s] to make certain that the aim set is achieved. It is the interaction between check and drill that determines whether we continue the exercise or pass on to another activity, as can easily be seen from observation of children playing marbles, hopscotch, or leapfrog or the pianist or the scientist at work. It is in the formation of mental patterns in which perception, action, and representation are intermingled that we find the mental structure. It is this that underlies the symbol and is the basis of our social intercourse. It is this that is a starting point for elaboration into a more developed structure.

(Gattegno, 1963, p. 41)

There are similarities with how other authors describe how mental processes and actions become objects through *reification* (see p. 167).

Mathematical thinking as problem solving: George Polya

Polya was a brilliant mathematician who emigrated to the USA where he contributed to the development of new mathematical ideas. Through his teacher education courses and his books on mathematical thinking, which are full of wisdom and insight, he profoundly influenced mathematics teaching in the USA. By reflecting on how he thought as a way of improving that thinking, he made reflection on and discussion about forms and types of mathematical thinking respectable.

Getting food is usually no problem in modern life. If I get hungry at home, I grab something in the refrigerator, and I go to a coffee shop or some other shop if I am in town. It is a different matter, however, if the refrigerator is empty or I happen to be in town without money; in such a case, getting food becomes a problem. In general, a desire may or may not lead to a problem. If the desire brings to my mind immediately, without any difficulty, some obvious action that is likely to attain the desired object, there is no problem. If, however, no such action occurs to me, there is a problem. Thus, to have a problem means: *to search consciously for some action appropriate to attain a clearly conceived, but not immediately attainable, aim.* To solve the problem means to find such action.

A problem is a 'great' problem if it is very difficult, it is just a 'little' problem if it is just a little difficult. Yet some degree of difficulty belongs to the very notion of a problem: where there is no difficulty, there is no problem.

... the solution of any problem appears to us somehow as finding a way: a way out of a difficulty, a way around an obstacle.

(Polya, 1962, p. 117)

Note the role of *epistemological obstacles* (see p. 303).

Mathematical thinking is the use of natural powers of sense-making applied to ... ; to what? This is the difficulty, since it is hard to specify the content of mathematics without ending up in a circular description: mathematical thinking is applying powers to mathematical topics; mathematical topics arise as the result of thinking mathematically! Polya plumps for problem solving, though it is just as hard to specify what makes a problem mathematical, or what it means to tackle a problem mathematically. The circle won't go away! To break out of such a circle seems to require rather abstruse circumlocutions, much as Humberto Maturana, for example, who uses highly abstract language to try to capture the essence of learning (see p. 70).

What is know-how in mathematics? The ability to solve problems – not merely routine problems but problems requiring some degree of independence, judgment, originality, creativity. Therefore, the first and foremost duty of the high school in teaching mathematics is to emphasize *methodical ... problem solving.*

(Polya, 1962, pp. xi–xii)

Mathematics as problem solving: Paul Halmos

... the mathematician's main reason for existence is to solve problems, and that, therefore, what mathematics *really* consists of is problems and solutions.

(Halmos, 1980, p. 519)

The major part of every meaningful life is the solution of problems; ... It is the duty of all teachers, and of teachers of mathematics in particular, to expose their students to problems much more than to facts.

[...]

One of the hardest parts of problem solving is to ask the right question, and the only way to learn to do so is to practise.

(ibid., pp. 523–4)

> A teacher who is not always thinking about solving problems – ones he does not know the answer to – is psychologically simply not prepared to teach problem solving to his students.
>
> (Halmos, 1985, p. 322)

Mathematical thinking: John Mason, Leone Burton and Kaye Stacey

Leone Burton (b. Australia, 1936–) and Kaye Stacey (b. Australia, 1948–) both studied and taught mathematics, but while Stacey maintains her roots in mathematics, Burton has moved into more general educational issues and how they pertain to mathematics education. In what has proved to be a classic text, Mason, Burton and Stacey put together advice on how to think mathematically through engaging readers in the act of thinking for themselves.

> Three kinds of involvement are required [to think mathematically]: physical, emotional and intellectual.
>
> Probably the single most important lesson to be learned is that being stuck is an honourable state and is an essential part of improving thinking. However, to get the most out of being stuck, it is not enough to think for a few minutes and then read on. Take time to ponder the question, and continue reading only when you are convinced that you have tried all possible alleys. Time taken to ponder the question and to try several approaches is time well spent.
>
> (Mason, Burton and Stacey, 1982, pp. ix–x)

The authors went on to announce five assumptions: that everyone *can* think mathematically, and that mathematical thinking is *provoked* by contradiction, attention and surprise, *supported* by an atmosphere of questioning, challenging and reflecting, and can be improved by *practice with reflection*. Finally, mathematical thinking helps in understanding *yourself* and the world.

> Thinking mathematically is not an end in itself. It is a process by which we increase our understanding of the world and extend our choices. Because it is a way of proceeding, it has widespread application, not only to attacking problems which are mathematical or scientific, but more generally. However, sustaining mathematical thinking requires more than just getting answers to questions, no matter how elegant the solution or how difficult the question. ...
>
> (ibid., p. 154)

Awareness: Caleb Gattegno

One of Gattegno's principal themes was the education of awareness. In awareness he included things that the body does of which the mind is not conscious, envisaging the person as a whole – body, mind and emotions together. He chose to describe subject matter in terms of awareness and how it might be educated.

> As soon as we can shut our eyes and evoke images we can act virtually upon these images to make them do some of the things we want and which are compatible with some of the attributes retained in the images.
> [...]
> ... As soon as we see that because mathematics is of the mind we must concern ourselves with the inner life of our students and, in particular ... with their awareness of the dynamics of the mind, we cast an entirely new light on the subject and on its transformation into life-giving activities which contribute to each of our students' personal evolution and hence a more responsible situating of themselves in the future descending upon us.
>
> (Gattegno, 1983, p. 34–5)

Gattegno had a lot to say about awareness, because for him it was much more than consciousness. It is the basis of all our functioning, conscious and unconscious. To become a teacher, one must become aware *of* relevant awarenesses in oneself in order to be able to prompt learners to educate their own awareness.

> [Teachers need to] make themselves vulnerable to the awareness of awareness, and to mathematization, rather than to the historical content of mathematics. They need to give themselves an opportunity to experience their own creativity, and when they are in contact with it, to turn to their students to give them the opportunity as well.
>
> (Gattegno, 1988, p. 167)

Horizontal and vertical mathematisation: Hans Freudenthal and Adrian Treffers

It is not always easy to distinguish between pure and applied mathematics, since pure mathematics is the result of applying mathematical thinking within mathematics itself. The distinction between concepts and applications has dogged mathematics education for centuries, despite various attempts to reunify them within school (for example, as *real problem solving* or *authentic* mathematics, see p. 108). Theory first and application later has been the practice for centuries (see p. 203). Treffers, a student and colleague of Freudenthal, responded to this by making a distinction between *horizontal* and *vertical* mathematising:

> Horizontal mathematisation leads from the world of *life* to the world of *symbols*. In the world of life one lives, acts (and suffers); in the other

one, symbols are shaped, reshaped, and manipulated, mechanically, comprehendingly, reflectingly; this is vertical mathematisation.

(Freudenthal, 1991, pp. 41–2)

Freudenthal reported that initially he reacted against this distinction, but that over time he came to see that it could be useful, as long as it was not taken as rigid and structural, but rather as partial and flexible. This lead him to extract two principles:

- Choosing learning situations within the learner's current reality, appropriate for horizontal mathematising.
- Offering means and tools for vertical mathematising.

(ibid., p. 56)

Mathematical modelling: Open University

In the 1970s, when modelling was being stressed as an important but overlooked aspect of learning mathematics, The Open University course M100 introduced a seven-phase 'model of modelling' which was taken up in many institutions:

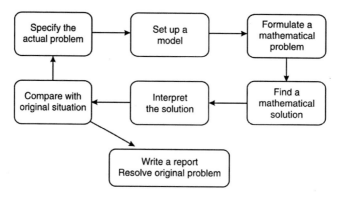

The seven phases of modelling were identified in order to help learners recognise what they were doing, and to provide a structure for use if they got lost. Notice the implicit correspondence between the three columns in the upper part of the figure and *three worlds* (see p. 73). Each of the phases can be elaborated:

- Specifying the actual problem is not as simple as it sounds. Mathematicians like to be told the original problem and situation rather than trying to work with someone else's model.
- Setting up a model is about imagining the situation and stressing only some of the features and factors (keep it simple is a good motto), then locating the quantities and relationships which seem to be central to the problem.

- Formulating a mathematical problem involves moving to the world of symbols and equations.
- Finding a mathematical solution may involve altering the mathematical problem until it becomes solvable, or tractable in some way.
- Interpreting the solution involves interpreting alterations made in the original, and identifying what the symbols represent.
- Comparing with the original situation involves checking to see if the proposed solution offers a satisfactory resolution of the original problem or whether the simplifications have rendered it too rough, in which case the modelling cycle is repeated.
- When a satisfactory or good-enough resolution is reached, a report is written and the original problem resolved.

Although displayed as a cycle, there is often spontaneous to-ing and fro-ing between the various phases, or rather, between the mathematical world and the world of the problem.

Mathematical modelling: John Mason

Mathematical modelling and, indeed, mathematical thinking, give structure to what we perceive, and also to how we perceive:

> ... the act of asking a question already comes from a way of perceiving, and so contains the seeds of its possible resolutions. For example it is well known that when someone acquires a hammer, the world divides itself into nails and non-nails: we perceive the world through the affordances (Greeno *et al.*, 1993) provided by the tools with which we are confident. ...
>
> Modelling is thus a co-emergent activity: the modeller perceives problematicity through the framework and structures of their past experience, the tools which are extensions of their thinking, and their domains of confidence. A model emerges, sometimes extending that expertise, that facility, that perception, that sensitivity, those tools, and sometimes shaping what is perceived as problematic, as it develops.
>
> Once formulated, a model is both frame and picture, both form and content. A particular model involves a way of seeing (the movement from one 'world' to another) as well as what is seen. Once constructed, a model channels thinking through its structure, through its particular stressings and ignorings, as well as illuminating and supporting analysis.
>
> (Mason, 2001, p. 39)

See also Wigner (p. 97).

There are significant issues about presenting models to learners, engaging learners in the act of modelling, and helping them to recognise it when they are doing it.

When a model is presented, there is more than just the model itself: there are choices and assumptions to be made explicit and questioned, there is the issue of whether the model adequately models the original problem, and there is the issue of whether the conclusions drawn are appropriate. Then there are the socio-political questions of who benefits from this particular model being used. Students need to be introduced to all of these aspects of models. But we also present models in order to support students in appreciating how to go about modelling. So each model acts as a case study for students. Or does it? ...

[...]

How does the student detect what is modelling, what is model, and what is mathematics (in which world are they supposed to be operating)? What is process and what is product? What is the student supposed to learn (memorise, learn from, learn about, ...)?

(ibid., pp. 57–8)

There are similarities with the issue of when an example is *exemplary* for learners (see Sierpinska, p. 173).

Modelling and mathematisation: David Wheeler

David Wheeler (b. Wiltshire, 1925–2000) was a teacher and mathematics educator. He was, with Gattegno, one of the founder members of the Association of Teachers of Mathematics and he edited the journal of the association for many years. He then went to Canada and founded the journal *For The Learning Of Mathematics* which is highly respected for its wide range of thoughtful articles.

As already indicated, modelling is usually identified with setting up a mathematical version of a situation in order to resolve some problem. Mathematisation is a more general process of perceiving the world through the lenses of mathematics: seeing relationships, properties and structures. Here Wheeler extols mathematisation.

It is more useful to know how to mathematize than to know a lot of mathematics. Teachers, in particular, would benefit by looking at their task in terms of teaching their students to mathematize rather than teaching them some mathematics.

(Wheeler, 1982, p. 45, quoting a 1974 paper of his)

Wheeler also observes that like speaking, mathematising is hard to catch as it happens.

There are similarities between teaching mathematising and *didactic phenomenology* (see p. 202) in the sense that the teacher constructs situations in which the learner can, perhaps with help and guidance, mathematise. See also *using situations* (p. 249).

To think mathematically is to mathematise situations and apply (mathematical) powers in order to model situations inside and outside of mathematics itself. It means to pose and resolve problems by following chains of necessary deductions, even if you sometimes work empirically in order to locate appropriate conjectures.

Mathematical themes

There are a number of mathematical themes which pervade mathematics and which have been identified by many different thinkers over the centuries. They provide connections between apparently disparate topics, firming up a sense of connection arising because of and through the use of the same powers and similar ways of working in apparently distinct topics.

Doing and undoing, reversing

If someone starts with a number which they do not reveal to you and then performs a sequence of calculations and tells you the answer, can you reconstruct the starting number by using their operations? If the operations can be reversed, that is, undone, then the number can be reconstructed, which is the basis for solving equations. When you can get the answer to a question, it is useful to ask yourself, could you reconstruct the question? For example, $3 \times 4 = 12$, but asking $12 = ? \times ?$ leads to factoring and prime numbers. Finding the remainder on dividing 15 by 7 is 'doing'; finding all those numbers which leave a remainder of 1 on dividing by 7 leads to algebra.

When a 'doing' leads to a particular, an 'undoing' is likely to lead to a collection of particulars. Indeed, many of the insightful developments in mathematics have arisen from people converting a doing-question into an undoing question.

Invariance amidst change

Most mathematical facts are actually statements about something being invariant while something else changes. The sum of the angles of a planar triangle is always 180 degrees (invariant), no matter how the shape of the triangle changes. The product of two odd numbers is always odd, no matter which odd numbers are chosen. Whenever an assertion is encountered, it is worth asking yourself what it is that is permitted to change while leaving a particular invariant unchanged. This question is valuable because attention often is focused on the invariant rather than on the permissible range of change of different features.

A single exercise or problem is a task. Asking yourself what could be changed and still have the same approach or technique would apply opens up *dimensions-of-possible-variation* (see p. 56); asking what sorts of change are possible in any one such dimension opens up range-of-change, leading to the notion of variable and parameter. Together these two ideas transform a set of exercises from a sequence of tasks for learners to work through piecemeal, to a doorway into a domain of generality.

Invariance: Eugene Wigner

Eugene Wigner (b. Hungary, 1902–1995) emigrated to the USA in the 1930s. He was an applied mathematician who confessed to being amazed at how effective mathematics is in modelling the material world (see p. 74 and p. 97).

> ... One ... regularity, discovered by Galileo, is that two rocks, dropped at the same time from the same height, reach the ground at the same time. The laws of nature are concerned with such regularities. Galileo's regularity is a prototype of a large class of regularities. It is a surprising regularity ... .
>
> The first reason that it is surprising is that it is true not only in Pisa, and in Galileo's time, it is true everywhere on the Earth, was always true, and will always be true. This property of the regularity is a recognized invariance property and ... without [these] ... , physics would not be possible. The second surprising feature is that the regularity which we are discussing is independent of so many conditions which could have an effect on it. It is valid no matter whether it rains or not, whether the experiment is carried out in a room or from the Leaning Tower, no matter whether the person who drops the rocks is a man or a woman. It is valid even if the two rocks are dropped, simultaneously and from the same height, by two different people. There are, obviously, innumerable other conditions which are all immaterial from the point of view of the validity of Galileo's regularity. The irrelevancy of so many circumstances which could play a role in the phenomenon observed has also been called an invariance. However, this invariance ... cannot be formulated as a general principle. The exploration of the conditions which do, and which do not, influence a phenomenon is part of the early experimental exploration of a field. It is the skill and ingenuity of the experimenter which show him phenomena which depend on a relatively narrow set of relatively easily realizable and reproducible conditions. ...
>
> (Wigner, 1960 webref)

There are similarities with *dimensions-of-possible-variation* (see p. 56).

Same and different: Colin Banwell, Dick Tahta and Ken Saunders

Banwell, Tahta and Saunders collaborated to produce a rich resource of problematic situations as the starting points for mathematical investigation and exploration, leading to most topics in the curriculum. It has served as inspiration for the many books that have followed, with most of the classic tasks being used traceable back to this collection.

… mathematics has inevitably commenced when it is decided how things are to be treated as the same. Among other issues, this raises the matter of how many different things there are. Equivalence is a choice at our disposal; but when a choice is made, counting must yield a unique answer. Here is the essence of the activity. We are free to choose bounds and may then explore the inexorable implications of our choice. But the activity must include the choice as well as the exploration.

(Banwell, Saunders and Tahta, 1972, p. 67)

Seeking 'same and different' is a potent way to explore invariance (see also p. 127).

Freedom and constraint

Most mathematical problems begin with something (perhaps a number, perhaps a shape) which is indefinite or arbitrary. Constraints are then imposed. With each imposed constraint, there is the question of whether there is sufficient freedom to permit some objects to meet that constraint. Thus, equations and inequalities are examples of constraints imposed upon initial freedom.

Whenever learners are asked to find an answer, they are being asked to construct a mathematical object subject to some constraints. If instead of seeing mathematics as being about the getting of answers, it is regarded as a constructive enterprise, in which techniques are developed to facilitate some constructions, then perhaps more learners would appreciate the essential creativity in mathematics, and be able to experience the pleasure mathematics affords.

Ordering and classifying, stressing and ignoring

Putting things in order, which involves comparing and contrasting, can be seen in the play of very young children, in the organisation of collections of adolescents, and in the structure of mathematics. We succeed as organisms because we can classify, that is, we can discriminate and recognise similarities and differences, which we do by stressing some features and ignoring others. This ability to stress-and-ignore at the same time is the basis for specialising and generalising, for imagining and expressing, and for ordering and classifying.

Extending and contracting meaning

When children first meet numbers, those numbers are whole, counting numbers, and hence positive. Then they meet zero, and negatives, and fractions, and decimals. The word *number* expands with each new encounter.

When we do not know something, we tend to label it. So π labels a particular ratio (circumference of any circle to its diameter: notice the invariance amidst change). We use π to refer to the number even though we know just a few billion of its decimal digits. So we associate properties of a number with a name, even when the name is rather inexplicit. Similarly, $\sqrt{3}$ is a name for something which is positive and squares to 3: it is known only by its properties. Thus we extend the meaning of words and symbols as we learn new properties, or meet new objects which also have the same properties (in the case of numbers).

We also focus meaning. Words used in common speech often have a technical meaning in mathematics which is narrower and more precise. Thus 'He only ate a fraction of the cake' is not a mathematical use of fraction, because this idiom assumes a number between 0 and 1, whereas mathematically a fraction can be the result of dividing any integer by any non-zero integer.

See also Davis and Hersh (1981).

The study of mathematics may be helped by noticing the underlying themes which weave across topics. Recurring themes include Doing and Undoing, Invariance Amidst Change, Freedom and Constraint, Ordering and Classifying, Stressing and Ignoring, Extending and Contracting Meaning.

Mathematical techniques and procedures

Teaching rules or revealing rules: Herbert Spencer

Spencer was an early advocate of using learners' powers. Here he reports on the demise of rote-teaching and the beginnings of getting learners to generalise for themselves.

> Along with rote-teaching, is declining also the nearly-allied teaching by rules. The particulars first, and then the generalizations, is the new method ... which, though 'the reverse of the method usually followed, which consists in giving the pupil the rule first' is yet proved by experience to be the right one. Rule-teaching is now condemned as imparting a merely empirical knowledge – as producing an appearance of understanding without the reality. To give the net product of inquiry without the inquiry that leads to it, is found to be both enervating and inefficient. General truths to be of due and permanent use, must be earned. ... While the rule-taught youth is at sea when beyond his rules, the youth instructed in principles solves a new case as readily as an old one.
>
> (Spencer, 1878, pp. 56–7)

Note the similarities with *training behaviour* and *educating awareness* (see p. 61 and p. 204). See also *rote learning* (p. 152) and *instrumental understanding* (p. 295).

Inductive method: Warren Colburn

Warren Colburn (b. Massachusetts, 1793–1833) was a prolific author of arithmetic and algebra texts in the USA. In 1825 he published an algebra text based upon what came to be called 'the inductive method of instruction', inspired by Herbert Spencer's ideas. The term *inductive* came to refer to learners detecting and expressing similarities and differences for themselves, and so reaching and expressing their own generalities. This, Colburn said, was in contrast to a *deductive* approach in which definitions, rules and principles were to be committed to memory, followed by a few illustrative examples, and then applied to exercises.

The inductive approach began a movement to displace '*recitation* from memory' which had characterised much of mathematics learning for many centuries (see p. 37). Instead, learners were exposed, using mental and then slate-based exercises, to simple cases which built up to more complex cases. Following principles adumbrated by Pestalozzi (see p. 39), Colburn tried to engage the learner explicitly in making generalisations.

> ... The manner of solving the examples in each section is particularly explained. All the most difficult of the practical examples are solved in such a manner, as to show the principles by which they were performed. Care has been taken to select examples for solution, that will explain those which are not solved. Many remarks with regard to the manner of illustrating the principles to pupils, are inserted in their proper places.
> [...]
> The reasoning used in performing these small examples is precisely the same as that used upon large ones. And when any one finds a difficulty in solving a question, he will remove it much sooner and much more effectively, by taking a very small example of the same kind, and observing how he does it, than by [resorting] to a rule.
>
> Colburn, 1863, pp. 109–10

Note the emphasis on observing yourself.

See also *practice makes perfect* (p. 176) and *discovery* learning (p. 224). For examples to be useful for induction they need to be seen as *exemplary* (see p. 173). Later texts merged the deductive and the inductive, suggesting that a varied diet might be more effective. There may be no 'best' mixture of methods.

Rote learning is usually contrasted with understanding, but see p. 295. Teachers might teach deductively or inductively: teaching rules first and applications later, or offering examples from which learners use their own powers with guidance. A mixed approach might be thought most likely to benefit a variety of learners.

Mathematical topics

Topics are specified by the curriculum, usually according to what will ultimately be examined. Under this heading we probe beneath the surface and
look for coherences within topics, and ways of thinking about topics which
contribute to *psychologising the subject matter* (see p. 45 and p. 203).

First some questions:

- What is to be taught to whom? What is the nature of the difference
  between what they know and expect and what they want to know? What
  difficulties and changes in meaning are likely to be required? What ways
  of working are familiar?
- When and under what condition (time of day, time of year etc.; energy
  levels of students, available technology, ...) is the teaching to take
  place?
- How (in what modes of interaction, in what sized groups, etc.)?
- In what context (one-off; ongoing class or group; for examination preparation; for using powers; for sharpening techniques, ...)?

Furthermore,

- Why might students choose to be taught? (Socio-institutional pressure
  and requirements; necessity to master tools, desire to understand,
  assessment driven; who benefits from learners being taught this topic?)
- What actions (shifts of attention, shifts of vocabulary, shifts of awareness) are required? What actions can be performed on what confidently
  manipulable objects?
- What activities would be likely to provoke requisite shifts? What specific
  gambits/devices might serve the purposes?
- What potentialities are present (for each task, each example, each act of
  teaching)? What is the least and the most that are likely to happen; what
  is fed by, and what feeds the functioning of each act? What is present in
  the group?
- What modes of interaction are appropriate for the particular situation
  (students, content, teacher, environment, goals, topic and concept
  image)?
- What transformations are sought and how will they come about?

Concepts

Mathematical topics draw upon concepts which have proved fruitful for
stating and resolving problems in the past. It is however very difficult to be
precise about just what a concept is!

Concepts: Hans Freudenthal

Freudenthal used an invitation to visit China to give a series of lectures as an opportunity to review a lifetime of investigation into the teaching and learning of mathematics. Here he tackles the notion of *concept*, which so readily slips into use in educational discussions.

> Cognition does not start with concepts, but the other way around: concepts are the *result* of cognitive processes. Mathematics allows explicit definitions at an earlier stage than any other field of knowledge. For instance, 'odd' and 'even' can be defined on the basis of 'whole number'. ... But what about 'whole number'? It is generated by a process, that of counting, rather than by an explicit definition, only to become a matter of common sense rather than a concept.
>   ... it has become clear to increasingly more people that, where non-mathematicians are concerned, teaching the concept of X is not the appropriate way to teach X. Cautious researchers now admit that concepts are preceded by something less formal, by initiations, preconcepts, or whatever they call it, which in the long run means that the proper goal is still that of teaching concepts. In my view, the primordial and – in most cases for most people – the final goal of teaching and learning is *mental objects*. I particularly like this term because it can be extrapolated to a term that describes how these objects are handled, namely by *mental operations*.
>
> (Freudenthal, 1991, pp. 18–19)

Conceptual fields: Gerard Vergnaud

Gerard Vergnaud (b. France, 1933–) was a student of Piaget and is a leading figure internationally in research in psychology, with special attention to mathematics. He is director of research of the National French Research Institute.

> Piaget has demonstrated that knowledge and intelligence develop over a long period of time, but he has done this by analyzing children's development in terms of general capacities of intelligence, mainly logical, without paying enough attention to specific contents of knowledge. It is the need to understand better the acquisition and development of specific knowledge and skills, in relation to situations and problems, that has led me to introduce the framework of conceptual fields. A *conceptual field* is a set of problems ... for the treatment of which concepts, procedures, and representations of different but narrowly interconnected types are necessary.
>
> (Vergnaud, 1983, p. 127)

By delineating conceptual fields it is possible both to focus attention on a richly interconnected field of experience, and at the same time to become aware of significant differences between the thinking required in different conceptual fields. Thus multiplication is not just repeated addition; indeed, seeing multiplication simply as repeated addition may prevent learners from encountering the distinctive thinking required in the conceptual field of multiplicative structures. See Vergnaud (1982) for additive structures, and Vergnaud (1983) for multiplicative structures.

Concept image: David Tall and Shlomo Vinner

David Tall (b. Northamptonshire, 1941–) is a mathematician-turned-educator who has led the study of advanced mathematical thinking as well as having undertaken careful study of mathematics learning in secondary schools. Shlomo Vinner (b. Jerusalem, 1936–) is also a mathematician-educator, and together they have pursued the study of mathematics education at tertiary level.

What does it mean to 'have a concept'? Tall and Vinner observed that when a technical term is used, various images and propensities come to mind, giving access to ways of thinking and to specific techniques which a moment before had not been present. The totality of images and competences which are associated with a term form the *concept image* of that term.

> Many concepts which we use happily are not formally defined at all, we learn to recognise them by experience and usage in appropriate contexts. Later these concepts may be refined in their meaning and interpreted with increasing subtlety with or without the luxury of a precise definition. Usually in this process the concept is given a symbol or name which enables it to be communicated and aids in its mental manipulation. But the total cognitive structure which colours the meaning of the concept is far greater than the evocation of a single symbol. It is more than any mental picture, be it pictorial, symbolic or otherwise. During the mental processes of recalling and manipulating a concept, many associated processes are brought into play, consciously and unconsciously affecting the meaning and usage.
>
> We shall use the term *concept image* to describe the total cognitive structure that is associated with the concept, which includes all the mental pictures and associated properties and processes. It is built up over the years through experiences of all kinds, changing as the individual meets new stimuli and matures.
>
> For instance the concept of subtraction is usually first met as a process involving positive whole numbers. At this stage children may observe that subtraction of a number always *reduces* the answer. For such a child this observation is part of his concept image and may cause problems later on should subtraction of negative numbers be encountered. For this reason all mental attributes associated with a concept, whether they be conscious or unconscious, should be included in the concept image; they may contain the seeds of future conflict.
>
> (Tall and Vinner, 1981)

Concept images can be the source of disturbances when incompatible aspects are juxtaposed:

> We shall call the portion of the concept image which is activated at a particular time the *evoked concept image*. At different times, seemingly conflicting images may be evoked. Only when conflicting aspects are evoked *simultaneously* need there be any actual sense of conflict or confusion. Children doing mathematics often use different processes according to the context, making different errors depending on the specific problem under consideration. For instance adding $\frac{1}{2} + \frac{1}{4}$ may be performed correctly but when confronted by $\frac{1}{2} + \frac{1}{3}$ an erroneous method may be used. Such a child need see no conflict in the different methods, he simply utilises the method he considers appropriate on each occasion.
>
> The definition of a concept (if it has one) is quite a different matter. We shall regard the *concept definition* to be a form of words used to specify that concept. It may be learnt by an individual in a rote fashion or more meaningfully learnt and related to a greater or lesser degree to the concept as a whole. It may also be a personal reconstruction by the student of a definition. It is then the form of words that the student uses for his own explanation of his (evoked) concept image. Whether the concept definition is given to him or constructed by himself, he may vary it from time to time. In this way a *personal* concept definition can differ from a *formal* concept definition, the latter being a concept definition which is accepted by the mathematical community at large.
>
> For each individual a concept definition generates its own concept image (which might, in a flight of fancy be called the *concept definition image*). This is, of course, part of the concept image. In some individuals it may be empty, or virtually non-existent. In others it may, or may not, be coherently related to other parts of the concept image.
>
> (ibid.)

Image schemata: Willi Dörfler

Dörfler drew attention to an important constructivist awareness concerning the role of drawings as carriers of meaning:

> ... an image schemata ... cannot be shared with anybody else, only the carriers can be communicated and in some cases the pertinent cognitive manipulations have a corresponding material way of manipulating the carrier. The image schema is just the specific way of viewing, interpreting, using, transforming, etc., the carrier. Therefore it is absolutely misleading to regard the concrete carriers to 'represent' the respective concept. ... much more appropriate to say that the individuals ... *present the concept to themselves*, make the concept present, cognitively and mentally.
>
> (Dörfler, 1991, p. 21)

In other words, teaching is not a matter of constructing and presenting learners with *representations* of ideas or ideals, but rather of bringing into their presence connections and images which then contribute to learners' construction of understanding (see also *reification*, p. 167).

Topic structure

Didactic phenomenology: Hans Freudenthal

Freudenthal's central focus was the location and elaboration of phenomena which would, on the one hand, be familiar to learners at appropriate ages and, on the other hand, could lead to the exposure, elaboration, and formalisation of the mathematical ideas commonly found in school mathematics. He analysed deeply the structure of individual mathematical topics from the point of view of the learner. He sought especially the prior experiences which the topic formalises, in order to construct tasks which would bring the topic to the attention of learners, and from which they could, with guidance and support, reconstruct the essential ideas themselves. His most famous work captures this in its title, *Didactical Phenomenology*, relating as it does to teaching based on learners' prior experiences (Freudenthal, 1983).

Freudenthal first introduced what he calls *inversion* and *conversion* which he identified as 'mathematical virtues', as background to and justification for his approach. Note the similarities with *transposition didactique* (see p. 83).

> No mathematical idea has ever been published in the way it was discovered. Techniques have been developed and are used, if a problem has been solved, to turn the solution procedure upside down, or if it is a larger complex of statements and theories, to turn definitions into propositions, and propositions into definitions, the hot invention into icy beauty. This then if it has affected teaching matter, is the *didactical* inversion ... [which may not be helpful] ... one should recognise that the young learner is entitled to recapitulate in a fashion the learning process of mankind. Not in the trivial abridged version, but equally we cannot require the new generation to start just at the point where their predecessors left off.
>
> Our mathematical concepts, structures, ideas have been invented as tools to organise the phenomena of the physical, social and mental world. *Phenomenology* of a mathematical concept, structure or idea means describing it in its relation to the phenomena for which it was created, and to which it has been extended in the learning process of mankind, ... it is *didactical phenomenology*, a way to show the teacher the places where the learner might step into the learning process of mankind.
>
> (Freudenthal, 1983, p. ix)

Note the similarities with Gattegno's use of *awareness* (p. 61), and with the SoaT framework (see p. 203). Having distinguished between mental objects and concepts (see p. 60), Freudenthal saw concepts as arising from the manipulation of mental objects. Freudenthal refers to Bruner's three forms of representation (see p. 260). Then he criticises Dienes' *multiple embodiments* (see p. 249).

> The fact that manipulating mental objects precedes making concepts explicit seems to me more important than the division of representations into enactive, ikonic and symbolic. In each particular case one should try to establish criteria that ought to be fulfilled if an object is to be considered as mentally constituted. ...
>
> In opposition to concept attainment by concrete embodiments I have placed the constitution of mental objects based on phenomenology. In the first approach the concretisations have a transitory significance. Cake dividing may be forgotten as soon as the learner masters the fractions algorithmically. In contradistinction to this approach, the material that serves to mentally constitute fractions has a lasting and definitive value. 'First concepts and applications afterwards' as it happens in the approach of concept attainment is a strategy that is virtually inverted in the approach by constitution of mental objects.
>
> (ibid., p. 33)

Freudenthal advocated starting with situations which are or can become 'real' to learners through their experience (see *realistic mathematics education*, p. 110). He himself linked his notion of mental objects to Fischbein's *intuitions* (see p. 63), saying that he prefered not to use Fischbein's term because of other associations with it.

Structure-of-a-topic: The Open University

In seeking to provide a structure which would help teachers gain an overview of a topic or concept, members of the Centre for Mathematics Education at The Open University devised a three-thread or three-axis structure based on interweaving the traditional aspects of the psyche: enaction or behaviour, affect and emotion, cognition and awareness. It arose through reflection on their own *concept images* juxtaposed with the three aspects of the *psyche* (see p. 32) and informed by Gattegno's memorable claim: 'Only awareness is educable'.

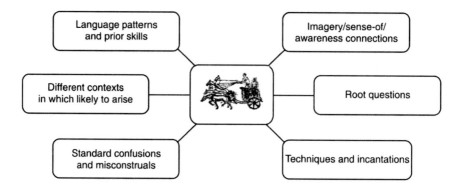

The horizontal thread encompasses the motivational–emotional. This thread stresses both the contexts in which the idea or topic originally arose, (even if it is a slightly fabricated or simplified story for students to understand), and in which it has been known to appear. It encompasses the virtue of surprising students, whether by challenging a preconception, or indicating an unexpected result. One of the roles of this overall framework is to support locating the surprise which helped to turn this topic from an ordinary result of perhaps passing interest into an actual topic. ...

The behavioural thread stresses the terms which students may already know or use in a less formal manner, language patterns (terms, phrases, clauses), both those which the students already use but less precisely, and those which are the marks of competence and understanding. It includes also specific manipulative techniques and any 'inner incantations' which a relative expert may employ when employing those techniques.

The awareness thread includes mental images, associations and connections which the teacher would like the students to develop, transitions from process to object which are entailed by or employed in the topic or idea, as well as standard confusions or misconceptions which students are likely to form because others have done so in the past. This may include historical analysis of obstacles encountered during the precising of the topic or idea.

(Bachelard, 1938)

The image of interweaving the threads is intended to emphasise the importance of mutual interaction and support between all three aspects. The framework can be summarised by the expressions 'harnessing emotion', 'training behaviour', and 'educating awareness', drawing on the central image of the psyche as analogous to a chariot (see p. 33). When one or more of awareness, behaviour, and emotion is pushed to the background, student experience is impoverished, and learning made more difficult.

This framework is based on the image of a chariot and brings together many of the ideas presented in previous chapters concerning *three worlds* (see p. 73), *disturbance* and *surprise* (see p. 55, p. 101 and p. 161), *concept image* (see p. 200), three aspects of the *psyche* (see p. 32), *motivation* (see p. 99), *obstacles* (see p. 303) and *awareness* (see p. 61 and 161), among others.

The *Structure-of-a-topic* framework was originally described in a series of booklets under the title of *Preparing To Teach a Topic* (Griffin and Gates, 1989; see also Mason, 2002).

Developing thinking: Floyd et al.

In one of the courses prepared by the Centre for Mathematics Education at the Open University in the 1980s, attention was drawn to the many different language patterns (and associated perspectives) which accompany a single topic and to the ensuing abstraction. The next extract starts with the language patterns for subtraction.

> *Surface understanding*: difference between; more than, less than; take away; counting on/back; it's the reverse of addition.
>
> *Deep understanding*: subtraction is the root, common to all.
>
> Within each aspect of subtraction in turn, when children begin to identify the one thing that all the activities have in common, and in spite of variations in equipment or the game being played, they are beginning to abstract the particular subtraction aspect under consideration. When they do the same thing across all the activities used in developing each and every aspect of subtraction, they are distilling the very essence of the subtraction process itself. Only then can they be said to have developed a sense of subtraction.
>
> Implicit in all the foregoing is the view that, by structuring children's learning experiences and by the skilful use of open-ended, self-organizing questions, they can be guided to the point where they can and do distil the essence of subtraction for themselves. If they don't ask the next question of themselves, they can be confronted with it: What do all these activities have in common?
>
> (Floyd *et al.*, 1982, pp. 15–16)

The children might need further prompting, but it is important that the child still does the thinking.

> The technique of juxtaposing a lot of specific cases like this makes it easier for the learner to pull out the sameness. This is what [is meant] by 'consciously teaching' a sense of subtraction. The fact that in all but one case we started with the same numbers, 7 and 2, and produced the same answer, 5, indicates that the same process may be going on each time. It is that process that we call *subtraction*. The one odd example is

explained by the insight that it is possible to find the answer to subtraction sum by performing a related addition.

Generalizing from a lot of special cases is a central part of thinking mathematically. By confronting children with these open questions and not telling them what the sameness is you let them do the abstracting. If you do this many times as part of a basic approach to teaching mathematical concepts, you'll find the children begin to think in this way for themselves. That is, they begin to *develop mathematical thinking*.

(ibid., p. 16)

There are similarities with *same and different* (see p. 128 and p. 194).

The language of concepts may distance us from more important mental objects; concepts cluster around conceptual-fields; words denoting concepts evoke concept images.

The *Structure-of-a-topic* framework incorporates and elaborates the notion of concept image and provides a structure to inform the preparation of lessons concerning any topic. The framework provides a collection of questions to use to interrogate the essence of a topic, to assist in *psychologising the subject matter* as Dewey would put it.

What learners learn

Learners are given tasks so that they will encounter and make sense of topics (including typical problems and techniques for solving them). So what do learners actually learn from the tasks they are set? Not always quite what the teacher expects!

Learners do not always learn what is taught!: Margaret Brown and Brenda Denvir

Denvir and Brown studied changes in what low-attaining learners seemed to learn as the result of being taught a particular topic. They concluded that, in the short term, many learners actually seem to improve performance on a variety of tasks, not always those connected with what was taught. Over the longer term, performance improved not only in connection with what was taught, but also on other apparently unrelated items. This suggests that learning is a complex process which may not be enhanced by narrow teaching-and-testing, and certainly not usefully judged in this way.

1　Children must be active, both in interacting with the physical world and in reflecting on these interactions.
2　Ideas and materials presented must be related to what children already know, both to the types of reasoning available … and to their

previous experiences ... in order to achieve 'meaningful learning' (Ausubel, 1978) and 'relational understanding' (Skemp, 1976).

3   In order to achieve integration of skills whereby new skills are developed, there will need to be repetition of the mental process involved in appropriate tasks.

4   In order to acquire mathematical concepts, children will need it, as Dienes (1960) suggested, a variety of examples of those concepts in different mathematical forms, different contexts and, possibly, in the different modes.

5   It is likely that as Bryant (1982) and Lawler (1981) suggest, children learn when different intellectual strategies turn out to produce the same result, especially if, in Lawler's words 'none was anticipated'.

(Denvir and Brown, 1986a, p. 144)

The study involved an analysis of mathematical and conceptual links between ideas, displayed as a hierarchical network.

... the amount of progress made may be related to differences in response during the teaching programme.

1   This work supports the view that, in order to learn, the child needs to engage with the ideas in a manner and at a level which is meaningful. Such commitment can be encouraged but cannot be imposed by the teacher.

2   It appeared that whilst abler children may perceive relationships which are not made explicit, the low attainer may need to engage in both practical activities and discussion which explicitly draw attention to such relationships.

3   The hierarchical framework can describe children's present knowledge and suggest which further skills they are most likely to acquire and thereby inform the design of teaching activities. However it cannot predict which skills or how many skills each child will acquire, so the teaching should not be too prescriptive or rigid in its assumptions about what may be learned.

4   Children were not relaxed in the one-to-one teaching sessions. Whilst their attention needs to be focused on the mathematics, their thoughts about it need to be spontaneous.

... [as a result] there were two major changes:

1   In order to promote discussion and to limit children's self-consciousness, [the researchers] decided that pupils would be taught in a group instead of individually. This would also have the advantage of being more readily transferred to normal classroom practice.

2   Children would be given general number activities which embodied concepts which they had already grasped as well as concepts which

they might acquire. Where appropriate, new skills or concepts would be suggested but there would be a less specific intention to teach particular points.

(ibid., pp. 156–7)

... the children did not always learn precisely what they were taught so attempts to match exactly the task to the child may not always have the expected outcome. The effectiveness of group teaching depended on activities being at a suitable level for all the children.

(ibid., p. 163)

Learners pick up teacher attitudes towards mathematics, and either assimilate them, or react against them. They also pick up messages about what is required to minimise hassle and get through lessons. Some learners are motivated to work out what they have to do to succeed or to have an 'easy life'. (Compare this with the *hidden curriculum*, p. 104.)

Misunderstandings

Learners inevitably make mistakes. They get hold of one aspect of an idea and assume they have got it all or sometimes they get the wrong end of the stick entirely. But teachers can learn from learners' mistakes, just as learners can (see also Balacheff, p. 252).

Mistakes: Alain Bouvier

Bouvier investigated the question of what to do about learners' mistakes.

Students' mistakes bother us. This assertion has become a sort of leit-motif at many meetings of mathematics teachers. Why is this? Do we see in students' *mistakes* the sign of *our* failure?

The same mistakes appear very frequently, persisting across classes, resisting 'correction' week after week, as if there were certain 'invariants', as if our teaching where unwittingly teaching mistakes. What is going on here? Why do some kinds of learning, like learning our mother tongue, seem to be successful on a grand scale, while the learning of mathematics is much less successful in spite of many hours of teaching spread over many years?

Let us take a simple example, the calculation of 2^3. Among the possible responses, two are common: $2^3 = 6$ and $2^3 = 5$. In many cases we have only to ask a student who has written one of these, 'Are you sure?' or 'Why?', for him to change his response immediately to the expected answer.

(Bouvier, 1987, p. 17)

There are similarities with *reversal* (see p. 178).

Some teachers may say that the student made a careless mistake; but, especially since Freud, we know that the smallest 'slip of the tongue' has significance. Moreover, although we may meet $2^3 = 6$ or $2^3 = 5$, we never seem to meet $2^3 = 37$ or $2^3 = 100$ [or $2^3 = 2000$?]. *Mistakes are not the result of chance.* They show that the student has used a particular logic, though not the appropriate one.

Others may say that the student 'confused' 2^3 with $2 \times 3 = 6$. Such explanations explain nothing! Do you know any child who would ... confuse two drawings [a house and a boat] ... ?

(ibid., p. 17)

Bouvier went on to suggest that there was a need to study learners' conceptions (*concept images*, see p. 200), and that to use these effectively the teachers need to study their own concept images.

Mistakes: Caleb Gattegno

Gattegno was adamant that learners' mistakes are the responsibility of the teacher, and a vital source of stimulation and information for teachers.

Though obviously we ultimately come to the point at which the mistakes must be corrected and the possibility of their recurrence eliminated, I would suggest that we should do well to curb our tendency to correct, and develop the habit of incorporating into our lessons the observations that we cannot fail to make in marking homework or in using an oral approach with our classes.

It is man's privilege to make mistakes; only through experience, experience that is often painful, does man learn and acquire some degree of wisdom. In the teaching of mathematics, the opportunity for gaining true understanding through experience is too often reduced to the minimum. There is always someone who knows, who can produce the right answer, which is imposed upon those who cannot. But how often must the teacher make the same correction, and how many children reach the end of their school career under the impression that only their more fortunate fellows who are 'mathematical' can hope to avoid the mistakes which to them are inevitable?

(Gattegno, 1963, pp. 23–4)

Note parallels with *learning from experience* (see p. 263). The *Structure-of-a-topic* framework (see p. 203) follows Gattegno in suggesting collecting learner mistakes and conceptions with each topic in preparation for future planning.

As an example, the comprehensive study undertaken in the UK in the 1980s, under the heading of CSMS (Concepts in Secondary Mathematics and Science, Hart *et al.*, 1981) started with a test administered to hundreds of secondary students. Their errors were often so interesting that follow-up interviews were conducted, revealing all sorts of clever conjectures that learners make, and curious conclusions that they come to in their attempts to make sense of what they (think they) heard or saw in lessons.

Bugs: Kurt van Lehn

Van Lehn, with his supervisor, John Seeley Brown, adopted a computer-based perspective when investigating children's errors in subtraction. Human beings do not usually 'crash' when a problem arises, rather they work around it. Van Lehn and Seeley Brown explored the possibility that learners pieced together fragments of procedures picked up at different times and in different situations. By classifying such sub-procedural fragments they were able to account for about 60 per cent of children's performances on subtraction problems. The key to their approach is that children's errors are far from wilful. Rather the errors are due to attempts to use fragments of procedures partly remembered.

> The procedure-following assumption: During test-taking situations, students solve arithmetic problems by following a procedure (or trying to) rather than by searching for a sequence of operators to transform the problem's initial state into a final, desired state.
>
> To put it another way, the knowledge that students carry into the test-taking situation (or any other situation where an expert is not readily available) consists of a procedure (or plan or search control knowledge) and perhaps some weak specifications of the syntax of the final state (for example, how long the answer should be). When their procedure fails to uniquely specify what to do next (that is, they reach an impasse), then it would be irrational of them to abandon their procedure and rely exclusively on their final state description because, in the case of subtraction, that final state description is very weak. Thus even if search control knowledge fails, then students probably do not search in the traditional sense of finding operations to achieve a known final state. Rather they perform a search of a different kind, which seeks an expedient way to overcome the impasse and return control to the procedure/search control knowledge. Thus the motive behind the students' activity is not so much to achieve a final state, because they do not have a good specification of what that is. Rather their motive is to follow a procedure as closely as possible.
>
> (van Lehn, 1990, pp. 36–7)

Students do not have knowledge of the design ... of mathematical calculation procedures. Their knowledge consists only of the procedure itself.

(ibid., p. 40)

Van Lehn suggested four kinds of impasse:

- *Decision impasses*: the procedure calls for a decision which cannot currently be made. The procedure has to be suspended in order to resolve the impasse
- *Reference impasses*: lack of unique identity of an object being referred to.
- *Primitive impasses*: descriptions of procedures always have primitive acts. They are mentioned but not described by the procedure. It is assumed that one already knows how to carry out pursuant primitive actions. If a production cannot be performed, then the impasse is classified as a primitive failure.
- *Critic impasses*: a critic is triggered when the procedure is about to do something that is known to be wrong. For instance, one possible critic for subtraction is that all the digits in the subtrahend and the minuend must be used at some time during the course of problem solving. If the procedure tries to finish before using all the digits, the critic triggers, and an impasse occurs. (Based on van Lehn, 1990, p. 41.)

What happens when an impasse is encountered?

> The *impasse-repair assumption*: when people reach an impasse while executing a procedure, they treat the impasse as a problem, solve it, and continue executing the procedure. The solution to an impasse is called a *repair*. ...
>
> (van Lehn, 1990, p. 42)

> The *common-knowledge assumption*: repair strategies are task-general methods, most of which are familiar to most subjects.
>
> (ibid., p. 43)

> The *impasse-repair independence assumption*: subject strategies for selecting repair strategies at impasses are so variable that aggregate selection data can be approximated by random choices that are independent of the type of impasse and the surrounding situation.
>
> (ibid., p. 53)

> The *patches assumption:* subjects knowledge of a procedure may include patches [repairs].
>
> (ibid., p. 58)

These assumptions were the subject of van Lehn's inquiry. He and Brown were able to account for some 60 per cent of learner subtraction errors in terms of compound procedures assembled from fragments of taught procedures.

Learning from mistakes and misconceptions: Pearla Nesher

Pearla Nesher (b. Israel, 1930–) is a psychologist with particular interests in learning. She is a leading researcher in mathematics education in Israel. Here she considers the claim 'we learn from our mistakes'.

> We hold many beliefs that we are unaware of and which are part of our habits, yet once such a belief clashes with some counter-evidence or contradictory arguments, it becomes the focus of our attention and inquiry.
> [...]
> I found it very refreshing when visiting a second grade class to hear the following unusual dialogue:
> Ronit: (second grader with tears in her eyes): 'I did it wrong' (referring to her geometrical drawings). 'Never mind', said the teacher, 'what did we say about making mistakes?'. Ronit (without hesitation) answered: 'We learn from our mistakes'. 'So', added the teacher, 'don't cry and don't be sad, because we learn from our mistakes'.
> The phrase 'we learn from mistakes' was repeated over and over. The atmosphere in the classroom was pleasant and the use of this phrase was the way the children admitted making errors on a given task. At this point I became curious and anxious to know what children really did learn from their mistakes. ... The exercises consisted of a given shape and given axis of reflection ... ; the children first had to hypothesize (or guess) and draw the reflected figure in the place where they thought it would fall, and then to fold the paper along the reflection axis and by puncturing the original figure with a pin to see whether their drawing was right or wrong.
> [...]
> ... what did the children really learn from their mistakes? When each child who made an error was asked to explain to me what was learned from his or her mistake I could not elicit a clear answer. Instead the children repeated again and again that one learns from mistakes in a way that started to sound suspiciously like a parroting of the teacher's phrase. At this point it became clear to me that the teacher tolerated errors, but did not use them as a feedback mechanism for real learning on the basis of actual performance.
>
> (Nesher, 1987, p. 34)

Misconceptions can become a source for learner errors:

> ... the notion of misconception denotes a line of thinking that causes a series of errors all resulting from an incorrect underlying premise, rather than sporadic, unconnected and non-systematic errors. It is not always easy to follow the child's line of thinking and reveal how systematic and

consistent it is. Most studies, therefore, report on classification of errors [and difficulty], though this does not explain their source and therefore cannot be treated systematically. Or, when dealt with, it is on the basis of a mere surface-structure analysis of errors ... . When an erroneous principle is detected at [a] deeper level it can explain not a single, but a whole cluster, of errors. We tend to call such an erroneous guiding rule a *misconception*.

[...]

... misconceptions are hard to detect. This is because on some occasions the mistaken rule is disguised by a 'correct' answer. That is, the student may get the 'right' answer for the wrong reasons ... .

(ibid., pp. 35–6)

The language of misconceptions has never settled comfortably beside a view of learners as making the best sense they can of their experience. Misconceptions can only be so labelled by someone who has different, perhaps more socially accepted, conceptions or conceptions more consistent with other conceptions. (See also *diagnostic teaching*, p. 233.)

Errors are part of learning, indeed, discerning conflict between expectation and experience or between conjecture and evidence is a principal stimulus to learning (see *disturbance*, p. 55, and *conjecturing*, p. 139). Attending to the slips and conjectures made by learners reveals a good deal about their sense-making processes. Furthermore, common errors and misconceptions can serve as the basis for useful tasks (see *conflict-discussions*, p. 234).

Section 2

Guiding and directing learning

The previous section described learning as a process in which learners are themselves active. What then is the role of the teacher? There are many different teacher actions: proposing tasks; asking questions; telling learners things they need to know; initiating discussion; commenting on work; evaluating; urging learners to practice in order to automate techniques. All of these actions are, of course, dedicated to stimulating and prompting learners to take initiative, and to become mathematically active. There is a multitude of additional teacher actions involving discipline and institutional practices such as homework setting and counselling, as well as preparation and record keeping, which are beyond the scope of this book. The extracts chosen concentrate on the choice and structure of mathematical tasks, and on what possibilities they afford for pedagogical interaction between teacher and learner.

In proposing a mathematical task, teachers have a sense of what they want or expect the pupils to do with it and get from it. They are aware of what aspects they intend to stress, and where it fits into the work of the day, term, year, as well as into any legislated description such as a national curriculum. What makes one teacher stress one aspect and a second stress another? How do pupils work out what is expected of them?

This section looks at the heart of teaching, specifically the subtle and not so subtle interactions with learners which contribute so much to their experience and yet which are so hard to analyse or research effectively. What factors influence which learners, and in what ways? As Freudenthal said, 'If a learning process is to be observed, the moments that count are its discontinuities, the jumps in the learning process' (Freudenthal, 1978, p. 78). What then can the teacher do? The extracts provide a number of different constructs for addressing these questions.

8   Teachers' roles

Introduction

Teaching is a highly complex activity, a fact not always appreciated by those who look at it from a distance. The first problem a teacher has is to surmount the negativity that surrounds teaching. Teachers and 'current teaching methods' are always the focus of complaint when an educational crisis surfaces. As early as 1928, Philip Ballard observed that:

> Rarely is a teacher satisfied with the arithmetic of his class. He is not allowed to be. Somebody always has something to say about it – generally something unpleasant. If it is not a colleague, it is probably an inspector; if it is neither of these, it is a parent or an employer. … What the teacher has to do is to grow a skin thin enough to let him know when he is hit, but thick enough to protect him from serious wounds. …
>
> (Ballard, 1928, p. ix)

Positioning

Complexity of teaching: Magdalene Lampert

Lampert studied her own teaching in fine detail over a full year with the aim of exposing the highly problematic nature of teaching.

> By taking a close look at the actions of a single teacher, teaching a single subject to a whole class over an entire academic year, I attempt to identify the problems that must be addressed in the work of teaching. Considering the nature of a teacher's actions as she addresses these problems, I try to explain what it is that is so hard about the work of teaching and what we might mean when we call this practice 'complex'. The single teacher I study here is myself. …
>
> Teachers face some students who do not want to learn what they want to teach, some who already know it, or think they do, and some who are poorly prepared to study what is taught. They must figure out how to

teach each student, while working with a class of students who are all different from one another. They have a limited amount of time to teach what needs to be taught, and they are interrupted often.

(Lampert, 2001, p. 1)

One reason why teachers are so often criticised is that they form the interface between society and young people; they are the agents through which society exercises control and direction over the coming generation. Consequently, society's ills are reflected sharply in the classroom. However, classrooms are thought to be where young people are most influenced; although that influence may be significant, it is often subtle and hard to predict.

Positioning: Rom Harré

Harré (b. New Zealand, 1927–) has had a varied career as a historian of science and a sociologist, as well as working in artificial intelligence. His books, no matter what the subject, are influential standards. As a sociologist, Harré with his colleague Luk van Langenhove (Harré and Langenhove, 1992; 1999) introduced and promoted the language of *positioning* to replace the language of *roles*: people are *positioned* by what other people say and do. You can be positioned as the 'one who knows', or as the 'one who never knows', as the 'silent one' or as the 'group clown', sometimes wittingly, and sometimes unwittingly, all as the result of group interaction. Sometimes positioning is temporary, but sometimes it is robust against change. Usually people do not realise how they are being positioned: their actions and thinking adjust to the roles and perspectives. Nor is it all one-way. Groups of people position individuals in the group, but the positioning of self and others evolves through the willing and unwilling responses of those individuals within the group.

Adolescents and children in institutions called schools immediately position the teacher as authority and warder: source and enemy. Learners are positioned as novices in general, and especially as low or high achievers, as 'good at this but not at that', as deficient in some ways and having strengths in others, and so on. How parents and teachers perceive individual learners and groups of learners exerts tremendous influence on those learners. Sometimes they react by striking out, often in unexpected and even unconnected ways; sometimes they go along with the positioning.

Positioning: Derek Edwards and Neil Mercer

Edwards and Mercer (see p. 97) have studied the language used between learners and between teachers and learners, trying to see how and under what circumstances learners and teachers position each other in classroom interactions.

It is largely within the teacher–pupil discourse through which the lesson is conducted that whatever understandings are eventually created are in the first place shaped, interpreted, made salient or peripheral, reinterpreted, and so on. And it is a process that remains essentially dominated by the teacher's own aims and expectations ... .

(Edwards and Mercer, 1987, p. 126)

Stances: Jerome Bruner

Bruner used the slightly different language of *stances* which learners and teachers might take or find themselves positioned into taking in various different classroom situations.

Each fact we encounter comes wrapped in stance marking . . . Some stances are invitations to the use of thought, reflection, elaboration, fantasy . . . if the teacher wishes to close down the process of wondering by flat declarations of fixed factuality, he or she can do so. The teacher can also open wide a topic . . . to speculation and negotiation.

(Bruner, 1986, p.126)

Examples of stances taken by teachers are captured in the catchy phrases *a guide on the side* in contrast to *a sage on the stage* (King, 1993), *a source of resource, a being in question,* and *discovered not covered* (Halmos, 1980, p. 523). Any single stance used exclusively is likely to become overly familiar and boring, while too much chopping and changing may prove unsettling for some learners.

Bruner's view, inspired by Vygotsky's theories (see p. 84), developed in a number of similar but different directions, under labels such as cognitive apprenticeship, enculturation, situated cognition, authentic mathematics, and real problem solving. Other perspectives, drawn from different sources, include investigative teaching and inquiry methods. Each of these labels is a form of stance or perspective which involves a way of describing interactions between teachers and learners, and which can be used to identify certain styles of interaction. Roles and stances are labels applied by observers; positioning is what happens in situations.

> Teachers operate with a range of positions or stances, in a complex social setting, which impacts significantly on learning.

Teachers, learners and mathematics

Teaching triads

Teachers teach learners mathematics, so there are three elements present in order to have a teaching situation: teacher, learner, and mathematics. Since it all takes place within a milieu (see p. 95), the triad has to be seen as operating within a context. Magdalene Lampert usefully elaborated on the triad of teacher–student–content by analysing the forces acting on and within each component (Lampert, 2001).

For some people, the context is not only vital, but is dominant (see *social constructivism*, p. 95). But there are other ways of looking at teaching.

A teaching triad: James Stigler and James Hiebert

Stigler and Hiebert were leading researchers in the international TIMSS study (see p. 40). International comparisons based on tests given to learners of roughly the same age led governments all over the world to institute curriculum reform, and led researchers to try to account for differences in performance.

> In Japanese lessons, there is the mathematics on one hand, and the students on the other. The students engage with the mathematics, and the teacher mediates the relationship between the two. In Germany, there is the mathematics as well, but the teacher owns the mathematics and parcels it out to students as he sees fit, giving facts and explanations at just the right time. In US lessons, there are the students and there is the teacher. I have trouble finding the mathematics; I just see interactions between students and teachers.
>
> (Stigler and Hiebert, 1999, pp. 25–6)

In some cases, teachers are in charge of the mathematics, and the mathematics is quite advanced, at least procedurally. Teachers often lead learners through a development of procedures for solving general classes of problems. Emphasis is on the technique, including both the rationale and the precision with which the procedure is executed. In other cases, teachers appear to take a less active role, allowing learners to invent their own procedures for solving problems. These problems can be quite demanding, both procedurally and conceptually. Problems are chosen to use procedures recently developed. In other instances, teachers present definitions and demonstrate procedures for solving specific problems; learners are then expected to memorise definitions and to practise procedures (based on Stigler and Hiebert, 1999, pp. 26–7).

Many teachers have set out to try to capture the essence of 'their approach', and to outline what makes particular approaches likely to be effective (see, for example, *Mathematics Teaching*, 139, 1992). There is, however, no totally convincing research to show that any one approach is better than others, only that when teachers are actively working on their teaching, encouraging learners to take an active part in lessons, the learners tend to do better on tests as well.

Six modes of interaction: John Mason

Tasks are what make subsequent interaction between teacher and learner possible. Useful activity is the means whereby the learner encounters signifi-cant mathematical ideas and themes, as well as, perhaps, aspects of them-selves, as described by the inner aspects of a task (see p. 241). For activity to be meaningful, some deeper action is necessary. The triad of teacher–learner–mathematical content, (or tutor–student–content) all within a milieu or environment (see p. 95) gives rise to an analysis of six different modes of interaction, based on ideas developed by J. G. Bennett (1956–1966; 1993). Three terms (teacher, learner, content) can occupy three roles (initiating, responding and mediating) which are needed for relationship and action to occur:

> In order to have what I call a balanced learning environment, there are six activities ... or modes of student–tutor[–content] interaction:
>
> Expounding   Exploring   Exercising
>
> Explaining   Examining   Expressing
>
> The columns are characterised by the source of the initiative: tutor, student and content. Since this is an unusual way of describing learning activities, a few words about each are in order.
>
> The first two modes, 'expounding' and 'explaining' are on the initiative of the tutor. The tutor expounds in the form of a lecture or in writing a text or in much of what we call tutorials. In a tutorial, a student asks a question and very quickly the tutor lapses into a lecturing mode. This can easily be detected in the tone of the tutor's voice. In a true tutorial explaining takes place when just one student is involved, with the tutor being perceptive of the student's individual needs. This is rather more difficult than it sounds! I have often found myself trying to drag a student into my conceptual world rather than trying to enter and remain in that of the student.
>
> The next two modes depend on the initiative of the student: 'explor-ing' and 'examining'. At some point initiative must pass to the student who begins to explore open-ended problems, to generalise for himself, and to begin what we call research. The role of the tutor is radically different from the previous modes because here his aim is to guide the student, to stimulate independent thought ... . The idea of projects and guided investigations are attempts to make use of the exploring mode.
>
> (Mason, 1979, p. 32)

Being aware of the different modes of interaction can assist in: staying with 'explaining' in tutorial mode rather than sliding into expounding; looking for opportunities to amplify learner experience of the desire to express and to exercise; getting learners to use their powers in creating and exploring.

There are other approaches to exploring such as inviting learners to make up their own problems like those used in class, or inviting them to construct examples of objects that meet certain constraints (see Watson and Mason, 2002).

> It may be surprising to find 'examining' under student initiative, but this is where I truly believe it belongs. ... a candidate submits himself for examination when he considers himself ready. ... an opportunity for a student to validate his own criteria of whether or not he is understanding the material. After all, a major part of teaching is to provide the student with his own criteria. ...
>
> The final two modes require the initiative to come from neither the student nor the tutor, but rather from the content which connects the tutor and the student: 'exercising' and 'expressing'.
>
> Of course when we are looking at the situation we think we see the initiative coming through the student. I say that the initiative for exercising really comes from content but expresses itself through the student ... . It is experienced as a force inside me, yet all embracing, and is quite different from a quick decision which doesn't last. There are techniques that must be mastered and there are concepts that need practice in recognising and manipulating. But it is defeating the purpose of the exercises to force the student, just as trying to push people to take physical exercise does not work [unless] they have a strong inner force which attracts them to it. Inappropriately forced, practice of academic material usually results in the kind of rote learning which so annoys teachers. ...
>
> The final mode is widely recognised but little acted upon. We all know that the best way to learn something is to try to express it to others, yet it is difficult to get students to express their [current] understanding. Indeed it is difficult enough to get them to ask a real question, one which has arisen inside them from significant contact with the material and which they have truly pondered.
>
> (Mason, 1979, p. 32)

The triad of teacher–student–content operates within a milieu and includes six different modes of possible interaction.

Tasks and classroom interactions cannot fruitfully be isolated from the whole situation in which they are embedded. Teachers with learners can develop classroom ethos or atmosphere, which means ways of working on mathematics, and ways of working with each other.

Teaching as ...

Guiding: John Holt

Holt discovered through close reflection on his own practice that his goals were not always the same as those of the learners in his classes:

> ... I used to feel that I was guiding and helping my students on a journey that they wanted to take but could not take without my help. I knew the way looked hard, but I assumed they could see the goal almost as clearly as I and that they were almost as eager to reach it. ... They were in school because they had to be, ...
>
> (Holt, 1964, pp. 37–8)

Guiding and reinvention: Hans Freudenthal

Addressing the question of how children as learners can become enculturated into the richness of a (mathematical) culture which has developed over thousands of years, Freudenthal suggested:

> Children should repeat the learning process of mankind, not as it factually took place but rather as it would have done if people in the past had known a bit more of what we know now.
>
> New generations continue what their forbearers wrought but they do not step in at the same level reached by their elders. ...
>
> ... guiding reinvention means striking a subtle balance between the freedom of inventing and the force of guiding, between allowing the learner to please himself and asking him to please the teacher. Moreover the learner's own free choice is already restricted by the 're' of 'reinvention'. The learner shall invent something that is new to him but well-known to the guide.
>
> (Freudenthal, 1991, p.48)

Note the similarity with the *teaching dilemma* (see p. 96).

> ... the learner should reinvent mathematising rather than mathematics; abstracting rather than abstractions; schematising rather than schemas; formalising rather than formulas; algorithmising rather than algorithms; verbalising rather than language – let us stop here, now that it is obvious what is meant.
>
> (ibid., p. 49)

Note the similarity with developing and extending learners' natural *powers* (see p. 115).

If the learner is guided to reinvent all this, then valuable knowledge and abilities will more easily be learned, retained, and transferred than if imposed.

(ibid., p. 49)

Guiding means striking a delicate balance between the force of teaching and the freedom of learning. It depends on such a perplexing manifold of hardly retrievable and only vaguely discernible variables that it seems inaccessible to any general approach. Observational reports on guiding may be a source of understanding and a help for teaching guidance. Unfortunately, most of the reports available are concerned with simple lessons or short sequences, and little is known about long-term learning processes.

(ibid., pp. 55–6)

Discovery learning: Government reports

'Discovery learning' grew out of the work of Dewey, Bruner and others. 'Discovery learning' has had multiple interpretations, ranging from 'learners have to discover everything for themselves with a minimum of guidance', to 'the teacher guides and cajoles the learners into rediscovering'. Consequently there has been considerable criticism, as well as support for 'discovery learning':

> [there is] unchallengeable evidence that sound and lasting learning can be achieved only through active participation. ... Although the discovery method takes longer in the initial stages ... far less practice is required to obtain and maintain the efficiency in computation when children have been able to make their own discoveries. ... When children explore for themselves they make discoveries which they want to communicate to their teacher and to other children and this results in frequent discussion. It is this change relationship which is the most important development of all.
>
> (Schools Council, 1965)

Integrated teaching: Heinrich Bauersfeld

Bauersfeld contrasted discovery learning with integrated teaching:

> *Discovery approach*: In explicitly defined situations, the student 'researcher' starts off from an introduction to working on prepared material, and finally ends up discussing and sharing findings in a whole-class session.
> *Integrated (culture) approach*: In *every* classroom situation, the students are expected to search for patterns, to assume regularities, and to relate developing or contrasting ideas, as well as to give reasons and arguments for the issue under discussion.
>
> (Bauersfeld, 1992, p. 23)

See also *scientific debate* (p. 277) and *conjecturing* (p. 139).

Learning through problems: Magdalene Lampert

Lampert's approach to teaching was to use problems. Her problems were not mere exercises, but problems arising from many different contexts. There are strong similarities with *investigative teaching* which flourished in the UK in the 1980s (Boaler, 1997; Ollerton and Watson, 2001), and various projects in different countries. Variations on this theme can be found in every generation over a hundred years or more.

It is worth recalling Polya's phases of learning (see p. 146):

> Let us summarize: *for efficient learning, an exploratory phase should precede the phase of verbalization and concept formation and, eventually, the material learned should be merged in, and contribute to, the integral mental attitude of the learner.*
> This is the *principle of consecutive phases.*

> (Polya, 1962, part 2, p. 104)

Listening: Brent Davis

Davis extolled the virtues of listening as a means of teaching:

> Occurring somewhere between the surety of the known and the uncertainty of the not-yet-known, the act of listening is similar to the project of education. It is, after all, when we are not certain that we are compelled to listen. Our listening is always and already in the transformative space of learning.
> (Davis, 1996, p. xxiv)

He went on to identify and develop three different forms of listening:

> *Evaluative listening:* … Within the mathematics classroom, this manner of listening is manifested in the detached, evaluative stance of the teacher who deviates little from intended plans, in whose classroom student contributions are judged as either right or wrong (and thus have little impact on lesson trajectories), and for whom listening is primarily the responsibility of the learner.
> *Interpretative listening:* … is founded on an awareness that an active interpretation – a sort of reaching out rather than taking in – is involved, whereby the listening is deliberate and aware of the fallibility of the sense being made.
> (ibid. pp. 52–3)

It is worth noting that the more involved and committed the teacher, the harder it is to maintain awareness of possible misinterpretation. These two modes are founded on a fundamental distinction between teacher and learner.

> *Hermeneutic listening*: ... is more negotiatory, engaging, messy, involving the hearer and the heard in a shared project [it] is an imaginative participation in the formation and transformation of experience through an ongoing interpretation of the taken-for-granted and the prejudices that frame perceptions and actions.
>
> (ibid., p. 53)

Listening in order to teach: Teacher report

After being involved in a year-long research project regarding listening, one teacher reported:

> I have become a better listener. Teachers are basically talkers who feel a strong desire to share their knowledge with other people. Children are no different. If we really make an effort to listen to our students, we will become the richer for it.
>
> (quoted in Cobb, Wood and Yackel, 1990, p. 135)

Subordinating teaching to learning: Caleb Gattegno

According to Gattegno, there are four tasks facing a teacher who wants to subordinate teaching to learning. In the following extracts, Gattegno had in mind a wide variety of situations, such as: things have multiple names; sense impressions act upon us and we upon them; we use direct experience for testing what we hear from others.

> ... *to become a person* who knows himself and others, as persons. This is no mere sentimental homily, but means that the teacher must recognize that beyond any individual's behaviors is a *will* which changes behaviors and integrates them.
>
> (Gattegno, 1970, p. 53)

> The second task of the teacher is to acknowledge the existence of *a sense of truth* which guides us all and is the basis of all our knowing.
>
> (ibid., p. 56)

> ... to find out *how knowing becomes knowledge*.
>   Since this problem applies to himself as well as to all others, what he needs to do is to watch himself making this transformation. ...
>
> (ibid., p. 60)

... the duty to consider the [principle of] *economy of learning*. ...
[...]

A reflection on the acts of living will show us that to live is to change time into experience. So time must be considered as what we are endowed with by the act of coming into the world and that consumption of time, if it is not to be destructive for the individual, should lead to some equivalent worth in terms of experience, which when accumulated, becomes growth.

(ibid., pp. 63–4)

The role of the teacher of mathematics is to recognize that a student who can speak has a large number of mental structures which can serve as the basis for awarenesses that will enable him to transform these structures into mathematical ones.

(ibid., p. 70)

Gattegno stressed the need for listening as a form of teaching – one of the instruments that teachers can use to inform themselves about what learners are doing and thinking (see p. 225). See also *conjecturing atmosphere*, p. 139, Maturana and Varela, p. 70, and Warden, p. 277.

Teaching can be seen as instructing, as guiding, as interacting, as fostering and sustaining mathematical thinking, even as listening, and it can be seen through the lenses of various metaphors (see Fox, p. 42). Listening can be evaluative or interpretative.

9 Initiating mathematical activity

Introduction

In this chapter the focus is on getting mathematical activity started. The chapter starts out with some principles, both philosophical and pragmatic. It then goes on to consider the practicalities of designing tasks, and selecting contexts and apparatus for learning.

Principles

The principles considered in the extracts in this section include the desirabliity of starting teaching with a question for learners to work on, the learners understanding the purpose of the mathematics behind the activity, and working from what learners already know and understand or have experienced.

Starting with a question: Paul Halmos

Paul Halmos (b. Hungary, 1916–) moved to the USA when he was eight. He became an eminent mathematician and is widely acknowledged as a brilliant expositor. He published an 'automathography' and has written many articles on the art of teaching. He was inspired by the teaching style of R. L. Moore (1882–1974), who provided graduate students with a list of theorems and required them to find the proofs, having agreed *not* to talk to each other outside of class or to consult textbooks. Most of the many famous mathematicians who went through Moore's class thought it was the best they had ever taken, though some found it inimical to their preferred ways of working.

> Let me emphasize one thing … . The way to begin all teaching is with a question. I try to remember that precept every time I begin to teach a course, and I try even to remember it every time I stand up to give a lecture … .
>
> Another part of the idea of the method is to concentrate attention on the definite, the concrete, the specific. Once a student understands,

really and truly understands, why 3 × 5 is the same as 5 × 3, then he quickly gets the automatic but nevertheless exciting and obvious conviction that 'it goes the same way' for all other numbers.

(Halmos, 1994, p. 852)

Note the similarities with making use of learners' powers to *generalise* (see p. 137 and p. 196). The purpose of an example is to afford access to a whole space of possibilities, not to focus attention on a particular example.

Halmos was convinced that learners have to come to see 'why' things are true for themselves (see also *teaching for understanding*, p. 293):

> What we can do is to point a student in the right directions, challenge him with problems, and thus make it possible for him to 'remember' the solutions. Once the solutions start being produced, we can comment on them, we can connect them with others, and we can encourage their generalizations. The worst we can do is to give polished lectures crammed full of the latest news from fat and expensive scholarly journals and books – that is, I am convinced, a waste of time.

(ibid., p. 851)

For Halmos, the most a teacher can do is create conditions and provide ways of working on mathematics. Most attempts at teaching end up interfering with learning, which resonates with Gattegno's booktitle: *What We Owe Children: The subordination of teaching to learning*.

Here are more observations from Halmos about teaching, which are consistent with his view that mathematics is centrally about *problem solving* (see p. 187).

> The best way to learn is to do; the worst way to teach is to talk.
> [...]
> A famous dictum of Polya's about problem solving is that if you can't solve the problem, then there is an easier problem that you [can] solve – find it! If you can teach that dictum to your students, teach it so that that they can teach it to theirs, you have solved the problem of creating teachers of problem solving. The hardest part of answering questions is to ask them; our job as teachers and teachers of teachers is to teach how to ask questions. It's easy to teach an engineer to use a differential equations cook book; what's hard is to teach him (and his teacher) what to do when the answer is not in the cook book. In that case, again, the chief problem is likely to be 'what is the problem?'. Find the right question to ask, and you're a long way toward solving the problem you're working on.

(Halmos, 1975, pp. 466–7)

Telling people things is nevertheless the most common form of instruction. *Constructivism* (see p. 54) was used to advocate movement away from lecturing towards investigations and discussion in order that learners would be supported in 'making sense', in 'constructing meaning'. But the constructivist notion that learners have to make their own sense, or to be enculturated into the practices (particularly the linguistic ones) of the community applies equally well to learners sitting in rows in lectures and learners exploring for themselves or engaging in scientific debate. What matters is whether the learners are in a position to be able to see, hear and make sense of what they are told and shown. Montaigne caught this point beautifully, if ornately:

> If only Nature would deign to open her breast one day and show us the means and the workings of her movements as they really are (first preparing our eyes to see them).
>
> (Montaigne, 1588, p. 602)

Montaigne went on to quote Plato as saying that 'nature is but enigmatic poetry', and that Nature intends to exercise our ingenuity. Our relationship to Nature through science is more developed since Montaigne's time than perhaps our relationship with (human) psyche. Preparing a learner to be able to see and hear is what Dewey was getting at in his phrase *psychologising the subject matter* (see also p. 45).

Psychologising the subject matter: John Dewey

Dewey argued strongly that effective education takes account of the interests, concerns, powers and potential of learners, and transforms the subject matter so that it is appropriate to the learner. Dewey called this *psychologising the subject matter*. Lee Shulman (see p. 41) adapted and built on this when he distinguished *pedagogic subject matter* as one of the types of knowledge required to be a teacher.

Here Dewey argues against the approach to curriculum design simply as laying out the subject matter clearly and logically.

> A psychological statement of experience follows its actual growth; it is historic; it notes steps actually taken, the uncertain and tortuous, as well as the efficient and successful. The logical point of view, on the other hand, assumes that the development has reached a certain positive stage of fulfilment. It neglects the process and considers the outcome. It summarizes and arranges, and thus separates the achieved results from the actual steps by which they were forthcoming in the first instance. We may compare the difference between the logical and the psychological to the difference between the notes which an explorer makes in a new country, blazing a trail and finding his way along as best he may, and the finished map that is constructed after the country has been thoroughly explored. The two are mutually dependent. Without the more or less accidental and devious paths traced by the explorer there would be no facts which could

be utilized in the making of the complete and related chart. But no one would get the benefit of the explorer's trip if it was not compared and checked up with similar wanderings undertaken by others; unless the new geographical facts learned, the streams crossed, the mountains climbed, etc., were viewed, not as mere incidents in the journey of the particular traveler, but (quite apart from the individual explorer's life) in relation to other similar facts already known. The map orders individual experiences, connecting them with one another irrespective of the local and temporal circumstances and accidents of their original discovery.

[...]

... But the map, a summary, an arranged and orderly view of previous experiences, serves as a guide to future experience; it gives direction; it facilitates control; it economizes effort, preventing useless wandering, and pointing out the paths which lead most quickly and most certainly to a desired result. Through the map every new traveler may get for his own journey the benefits of the results of others' explorations without the waste of energy and loss of time involved in their wanderings – wanderings which he himself would be obliged to repeat were it not for just the assistance of the objective and generalized record of their performances. ...

[...]

Hence the need of reinstating into experience the subject-matter of the studies, or branches of learning. It must be restored to the experience from which it has been abstracted. It needs to be *psychologized*; turned over, translated into the immediate and individual experiencing within which it has its origin and significance.

... The problem of the teacher is ... concerned with the subject-matter of the science as *representing a given stage and phase of the development of experience*. His problem is that of inducing a vital and personal experiencing. Hence, what concerns him, as teacher, is the ways in which that subject may become a part of experience; what there is in the child's present that is usable with reference to it; how such elements are to be used; how his own knowledge of the subject-matter may assist in interpreting the child's needs and doings, and determine the medium in which the child should be placed in order that his growth may be properly directed. He is concerned, not with the subject-matter as such, but with the subject-matter as a related factor in a total and growing experience. Thus to see it is to psychologize it.

(Dewey, 1902, pp. 19–23)

There are similarities with *educating awareness* (see p. 61 and p. 161) and with *didactical phenomenology* (see p. 202).

Dewey went on to criticise educational approaches that ignore the experience of the learner, and so fail to *psychologise the subject matter*.

It is the failure to keep in mind the double aspect of subject-matter which causes the curriculum and child to be set over against each other … . The subject-matter, just as it is for the scientist, has no direct relationship to the child's present experience. It stands outside of it. The danger here is not a merely theoretical one. We are practically threatened on all sides. Textbook and teacher vie with each other in presenting to the child the subject-matter as it stands to the specialist. Such modification and revision as it undergoes are a mere elimination of certain scientific difficulties, and the general reduction to a lower intellectual level. The material is not translated into life-terms, but is directly offered as a substitute for, or an external annex to, the child's present life.

(ibid., pp. 23–4)

There are similarities with attacks by Spencer on *rote learning* and *rule teaching* (see p. 152 and p. 196), and by Whitehead on *inert knowledge* (see p. 288).

Dewey then considered the implications of the failure to psychologise, particularly concerning too rapid use of symbols for experiences (what might also be referred to as *awarenesses*, see p. 61).

Three typical evils result: In the first place, the lack of any organic connection with what the child has already seen and felt and loved makes the material purely formal and symbolic. There is a sense in which it is impossible to value too highly the formal and the symbolic. The genuine form, the real symbol, serve as methods in the holding and discovery of truth. … But this happens only when the symbol really symbolizes – when it stands for and sums up in shorthand actual experiences which the individual has already gone through. A symbol which is induced from without, which has not been led up to in preliminary activities, is, as we say, a *bare* or *mere* symbol; it is dead and barren. …

The second evil … is lack of motivation. There are not only no facts or truths which have been previously felt … with which to appropriate and assimilate the new, but there is no craving, no need, no demand. When the subject-matter has been psychologized, that is, viewed as an outgrowth of present tendencies and activities, it is easy to locate in the present some obstacle, intellectual, practical, or ethical, which can be handled more adequately if the truth in question be mastered. This need supplies motive for the learning. An end which is the child's own carries him on to possess the means of its accomplishment. But when material is directly supplied in the form of a lesson to be learned as a lesson, the connecting links of need and aim are conspicuous for their absence.

(ibid., pp. 24–5)

There are similarities with the *transposition didactique* (see p. 83), and the role of *obstacles* (see p. 303) and *disturbance* (see p. 55).

The third evil is that even the most scientific matter, arranged in most logical fashion, loses this quality, when presented in external, ready-made fashion, by the time it gets to the child. It has to undergo some modification in order to shut out some phases too hard to grasp, and to reduce some of the attendant difficulties. What happens? ... The really thought-provoking character is obscured, and the organizing function disappears. Or, as we commonly say, the child's reasoning powers, the faculty of abstraction and generalization, are not adequately developed.

(ibid., p. 26)

Note the reference to learners' *powers* (see p. 115 and p. 233). The principal role of the curriculum developer and the teacher is to *psychologise the subject matter.* The *Structure-of-a-topic* framework (see p. 203) can be helpful in this regard.

Finally, Dewey returned to learners' powers.

It is his present powers which are to assert themselves; his present capacities which are to be exercised; his present attitudes which are to be realized. But save as the teacher knows, knows wisely and thoroughly, the race-expression which is embodied in that thing we call the Curriculum, the teacher knows neither what the present power, capacity, or attitude is, nor yet how it is to be asserted, exercised, and realized.

(ibid., p. 31)

This passage captures the essence of most attempts to reform education. It was a rallying cry for what in the 1970s became the child-centred curriculum, itself criticised for leading to practices that allowed children to proceed at their own pace without making full use of their powers. It summarises the key constructs that lie at the heart of effective teaching and successful learning.

Diagnostic teaching: Alan Bell

Alan Bell (b. Kent, 1929–) has been researching mathematics classrooms for many years as a member of the influential Shell Centre at the University of Nottingham.

The Diagnostic Teaching project began by identifying a multitude of common errors and misconceptions underlying those errors in arithmetic, and problems which proved difficult because learners often choose an inappropriate operation. Teaching material was then prepared, specifically targeted at 'notational misconceptions, numerical misconceptions, and the invariance of quantity relations in problems in contexts such as price and speed' (Bell, 1986, p. 26).

By invariance here, the author meant, for example, that (average) distance always equals (average) speed multiplied by time.

... a short start activity ... would lead to the exposure of such misconceptions as are present in the pupils' schemes and ideas. So it could be said that we deliberately gave them questions which at least some pupils would get wrong; and without forewarning them of possible hazards. The principle was that if there is an underlying misconception, then it's 'better out than in'; it needs to be seen and subjected to critical peer group discussion. Of course, establishing a classroom atmosphere in which this is an accepted activity is not a trivial matter, and it may take some time.

[...]

... The working assumption was that if the difficulties with notation and the numerical misconceptions could be overcome, then correct choices of operation would be made. ...

... we saw the 'conflict-discussion' as the main learning experience, and the written-work as introductory, giving the opportunity for opening up the situation and allowing some mistakes to be made which led to conflicts and hence the discussion. Following the discussions we gave some written work to 'consolidate' the understanding gained. This consisted of similar problems but with feedback enabling immediate correction to be made if necessary.

... Perhaps the most striking observation from all this work is that back-sliding is the norm. Even after clearly effective lessons with learning visibly taking place, in the next lesson most of the class could slip again into the original error. True, the second recovery was quicker than the first. The method of conflict-discussion promises to provide a more effective way of dealing with this widely recognised phenomenon than simply reteaching. The same key conceptual points do need to be the focus of discussion repeatedly; but they need to appear in different contexts and modes of presentation.

(ibid., pp. 27–9)

The authors' first attempts produced tasks that proved to be too rigid. But what did develop was discussion around various alternatives. They ended up with a chart with cards containing numbers, statements in words concerning operations, and symbolic representations of those operations. Groups of learners then sorted the cards onto a chart, seeking agreement as to where cards belonged.

In a follow-up article (there were to be a further three articles), Bell reported on getting learners to make up their own questions and to mark and comment on the homework of a fictitious learner who made many classic mistakes.

In general these are hard tasks; though the difficulty decreases with familiarity. Our conclusion from our research has been that this is what is required to provoke worthwhile discussion and to strengthen understanding. ...

[...]

Students' early attempts to make up questions showed a surprising level of difficulty. Frequently the questions were unanswerable. Sometimes they simply gave data but asked no question; in other cases they gave insufficient information. ...

In later attempts students gave more coherent questions, and these showed up some important misconceptions [especially when they gave their own answers!].

[...]

In another form of making up questions, ... students were given a set of related quantities, but just one numerical value, and were asked to write *two* possible questions, one containing easy numbers, and one with hard numbers. This gave the students the challenge of recognising what were 'hard numbers' in these problems, as well as having to operate with them.

These tasks offer a variety of different demands and constraints; each has some element of freedom for creativity, and also some means of ensuring that the more difficult number and quantity combinations are faced as well as the easier ones.

(Bell, 1987, pp. 21–2)

Principles: Alan Bell

Bell subsequently considered how activity can be turned into learning:

Most uses of mathematics involve a cycle of mathematization, manipulation, and interpretation – that is, recognizing in the given situation the relevance of some mathematical relationship, expressing this relation symbolically, manipulating the symbolic expression to reveal some new aspect, and interpreting this new aspect or giving some fresh insight into it in the given situation. ...

[...]

Given that the pupils are to be offered activities which embody the characteristic mathematical strategies, and which embrace the major concepts of the subject, what needs to be done to turn these into *learning* experiences? That is, what can we do to make it more likely that the pupils will actually perform better when they meet these or similar tasks again? Learning is not just success in the present task but improvement in capability. This factor has been neglected in some recent pedagogies, which assume that a sequence of gently graded problem-solving tasks results in learning.

... to develop the strategy of generalizing one would offer a set of experiences, of different types, in different contexts and in different conceptual fields, but each requiring the forming and expressing of some generalization, and one would draw attention to the characteristic features of the process. Particular skills or concepts would be dealt with in a similar way. It is thus appropriate to alternate general exploratory activities with work focused on related specific concepts, strategies, or skills.

In some respects, the requirements conflict. For example, in an activity aimed at developing the ability to carry through an investigation in which one follows up each discovery by choosing an appropriate question to tackle next, one cannot control which concepts and skills will be involved in the work as it progresses. Conversely, when the aim is to work on some particular concepts and skills, it is necessary for the discussion to be guided so as to explore the various aspects of those concepts; one cannot at the same time allow the inquiry to take its direction from what appears the most relevant question to ask next.

(Bell, 1993, pp. 6–8)

Bell then offered some explicit principles for designing teaching:

… First one chooses a *situation* which embodies, in some *contexts,* the concepts and relations of the *conceptual field* in which it is desired to work. Within the situation, *tasks* are proposed to the learners which bring into play the concepts and relations. It is necessary that the learner shall know when the task is correctly performed; hence some form of *feedback* is required. When *errors* occur, arising from some *misconception*, it is appropriate to expose the *cognitive conflict* and to help the learner to achieve a resolution. This is one type of *intervention* which the teacher may make to assist the learning process.

(ibid., pp. 8–9)

Note how Bell made reference in the passage to many of the ideas presented elsewhere in this reader.

Another general mode of intervention is in adjusting the *degree of challenge* offered to the learner by the task; the extent to which the task itself provides this flexibility is a significant task feature. The next requirement is for ways of developing a single starting task into a multiple task, bringing the learner to experience a rich variety of relations within the field. Typically, this can be done by making *changes of element* (e.g., type of number), *structure*, and *context*. The *degree of intensity* of this complex of learning experiences is an important factor. *Reflection* and *review* are other key principles; they imply the perception and study not only of the basic concepts and relations within the tasks but also of the properties of the different types of problem within the field and of the methods of solution found – meta-knowledge of the tasks and of the activity.

(ibid., pp. 8–9)

There are similarities with *dimensions-of-possible-variation* (see p. 56).

A fundamental fact about learned material is that richly connected bodies of knowledge are well retained; isolated elements are quickly lost.

(ibid., p. 9)

Compare this with *situated cognition* (see p. 86), *rote learning* (see p. 151), and *knowing* (p. 289) and *understanding* (p. 293).

> In conflict-discussion lessons ... feedback is an integral part of the process of discussion ... . In other tasks, including games, the mode is predict and check ... .
>
> *Refection* and *Review*: Exploring relationships and resolving conflicts through discussion are in themselves reflective activities. Here we imply something more – a more global reflection on the process of performing the task and identifying the crucial steps, and on the new knowledge gained and how it fits into one's existing body of knowledge. This development of *awareness* is important in labelling the newly gained knowledge in memory in such a way as to make it accessible on relevant future occasions.
>
> [...]
>
> *Intensity*: It is well known that repetition is an essential element in learning. Questions remain concerning the effects of the degree of variety in the set of tasks; some of these are implicit in the foregoing discussion. There is clearly no general answer to this question, but there is evidence in some experiments that what might be regarded as excessive repetition has resulted in striking gains. It is also clear that while repeated *memorization* tasks may produce short-lived results, intensive *insight-demanding* tasks produce longer-term gains.
>
> [...]
>
> *Feedback*: In some cases feedback is intrinsic to the task; in other cases, a predict-and-check-mode may be possible – for example, a mental calculation may be compared with a calculator result. In some games, the opponent may challenge a doubtful answer. ... Sometimes definite feedback of correctness is difficult or impossible, but provision can be made for discussion of the task in pairs, or in a group, so that at least some errors and misconceptions can be detected.

(ibid., pp. 15–19)

Principles: Jan van den Brink

Van den Brink took the principles suggested by Alan Bell and colleagues, and illustrated some while challenging others by using examples.

- Richly connected bodies of knowledge are well retained;
- Discussion of a few hard critical problems is more effective than progress through a sequence of many easy questions;

- Pure practice increases fluency but does not develop understanding
  (… our pupils' demonstrated that striking surprises are important for
  developing understanding);
- Scope for pupil choice and creative productions can provide both
  motivation and challenge at the pupils' own level;
- Establishment of multiple connections is helped by exploring fully
  the relationships in one context before moving to another context (I
  [van den Brink] do not agree with this principle. … There ought to be
  merely a mutual influence between formal contexts and daily ones.)

(van den Brink, 1993, pp. 62–3)

The age-old disagreement about relevance and the role of familiar context
appears again (see also p. 82, p. 110, p. 264 and p. 292).
  Van den Brink also added two more principles:

- Correcting the unexpected conflicts and surprises (mostly opposites
  of well-known relations) is powerful learning.
- Criticizing by teachers improves teaching … the role of the teachers in
  criticizing [draft] textbooks improved the teaching material.

(ibid., p. 63)

> Psychologising the subject matter is what teachers can do for learners: estab-
> lishing an environment in which they encounter cognitive conflicts.

Tasks

In this section, tasks are considered as devices for intiating activity. Tasks
are drawn, usually by the teacher from a task-space full of possible variation. The section includes a classification of types of task and a consider-
ation of the possibility of the learner becoming aware of the dimensions-of-
possible-variation.

Structure of tasks

Task and activity: Bent Christiansen and G. Walther

Christiansen and Walther drew on Vygotsky's notion of *activity* to distinguish between a task that is proposed and the activity that may arise from
engaging in (some version of) that task. See also *teaching dilemma* (p. 96).

> The tasks and the activities establish so to speak the 'meeting place'
> between teacher and learner.
>
> (Christiansen and Walther, 1986, p. 246)

... students – by means of tasks set by the teacher – may be *initiated* into an appropriate spectrum of mathematical activity. However, a number of teacher-actions are needed in each case to ensure that the educational activity in question results in learning as intended. ... any activity proceeds through goal directed actions which are 'inherent' in, but not 'given by' the task; ... specific tasks are needed to motivate specific types of activity (e.g. of exploratory or problem-solving types); ... any activity contributes to learning of different types and at different cognitive levels; ... specific teacher-actions are needed to ensure that personal knowledge is developed in an appropriate degree into shared knowledge.

(ibid., pp. 253–4)

Learners have to interpret any task, and will naturally do so in terms of what they can imagine themselves doing. Alternatively, they may wait until the task is specified in such detail that they can undertake it but without having to engage, which amounts to a form of *funnelling* (see p. 274).

... even when students work on assigned tasks supported by carefully established educational contexts and by corresponding teacher-actions, learning as intended does not follow automatically from their activity on the tasks. ...

[A learner's engagement with a task is influenced by] the individual's interest in the task, his motivation for acting, his attitudes towards the teacher and the school, his conceptions of learning and of mathematics. And ... whether he *reflects* on his actions and on his own learning.

(ibid., p. 262)

Task design: Konrad Krainer

Konrad Krainer is an academic at the University of Klagenfurt, in Austria. His interests span educational management and mathematics education. Here he raises the endemic tensions facing any teacher or curriculum developer.

How should mathematics instruction be organized? This is one of the most important questions to be dealt with in mathematics education. There are two extreme answers to this question.

The first sees mathematics as a highly complex and highly developed science which offers, however, polished and stable ideas and theories in areas understandable for pupils ... . Therefore, it is easy to build up well-established ('secured') courses for mathematics ... . According to the second answer to this question, pupils bring a variety of relevant practical experiences, associations, intuitions, and so on to mathematics instruction. If the spontaneity and creativity of the pupils are taken seriously it is – from a psychological point of view – necessary to have a certain insecurity of mathematics courses … .

[…]

This dilemma cannot be resolved by a didactical theory. The situation remains one of conflict because both extremes embody meaningful demands: on the one hand, the demand for economical efficiency and for well-developed 'motorways', and on the other hand, the demand that the pupils should investigate and discover for themselves and have the freedom to 'pave' their own ways.

(Krainer, 1993, pp. 66–7)

Compare this with the *didactic tension* emerging from the *contrat didactique* (Brousseau, p. 79).

Krainer applied his more general perspective to the design of 'powerful' mathematical tasks, identifying various properties that should be incorporated in the tasks.

1a *Team spirit*: … [the] tasks should be well interconnected with other tasks. The 'horizontal' connection of tasks can be seen as a contribution to the security of mathematics courses.
1b *Self-dynamics*: … tasks facilitate the generation of further interesting questions. The 'vertical' extension of tasks to open situations can be seen as a contribution to the insecurity of mathematics courses.

   Powerful tasks therefore embody the dilemma security–insecurity as a constituting element.
2a *High level of acting*: … the initiation of active processes of concept formation which are accompanied by relevant ('concept generating') actions.
2b *High level of reflecting*: … acting and reflecting should always be seen as closely linked. An important aspect of reflection refers to further questions from the learners (which in their turn could lead to new actions).

These two [sets of] properties express the philosophy that learners should be seen not only as consumers but also as producers of knowledge. The teacher's task is to organize an active confrontation of the pupils with mathematics. Powerful tasks are important points of contact between the actions of the teacher and those of the learner.

(ibid., p. 68)

Here Krainer is advocating thinking of tasks as systems of tasks, never complete, but indicating directions of possible development and challenge. This fits with the notion of tasks as samples from a task-domain or task-space in which individual tasks arise as choices made in a variety of *dimensions-of-possible-variation,* within a range-of-permissible-change (see p. 57). The task-domain consists of all possible variations, and it is to the advantage of the learner as well as the teacher to become aware of that space. Indeed, each individual will have their own version of a task-space, consisting of the dimensions-of-possible-variation and the range-of-permissible-change within each of those dimensions of which they are aware.

Framing tasks: Paolo Boero

Paolo Boero (b. Italy, 1941–) is a leading mathematics educator and researcher, known for his detailed research into the design and analysis of tasks for use in schools. Boero used the notion of a *field of experience* to go beyond mere context, appealing to what learners already have experienced and from which rich mathematical ideas can emerge:

> The field of experience of sunshadows is a context in which students can naturally explore problem situations in different dynamical ways. In order to study the relationships between sun, shadow and the object which produces the shadow, one can imagine (and, if necessary, perform a concrete simulation of) the movement of the sun, of the observer and of the objects which produce the shadows.
>
> The field of experience of sunshadows was chosen because it offers the possibility of producing, in open problem solving situations, conjectures which are meaningful from a space geometry point of view, not easy to be proved and without the possibility of substituting proof with the realization of drawings.
>
> (Boero *et al.*, 1996 webref)

Outer and inner aspects of tasks: Dick Tahta and John Mason

From his work with learners on watching and making mathematical animations, Tahta drew attention to a distinction between the overt or outer task which is set, and the inner aspects which are expected to emerge through activity arising from that task. This notion can be developed even further to include meta-aspects of tasks:

> Tahta (1980; 1981) distinguished *inner* and *outer* meaning of tasks, and to these I add *meta* meaning. *Outer* meanings have to do with explicit content such as known mathematical results described in terms of a mathematical label which purports to summarise a mathematical story. To exploit the outer meaning of a task, it makes sense to engage students in story telling by reconstructing what they have seen by giving brief-but-vivid accounts of fragments from the task

activity, and weaving that into a story which accounts for those fragments. Throughout this story weaving, negotiation with others plays a
crucial role.

Inner meaning refers to global awareness such as multiplicity of definitions or of perspective, the linking together of previously disparate
elements into one continuous family, the perception of an infinite class
of elements as a single entity, the choosing of constraints and the effect
of those constraints, the stressing of different points of view that yield an
invariant result, the simultaneous holding of several points of view by
means of one invariant. ...

Meta meaning refers to the opportunities provided by any mathematical exercise to observe one's own behaviour and propensities, and
thereby perhaps to increase sensitivity so as to inform action in the
future.

(Mason, 1992, p. 12)

Task design: David Wood, Jerome Bruner and Gail Ross

David Wood and his colleagues were designing research tasks for young
children in order to explore the ways in which mothers supported or tutored
their children in the face of difficulties.

> The task set the children was designed with several objectives in mind.
> First and foremost, it had to be both entertaining and challenging to the
> child while also proving sufficiently complex to ensure that his behav-
> iour over time could develop and change. It had to be 'feature rich' in
> the sense of possessing a variety of relevant components. We tried to
> make its underlying structure repetitive so that experience at one point
> in task mastery could potentially be applied to later activity, and a child
> could benefit from after-the-fact knowledge or hindsight. But the task
> had not to be so difficult as to lie completely beyond the capability of
> any of the children. And finally, we did not want to make too great
> demands upon the child's manipulatory skills and sheer physical
> strength.

(Wood, Bruner and Ross, 1976, p. 91)

See also p. 266 and p. 268 for principles Wood *et al.* developed from their
studies concerning tutoring, especially *scaffolding*.

Task types

There are many different ways of classifying types of tasks. They can be seen
in terms of:

- A phenomenon to be explored and explained (in the material world outside school, in common experience, on an electronic screen, in mental imagery, in symbols);
- Instructions to follow on self-chosen objects which contribute to collective data that then become a phenomenon to be explained;
- Routine exercises which can be opened out in various ways;
- Invitations to construct objects meeting various constraints, as a step towards appreciating a general class of objects rather than simply particular cases;
- Invitations to construct problems for the learners' peers, the teacher, or other adults, in order to encourage thinking about the class of 'problems like this' and the technique for resolving them, as a step towards appreciating a general class of problem.

This perspective stresses the source of something on which to work. Tasks can also be classified in terms of what learners are invited to do. For example, use data obtained from the Internet, from a book or self-collected; seek advice in response to questions posed by other (possibly imaginary) learners; sort or classify objects, statements or expressions; construct physical, mental or symbolic objects; interpret diagrams, graphs, and expressions; explore the significance of some way of doing things such as a scoring mechanism in some sport.

Task dimensions: Doug Clarke

A variety of task dimensions have been studied and used by researchers and curriculum developers. Working in Australia, Clarke and his colleagues (Clarke, webref) have developed criteria for rich assessment tasks, including that: the tasks connect with and arise naturally from the topics to be taught, they are manageable in the time; they have multiple outcomes and are susceptible to multiple approaches; the way of working encourages group work and communication as well as individual work; they authentically represent use of skills and knowledge in the future.

Like Clarke, Higgins also made use of dimensions concerning rich or impoverished tasks laid out by Steve Leinwand and Grant Wiggins (see Stenmark, 1991; Higgins, webref) by using distinctions that are often in tension. Each row below is seen as a spectrum. It is not a matter of ruling out tasks that fail to meet the requirements of the left-hand end of each distinction, but rather to use these as ideals to be approached along a spectrum from right to left in as many categories as possible.

ESSENTIAL	Fits into the core of the curriculum Represents a 'big idea'	TANGENTIAL
AUTHENTIC	Uses processes appropriate to the discipline Learners value outcome of process	CONTRIVED
RICH	Leads to other problems Raises other questions Has multiple possibilities	SUPERFICIAL
ENGAGING	Thought-provoking; fosters persistence	UNINTERESTING
ACTIVE	Learner is worker and decision maker; learners interact with other learners; learners construct meaning and deepen understanding	PASSIVE
FEASIBLE	Can be done within school and homework time; developmentally appropriate for learners; safe	INFEASIBLE
EQUITABLE	Develops thinking in a variety of styles; contributes to positive attitudes	INEQUITABLE
OPEN	Has more than one right answer; has multiple avenues of approach making it accessible to all learners	CLOSED

(Adapted from Higgins, webref)

The terms used for these distinctions display a strong bias and commitment to tasks used for assessment purposes. Further dimensions are needed for tasks that are designed to work on, develop and probe facility with routine techniques, and for tasks designed to expose learners to new concepts or to encounter pervasive *themes* (see p. 193) or the development of *powers* (see p. 115). See also Ahmed (1987). Although tasks are often classified as either open or closed as in the last row of the table, (or even open-ended or open-fronted), it is not the task that is open or closed, but the people who work on it who open it out or close it down. What matters is not so much the type of the task, as the activity which arises from it and the possibilities afforded.

Opening up tasks: Sherman Stein

Stein, who wrote about how algorithms drive out thought (see p. 177), went on to advocate 'open field' tasks.

> What is the point of ... [an] exercise? Is it to check a definition [is understood] or a theorem or the execution of an algorithm? ... Blinders are placed on the student to focus attention on particular facts or skills. For

instance we ask students to factor $x^4 - 1$. An open field exercise puts no blinders on the student. We might ask 'for which positive integers n does $x^2 - 1$ divide $x^n - 1$?' An open-field exercise may not connect with the section covered that day; it may not even be related to the course. Such an exercise may require the student to devise experiments, make a conjecture, and prove it.

(Stein, 1987, pp. 3–4)

The notion of *dimensions-of-possible-variation* (p. 57) provides a language for discussing with learners how they can open up any task for themselves: what things could be varied, yet the task remains much the same?

Distinguishing tasks as set (and as conceived by author and by teacher) from activity arising from work on those tasks (as construed by learners) helps to free teachers from expectations that learners will all do the same thing in the same way, and to open up sensitivity to the richness of what emerges. This will also facilitate awareness of the kinds of questions to ask which might promote particular mathematical awarenesses and thinking. Seeing tasks as having inner and meta-aspects, as well as outer overt form, opens up thinking about tasks in relation to the *Structure-of-a-topic* framework. Tasks can arise from a field of experience rather than from a simple context.

Situations and apparatus

The use of situations which arise as a context for mathematics has been advocated by many authors with different justifications (see *authentic activity*, p. 108, *real problem solving*, p. 114, *realistic mathematics*, p. 110); furthermore, the use of physical apparatus to create situations and to support the learning of mathematics has been advocated since ancient times (see Plato p. 34). It transpires that the use of apparatus, or *cultural tools* (see p. 85) is highly problematic. The extracts in this section explore this issue.

Making use of situations

For an expert, mathematics appears to be embedded within the apparatus, but a learner has to distinguish what is mathematical from what is happenstance and particular to the situation involving the apparatus. In a very real sense, the concept has to be understood, at least to some extent, in order to appreciate how the apparatus displays or reveals the mathematical ideas.

> … when a teacher presents a child with some apparatus or materials …
> he [or she] typically has in mind some one particular conception of what
> he [or she] presents in this way. But then the incredible assumption
> seems to be made that the teacher's conception of the situation

somehow confers a special uniqueness on it such that the children must also quite inevitably conceive of it in this way too.

(Dearden, 1967, pp. 145–6,
quoted in Cobb, Yackel, and Wood, 1992, p. 9)

Affordances: James Gibson and James Greeno

James Gibson (Ohio, 1904–1979) was an American psychologist particularly interested in perception. He coined the term *affordance* to refer to the complex interrelationship between animal and environment.

> The affordances of the environment are what it offers the animal, what it provides or furnishes, either for good or ill. The verb 'to afford' is found in the dictionary, but the noun 'affordance' is not. I have made it up. I mean by it something that refers to both the environment and the animal in a way that no existing term does. It implies the complementarity of the animal and the environment ...
>
> (Gibson, 1979, p. 127)

James Greeno (b. South Dakota, 1935–) is an American sociologist-psychologist and mathematics educator. He developed Gibson's notion of *affordances* within mathematics education, which for him involved shifting attention from individuals to interactions:

> [In situativity theory] ... cognitive processes are analyzed as relations between agents and other systems. This theoretical shift does not imply a denial of individual cognition as a theoretically important process. It does, however, involve a shift of the level of primary focus of cognitive analyses from processes that can be attributed to individual agents to interactive processes in which agents participate, cooperatively, with other agents and with the physical systems that they interact with.
>   [...]
> ... In any interaction involving an agent with some other system, conditions that enable the interaction include some properties of the agent along with some properties of the other system. ... The term affordance refers to whatever it is about the environment that contributes to the kind of interaction that occurs. One also needs a term that refers to whatever it is about the agent that contributes to the kind of interaction that occurs. [Terms used include *ability*, *effectivity*, and *aptitude*.] ...
> Affordances and abilities, (or effectivities or aptitudes) are, in this view, inherently relational. An affordance relates attributes of something in the environment to an interactive activity by an agent who has some ability, and an ability relates attributes of an agent to an interactive activity with something in the environment that has some affordance. The relativity of affordances and abilities is fundamental. Neither an

affordance nor an ability is specifiable in the absence of specifying the other. It does not go far enough to say that an ability depends on the context of environmental characteristics, or that an affordance depends on the context of an agent's characteristics. The concepts are codefining, and neither of them is coherent, absent the other, any more than the physical concept of motion or frame of reference make sense without both of them.

(Greeno, 1994, pp. 337–8)

Along with affordances there are constraints and attunements (what individuals are disposed or attuned to recognise as possibilities), including *powers* (see p. 115). Affordances are constrained as well as enabled by tools, rules, custom, language and power, so the actual possibilities are a subset of what might be possible. There is a complex interplay between what could be possible, what is possible and what is seen as possible.

Play: Zoltan Dienes

Dienes strongly advocated exposing learners to multiple embodiments (several different situations in which the same idea arises) so that they can abstract the essence, just as three pens, three crayons, or three teddies are abstracted to 'three' quite naturally and spontaneously by young children:

> Many people have suggested before … the natural way in which children acquire knowledge is through play in some form or another. It is not at all clear, however, what the processes are that lead from play to the purer forms of cognition such as construction of classifications, generalizations, logical classifications and deductions.
>
> (Dienes, 1963, p. 21)

There are similarities with the role of intention in *activity theory* (see p. 84).

Dienes then went on to distinguish three types of play: *exploratory-manipulative*, which is curiosity-prompted play without specific aim or direction; *representational* play in which the objects begin to stand for something they are not, bringing imagination into 'play'; and the *search for regularities*.

> Manipulative play may quite imperceptibly move over to a search for regularities. When a rule or rules are found, play may occur which uses these rules. Children delight in regularities, and the formulation of a rule-structure is a kind of closure which ties up all the loose ends of past experience. Children feel safe within such a rule-structure. Once it's been thoroughly mastered, and has become part of the currency of play, the closure is often reopened by asking questions. In this case the rules

themselves will be the objects of manipulation and situation is open again at a higher level.

(ibid., p. 23)

Dienes is making use of *invariance* (see p. 132 and p. 193), and there are similarities with *modelling* (see p. 190), and Polya's three phases of *exploring, formalising* and *assimilating* (see p. 147).

Activity: Geoff Giles

Geoff Giles (b. Scotland, 1929–) was the founding director of the DIME project. He is a prolific generator of mathematical tasks and cultural tools, such as angle measurers and tiles, for generating useful mathematical activity.

> ... The teacher provides the situation in which the activity takes place. The situation contained, explicitly or implicitly, a problem, i.e., the situation provokes the child into activity. This activity is not to be effected by direct intervention of the teacher and thus depends only on the initial situation.
>
> (Giles, 1966, p. 9)

> Activity may not be mathematical. Operating a record player is not in itself a musical activity although it may be closely connected. Similarly, playing with coloured rods might involve no mathematical activity. (They might represent soldiers, or flowers in a garden.) Mathematics exists in the mind, and so mathematical activity is a mental activity. We cannot observe it directly; we can only infer that it is taking place from behaviour.
>
>   Activity may be mathematical and yet not desirable. Tackling a problem involving two taps filling a bath with no plug is a mathematical activity but is undesirable.
>
> (ibid., p. 10)

Appropriate tasks: Herbert Spencer

Spencer was an early advocate of learner exploration (see p. 116). He raised the question behind criticism of *discovery learning* (see p. 143):

> If it be true that the mind, like the body ... unfolds spontaneously – if its successive desires for this or that kind of information arise when these are severally required for its nutrition – if there thus exists in itself a prompter to the right species of activity at the right time – why interfere in any way? Why not leave children *wholly* to the discipline of nature? ... This is an awkward-looking question.
>
> (Spencer, 1878, pp. 62–3)

Spencer drew attention to the way in which adults provide children with appropriate tasks and equipment, but the development is through a learner's own use of their muscles and coordination. He proposed a parallel with intellectual development (see *powers*, p. 115).

> ... Thus, in providing from day to day the right kind of facts, prepared in the right manner, and giving them in due abundance at appropriate intervals, there is as much scope for active ministration to a child's mind as to its body.
>
> (Spencer, 1878, p. 64)

Using situations: Colin Banwell, Ken Saunders and Dick Tahta

Banwell and his colleagues described the conditions they consider necessary for situations to be fruitful mathematically:

> To be most fruitful, ... situations should be able to be developed in many different directions. They must be able to be initiated simply, immediately, and with a minimum demand upon existing vocabulary or technique. For there to be any creative response, they must be presented with flexible and experimental intent, often with deliberate ambiguity.
>
> ... working from situations ... is not the same as working from problems. Part of the activity is, in fact, the formulation of [local] problems that may arise out of the definitions and rules that are developed in the discussion of the situation. Students will readily wish to solve problems that they have created themselves and such solutions are part of the work that follows from the starting point.
>
> (Banwell, Saunders and Tahta, 1972, p. 66)

Many teachers have found that learner-generated tasks are more engaging than worksheets and textbook tasks.

> ... In selecting, or recognizing, starting points that will be fruitful, the teacher may wish to see a [good] balance between those that are genuinely open for himself as well as his students, and those that he knows through experience or insight are very likely to lead to structures already known to him if not to students. In the latter case, it may be difficult for him to restrain his influence on the choices that have to be made. We do not suggest that he should not make choices, but think it is important that he should not only know when this is happening but be able to show it.
>
> (ibid., p. 66)

When a teacher 'knows' what learners could encounter, the *desire* that the learners do encounter it can turn into a strong temptation to make sure that this happens (see p. 96). Banwell and his colleagues were advocating that teachers be aware of, and be able to justify, the choices that they make.

Using situations: Janet Ainley

Ainley has been a primary school teacher, teacher educator, and researcher. She worked for some time with Skemp as a research fellow. Here she neatly captures a teaching dilemma between using situations as they arise, and sticking to a prepared plan. Using situations as they arise can be taken to extremes: either ignoring interests that have attracted learners' attention, or on the other hand, being swayed and driven by whims in an attempt to make and maintain contact with the learners' interests.

> *Dead Birds*: Pat likes to harness the children's enthusiasms and interests in the classroom, and tries to integrate work in all areas of the curriculum. Activities are rarely planned in advance, because this might impose adult interests on the children. Instead, all the work stems from what the children bring to the classroom. Often this is in the form of stories from their experiences at home, but occasionally they literally bring into school starting points from which work in a range of subjects may develop.
>
> For example, one day a child found a dead bird on the way to school, and brought it to show to Pat and the rest of the class. Everything else was abandoned as the children became absorbed in studying this find. Lots of writing and artwork were inspired by the dead bird, but Pat was also pleased with the mathematical activities that the children did. They had been doing some weighing activities earlier in the week, so some of them decided to weigh the bird, using a variety of informal units. The maths table in the classroom was well equipped with measuring instruments, and other children wanted to use these to measure various parts of the bird. One group pulled out some of its feathers and timed them with a stop-watch as they dropped to the ground. ...
>
> *Easter Bunnies*: Chris is also very concerned to link the mathematics that the children do to other curriculum areas. The class follow a mathematics scheme, but children work at their own pace through the textbooks. The books are a bit dull, and Chris likes to make extra teaching materials for the class, following the progression in the textbook, but relating mathematics to topics that the class are working on in other areas.
>
> Chris is a good artist, and makes attractive worksheets, which the children always enjoy using. Towards the end of the spring term last year, the class were preparing for Easter. In mathematics, many of the children were doing multiplication and division, so Chris adapted the exercises in the textbook and made worksheets of problems involving Easter

bunnies. For the group that had got up to the section in the textbook on money problems, Chris' worksheets were all about buying Easter eggs.

(Ainley, 1982, p. 7)

Rich contexts: Hans Freudenthal

Freudenthal mused on how *context-rich* mathematics instruction became *rich contexts*, perhaps influenced by the notion of *rich structures*. Here he lists features of context-rich tasks.

> *Fraught with relations* was the term I chose for the mathematics I wanted to be taught. In the meantime that term has become mathematics in *rich contexts*. ...
>
> [...]
>
> *Location*: a meaningful gathering of situations, which can be handled separately, or in more or less close connection with each other. ...
>
> *Story*: ... rather than a gathering, something that, reeled off as a succession of worksheets, is structured in time. It may be a true story or fiction, a classic or invented *ad hoc*. [For example, a giant leaves traces of visiting the classroom and from his footprint his size is gauged, the amount of food he needs, etc., and then messages appear from him asking various questions.]
>
> *Project*: ... reality to be created [through making something].
>
> *Theme*: ... a mathematically oriented strand of subject matter with varying relations to reality [such as 'light and shadow' or 'exponential functions'].
>
> *Clippings*: mainly from newspapers and weeklies, but also from books and other media. ...
>
> Contexts were defined as domains of reality disclosed to the learner in order to be mathematised. In the cases of *location, story, project,* and *theme* such domains are purposefully – sometimes artificially – delimited by the teacher or developer, who wants the learner to reinvent certain processes and products of mathematising. The case of *clippings* is a bit different. Here it is not a domain but a small piece that is cut out, although its paradigmatical value for mathematising and for acquiring a mathematical attitude may be enormous in comparison.
>
> But in all cases it should be kept in mind that context is not a mere garment clothing nude mathematics, and mathematising is quite another thing than simply unbuttoning this garment. ... Viewing context as noise, apt to disturb the clear mathematical message, is wrong; the context itself is the message, and mathematics a means of decoding.

(Freudenthal, 1991, pp. 73–5)

Angle as problématique: Nicolas Balacheff

The following extracts are taken from a paper in which Balacheff sketched the background assumptions of his approach, and applied the approach to the case of the size of angles and the invariance of the sum of the angles of a triangle.

First, some of the background, then a proposal to make use of the learners' initial wrong conceptions by identifying four constraints.

> Pupils' conceptions of the notion of angle are likely to lead them to assert that the larger the triangle, the larger the sum of the angles ... . Because of this conception, the value of a proof proposed by the teacher, even after some manipulations [learners folding triangles, etc.] are doubtful, because (a) the assertion itself might appear arbitrary insofar as results like 182° or 178° are pragmatically as good candidates as 180°, and (b) the pupils will be left with an open conflict between their intuition ... and the authority of the proposed proof.
>   [...]
>
> 1   It is not possible to tell the pupils beforehand that the purpose of the sequence will be to establish that the sum of the angles of a triangle is 180°. That would destroy the problem, because the assertion would no longer be considered as a conjecture; the student knows the teacher always tells the truth. This is a classic example of one of the basic beliefs held in the didactical contract.
> 2   The validity of the measurement of a particular set of triangles as a means to establish the conjecture should be dismissed. But this decision should be taken by the pupils on their own and not imposed by the teacher; otherwise they will seek a proof that is acceptable to the teacher.
> 3   The situation we design should elicit the pupils' conceptions about the relations between the size of a triangle and the value of the sum of its angles, because it is from the contradiction between this conception and the fact that the sums are around 180° that the conjecture could stem. This requires a situation for action.
> 4   We should provide the classroom with a situation for validation oriented toward the construction of a proof of the conjecture. That supposes a didactical contract in which the pupils have the responsibility for the truth of the conjecture. This is possible only if they have had the responsibility for forming the statement of the conjecture itself.
>
>   (Balacheff, 1990, p. 265)

Note the problem of being explicit with learners about the objectives of a lesson (see also *inner and outer* aspects of tasks, p. 241).

Pros and cons of apparatus

Multiple embodiment: Zoltan Dienes

Dienes was led to what he called the perceptual variability principle and to the mathematical variability principle:

> … to abstract a mathematical structure effectively, one must meet it in a number of different situations to perceive its purely structural properties. … [As] every mathematical concept involved essential variables, *all* these mathematical variables need to be varied if the full generality of the mathematical concept is to be achieved. The application of the perceptual variability principle ensures efficient abstraction; the application of the mathematical variability principle ensures efficient generalization. By abstraction I mean understanding the structure's applicable breadth; and by generalization, grasping the full extent of the mathematical class, usually of numbers, for which the expression of the rule-structure is valid. Effective mathematical thinking must take into account the abstraction and the generalization process.
>
> (Dienes, 1963, pp. 158–9)

Note the use of *abstraction* and *generalisation* (see p. 59 and p. 185). Note also the similarities with *invariance* as a theme in mathematics (see p. 193) and with *dimensions-of-possible-variation* (see p. 56). There were problems however, in applying and testing these principles.

Dienes reported:

> We assumed throughout our experiments that abstraction would arise from a multiple embodiment of the concepts to be abstracted. By this I mean that situations physically equivalent to the concept-structure to be learned would, if handled according to specific instructions leading towards the structure, result in abstracting the common structure from all the physical situations. We thought that when this had been accomplished, symbolism could be introduced to describe the structure just abstracted. But as we observed the children going through such 'abstraction exercises', it soon became clear that the picture was far more complex than we had assumed.
>
> At first there was the theoretical difficulty of finding the criterion for determining whether a concept had been learned as an abstract structure or not. According to our first 'simple-minded' theory, abstraction was tested by children's ability to transfer a mathematical structure embodied in one situation to a different embodiment. … there are certain difficulties about this procedure, and, even theoretically, in order to make the procedure valid some method of comparing embodiments would have to be devised. Clearly some embodiments are closer to each other than

others: in one case, for example, only a small number of the attributes [relevant] to the structure may have been varied, and in another a large number of these attributes might have been varied. It seems that it would be possible to make an embodiment so 'noisy' that extracting the looked-for mathematical structure might be well-nigh impossible.

(ibid., pp. 68–9)

See also Dienes on generalization and symbols (p. 136).

Not everyone agrees with the universal value of using apparatus in classrooms. Embodiment is a feature of the perceiver, not the apparatus itself. (See also *mathematising*, p. 256 and p. 283.)

Blocks abstract for some: John Holt

... Children who already understand base and place value, even if only intuitively, could see the connections between written numerals and these blocks. ... But children who could not do these problems without the blocks didn't have a clue about how to do them with the blocks.

... They found the blocks, ... as abstract, as disconnected from reality, mysterious, arbitrary, and capricious as the numbers these blocks were supposed to bring to life.

(Holt, 1964, pp. 218–19)

Passing over situated knowledge: Koeno Gravemeijer

Even though actions on objects, which may, of course, be mental or symbolic as well as material, lie at the heart of learning, the use of apparatus to *embody* mathematical concepts has been more praised than used. Dienes was not the only person to encounter problems in researching the use of apparatus. Koeno Gravemeijer is a Dutch mathematics educator and researcher who worked with Hans Freudenthal, and continues his work at the Freudenthal Institute. Here he summarises his position after giving many examples:

... the use of manipulatives does not really help students attain mathematical insight. ... [The reason put forward is that] the mathematics *embedded in the models* is not concrete for the students. ... the manipulatives approach passes over the situated, informal knowledge of the students. ...

(Gravemeijer, 1994, p. 77)

Beginning with the concrete: John Dewey

Here Dewey works on the distinction between the concrete and the abstract, and challenges the notion that apparatus in itself aids learning (see also Dewey, p. 45, and Gattegno, p. 134).

Since the *concrete* denotes thinking applied to activities for the sake of dealing with difficulties that present themselves practically, 'begin with the concrete' signifies that we should, at the outset of any new experience in learning, make much of what is already familiar, and if possible connect the new topics and principles with the pursuit of an end in some active occupation. We do not 'follow the order of nature' when we multiply mere sensations or accumulate physical objects. Instruction in number is not concrete merely because splints or beans or dots are employed. Whenever the use and bearing of number relations are clearly perceived, a number idea is concrete even if figures alone are used. Just what sort of symbol it is best to use at the given time – whether blocks, or lines, or figures – is entirely a matter of adjustment to a given case. If the physical things used in teaching number or geography or anything else do not leave the mind illuminated with recognition of a *meaning* beyond themselves, the instruction that uses them is as abstruse as that which doles out ready-made definitions and rules, for it distracts attention from ideas to mere physical excitations.

(Dewey, 1933, pp. 224–5)

There are interesting parallels with Mason (1980) where he suggested that symbols can actually be 'concrete', imagistic or symbolic, or all three simultaneously.

The notion that we have only to put physical objects before the senses in order to impress ideas upon the mind amounts almost to a superstition. The introduction of object lessons and sense-training scored a distinct advance over the prior method of linguistic symbols, but this advance tended to blind educators to the fact that only a halfway step had been taken. Things and sensations develop the child, indeed, but only when he *uses* them in mastering his body and coordinating his actions. Continuous occupations involve the use of natural materials, tools, modes of energy, and do it in a way that compels thinking as to how they relate to one another and to the realization of ends. But the mere isolated presentation of things to sense remains barren and dead.

(Dewey, 1993, p. 225)

Appropriateness?: Kath Hart

Kath Hart (b. London, 1934–) achieved the first Ph.D in mathematics education in England. She advocated the design of textbooks and tasks on the basis of research, and led various teams to that end herself (Hart, 1981; 1984). Here she challenges the use of apparatus:

Before we recommend to teachers that they use manipulatives we should advise them to view the appropriateness and limitations of the materials for the purpose of leading to and authenticating a part of formal mathematics.

[...]

We need to research when manipulatives are appropriate as well as the balance of time given to different activities within the same scheme.

(Hart, 1993, pp. 27–8)

Hart's researches showed that time spent on the apparatus was rarely matched with time spent articulating the formula or rule. Furthermore, children with difficulties in applying rules were often sent back to concrete aids, which presupposed that they remembered the connection and that they could re-invent the it.

Need for sense-making first: Grayson Wheatley

Although the use of apparatus is promoted to counter learners' sense of abstractness, alienation and irrelevance, Wheatley suggested that abstraction is inescapable (see also *alien*, p. 102, and *motivation*, p. 99), and that an effective approach promotes sense-making first and foremost.

> Often the use of manipulatives is supposed to make the abstract formulations of mathematics comprehensible to students. Using concrete objects to 'show' students a mathematical concept or relationship is still based on the 'abstract-first' conception of learning. When, as Gravemeijer (1990) suggests, emphasis is placed on mathematizing from potentially meaningful situations, students have the opportunity to construct experience-based knowledge. ... In mathematics learning, the intention to make sense is essential (Erlwanger, 1973). Neither the abstract-first nor procedures-first approach to learning fosters the intention to make sense. ...
>
> (Wheatley, 1992, p. 533)

> Often when manipulatives are used in teaching mathematics, the teacher demonstrates *the* way they are to be used and students are left little freedom to give meaning to the experience in ways that make sense to them; the way the materials are to be used is prescribed. There is the mistaken belief on the part of the teacher that the mathematics is apparent in the materials, for example, 'base 10' blocks (Cobb, Yackel and Wood, 1992). This is based on the belief that mathematics is 'out there' and that models 'show' the concepts. The demonstration with concrete materials is quite appealing because the concepts are so vivid for those who have *already* made the construction. Thus there is the mistaken belief that since we, as adults, can see the mathematics in the blocks, the students will too. But the 'seeing' requires the very construction the activity is intended to teach.
>
> (ibid., p. 534)

Where apparatus can become an obstacle rather than an aid there are similarities with Fischbein's analysis of *intuition* (see p. 63).

Empirical abstraction: Jean Piaget

Piaget writes about deriving information from apparatus.

> It is notable ... that empirical abstraction, whatever the level involved, never comes into operation by itself. In order to derive information from an object, and even if it can only be drawn from that object, the use of an assimilatory apparatus is indispensable. This assimilatory apparatus is of a mathematical nature ... a whole range of instruments ... which is necessary to the very 'reading' of experience itself and which is independent of other interpretations which will follow. These recording instruments make possible only the empirical type of abstraction, but it is clear that they themselves are not derived from the object, since they constitute the conditions preliminary to the subject's cognitive grasp of that object. They are thus due to the subject's own activities, and, as such, they arise from previous reflecting abstraction. This will be true ... even if the empirical abstraction which they make possible subsequently draws its products from the external object alone.
>
> (Piaget, 1980, pp. 90–1)

Assimilation is a key process of Piaget (see p. 149), as is *reflective abstraction* (see p. 171).

Manipulatives: Patricia Moyer-Packenham

Moyer-Packenham taught in elementary school for ten years before moving into teacher education in both mathematics and science leadership.

> ... Manipulatives are not, of themselves, carriers of meaning for insight. 'Although kinesthetic experience can enhance perception and thinking, understanding does not travel through the finger tips and up the arm' (Ball, 1992, p. 47). It is through their use as tools that students have the opportunity to gain insight into their experience with them. Research has shown that for children to use concrete representation effectively without increased demands on their processing capacity, they must know the materials well enough to use them automatically (Boulton-Lewis, 1998). If the user is constantly aware of the artifact then it is not a tool, for it is not serving the purpose of enabling some desired activity which moves one toward a desired goal state (Winograd and Flores, 1986). ...
>
> Students sometimes learn to use manipulatives in a rote manner, with little or no learning of the mathematical concepts behind the procedures (Hiebert and Wearne, 1992) and the inability to link their actions with

manipulatives to abstract symbols (Thompson and Thompson, 1990). This is because the manipulative is simply the manufacturer's representation of a mathematical concept that may be used for different purposes in various contexts with varying degrees of 'transparency'. ...

(Moyer, 2001, pp. 176–177)

So *rote* learning can apply to manipulating physical objects as well as to symbols as marks on paper. It is not just apparatus that requires interpretation:

Algebraic symbols do not speak for themselves. What one actually sees in them depends on the requirements of a specific problem to which they are applied. Not less important, it depends on what one is *prepared* to notice and *able* to perceive.

(Sfard, 1994, p. 192)

Moyer-Packenham pointed out that the teacher's attitude and reasons for using apparatus is likely to influence the affordances (see p. 246) available in the situation. In a small study of pre-service teachers' views about apparatus, she found a persistent orientation towards the 'fun dimensions'.

In many instances teachers indicated that the use of manipulatives was 'fun'. Initially the term 'fun' seemed to indicate that teachers and students found enjoyment in using the manipulatives during mathematics teaching and learning. Further analysis of the data suggested that embedded in teachers' use of the word 'fun' were some unexamined notions that inhibit the use of manipulatives in mathematics instruction. Teachers made subtle distinctions between 'real math' and 'fun math', using the term 'real math' to refer to lesson segments where they taught rules, procedures and algorithms using textbooks, notebooks, worksheets, and paper-and-pencil tasks. The term 'fun math' was used when teachers described parts of the lesson where students were having fun with the manipulatives.

Moyer, 2001, p. 185)

See also *activity theory* and the mediation of tools (p. 85 and p. 220).

Advance organisers: David Ausubel

However tasks are presented, many learners find it helpful to have an overview of what is expected before they dive into details. Ausubel, an America psychologist much influenced by Piaget, called these *advance organisers*. They have become institutionalised in radio and television programmes in which you are told what the programme is about or what someone is going to say (advance organiser, sign posting), then there is the substance of the programme, followed by a summary of what it was about or what the person said.

… These organizers are introduced in advance of learning itself, and are also presented at a higher level of abstraction, generality, and inclusiveness; and since the substantive content of a given organizer or series of organizers is selected on the basis of their suitability for explaining, integrating, and interrelating the material they precede … , this strategy simultaneously satisfies the substantive as well as the programming criteria for enhancing the organization strength of cognitive structure.

(Ausubel, 1963, p. 81)

Affordances are possibilities due to relationship between person and situation, so tasks and texts, and particularly, apparatus, only have affordances in the context of particular people making use of them. Secondary play is an important part of encountering and getting to know any object, whether apparatus, images, or symbols.

Various dimensions of tasks each provide a spectrum of possibilities, all directed towards engaging the learner in exploring, connecting and experiencing. Apparatus (examples in the material world) may help link to learner experience, but has to be transcended and left behind (move into mental and symbolic worlds) for useful learning to occur. Apparatus use can be an obstacle to learning, particularly where teachers treat apparatus as 'for fun' rather than drawing out mathematical structure.

10 Sustaining mathematical activity

Introduction

This chapter addresses the core of teaching. Several frameworks that have proved to be useful in planning lessons are introduced, building on previous chapters.

> The structure of any domain of knowledge may be characterized in three ways, each affecting the ability of any learner to master it: the *mode of representation* in which it is put, its *economy*, and its effective *power*. Mode, economy, and power vary in relation to different ages, to different 'styles' among learners, and to different subject matters.
>
> (Bruner, 1966, p. 44)

Integrating frameworks

Four closely interlinked frameworks are considered here. The words in each framework have been chosen to trigger the framework into mind while planning lessons and, in the midst of a lesson, to act as a reminder about what actions could be chosen to support effective learning rather than following automated and habitual routines.

Enactive–Iconic–Symbolic (EIS): Jerome Bruner

The EIS framework is an expression of *three worlds* of experience (see p. 73).

> Any domain of knowledge (or any problem within that domain of knowledge) can be represented in three ways: by a set of actions appropriate for achieving a certain result (enactive representation); by a set of summary images or graphics that stand for a concept without defining it fully (iconic representation); and by a set of symbolic or logical propositions drawn from a symbolic system that is governed by rules or laws for forming and transforming propositions (symbolic representation). The distinction can most conveniently be made completely in terms of a

balance beam, … . A quite young child can plainly act on the basis of the 'principles' of a balance beam, and indicates he could do so by being able to handle himself on a see-saw. He knows that to get his side to go down farther he has to move out farther from the center. A somewhat older child can represent the balance beam to himself either by a model on which rings can be hung and balanced or by a drawing. The 'image' of the balance beam can be varyingly refined, with fewer and fewer irrelevant details present, as in the typical diagrams in an introductory textbook in physics. Finally, a balance beam can be described in ordinary English, without diagrammatic aids, or it can be even better described mathematically by reference to Newton's Law of Moments in inertial physics. Needless to say, actions, pictures, and symbols vary in difficulty and utility for people of different ages, different backgrounds, different styles.

(Bruner, 1966, pp. 44–5)

What does it mean to translate experience into a model of the world? … there are probably three ways in which human beings accomplish this feat. The first is through action. We know many things for which we have no imagery and no words, and they are very hard to teach anybody by the use of either words or diagrams and pictures. If you tried to coach somebody at tennis or skiing or to teach a child to ride a bike, you will have been struck by the wordlessness and the diagrammatic impotence of the teaching process. … There is a second system of representation that depends upon visual or other sensory organization and upon the use of summarizing images. … We have come to talk about the first form of representation as *enactive*, the second as *iconic*. Iconic representation is principally governed by principles of perceptual organization and by … economical transformations in perceptual organization … – techniques for filling in, completing, extrapolating. Enactive representation is based, it seems, upon a learning of responses and forms of habituation.

Finally, there is representation in words or language. Its hallmark is that it is *symbolic* in nature, with certain features of symbolic systems that are only now coming to be understood. Symbols (words) are arbitrary, … they are remote in reference, and they are almost always highly productive or generative in the sense that a language or any symbol system has rules for the formation and transformation of sentences that can turn reality over on its beam ends beyond what is possible through actions or images. A language, for example, permits us to introduce lawful syntactic transformations that make it easy and useful to approach declarative propositions about reality in a most striking way. We observe an event and encode it – the dog bit the man. From this utterance we can travel to a range of possible recodings – did the dog bite the man or did he not? If he had not what would have happened? And so on. …

I should also mention one other property of a symbolic system – its compactibility – a property that permits condensations [formulae] ... .

(ibid., pp. 10–12)

Here Bruner is acknowledging the importance of the use of language to distance the speaker from an action ('everything said is said by an observer', see p. 70).

How transitions are effected – from enactive presentation to iconic, and from both of these to symbolic – is a moot and troubled question. To put the matter very briefly, it would seem as if some sort of image formation or schema formation – whatever we should call the device that renders a sequence of actions simultaneous, renders it into an immediate representation – comes rather automatically as an accompaniment of response to stabilization. But how the nervous system converts a sequence of responses into an image or schema is simply not understood.

(ibid., p. 14)

Bruner was pointing to the fundamental problem of how it is that a sequence of impressions becomes a self-contained entity with stressing and ignoring producing a sense of sameness and of difference in relation to past experience (see *reification*, p. 167, and *discernment*, p. 55). Bruner advocated paying attention to transitions between enactive participation (learners doing things like moving or counting bricks, even doing calculations in the head or on a calculator) and iconic participation, imagining without actually doing. The word 'transition' should not be taken as describing a once and for all shift between worlds, but rather a gradual shift as to which world is dominant at the time. A similar 'transition' takes place between the iconic and the symbolic as the 'doing' is recorded in general terms, formalised in some way.

The following three frameworks were developed for an Open University course for teachers in the 1980s to support teachers in the developments which Bruner suggests are problematic.

Do–Talk–Record (DTR)

The *Do–Talk–Record* framework (and variants such as *See–Say–Record*) was proposed as useful for remembering to get learners talking about their ideas before rushing into symbols and written records, and for justifying spending time in this way. The idea is expressed as:

Action and concrete experience of a process, linked through language development and much discussion, support pictures of that action and words which describe the process, which in turn is linked as a result of frequent use and successive shorthanding to standard notation and layout of an algorithm.

(based on Floyd *et al.*, 1982, Block 1, p. 23)

Note the similarity with other versions of *reification* (see p. 167).

> Students on EM235 were led to a framework of Do–Talk–Record in order
> to draw attention to the desirability of learners acting upon familiar
> objects and talking about what they are doing in order to develop and
> integrate the basic language patterns of the topic into their own func-
> tioning. Recording is then motivated by giving instructions to others as
> to how and when to perform the same actions using longhand stories
> and pictures, and then, through successive shorthanding, to approach
> standard notation and layout.
>
> (based on Floyd *et al.*, 1982, Block 1, p. 24)

> New ideas take time to grasp. Useful activities are ones which provide
> plenty of opportunity for rehearsing language, rather than filling in
> blanks in a worksheet. For example, games in which each learner can
> check that others are using the language appropriately, providing varia-
> tions of activities in order to keep learners in a situation long enough for
> them to become fluent in the use of the language.
>
> (based on Floyd *et al.*, 1982, Block 1, p. 48)

See–Experience–Master (SEM)

No idea is grasped or appreciated on first or even second encounter. The
SEM framework, also used on The Open University Course EM235, can serve
as a reminder not to expect too much of learners too quickly.

> First encounters with any idea are at best transitory. A word you do not
> recognize flashes by in a conversation; a concept you vaguely recognize
> gets used several times, but you have no clear idea of its full import; a task is
> set and although you can work out what to do you are not at all clear what
> it is really about or why it works, or even, perhaps, what it achieves. It is
> unreasonable then to expect learners to grasp ideas on first encounter.
>
> However, as you get more experience with a concept or a technique,
> it gradually starts to fit in with what you already know. You start to
> assimilate it into your familiar ways of thinking, or you find yourself
> adjusting your thinking to accommodate the new idea. ... Familiarity
> and facility arise only after considerable experience *and*, usually, reflec-
> tion on that experience. For one thing we do not seem to learn from
> experience is that we do not often learn from experience alone. Some-
> thing else is required.
>
> Sometimes you find that after a period of time, what seemed awkward
> and a struggle suddenly comes easily. Learning can be thought of as a
> maturation process, like the baking of bread and the brewing of beer:
> some transformation is required which cannot be rushed.
>
> (based on Floyd *et al.*, 1982, Blocks 2 & 4)

Transitions between the three modes of representations in the three worlds introduced by Bruner can be enhanced and supported by paying attention to the purpose of 'doing', of manipulating confidence-inspiring entities, namely, to get a sense of what the particular is indicating might be true in general, and eventually articulating this. A new concept is appreciated by reference to familiar examples and how the examples illustrate the concept; a difficult problem is tackled by simplifying and particularising it so as to get a sense of what might be going on, before returning to the more difficult or more general case; a tricky technique is mastered by applying it to familiar cases and then to less and less familiar cases as a sense of what the technique does and how it works and is used, develops, eventually coming to articulation (you express it for yourself).

Manipulating–Getting-a-sense-of–Articulating (MGA) spiral

This next framework was also developed by Floyd *et al.* (1982) and elaborated in various places, though the ideas have ancient roots in the wisdom of teachers through the ages. Its role is to serve as a reminder of the purpose of 'doing things' beyond the mere accomplishment of the task, and to offer a metaphor for the complex layering process which we call experience and learning.

> Picture mathematical thinking on a helix which loops round and round. Each loop represents an opportunity to extend understanding by encountering an idea, an object, a diagram, or symbol with enough surprise or curiosity to impel exploration of it by *manipulating*. The level at which manipulation begins must be concrete and confidence inspiring and the results of the manipulation will then be available for interpretation. Tension provoked by the gap which opens between what is expected and what actually happens provides a force to keep the process going and some *sense* of pattern or connectedness releases the tension into achievement, wonder, pleasure, further surprise or curiosity which drives the process on. While the sense of what is happening remains vague, more specialization is required until the force of the sense is expressed in the articulation of a generalization. Articulations do not have to be verbal. They might well be concrete, diagrammatic or symbolic but they will crystallize whenever is the essence underlying the sense which has been achieved as a result of the manipulations. And achieved articulation immediately becomes available for new manipulating, and the wrap-around of the helix. Each successive loop assumes that the thinker is operating at a deeper level of complexity. The connectedness of the loops always permits the thinker the opportunity to track back to previous levels and therefore to revise articulating that might have begun to wobble.

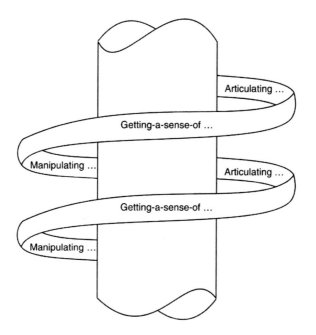

(Mason, Burton and Stacey, 1982, pp. 155–6)

Interconnections

Bruner's three modes of *representation* (EIS) allied to the *three worlds* (see p. 73) are embedded in what the MGA spiral offers:

> *Turning to enactive elements to explore the meaning of symbols or concepts; Using enactive elements to try to get a sense of pattern; Asking for images, metaphors, diagrams to illustrate what is going on; crystallizing understanding in symbolic form; practising with examples to move the symbolic form into enactive elements.*
>
> (Mason, 1980, p. 11)

These in turn are related to *Do–Talk–Record* (see p. 262) as a summary of conjecturing (see p. 139):

1 Do examples (Specialize) using entities with which you are entirely confident, which you can manipuilate easily while part of your attention remains focused on your primary goal.
2 Try to get a sense of underlying pattern or relationship. Often diagrams or metaphors will help here – have you seen a similar problem or idea? An analogous one?

3 Try to articulate the pattern you sense. Keep refining the articulation until it can be checked on examples [taking you] back to 1 again.

(ibid., p. 10)

The first is mostly *doing* (but with attention: recall the *two birds*, p. 32) affording opportunity for *seeing* (encountering) new ideas, *experiencing* themes and ideas met previously (as well as contexts and ways of speaking and so on – see *Structure-of-a-topic*, p. 203), and gaining *mastery* of techniques already encountered. The second is enhanced by *talking* (to yourself and to others) in order to get a sense of the pattern or multiple relationships, to experience multiple *dimensions-of-possible-variation* (see p. 56) which make up or contribute to the concept involved. It supports *educating awareness* (see p. 61 and p. 204). The third, articulating, leads to *recording* and formalisation, through recognition of properties independent of the particular objects used, and hence to appreciation of generality. Note connections with *reification* (see p. 167).

For a summary and synthesis of the three frameworks, see Floyd *et al.* (1982, Block 4, pp. 20–27).

The three forms of representation, *Enactive–Iconic–Symbol*, correspond to the three worlds. To fully encounter an idea learners need to engage in *Doing–Talking–Recording*, but it is important not to rush to recording. *See–Experience–Master* is a reminder not to expect too much from early encounters: teaching takes place *in* time while learning takes place *over* time.

Manipulate–Get-a-sense-of–Articulate, *Do–Talk–Record*, *Enactive–Iconic–Symbolic* and *See–Experience–Master* together provide a rich collection of triggers to sensitise awareness of opportunities when planning and in the midst of lessons.

Teacher intervention

Scaffolding

The heart of teaching lies in teacher interventions. But how to describe these interventions let alone recommend some over others is highly problematic.

The hardest part of teaching by challenging is to keep your mouth shut, to hold back. Don't *say*, ask! Don't replace the wrong *A* by the right *B*, but ask, 'Where did *A* come from?' Keep asking 'Is that right?, Are you sure?' Don't say 'No'; ask 'Why?'

(Halmos, 1985, p. 272)

Scaffolding: David Wood, Jerome Bruner and Gail Ross

Wood, Bruner and Ross introduced the term *scaffolding* into educational literature. The term has been used in a wide range of senses, though originally it was intended to describe how a teacher works in relation to Vygotsky's notion of the *zone of proximal development* (see p. 88).

> Well-executed scaffolding begins by luring the child into actions that produce recognizable-for-him solutions. Once that is achieved, the tutor can interpret discrepancies to the child. Finally, the tutor stands in a confirmatory role until the tutee is checked out to fly on his own … .
>
> (Wood, Bruner and Ross, 1976, p. 96)

1 *Recruitment.* The tutor's first and obvious task is to enlist the problem solver's interest in and adherence to the requirements of that task. …
2 *Reduction in degrees of freedom.* This involves simplifying the task by reducing the number of constituent acts required to reach solution. …
3 *Direction maintenance.* Learners lag and regress to other aims, given limits in their interests and capacities. The tutor has the role of keeping them in pursuit of a particular objective. Partly it involves keeping the child 'in the field' and partly a deployment of zest and sympathy to keep him motivated. …

> (ibid., p. 98)

This is part of being 'consciousness for two' (see p. 88).

4 *Marking critical features.* A tutor by a variety of means marks or accentuates certain features of the task that are relevant. His marking provides information about the discrepancy between what the child has produced and what he would recognize as a correct production. His task is to interpret discrepancies.

> (ibid., p. 98)

Note parallels with *stressing* and *ignoring* (see p. 127) and *structure of attention* (see p. 60).

5 *Frustration control.* There should be some such maxim as 'Problem solving should be less dangerous or stressful with the tutor than without'. Whether this is accomplished by 'face saving' for errors or by exploiting the learner's 'wish to please' or by other means, is of only minor importance. The major risk is in creating too much dependency on the tutor.
6 *Demonstration.* Demonstrating or 'modeling' solutions to a task, when closely observed, involves considerably more than simply performing in the presence of the tutee. It often involves an 'idealization' of the act to be performed and it may involve completion or even explication of a solution already partially executed by the tutee himself. In this sense, the tutor is 'imitating' in idealized form an attempted solution tried (or assumed to be tried) by the tutee in the

expectation that the learner will then 'imitate' it back in a more appropriate form.

(ibid., p. 98)

Scaffolding: David Wood and David Middleton

David Wood has devoted his entire career to exploring aspects of tutoring as it happens between mothers and young children, and between teachers and young children. However much of what is observed applies to tutoring at all ages.

> The child, of course, is no passive observer ... . The change and develop-
> ment of his abilities are not to be viewed as 'copying' or imitation in the
> sense that he merely matches his behaviour to that of another. Rather, ...
> he emerges as an active, selective agent, more akin to a 'rule-inducer' than
> a mere copier of action patterns (Wood and Middleton, 1975). However, it
> is our contention that any process of rule induction or problem-solving on
> his part can, and indeed often must, be facilitated by the intervention of
> another who is more expert in the situation than he is. It is the aim of the
> present study to examine in some detail the strategies which the mothers
> display when they attempt to fulfil this instructional role.
>
> [...]
>
> Clearly, when a child is alone success demands that he perform ...
> operations himself. But when a mother intervenes to help him she may
> take over one or more of them. By so doing, she may leave the child
> relatively free to concentrate all his attention and effort upon a narrower
> range of alternatives within the task. Where, for example, she asks him
> in general terms for some activity, 'Can you make some more like this
> one?', she merely suggests a relatively short-term goal to the child,
> leaving to him the task of determining the parameters for search,
> searching, assembling and evaluating. Or she might ask for something
> more specific like a 'big one', further constraining his actions by deter-
> mining not only a goal but at the least some of its attributes.
>
> (Wood and Middleton, 1975, pp. 181–2)

This is part of being 'consciousness-for-two' (see p. 88). This leads to a core problem in teaching: when and how to intervene?

> The crucial problem facing an instructor, of course, is deciding at what
> level to intervene. How many operations should she ask of the child and
> how many should she do herself? On the one hand, she should not want
> to see him 'swamped' by too many possibilities, but neither too should
> she wish to stifle his performance by doing too much herself. ... Ideally,
> the instructor should engineer discrepancies for the child by constantly
> showing or requesting goals which he can currently recognize but not

produce. In this way, he can lead the child to suitably constrained problem-solving activity.

(ibid. p. 182x)

Note the recourse to *disturbance* (see p. 55, p. 101 and p. 161). However desirable, 'doing for learners only what they cannot yet do for themselves' is not an easy path to follow.

> ... we suggest that, although any effective instruction requires the child to do more than he is immediately capable of, it must not ask him for too much. Ideally, the child should be asked to add one extra operation or decision to those which he is presently performing. This level of intervention we have termed the 'region of sensitivity to instruction' and our hypothesis is that the most effective instructors will concentrate their instructional activity within this region.

(ibid., p. 182)

The 'region of sensitivity to instruction' is informed by the notion of near-simultaneity of variation within *dimensions-of-possible-variation* (see p. 56). The purpose of scaffolding is to provide temporary support, which must therefore fade as the learner gradually takes over. Otherwise the learner is trained in dependency rather than gaining independence.

Questioning questioning

One obvious form of *scaffolding* (see p. 266) is asking questions. Asking learners questions is entirely natural, even if not always productive or effective.

Moving beyond the particular: Jerome Bruner

> ... if you ... are convinced that the best learning occurs when the teacher helps lead the pupil to discover generalizations on her own, you're likely to run into an established cultural belief that the teacher is an authority who is supposed to *tell* the child what the general case is, while the child should be occupying herself with memorizing the particulars. And if you study how most classrooms are conducted, you will often find that most of the teacher's questions to pupils are about particulars that can be answered in a few words or even by 'yes' or 'no'. So your introduction of an innovation in teaching will necessarily involve changing the folk psychological and folk pedagogical theories of teachers – and, to a surprising extent, of pupils as well.

(Bruner, 1996, p. 46)

Questioning: Janet Ainley

Question asking turns out to be very complicated, largely because what appears to be a question can be an instruction, and what appears to be an instruction can be a question. Furthermore the purpose of asking questions can be very varied. Here Ainley, who worked with Skemp, analyses the nature and purposes of questions.

> ... The students know that the teacher already knows the answer to the questions she is asking. Asking questions to which you already know the answer is a very odd linguistic activity, almost entirely restricted to classrooms, or at least to teaching situations. In other circumstances it would rightly be considered bizarre, except as a conversational gambit (where it is not apparent to the person you are talking to that you do know the answer). And yet this activity is what is generally meant by 'questioning' children. It is part of the 'school game' and teachers and students both know its purpose: the teacher does not want to find out information, but rather to ascertain whether or not the students know the answers. ...
>
> [...]
>
> ... what constitutes an open rather than a closed question, since being open or closed seems not to be so much an attribute of the question per se as something read into it by the questioner or the hearer. Teacher and pupils may have different perceptions of this distinction, and students' perception may be altered by the way in which their answers are handled. The purpose of these questions is not to gain new information. This is well known to the students, who may very well perceive such a question as a closed one, that is, as having only one correct answer. When starting off investigations ... I often ask, 'How many different ones can you find?' My intention is to open up the investigation, but some hearers will take this as a closed question, requiring an exact numerical answer. ...
>
> ... There is an important sense in which *any* type of questioning conveys information. By asking questions you indicate what is of interest to you. When the teacher asks a question, she is drawing attention to those aspects of the situation which are important. This is true even with more open questions. A teacher's question conveys the message 'there's something important here, and you should know about it'. Again, this is emphasised by the fact that the student believes the teacher already knows the answer(s). One reason for asking such a question is precisely to draw attention to something.
>
> [...]
>
> ... There seem to be, in very general terms, three distinct types of activities which have the same syntactic form, but serve different purposes. These we might call,

- *genuine questions* – asked because you want to know the answer;
- *test questions* – asked when you already know the answer, to find out if the other person knows it;
- *provoking questions* – asked to draw attention to something you want the person to think about.

(Ainley, 1987, pp. 25–6)

Open and closed questions: Anne Watson

As we have seen, questions are often described as either *open* or *closed*, but it is not at all clear that open questions are more effective in involving learners than are closed questions, or vice versa.

An open question is usually taken to mean one with several answers, to which many learners can contribute, but contrast these two open questions:

If the answer is 4, what could the question be?

I want you to make up three questions to which the answer is 4, and each question must come from a different topic we have studied this term.

The first question is wide open, and is likely to generate low level arithmetical operations using small whole numbers. The second is more constrained and denies the possibility of sticking with simple operations; learners are forced to think beyond the obvious. Both are open, with the advantages of open questions, but one is more likely to involve grappling with concepts than the other.

Compare the first open question to this closed question:

What number is a square number, and is also the number of sides of a shape which can be made by sticking two congruent triangles together edge-to-edge?

The latter question is closed, but encourages engagement with concepts. The almost Orwellian mantra 'open-good; closed-bad' is clearly misleading.

(Watson, 2002, pp. 34–5)

Learners who are used to directed instructions may at first be flummoxed by questions which invite them to make choices. But over a period of time when they find that they are permitted to make choices, their creativity and adventurousness is likely to open out.

Any question can be closed down so that a single yes or no is all that is required, and learners get quite good at guessing which it is likely to be by the tone of voice of the questioner, pauses and emphasis and so on. It is equally the case that any question or instruction, no matter how narrow and restrictive, can be opened out. One obvious device is to ask learners to answer the question in as many *different* ways as possible. Another is to ask them to consider various *dimensions-of-possible-variation* and to make up their own questions to illustrate these different dimensions (see p. 56).

Sources of questions: John Mason

Questions are often asked because of some internal prompt:

> *Conjecture*: an adult asks a learner a question when the adult, in the company of the learner, experiences a shift in the focus of their own attention. The question is intended to reproduce that shift of focus in the learner.
>
> In particular, enquiry-questions are asked when people become aware that they are uncertain, confused, stuck, struck by something they cannot account for or realise that some expectation is contradicted.
>
> (Mason, 2002b, p. 248)

Learners' habits: John Holt

Children can develop deeply ingrained habits that serve them well in most classrooms. There may be circumstances in which these habits are not helpful, but it takes a determined teacher to break out of the potential straightjacket.

John Holt describes his interactions with a learner, revealing some of the habits to which the learner resorted:

> This child *must* be right. She cannot bear to be wrong, or even to imagine that she might be wrong. When she is wrong, as she often is, the only thing to do is to forget it as quickly as possible. Naturally she will not tell herself that she is wrong; it is bad enough when others tell her. When she is told to do something, she does it quickly and fearfully, hands it to some higher authority, and awaits the magic words, 'right', or 'wrong'. If the word is 'right', she does not have to think about the problem any more; if the word is 'wrong', she does not want to, cannot bring herself to think about it.
>
> This fear leads her to other strategies, which other children use as well. She knows that in a recitation period, the teacher's attention is divided among twenty students. She also knows the teacher's strategy of asking questions of students who seem confused, or not paying attention. She therefore feels safe waving her hand in the air, as if she were bursting to tell the answer, whether she really knows it or not. This is her safe way of telling me that she, at least, knows all about whatever is going on in class. When someone else answers correctly she nods her head in emphatic agreement. Sometimes she even adds a comment, though her expression and tone of voice show that she feels this is risky.

It is also interesting to note that she does not raise her hand unless there are at least half a dozen other hands up. ...

[...]

... A teacher who asks a question is tuned to the right answer, ready to hear it, eager to hear it, since it will tell him that his teaching is good and that he can go on to the next topic. He will assume that anything that sounds close to the right answer is meant to be the right answer. So, for a student who is not sure of the answer, a mumble may be his best bet.

(Holt, 1964, pp. 12–13)

One of the purposes of questioning is to draw learner attention to mistakes, and to discover whether they are slips or indicators of confusion or inappropriate generalisation and reconstruction. See *mistakes*, p. 208 and p. 303, for how to learn from learner mistakes.

Questioning: Amy Martino and Carolyn Maher

Carolyn Maher (b. New Jersey, 1941–) has been researching details of classroom interactions for many years. Here, writing with a colleague, she summarises some of her research about questioning.

... Over the course of years, we have observed that a very special combination of student, teacher, task, and environment fosters individual cognitive growth in the mathematics classroom. To begin, students need a classroom environment that allows them time for exploration and reinvention. The teacher in this type of class embraces the ideal that students must express their current thinking. This thinking is then carefully considered by both teacher and peers. How is this done? It begins with teacher modeling, and very gradually this careful listening and exchange of ideas becomes the accepted mode of communication used by all members of this community. Students begin to realize that discussing their ideas and concerns with the community aids them in advancing their own thinking. In order for this part of the learning process to occur, students must be willing to engage with new ideas, build models, listen to input from other sources, and sometimes expose their own confusions or misconceptions. This means that the student in this learning environment is constantly rejecting, incorporating, or withholding judgement on new ideas that arise from discussion. Naturally, this is all based upon the premise that the student cares about understanding what he/she is studying.

(Martino and Maher, 1999, pp. 53–4)

The paper has numerous examples from the research. There are similarities with *conjecturing* (see p. 139), and making use of *listening* (p. 225).

Funnelling: John Holt

Inspecting his own teaching closely, Holt discovered that learners know that not every question has to be answered. Some learn to play the teacher-questioning game all too well: For example,

> They are very good at … getting other people to do their tasks for them. I remember the day not long ago when Ruth opened my eyes. We had been doing math, and I was pleased with myself because, instead of telling her answers and showing her how to do problems, I was 'making her think' by asking her questions. It was slow work. Question after question met only silence. She said nothing, did nothing, just sat and looked at me through those glasses, and waited. Each time, I had to think of a question easier and more pointed than the last, until I finally found one so easy that she would feel safe in answering it. So we inched our way along until suddenly, looking at her as I waited for an answer to a question, I saw with a start that she was not at all puzzled by what I had asked her. In fact, she was not even thinking about it. She was coolly appraising me, weighing my patience, waiting for the next, sure-to-be-easier question. I thought, 'I've been had!' The girl had learned how to make me do her work for her, just as she had learned to make all her previous teachers do the same thing. If I wouldn't tell her the answers, very well, she would just let me question her right up to them.
>
> (Holt, 1964, p. 24)

What happened to John Holt happens to every teacher at some time. Heinrich Bauersfeld called this phenomenon *funnelling*.

Funnelling: Heinrich Bauersfeld

- The teacher recognizes a student with difficulties; …
- The teacher opens with a short question in order to stimulate self-correction. He receives an unsatisfactory reaction.
- The teacher then goes further back to collect and clear prerequisites for the insight, aiming at an 'adequate' reaction from the student. *Adequate* at this stage is already an approximate fit with the teacher's expectation.
- Continued deviant answering on the student's side meets on the teacher's side a growing concentration on the stimulation of the 'adequate' answer through more precise, that is, narrower, questions. Thus the standard for 'adequateness' deteriorates, the quality of the discussion decreases.
- Step by step the teacher, in fact, through what he does, reduces his presumption of the student's actual abilities and self-government in a way that is quite the opposite to his intentions and in contradiction even to his subjective perception of his own action (he sees himself 'providing for individual guidance').

- The student realizes both the simplified but stiffer demands and the growing tension … [which] intensifies with teacher and student.
- When the deterioration has come down to the simplest exacting recitation or completion by the student, the culmination is reached. Just one expected word from the student can bring the teacher to a presentation of the complete solution himself.

(Bauersfeld, 1988, p. 36)

Bauersfeld noted that the longer such a pattern continues, the less likely it is to break off before reaching the end where the teacher essentially gives away the answer that has been sought all along. (See also Bauersfeld, 1980; Wood, 1998.)

Effect on thinkers: John Holt

John Holt concludes that learners are not always in class with the intention of learning (see *purposes*, p. 42).

> Schools and teachers seem generally to be as blind to children's strategies as I was. Otherwise, they would teach their courses and assign their tasks so that students who really thought about the meaning of the subject would have the best chance of succeeding, while those who tried to do the tasks by illegitimate means, without thinking or understanding, would be foiled. But the reverse seems to be the case. Schools give every encouragement to *producers*, the kids whose idea is to get 'right answers' by any and all means. In a system that runs on 'right answers', they can hardly help it. And these schools are often very discouraging places for *thinkers*.

(Holt, 1964, p. 25)

A useful overview of various language games like funnelling can be found in Bauersfeld (1995).

Topaze effect: Guy Brousseau

Guy Brousseau described funnelling by reference to a character in Marcel Pagnol's famous French play in which the character Topaze is giving a dictation test to a learner. For difficult words he pronounces the words letter by letter, thereby permitting the learner to spell correctly without effort.

> The answer that the student must give is determined in advance; the teacher chooses questions to which this answer can be given. Of course, the knowledge necessary to produce these answers changes, as does its meaning. … If the target knowledge disappears completely, we have the *Topaze* effect.

(Brousseau, 1997, p. 25)

Exerting control: Philip Jackson

Philip Jackson is an experienced and sensitive observer and recorder of incidents in classrooms. Here is just a brief extract analysing several incidents (not included here) which show how sensitive questioning has an important role in socialising learners to become aware of themselves and their actions. 'Visiting' means going to someone else's desk and chatting.

> ... the children being questioned are invited by the teacher to step outside their own skin, to see their actions from an external perspective and often to give them a name or label from that perspective. The invitation may take the form of a fairly neutral query, as when the children are simply asked, 'What are you doing?' or it may provide them with options to use in their description, as when Mrs Martin asks, 'Are you visiting or helping?' Occasionally Mrs Martin offers her own perspective, which reveals to the children how their actions are actually seen by someone else, as when she says, 'I thought you were (looking for something)'.
>
> Being questioned in this way encourages the children to become judges of their own actions. Yet the freedom to make those judgments, as the process also makes clear, is by no means unconstrained. The categories by which to judge are often set in advance and are usually few in number. There are other people present who are doing the judging as well – the teacher, one's classmates who are looking on, and sometimes an adult observer or two – which means that one's own judgment may not only be tested against those of others but may sometimes be contested, called into question, disagreed with. The public nature of the process, the fact that the children are asked not only to judge, but also to *announce* their judgments in a voice that all can hear, not only opens the door to falsifying one's response, it also entails an act of commitment, a form of giving one's word. In short, it calls upon the children to see themselves, if not as others see them, then at least as they choose in that particular circumstance to be seen by others.
>
> (Jackson, 1992, p. 52)

Other good sources of classroom incidents include Holt (1964; 1967; 1970) and Armstrong (1980).

Scaffolding and fading, dependence and independence are of central concern in intervention. Acting as 'consciousness for two' requires skilful and sensitive intervention.

Learners already expect there to be a predetermined answer to question, which can be genuine, testing or provoking. Funnelling is an easy trap to fall into, especially when trying to 'make it easy' for learners, driven by a strong desire to make sure that they 'understand'.

Mathematical discussion

Developing practices that were inspired by contact with Vygotsky's ideas, Bruner and his colleagues noticed that one role of a teacher when interacting with learners is to act as a *consciousness for two* (see p. 88). By resisting doing for the learners what they can already do for themselves, the teacher can hold awareness of goals while the learner pursues subgoals.

Discussion: Janette Warden

Generating considered and considerate discussion in the classroom takes time and attention:

> Before the children will give each other their full attention when engaged in a group discussion I find that I have to get across that every member of the class is entitled to my full attention when they are reading to me; being helped by me; or simply talking to me. On a number of occasions, with a new class, whilst, say, hearing a child read another child has come to ask a question, or, for help, and interrupts, I stop and tell the child not to interrupt but to wait. Afterwards I explain that it is not easy to listen to two people at the same time, and, that if we are listening properly we want to give our full attention to what is being said to us.
>
> During these 'settling in' days, whilst I am still working with the class as a group or with individual children, in order to help the children gain confidence in their own judgments and ideas I constantly ask questions such as 'Well what do you think?' or 'Can you explain to me how you did this?' Later on when group work is more established I still ask these questions. They really help them to start thinking for themselves, often for the first time!
>
> (Warden, 1981, pp. 249–50)

Scientific debate: Marc Legrand

Marc Legrand (b. France, 1943–) was uninterested in mathematics until his twenties when, under the influence of a particular teacher, he himself engaged in *scientific debate*. With teacher and researcher colleagues he has developed techniques for engaging undergraduates explicitly in *scientific debate* which he justifies as an epistemological principle:

> A person who has not had sufficient occasion actually to play, in its full grandeur, a genuine game of science has very little chance of interesting himself in the essential reasoning process of science, of understanding what the results of this reasoning really have to offer (understanding the power, but also the limitations, of its algorithms and modes of thought),

and consequently of finding relevant ways of using those results to find a scientific solution to his own problems.

(Legrand, 1995, quoted in translation in Warfield, webref)

Scientific debate means an interaction in which conjectures are formulated, proposed, challenged, tested and justified (see *conjecturing atmosphere*, p. 141). Learners are seen as participants in a scientific community whose methods of development include conjectures and modifications and proofs and refutations (Lakatos, 1976). Scientific debates can arise spontaneously when learners query a statement. Scientific debates can also be provoked intentionally by asking learners to make a conjecture regarding some problematic issue.

The essence of a scientific debate and of a conjecturing atmosphere is that people are eager to try ideas out and are neither embarrassed nor ashamed to make a mistake: everything said is offered as a conjecture, with the intention of modifying it if necessary (in contrast to an ethos in which things are only said when the sayer is confident they are correct). Those who are uncertain about some detail often choose to speak, while those who are confident often choose to listen and then to suggest modifications through counter-examples, images, questions and suggestions. The intention is to create the conditions under which fruitful mathematics is done at any level of sophistication.

It takes time to accustom learners to mathematical discussion, but it is an essential part of *teacher–learner–content interaction* (see p. 221) and it supports and makes use of learners powers to *conjecture* (see p. 139) and to justify.

Scientific debate: Derek Holton

Derek Holton (b. Buckinghamshire, 1941–) is now a New Zealand mathematician and prolific author of pamphlets aimed at helping aspiring young mathematicians engage in mathematical thinking and also to prepare themselves to participate in the annual international mathematical Olympiads. Here he summarises the notion of *scientific debate*.

> Under *le débat scientifique*, (see Legrand, 1993) students are seen as participants in a scientific community whose methods of development include conjectures, proofs and regulations. Scientific debates can arise spontaneously, as when a student asks a question, or can be intentionally provoked. The guiding principles for scientific debate include:
>
> * *disturbance*: students must encounter and deal with conflict;
> * *inclusiveness*: everyone should have an opportunity to understand what we try to teach; and

- *collectivity*: collective resolution of issues shows how to work with contradictions and to respect the views of others.

Now it may seem strange that what is labelled 'scientific' has such a strong social underpinning. Maybe this can be explained by noting that the point of the exercise is to allow students to engage in 'scientific debate'. This requires an atmosphere where conjecturing is supported, where students feel free to put forward their ideas, where they are not embarrassed to make a mistake, and where they feel that they are able to modify the ideas of others. In order to generate an atmosphere in which valuable debate may take place, students and staff must value certain social principles such as respect for each other's views.

(Holton, webref)

Note the role of *disturbance* (see p. 55, p. 101 and p. 161) and collective or social involvement in a *community of practice* (see p. 95).

Scientific debate is a form of conjecturing atmosphere within which mathematical thinking thrives and develops.

---

11 Concluding mathematical activity

Introduction

Mathematical activity usually concludes with reflection.

Reflection is advocated by very many authors. For example, Polya (1957) proposed four phases of problem solving: understanding the problem, making a plan, carrying out the plan, and looking back (reflection): simple advice, but not so easy to carry through. As many have observed, reflection is 'more honoured in the breach than the observance'.

Mason, Burton and Stacey (1982) expanded Polya's four phases to seven in order to try to make the identification of different phases more useful: getting started, getting involved, mulling, keeping going, insight, being sceptical, and contemplating.

In the Project for Enhancing Effective Learning (PEEL) in Australia (Northfield and Baird, 1992), learners were encouraged to keep diaries and to reflect on their activities; the difficult part in this project was to sustain overt reflection as a classroom practice (see also Waywood, 1992, 1994).

Li (1999, p. 33) observed from his Chinese perspective that reflection is only useful if there is something specific on which to reflect. He considered that manipulative facility and competence are prerequisites for effective reflection.

Reflection

Reflection: John Dewey

> ... *reflective* thinking, in distinction from other operations to which we apply the name of thought, involves (1) a state of doubt, hesitation, perplexity, mental difficulty, in which thinking originates, and (2) an act of searching, hunting, inquiring, to find material that will resolve the doubt, settle and dispose of the perplexity.
>
> (Dewey, 1933, p. 12)

> ... Thinking begins in what may fairly enough be called a *forked-road* situation, a situation that is ambiguous, that presents a dilemma, that

proposes alternatives. As long as our activity glides smoothly along from one thing to another, or as long as we permit our imagination to entertain fantasies at pleasure, there is no call for reflection. Difficulty or obstruction in the way of reaching a belief brings us, however, to a pause. In the suspense of uncertainty, we metaphorically climb a tree; we try to find some standpoint from which we may survey additional facts and, getting a more commanding view of the situation, decide how the facts stand related to one another.

(ibid., p. 14)

There are similarities with *disturbance* (see p. 55, p. 101 and p. 161).

… General appeals to a child (or to a grown-up) to think, irrespective of the existence in his own experience of some difficulty that troubles him and disturbs his equilibrium, are as futile as advice to lift himself by his boot-straps.

(ibid., p. 15)

Dewey distinguished between reaction to a situation, and thoughtful reflective response:

There may, however, be a state of perplexity and also previous experience out of which suggestions emerge, and yet thinking need not be reflective. For the person may not be sufficiently *critical* about the ideas that occur to him. He may jump at a conclusion without weighing the grounds on which it rests; he may forego or unduly shorten the act of hunting, inquiring; he may take the first 'answer', or solution, that comes to him because of mental sloth, torpor, impatience to get something settled. One can think reflectively only when one is willing to endure suspense and to undergo the trouble of searching. … It is at the point where examination and test enter into an investigation that the difference between reflective thought and bad thinking comes in. To be genuinely thoughtful, we must be willing to sustain and protract that state of doubt which is the stimulus to thorough inquiry, so as not to accept an idea or make a positive assertion of a belief until justifying reasons have been found.

(ibid., p. 16)

Reflection: Richard Skemp

Richard Skemp was led from considering reflection into territory similar to that of Gattegno and Bruner in relation to language as a means to distance the speaker–thinker–reflector from the action. This echoes Maturana's notion that *everything said is said by an observer* (see p. 70). Skemp proposed that reflection is enhanced when labels are used.

[Reflective activity] involves becoming aware of one's own concepts and schemas, perceiving their relationships and structure; and manipulating these in various ways. ... the intervening processes are cognitive, and make possible the overall activity which we call reflective intelligence. ...

The process of becoming aware of one's concepts for the first time seems to be quite a difficult one. ... the overall development of this ability extends over a number of the years of childhood. But even in persons with highly developed reflective ability, it is still a struggle to make newly formed, or forming, ideas conscious.

... *It is largely by the use of symbols that we achieve voluntary control over our thoughts.*

Verbal thinking (which can be extended to include algebraic and any other pronounceable symbols) is internalized speech; as may be confirmed by watching the transitional stages in children. The use of pronounceable symbols for thinking is closely related to communication; one might describe it as communication with oneself. So becoming conscious of one's thoughts seems to be a short-circuiting of the process of hearing oneself tell them to someone else. This view is supported by a common observation that actually doing so to a patient listener (thinking aloud) is nearly always helpful when one is working on a problem. Visual thinking is a much more individual matter ...

(Skemp, 1971, pp. 82–3)

Reflection: Hans Freudenthal

Freudenthal suggested that reflection is going on all the time:

> ... when I use the word 'reflection', I mean mirroring oneself in someone else in order to look through his skin, to explore him, to take him in. And, consequently, since somebody else is like oneself – a human – this is an experience about human behaviour and, finally, knowledge about one's own behaviour. So from mirroring oneself in someone else follows – as the night the day – the mirroring of oneself in one's own person, that is, introspection. It becomes reflecting on oneself, on what one did, felt, imagined, thought, on what one is doing, feeling, imagining, thinking. Reflecting, once started, is an activity we perform every moment, in order to determine our course of action, yet, as a mental exercise, it can become an aim in itself.

(Freudenthal, 1991, p. 104)

There is however a difference between awareness of the active one of the *two birds* and the reflections available from the second bird as witness (see p. 32).

Freudenthal identified several modes of reflection, which he saw as a process of shifting one's standpoint, where the shifting may take place in time, location, or any other mental dimension:

- *Reciprocal shifting*: shifting from A to B in order to look back at A (looking in a mirror, getting older, making a mental reservation about something);
- *Directed shifting*: shifting from A to B while considering C (breaking a process down into steps);
- *Parallel shifting*: shifting A's environment to B's.

(based on Freudenthal, 1991, p. 105)

See also Freudenthal's remarks concerning the van Hieles (p. 163).

Anne Watson has pointed out that mathematical reflection can be realised as a rotation if you move up one spatial dimension; psychological reflection similarly involves moving into a different place or dimension, such as Dewey's metaphorical tree.

Reflection: Caleb Gattegno

Gattegno's writing is rarely clear on first reading, but it is worth the effort to probe beneath the laconic style which packs ideas into short spaces. Here he connects reflection, which he sees as a sophisticated activity, with his favourite theme of awareness (see p. 61).

> ... Reflection does not automatically yield its nature so that it can be acknowledged at once as the awareness of awareness because of the movement's concentration on the substance of the reflection, but it can be seen for what it is, once the self reaches the dynamics instead of the content. Stressing and ignoring, the primitive tools of both plants and animals, also pervade man's existence and permit or forbid access to what is available. Once one is aware of reflection, this could have yielded the awareness of awareness had the thinker ignored the content and stressed the dynamics.

(Gattegno, 1987, p. 40)

Note the parallels with Dewey's views on reflection, though Gattegno is using reflection to probe even more deeply.

Reflection: Paul Cobb, Kay McClain and Joy Whitenack

> ... reflective discourse ... is characterized by repeated shifts such that what the students and teacher do in action subsequently becomes an explicit object of discussion. In fact, we might have called it *mathematizing discourse* because there is a parallel between its structure and psychological accounts of mathematical development in which actions or processes are transformed into conceptual mathematical objects. In the course of the analysis, we also developed the related

construct of *collective reflection*. This latter notion refers to the joint or communal activity of making what was previously done in action an object of reflection.

(Cobb *et al.*, 1997, p. 258)

Cobb and his colleagues are pointing out similarities between reflection and *reification* (see p. 167), related to what Piaget called *reflective abstraction* (see p. 171), and to the MGA spiral (see p. 264).

... The notion of reflective discourse ... helps clarify certain aspects of the teacher's role. In our view, one of the primary ways in which teachers can proactively support students' mathematical development is to guide and, as necessary, initiate shifts in the discourse such that what was previously done in action can become an explicit topic of conversation.

(ibid., p. 269)

There are similarities with shifts in the *structure of attention* (p. 60).

... initiating and guiding the development of reflective discourse requires considerable wisdom and judgment on the teacher's part. One can, for example, imagine a scenario in which a teacher persists in attempting to initiate a shift in the discourse when none of the students gives a response that involves reflection on prior activity. The very real danger is, of course, that an intended occasion for reflective discourse will degenerate into a social guessing game in which students try to infer what the teacher wants them to say and do (cf. Bauersfeld, 1980; Voight, 1985). In light of this possibility, the teacher's role in initiating shifts in the discourse might be thought of as probing to assess whether children can participate in the objectification of what they are currently doing. Such a formulation acknowledges the teacher's proactive role in guiding the development of reflective discourse while simultaneously stressing both that such discourse is an interactional accomplishment and that students necessarily have to make an active contribution to its development.

A second aspect of the teachers role ... is the way in which [the teacher] develop[s] symbolic records of the children's contributions. Of course one can imagine a scenario in which ways of notating could themselves have been a topic for explicit negotiation. For our purpose, the crucial point is not who initiated the development of the notational schemes, but the fact that the records grew out of the students' activity in a bottom-up manner ... , and that they appeared to play an important role in facilitating collective reflection on that prior activity.

(ibid., pp. 269–70)

This is one aspect of what the *Do–Talk–Record* framework is about (see p. 262).

> ... What is required is an analytical approach that is fine-grained enough to account for qualitative differences in individual children's thinking even as they participate in the same collective activities ... . Our rationale for positing an indirect linkage between social and psychological processes is therefore pragmatic and derives from our desire to account for ... differences in individual children's activity. As we have noted, this view implies that participation in an activity such as reflective discourse constitutes the conditions for the possibility of learning, but it is the students who actually do the learning. Participation in reflective discourse, therefore, can be seen both to enable and constrain mathematical development, but not to determine it.
>
> (ibid., p. 272)

Reflection: Kenneth Zeichner

Ken Zeichner (b. Pennsylvania, 1948–) is an educational researcher who has made reflection one of his core interests. Here he draws on three levels of reflection discerned in organisational psychology: technical, clarifying, and moral-ethical, based on Dewey's ideas:

> Van Maanen (1977) identifies three levels of reflection, each one embracing different criteria for choosing among alternative courses of action. At the first level of technical rationality ... , the dominant concern is with the efficient and effective application of educational knowledge for the purposes of obtaining ends which are accepted as given. At this level, neither the ends nor the institutional contexts of classroom, school, community, and society are treated as problematic.
>
> A second level of reflectivity, ... is based upon a conception of practical action whereby the problem is one of explicating and clarifying the assumptions and predispositions underlying practical affairs and assessing the educational consequences toward which an action leads. At this level, every action is seen as linked to particular value commitments, and the actor considers the worth of competing educational ends.
>
> The third level, critical reflection, incorporates moral and ethical criteria into the discourse about practical action. At this level the central questions ask which educational goals, experiences, and activities lead toward forms of life which are mediated by concerns for justice, equity, and concrete fulfillment, and whether current arrangements serve important human needs and satisfy important human purposes ... . Here both the teaching (ends and means) and the surrounding contexts are viewed as problematic – that is, as value-governed selections from a larger universe of possibilities.
>
> (Zeichner and Liston, 1987, pp. 24–5)

Reflection: Ingrid Pramling

Pramling develops her view of learning as *learning to experience the world* (see p. 61), into a list of principles, which include ways in which she uses reflection as a teaching strategy:

- Using reflection as a method in education. To get children to talk and reflect they must become involved in activities (material, situations, play, tasks, etc.) which directly influence them to think about and reflect upon the phenomena about which the teacher wants to develop their understanding. To get children to talk and reflect in concrete situations demands that teachers use types of questions that they do not normally use, but also to utilize drama, drawing, music, etc. for children to gestalt their understanding.
- Using variation of thought. The teacher must expose the ways in which children are thinking and use these as content in education. The teacher must then be aware that children learn from one another, which means that the differences between children are focused on instead of similarities. Exposing children to variation of thought can be achieved in many different ways, such as through drawing, drama, play, discussion, etc.

(Pramling, 1994)

Note links with *dimensions-of-possible-variation* (see p. 56).

Reflection: Grayson Wheatley

In mathematics learning, reflection is characterized by distancing oneself from the action of doing mathematics (Sigel, 1981). It is one thing to solve the problem and it is quite another to take one's own action as an object of reflection. In the process of reflection, schemes of schemes are constructed – the second-order construction. Persons who reflect have greater control over their thinking and can decide which of several paths to take, rather than simply being in the action.

It is not enough for students to complete tasks; we must encourage students to reflect on their activity. For example, being asked to justify a method of solution will often promote reflection. This may occur in the small-group setting when a learner partner asks, 'Will that work?' or it may occur in the whole-class discussion when the presenter is asked to clarify an explanation. Finally, carefully selected tasks cannot cause perturbation which results in reflection.

[...]

It is possible that students may be so active that they fail to reflect and thus do not learn. We can keep students so busy that they rarely have time to think about what they're doing, and they may fail to become aware of the methods and options. In fact, there is an implicit message that they are not supposed to think about what they are doing.

(Wheatley, 1992, pp. 535–6)

Wheatley proposes that optimal conditions for learning occur when individuals have to defend positions they have taken, and notes that social norms have to be negotiated, including:

1 Group members must assume the obligation of trying to make sense of the explanation;
2 Persons presenting a solution or explanation must present a self-generated solution;
3 ... group members recognize the obligation to construct a response to any challenge to their explanation [with] an explanation which incorporates a construction of the questioner;
4 The purpose of the dialogue is not to be right but to make sense;
5 The purpose of any question raised by a member of the group is to give meaning to the explanation; it is a sincere and genuine question.

(ibid., p. 539)

Compare with *scientific debate* (see p. 277) and *conjecturing atmosphere* (see p. 139).

Reflection is one of the ways of awakening the second bird in the image of two birds (see p. 32). It is the means whereby the driver of the carriage in the other image can keep the carriage in good condition, look after the horses, and generally be ready to take the owner wherever is required (see p. 33). It is the means by which it is possible to refresh oneself and to prepare to notice even more opportunities in the future.

Reflection is much praised but difficult to promote on an ongoing basis.

Being stuck is an honourable state.

Four phases of problem solving: understanding the problem, making a plan, carrying out the plan, and looking back.

Seven phases of problem solving: getting started, getting involved, mulling, keeping going, insight, being sceptical, and contemplating.

Reflection is a more general response to disturbance, to 'forked road' possibilities.

Three levels of reflection: technical, clarifying assumptions, and moral-ethical.

12 Having learned ... ?

Introduction

What is the point of activity arising from tasks? Does it constitute 'learning'? Presumably learners are expected to have learned something, though some authors argue that learning cannot be observed: while teaching takes place in time and can be observed, learning takes place over time as a process of maturation. Some argue that learning is what we do when we are asleep, as the brain sorts out the sense impressions of the day, linking some things into past experiences, and leaving others in relative isolation, which is almost tantamount to forgetting. Activity itself is activity: if there are changes in how actions are perceived, if connections and links are made, then perhaps learning has been facilitated. Since the aim of activity is to enable the growth of understanding, this chapter focuses on knowing, understanding, and obstacles to understanding.

Knowing

Denvir and Brown (1986) showed in their study that some learners improved performance on all sorts of tasks, not just the topics they were taught explicitly (see p. 206). This suggests a more general phenomenon, that effective learning of mathematics is more about developing sophistication than about acquiring batches of isolated skills. Performing some calculations in one domain may contribute to greater facility in another, ostensibly unrelated domain. Aiming teaching at step-by-step acquisition fails to make use of the more complex manner in which people develop skills, understanding, and insight.

Inert knowledge: Alfred North Whitehead

Whitehead described the central problem of all education as:

> ... the problem of keeping knowledge alive, of preventing it from becoming inert ...
>
> (Whitehead, 1932, p. 7)

... Education with inert ideas is not only useless; it is, above all things, harmful ... .

(ibid., p. 2)

The notion of inert knowledge (see also p. 35) has been taken up and examined by a multitude of authors seeking both explanation for it and strategies to overcome it (see Renkl *et al.*, 1996, for a survey; see also *rote* learning, p. 151).

Knowing: Gilbert Ryle

In his seminal work, Gilbert Ryle (1949) distinguished between *knowing-that* (factually), *knowing-how* (to perform acts), and *knowing-why* (having stories to account for phenomena and actions). To this can be added *knowing-to* (act in the moment as deemed appropriate).

Knowing-why means having some 'story' to account for *knowing-that* or *knowing-how*, but the story does not have to be valid or true in someone else's theories. What we really want is that learners *know-to* use techniques they have met and powers they have developed, in new situations.

These distinctions are not intended to be hard and fast. Some *know-how* depends on *knowing-that*, *knowing-to* draws upon *knowing-how*, and *knowing-why* encompasses *knowing-that* and *knowing-how*. But it is often the case that people apparently *know-that*, yet do not act on that knowledge; *know-how* but fail to recognise an opportunity to employ it; *know-why* something must be the case but do not use it, or do not use it effectively.

Learners can often solve routine problems of the type on which they have been trained, but as soon as they are given something more general or less familiar, or a task requiring several steps, they are mostly at sea. They do not appear to *know-to* use what they have learned. For example, Burkhardt (1981) suggested that it is unreasonable to expect learners to use tools for mathematical modelling which learners first encountered in the previous two or three years, and descriptions of the difficulty learners have with multi-step problems are legion. It takes time to integrate tools into your own functioning, to have them become 'ert' (as opposed to inert) in the sense of Whitehead.

Active, practical knowledge, knowledge that enables people to act creatively rather than merely react to stimuli with trained or habituated behaviour, involves *knowing-to* act, in the moment. This is what learners need in order to engage in problem solving where context is novel and resolution non-routine or multi-layered; this is what teachers need in order to provoke learners into educating their awareness as well as training their behaviour (see p. 204). Although teachers believe they are teaching learners to know actively, their experience suggests otherwise.

Greeno *et al.* (1993) use an analogy of motion: motion is not a property of the object as it depends upon a frame of reference. Rather, motion is a relation between a frame of reference and an object. So too knowing is not a static property of a person, but a dynamic and emergent relation between person and situation.

Knowing: Caleb Gattegno

Given his focus on *awareness* (p. 61), it is natural to find Gattegno basing his definition of knowing on it:

> Knowing is the awareness that one is aware of something, and according to whether we stress the something or the awareness, we progress in the subject, or in the education of our awareness. Movements in the education of our awareness may be short-lived or permanent. When short-lived, they are called flashes of intuition, bright ideas, sudden insights. When permanent, they make possible a familiarity with awareness and provide a chance to reach awareness of the awareness as a state of being acknowledged by the self.
>
> (Gattegno, 1987, p. 42)

Unformulated knowing: Brent Davis

Davis takes a strongly enactivist stance towards knowing and understanding, with a preference for phenomenological approaches to research, and with interests in mathematics education. Here he distinguishes *formulated* and *unformulated* knowing, based on a distinction of Charles Taylor (1991):

> … two sorts of action: formulated and unformulated. The former [Taylor] describes as those thoughts, behaviors, and bits of knowledge that we have written into the text of our experience – those we are aware of, speak of, and tend to link in narrative and causal chains. Such formulated actions, Taylor argues, represent only a small portion of our total action, even though they dominate our conscious awarenesses. The bulk of our moment-to-moment living is a matter of unformulated action – a negotiated movement through an interactive world during which our knowledge of that world and our way of being in that world are continuously enacted. The evidence of such knowledge and understandings is our survival, not our ability to identify, explain (narrate) our actions in formal terms.
>
> (Davis, 1996, pp. 44–5)

William James (1899, pp. 33–9) referred to unformulated actions as habits below the level of consciousness. Others have referred to them as automatic functionings, and even as a form of 'sleep walking' in that we have no conscious control over our reactions at those times. The watching bird is asleep (see p. 32). Teaching can be seen in terms of helping learners awaken that second bird in more situations; working to develop professional practice is similarly oriented to being more awake to opportunities and to being able to respond rather than react.

Unformulated knowing is akin to Vergnaud's *theorems-in-action* (see p. 63), what Polanyi (1958) called *tacit* knowing, and what both Vico (1744) and Bachelard (1958) referred to as *poetic* knowing. For Davis it is in the interplay between the formulated and the unformulated that learning takes place.

Knowing: Magdalene Lampert

> ... Magdalene Lampert posits that there are four types of mathematical knowledge: intuitive, concrete, computational, and principled conceptual knowledge (Lampert, 1986). Intuitive knowledge represents an understanding that is derived from specific contexts and relates only to those contexts. Computational knowledge enables one to perform activities with numerical symbols according to previously determined and generalizable rules. This is the most common form of mathematical knowledge presented in schools. Concrete knowledge involves knowing how to manipulate concrete objects or representations of them to solve a problem. Finally, principled conceptual knowledge represents the understanding of abstract principles and concepts that govern and define mathematical thinking and procedures.
>
> (Merseth, 1993; webref)

Merseth's article discusses a task very similar to the *L'âge du capitaine* (Baruk, 1985, see p. 15), which is about errors in mathematics more generally.

Transfer

One version of the question of how people come to *know-to* act in a new situation is the question of how and when people know to transfer something learned in one context to another context. How are learners to know to use a technique in an entirely new context? The usual response is that something in the new situation resonates with past experience, bringing the technique to the surface. But situations one person recognises may not be the sorts of situations which other people recognise. The term *transfer* was used initially by people working in the behaviourist tradition. Multiple attempts to locate conditions under which learners could transfer the use of some technique or idea to a new context failed to produce any concrete results (see Detterman and Sternberg, 1993). With the development of constructivism as a perspective from which to view learning, questions were raised about transfer as a viable notion. (See also *situated cognition*, p. 86.) From a *situated* perspective the issue of transfer becomes the issue of how situatedness broadens and extends: what is it that brings to mind knowing to act in a fresh situation different from that in which the technique has been used before?

Transfer: Lev Vygotsky

Vygotsky considers transitions between using a concept and describing or defining that concept which resonates with van Hiele *phases* (see p. 59) and *structure of attention* (see p. 60).

> The adolescent will form and use a concept quite correctly in a concrete situation but will find it strangely difficult to express that concept in words, and the verbal definition will, in most cases, be much narrower than might have been expected from the way he used the concept. The same discrepancy occurs also in adult thinking, even at very advanced levels. This confirms the assumption that concepts evolve in ways differing from deliberate conscious elaboration of experience in logical terms. Analysis of reality with the help of concepts precedes analysis of the concepts themselves. ...
>   [...]
> The greatest difficulty of all is the application of a concept, finally grasped and formulated on the abstract level, to new concrete situations that must be viewed in these abstract terms – a kind of transfer usually mastered only toward the end of the adolescent period. The transition from the abstract to concrete proves just as arduous for the youth as the earlier transition from the concrete to the abstract.
>
> (Vygotsky, 1962, pp. 79–80)

Transfer: Overview

Lave (1988) followed up the study by Nunes *et al.* (1993) with studies of adult numeracy skills as they left a supermarket (and posed in a supermarket context) and similar tasks posed in their homes. Again a difference in performance was observed, both in accuracy and in approach. This led to the notion of *situated cognition*: we learn things in a social context, and that context plays an important role in what is learned as well as in how it is learned (see also Brown, Collins and Duguid, 1989). Transfer then becomes a problem of how situated cognition expands the range of situatedness. In a new situation, unless there is something which triggers our attention from past experience, we are unlikely to think of, or to show evidence of transfer to, the new situation.

Knowing-to act in the moment using a particular action or strategy is more sophisticated than *knowing-that* something is true or *knowing-how* to do something when asked, and more demanding than *knowing-when* and *knowing-about*, or even *knowing-why*. All the forms of knowing are involved in understanding, which is a dynamic process and a response to a situation, not a static state.

When training behaviour, there is an issue of whether the learner can transfer that training to other contexts. When educating awareness, there is an issue of how narrowly situated the awareness is, how contextually bound, and how that situatedness can be reduced so that learners *know-to* use techniques in a broader range of situations.

Understanding

Some authors focus on knowing and knowledge, with *epistemology* being the study of how we come to know things. But learners of mathematics are expected to do more than simply know. They are expected to *understand*, to appreciate, to comprehend. It is often said that we should 'teach for understanding', in contrast to 'learning by rote', which Spencer and others so detested (see p. 151):

> There is a persistent belief in the merits of the goal, but designing school learning environments that successfully promote [learning with] understanding has been difficult.
>
> (Hiebert and Carpenter, 1992, p. 65)

But as we have seen (see p. 289), learning to do, and appreciating why that is what you do and why it works, often go hand in hand. Neither always precedes the other, and a constant diet in one direction stultifies learners rather than helps them. What then does it mean 'to understand', and how can understanding be evaluated?

What learners learn: David Wheeler

> It is frequently said that we should not teach children to learn mathematics by rote but that we should teach 'for understanding'. An obvious immediate comment to make is that we cannot imagine any teacher trying to teach for misunderstanding. *Of course* we must teach for understanding; but how do our pupils achieve it, and how do we know when they have?
>
> It seems as if children may arrive at understanding by different routes. Teaching children to learn by rote does not necessarily prevent them from eventually coming to understand, as some of us can testify. Many children apparently do not understand mathematics when taught by methods which require them mainly to imitate and memorise, but we

shall never be able to prove that they would have learned more successfully if taught another way since they are no longer available for an
experiment. But with both the children who have succeeded and the
children who have failed, it is apparent that the way mathematics has
been taught to them has not entirely controlled the mathematics that
they have learnt. Some children have understood more than was
presented to them, and some have not understood the little they were
shown.

(Wheeler, 1965, p. 47)

Note the parallel with the findings of Denvir and Brown (see p. 206), and the
contrast with other authors' views on *rote* learning (see p. 151).

> ... It is generally agreed that concepts are not conveyed by instruction,
> and that some more indirect teaching method is necessary. If concepts
> are abstractions, and if they are obtained by fastening onto the common
> elements in a number of situations, they can perhaps be taught by
> putting a variety of situations, all with the same significant feature, in
> front of the learner. Unfortunately there is no means of knowing in
> advance how many examples have to be presented, or any guarantee
> that the learner will not choose to concentrate on the irrelevant features
> when he is faced with a particular situation. A more fundamental objec-
> tion is that it is the person who has the concept who decides on a
> common feature and the ways in which it will be disguised. But what
> looks like a common feature to somebody who is in the know, may not
> look like one to somebody who isn't, and in practice any uncertainty
> about what to abstract is often settled by a procedure not very far
> removed from instruction.

(ibid., pp. 47–8)

Note parallels with thinking about *generalisation* and *abstraction* (see p. 132
and p. 144), and especially *same and different* (see p. 126). Wheeler's observations can be seen as a particular instance of the *transposition didactique*
(see p. 83), in that expert awareness is transformed into 'here, look at this;
this is what I am seeing'. See also *evaluating understanding* (see p. 305).

Understanding: Richard Skemp

> *To understand something means to assimilate it into an appropriate
> schema.* This explains the subjective nature of understanding and also
> makes clear that this is not usually an all-or-nothing state. We may
> achieve a subjective feeling of understanding by assimilation to an inap-
> propriate schema – the Greeks 'understood' thunderstorms by assimi-
> lating these noisy affairs to the schema of a large and powerful being,
> Zeus, getting angry and throwing things. In this case, an appropriate

schema involves the idea of an electric spark, so it was not until the eighteenth century that any real understanding of thunderstorms was possible. ... Better internal organization of a schema may also improve understanding, and clearly there is no stage at which this process is complete. One obstacle to the further increase of understanding is the belief that one already understands fully.

We can also see the deep-rooted conviction ... that it matters whether or not we understand something, is well founded. For this subjective feeling that we understand something, open to error though it may be, is in general a sign that we are therefore able to behave appropriately in a new class of situations.

(Skemp, 1971, pp. 46–7)

Relational understanding and instrumental understanding: Richard Skemp

The distinction between instrumental and relational understanding is usually attributed to Richard Skemp, who certainly developed and applied it in his writing and teaching.

It was brought to my attention some years ago by Steig Mellin-Olsen of Bergen University, that there are in current use two meanings [of reflection]. These he distinguishes by calling them 'relational understanding' and 'instrumental understanding'. By the former is meant what I have always meant by understanding ... knowing both what to do and why. Instrumental understanding I would until recently not have regarded as understanding at all. It is what I have in the past described as 'rules without reasons', without realising that for many pupils *and their teachers* the possession of such rule, and ability to use it, was what they meant by 'understanding'.

[...]

If it is accepted that these two categories are both well-filled, by those pupils and teachers whose goals are respectively relational and instrumental understanding (by the pupil), two questions arise. First, does this matter? And second, is one kind better than the other? For years I've taken for granted the answers to both these questions: briefly, 'Yes; relational'. But the existence of a large body of experienced teachers and a large number of texts belonging to the opposite camp has forced me to think more about why I hold this view. In the process of changing that judgment from an intuitive to a reflective one, I think I have learnt something useful. The two questions are not entirely separate ... .

[...]

Leaving aside for the moment whether one kind is better than the other, there are two kinds of mathematical mismatches which can occur:

1   Pupils whose goal is to understand instrumentally, taught by a teacher who wants them to understand relationally;
2   The other way about.

The first of these will cause fewer problems *short-term* to the pupils, though it will be frustrating to the teacher. The pupils just 'won't want to know' all the careful ground-work he gives in preparation for whatever is to be learned next, nor his careful explanations. All they want is some kind of rule for getting the answer. As soon as this is reached, they latch on to it and ignore the rest.

If the teacher asks a question that does not quite fit the rule, of course they will get it wrong. ...

(Skemp, 1976, pp. 20–1)

For example: 'What is the area of the field 20 cm by 15 yds? The reply was '300 square centimeters'. When asked why not 300 square yards, they answered: 'Because area is always in square centimeters'.

'Well is the enemy of better', and if pupils can get the right answers by the kind of thinking they are used to, they will not take kindly to suggestions that they should try for something beyond this.

(ibid., p. 22)

The *didactic contract* and *didactic tension* (see p. 79) are another formulation of this same idea.

Understanding: Victor Byers and Nicolas Herscovics

Victor Byers and Nicolas Herscovics (1935–1994) extended Skemp's two forms of understanding as a result of discussions with teachers. They added two further forms:

- *Instrumental understanding* is the ability to apply an appropriate remembered rule to the solution of a problem without knowing why the rule works.
- *Relational understanding* is the ability to deduce specific rules or procedures from more general mathematical relationships.
- *Intuitive understanding* is the ability to solve a problem without prior analysis of the problem.
- *Formal understanding* is the ability to connect mathematical symbolism and notation with relevant mathematical ideas and to combine these ideas into chains of reasoning.

(Byers and Herscovics, 1977, p. 26)

Their use of *intuitive* follows Bruner:

Intuition implies the act of grasping meaning or significance or structure of a problem without explicit reliance on the analytic apparatus of one's craft ... It precedes proof; indeed it is what the techniques of analysis and proof are designed to test and check.

(Bruner, 1965, p. 102, quoted in Byers and Herscovics, 1977, p. 25)

There are interesting comparisons to be made with Ryle, Skemp and others on types of knowing (see p. 289), and with Fischbein on *intuition* (see p. 63).

Modernising their expressions one might wish to do without the ambiguous notion of 'the ability' since understanding is now usually seen as relative to situation, time and place, and not something static possessed by an individual and available at all times, places, and in all situations. It is also worth noting that you can have a direct insight but struggle to express it in any other way; that you can have a sense of how the formal symbols are manipulated but not appreciate what it is about; that you can know all sorts of connections and links relationally yet not see that the technique applies in a new situation (the difference between *knowing-how* and *knowing-to*, see p. 289). Intuitive understanding of a situation is what can be located and developed into explicit and more formal expression (in Dewey's terms, *psychologising the subject matter*; in Freudenthal's terms, locating relevant *didactic phenomena*). See also *proceptual understanding* (p. 166).

Understanding: Edwina Rissland (Michener)

Born in New Jersey, Edwina Rissland (Michener) studied engineering students whom she was teaching at university, trying to find ways of easing their difficulties. She produced a categorisation of types of mathematical objects which learners need in order to understand a topic and to be able to use techniques effectively, which can be summarised as:

results (theorems, facts); examples (illustrative); and concepts (including formal and informal definitions and heuristic advice)

(Michener, 1978, p. 362)

Examples are connected with construction methods; results are connected with logical deductive reasoning; concepts are connected with pedagogical ordering (ibid., p. 364). Examples themselves have different uses:

start-up examples, reference examples (referred to repeatedly), model examples (paradigmatic, generic), counter-examples to conjectures and showing necessity of hypotheses in theorems

(ibid., pp. 366–8)

Then there are different levels of concepts, such as mega-principles (consider extreme cases, try zero) and counter-principles (watch out for division by zero) (ibid., pp. 368–9); and different levels of importance of results: key results, transitional results, culminating results (ibid., p. 369). By clarifying the role of examples, principles and results in these terms she found that learners were better able to make appropriate use of them in making sense of the mathematics.

Understanding: Jeremy Kilpatrick

Jeremy Kilpatrick (b. Iowa, 1935–) was a student of Polya's, and is a leading researcher in mathematics education. Here he and colleagues structure their comprehensive research-based analysis of the pedagogy of mathematics by seeing understanding as having five strands:

- *Conceptual understanding* – comprehension and mathematical concepts, operations, and relations;
- *Procedural fluency* – skill in carrying out procedures flexibly, accurately, efficiently, and appropriately;
- *Strategic competence* – ability to formulate, represent, and solve mathematical problems;
- *Adaptive reasoning* – capacity for logical thought, reflection, explanation, and justification;
- *Productive disposition* – habitual inclination to see mathematics as sensible, useful, and worthwhile, coupled with a belief in diligence and one's own efficacy.

What does a learner have when they are said to have learned something? Most of us find that we go on learning about things we thought we already knew about: for example, just what constitutes a *number* and how different types of numbers fit together, their properties, and so on, provides an endless field of enquiry.

The products of learning have cognitive, affective and enactive components: you have learned something if you can do things now you couldn't do before, perhaps more competently, but perhaps also more confidently, moving into the affective domain. There may be a greater disposition to think mathematically or to use mathematical thinking in more contexts, to be sensitised to recognise opportunities for using techniques and ways of thinking in new situations. Above all, one expects a stronger sense of understanding more, whatever that might mean.

(Kilpatrick *et al.*, 2001, p. 116)

Understanding: Susan Pirie and Tom Kieren

Susan Pirie (b. Kent, 1942–) and Tom Kieren (b. Minnesota, 1940–) together developed an onion-layer description of understanding, as a result of trying to observe it taking place. They noticed that understanding is not a continuous process, that sometimes people appear to go backwards, to retreat to previous ways of thinking, and then suddenly emerge with more sophisticated and deeper understanding: hence the layers of onion.

> The process of coming to know starts at a level we call 'primitive doing'. Action at this level may involve physical objects, figures, graphics or symbols. 'Primitive' here does not imply low-level mathematics, but rather a starting place for the growth of any particular mathematical understanding.
>
> The first recursion occurs when the learner begins to form images out of this 'doing'. The effective actions here involve 'image making'. At the next level these action-tied images are replaced by a form for the images. From the mathematical point of view it is this 'image having' which frees a person's mathematics from the need to take particular actions as examples. This is a first level of abstraction; but it is critical to note that it is the learner who makes this abstraction by recursively building on images based in action. For understanding to grow, these images cannot be imposed from the outside.
>
> (Pirie and Kieren, 1989, p. 8)

There are similarities with *reification* (see p. 167).

> Because knowing has to be *effective* action, the recursions do not stop here. The images can now be examined for specific or relevant properties. This may involve noticing distinctions, combinations, or connections between images. This level of 'property noticing' is the outermost level of unselfconscious knowing. (The word 'outer' has been carefully chosen to imply that the levels of understanding wrap around each other, as illustrated in [the] figure, and contain, indeed require, the possibility of access to all previous levels. Levels of understanding do not equate with higher or lower levels of mathematics.)

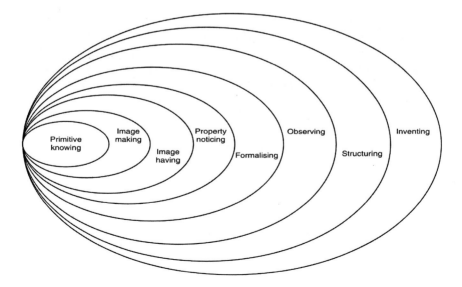

The next level of transcendent recursion entails thinking consciously about the noticed properties, abstracting common qualities and discarding the origins of one's mental action. It is at this level that full mathematical definitions can occur as one becomes aware of classes of objects that one has constructed from the formation of images and the abstraction of their properties.

(ibid., pp. 8–9)

Note parallels with van Hiele *levels* (see p. 59) and *structure of attention* (see p. 60).

One is now in a position to observe one's own thought structures and organise them consistently. One is aware of being aware, and can see the consequences of one's thoughts. It is clear at this point that while this outer level of understanding is transcendent, in other words fundamentally new in some way, it has to be consistent with all previous levels of knowing.

(ibid., p. 8)

There are similarities with *awareness of awareness* and the origins of disciplines (see p. 186 and p. 189).

For fuller understanding one must now be able to answer *why* the consequences of thoughts must be true. This calls for an awareness of associations and of sequence among one's previous thoughts, of their interdependence. In mathematical terms it might be setting one's thinking within an axiomatic structure.

All of these levels of recursion are referenced in a direct way to previous levels. Although new levels transcend or make one free of actions at an inner 'level', in some sense these actions on previous levels become initiating conditions which constrain one's knowing. At the highest level of recursion ... knowers act as free agents. We call this the level of inventing. Now one can choose to initiate a sequence or structure of thought which is a recursion on the previous one in the sense that it exists as a base, but is freely, yet compatibly, created. ...

(ibid., p. 8)

An important feature of their use of this onion image for tracking learners' experiences is that learners frequently 'fold back': they behave as if they had moved to an inner layer, before then moving out again, perhaps more securely. Note the similarities with the spiral model of *See–Experience–Master* (see p. 263) and with the van Hiele *levels* or *structure of attention* (see p. 59).

The National Council of Teachers of Mathematics standards states:

The learning principle: Students must learn mathematics with understanding, actively building new knowledge from experience and prior knowledge.

(NCTM, webref)

Understanding: Anne Watson

In synthesising research on understanding Watson distinguishes several different meanings for *understanding*, each of which plays a role in overall understanding:

- Knowing how to perform and use mathematics (instrumental and procedural);
- Knowing about usefulness in context (contextual);
- Relating mathematical concepts (relational);
- Knowing about underlying structures (transformable, generalized and abstract);
- Having overcome inherent obstacles.

(Watson, 2002a, p. 153)

She goes on to suggest strategies for promoting these different kinds of understanding.

Experience of understanding

Understanding is more of an experience than a behaviour, so some authors have tried to elaborate what that experience is like.

Understanding: Janet Duffin and Adrian Simpson

Janet Duffin and Adrian Simpson's article is unusual in that it tracks their exploration of their appreciation of what understanding feels like, stimulated by some classroom incidents, and in the light of reading of literature generally and one article specifically. What follows is a brief extract of some of their conclusions.

We named the three components of understanding *building*, *having*, and *enacting*. By the first component, we mean the formation of the connections between internal mental structures that we conjecture constitute the understanding which an individual has ready to be used to solve problems. With this meaning, it becomes clear that the mechanisms for the (formation and destruction) of these connections are already encapsulated within our theories of responses to natural, conflicting, and alien experiences.

The second component, which we term *having*, is the state of connections at any particular time. As teachers, it is this totality of connections (each having the potential to be used by the learner) that we are most interested in when we talk about a learner's understanding. It is important, at this point, to recognize that the emphasis on 'connections' gives the theory a different way of addressing the issue of whether understanding is 'all and nothing'. ...

[...]

By [*enacting* understanding] we mean the use of the connections available *in the moment* to solve a problem or construct a response to a question. The breadth of understanding which a learner *has* may be evidenced by the number of different possible starting points they have for solving a problem, while the depth of their understanding may be evidenced by the ways in which they can unpack each stage of their solution in ever more detail, with reference to more concepts.

[...]

We can try to determine the internal characteristics by asking ourselves and other learners the questions:

What do I feel when I (am building/have/am enacting) understanding?

And we can try to determine the external manifestations by asking ourselves and other teachers the questions:

What do I expect to be able to see in my students when I believe that they (are building/have/are enacting) their understanding?

(Duffin and Simpson, 2000, pp. 420–1)

Obstacles

Gaston Bachelard (b. France, 1884–1962) was a philosopher who focused on the development of scientific knowledge, informed by a wide range of interests and reading. There are several websites devoted to his memorable quotations. Several of them resonate with the notion of human powers, especially mental imagery (see p. 129).

Man is an imagining being.

The words of the world want to make sentences.

A word is a bud attempting to become a twig. How can one not dream while writing? It is the pen which dreams. The blank page gives the right to dream.

(Bachelard, webref)

Bachelard coined the notion of *epistemological obstacles* for difficulties learners experience in getting to grips with certain concepts due to their intrinsic complexity or sophistication.

It is not a question of considering external obstacles like the complexity or the transient nature of phenomena, nor of implicating weakness of the human senses and the human mind; it is in the very act of intimately

knowing that there appear by a sort of functional necessity sluggishness
and troubles ... we know against previous knowing.

(Bachelard, 1938, p. 13, quoted in Brousseau, 1997, p. 83)

Bachelard identifies through his study of physics a range of types of obstacle:
the obstacle of first experience which will later turn into experience to be
construed; the obstacle presented by previous general knowledge of the
situation; obstacles produced by the use of particular language; obstacles
arising from inappropriate images and associations; obstacles arising from
familiar techniques and actions; obstacles arising from inappropriate
anthropomorphisation, assumptions about what is real, and so on, and
obstacles arising from factual and quantitative knowledge.

His ideas were developed by Brousseau and Duroux and incorporated
into the theory of the *situation didactique* (see p. 79).

Epistemological obstacles and errors: Guy Brousseau

Brousseau links epistemological obstacles with errors learners routinely
make, noting that they often have valuable origins:

> ... errors and failures do not have the simplified role that we would like
> them to play. Errors are not only the effect of ignorance, of uncertainty,
> of chance, as espoused by empiricist or behaviourist learning theories,
> but the effect of a previous piece of knowledge which was interesting
> and successful, but which now is revealed as false or simply unadapted.
> Errors of this type are not erratic and unexpected, they constitute obsta-
> cles. As much in the teacher's functioning as in that of the student, the
> error is a component of the meaning of the acquired a piece of
> knowledge.
> [...]
> We assume, then, that the construction of meaning, as we understand
> it, implies a constant interaction between the student and problem-situa-
> tions, a dialectical interaction (because the subject anticipates and
> directs her actions) in which she engages her previous knowings,
> submits them to revision, modifies them, completes them or rejects them
> to form new conceptions. The main object of *didactique* is precisely to
> study the conditions that the situations or the problems put to the
> student must fulfil in order to foster the appearance, the working and the
> rejection of these successive conceptions.
> We can deduce from this discontinuous means of acquisition that the
> informational character of these situations must itself also change in
> jumps.
>
> (Brousseau, 1997, pp. 82–3)

Note the similarity with conjecturing and with *scientific debate* (see p. 277), and with Freudenthal's search for *discontinuities* (p. 177).

> What happens is that [errors] do not completely disappear all at once; they resist, they persist, then they reappear, and manifest themselves long after the subject has rejected the defective model from her conscious cognitive system. ...
>
> [...]
>
> The obstacle is of the same nature as knowledge, with objects, relationships, methods of understanding, predictions, with evidence, forgotten consequences, unexpected ramifications, etc. It will resist being rejected and, as it must, it will try to adapt itself locally, to modify itself at the least cost, to optimize itself in a reduced field, following a well-known process of accommodation.
>
> This is why there must be a sufficient flow of new situations which it cannot assimilate, which will destabilize it, make it ineffective, useless, wrong; which necessitate reconsidering it or rejecting it, forgetting it, cutting it up – up until its final manifestation.
>
> (ibid., pp. 84–5)

Brousseau goes on to discuss different origins of obstacles: neurological (due to brain functioning), didactical (due to manner or order of teaching), and epistemological (due to something inherently complex in what is being learned) (ibid., pp. 86–87). See also Duroux (1982).

Obstacles: Efraim Fischbein

Fischbein used the notion of obstacles in his study of intuition (see p. 63).

> It is highly illuminating to compare the obstacles, difficulties and distortions which have appeared in the history of mathematics with those which emerge during childhood and in the instructional process. Basically, the same types of conflicts may be identified. Intuitive factors – the quest for practicality, for behavioral interpretations, for visual, spatially consistent expressions – have profoundly influenced the historical development of the number concept, of the various geometries, of the infinitesimal calculus, of the concept of infinity, etc. Similar phenomena may be detected during the instructional process. This supports the hypothesis that intuitive forms of reasoning are not only a transitory stage in the development of intelligence. On the contrary, typical intuitive constraints influence our ways of solving and interpreting at every age. Even when dealing with highly abstract concepts, one tends to represent them almost automatically in a way which would render them intuitively accessible. We tend automatically to resort to behavioral and pictorial representations which can confer on abstract concepts the kind of manipulatory features

to which our reasoning is naturally adapted. It has been proved that even long after the student has acquired the adequate, highly abstract knowledge referring to a certain mathematical notion, the primitive, intuitive model on which this notion was originally built may continue to influence, tacitly, its use and interpretation.

(Fischbein, 1987, p. 212)

Evaluating understanding

Can understanding be assessed or evaluated?

Understanding: David Wheeler

How do we judge successful understanding? There are certain techniques – if that is not too grand a word – that we use. Probably the commonest involves asking the child to perform some task which appears to require understanding of what he has learnt. If the learning task was a computational process or algorithm, he will be asked to work some exercises based on the process. It is not unknown for these to be successfully done and yet for very similar exercises to be insoluble a month later. What has gone wrong? We often say that he cannot *really* have understood what he was doing the first time. Whether he did or not, our test of understanding was not adequate as we now want the child to be able to retain his ability to work the exercises over a period. We have substituted a more demanding requirement.

Possibly we have also met cases of children's inability to perform a task the first time round and an apparently spontaneous emergence of success later. It is as if germination had gone on unnoticed in the meanwhile. Introspection sometimes reveals cases in which we ourselves have suddenly understood – 'light dawned', 'it clicked' – after a delay in which no external stimulus seems to have acted. If *we* are able to learn something when we are not being taught, we can probably imagine the same thing happening to children. For both of these reasons it can be misleading to ask for a proof of comprehension immediately a piece of instruction has taken place.

Another test of understanding is the application of something learned to a new problem. This works pretty well as a positive test, but it is a weak indicator if it gives negative results. Failure to make the application may be due to the jump between the new situation and the old being too large. ...

[...]

It is not merely perverse to say that we could profitably think less about 'teaching for (the child's) understanding' and more about 'teaching for the teacher's understanding'. Only through attending to the second are we likely to make much progress with the first. And the unfortunate truth is that many of our ways of presenting mathematics in the classroom start from the assumption that we (the teachers) already understand and have nothing to learn. Not until we allow that this may not be the case do we find evidence of our ignorance underneath our noses.

(Wheeler, 1965, pp. 48–50)

Affecting learning: Jean Lave

... if teachers teach in order to affect learning, the only way to discover whether they are having effects and if so what those are, is to explore whether, and if so how, there are changes in the participation of learners learning in their various communities of practice. ...

... teachers need to know about the powerful identity-changing communities of practice of their students, which define the conditions of their work. It is a puzzle, however, as to where to find them, and how to recognize them ...

(Lave, 1996, pp. 158–9)

Evaluating learning requires agreement on what constitutes learning (see p. 30). For example, if learning includes developing sensitivities to notice more detail in different situations, then evaluation must include this component; if it includes changes in the structure of attention and the education of awareness, then evaluation must take this into account; if it includes performance of techniques with facility, then evaluation will take this into account; if it includes *knowing-to* use familiar techniques in new contexts, then evaluation must offer learners corresponding opportunities; if it includes *knowing-about*, then evaluation will include opportunities for learners to display connections and links, to account for phenomena and to construct relevant narratives; if it includes constructing mathematical objects which meet specified constraints, then evaluation will include this as a component.

Assessment: Paul Black and Dylan Wiliam

Paul Black is a scientist and science educator who has specialised in assessment practices. Dylan Wiliam is a sociologist who researches assessment, with an interest in mathematics education. They have formed the core of a team of people conducting extensive research into the role of teacher assessment (Black and Wiliam, 1998)

In a follow-up booklet (Black *et al.*, 2002) they highlight the importance of asking suitable questions, extending wait-time (which is easiest if the questions are genuine);

It is the nature, rather than the amount, that is critical when giving pupils feedback on both oral and written work. Research experiments have established that, whilst pupils' learning can be advanced by feedback through comments, the giving of marks – or grades – has a negative effect in that pupils ignore comments when marks are also given (Butler, 1988). These results often surprise teachers, but those who have abandoned the giving of marks find that their experience confirms the findings: pupils do engage more productively in improving their work.

(Black *et al.*, 2002, p. 8)

The Turing Test: Alan Turing

Alan Turing (b. London, 1912–1954) is best known for his work decoding the Enigma codes, and the first significant use of a modern computer. Turing's 1950 paper 'Computing machinery and intelligence' has become one of the most cited in philosophical literature. In it he proposes first a gender test, but then shows how the same format provides a test for 'human cognitive abilities', hence its interest concerning assessment.

> I propose ... a game which we call the 'imitation game'. It is played with three people, a man (A), a woman (B), and an interrogator (C) who may be of either sex. The interrogator stays in a room apart from the other two. The object of the game for the interrogator is to determine which of the other two is the man and which is the woman. He knows them by labels X and Y, and at the end of the game he says either 'X is A and Y is B' or 'X is B and Y is A'. The interrogator is allowed to put questions to A and B ...
> [...]
> In order that tones of voice may not help the interrogator the answers should be written, or better still, typewritten. The ideal arrangement is to have a teleprinter communicating between the two rooms. Alternatively the question and answers can be repeated by an intermediary. The object of the game for the third player (B) is to help the interrogator. The best strategy for her is probably to give truthful answers. She can add such things as 'I am the woman, don't listen to him!' to her answers, but it will avail nothing as the man can make similar remarks.
> We now ask the question, 'What will happen when a machine takes the part of A in this game?' Will the interrogator decide wrongly as often when the game is played like this as he does when the game is played between a man and a woman? These questions replace our original, 'Can machines think?'

(Turing, 1950 webref)

The Chinese Room: John Searle

John Searle (b. Colorado, 1932–) is a prolific contemporary philosopher who has consistently challenged the claims and approaches of 'the mind–brain as a computer' school of thought. He posed a similar problem to Turing's, called 'the

Chinese room'. The incoming symbols turn out to be data and questions about the data; the outgoing symbols are answers. Searle supposes that he gets good enough at using the rules that the answers are indistinguishable from those of a Chinese speaker. Despite this, he does not know any Chinese whatsoever.

> Suppose I am locked in a room. In this room there are two big bushel baskets full of Chinese symbols, together with a rule book in English for matching Chinese symbols from one basket with Chinese symbols from the other basket. The rules say things such as 'Reach into basket 1 and take out a squiggle-squiggle sign, and go [and] put that over next the squoggle-squoggle sign that you take from basket 2. ... Now let us suppose that the people outside the room send in more Chinese symbols together with more rules for shuffling and matching the symbols. But this time they also give me rules for passing back Chinese symbols to them. So, there I am in my Chinese room, shuffling these symbols around; symbols are coming in and I am passing symbols out according to the rule book. ... *if I don't understand Chinese in that situation, then neither does any other digital computer solely [by] virtue of being an appropriately programmed computer,* ...
>
> (Searle, 1987, p. 213)

Searle uses this image to argue that behaviour alone is not sufficient to identify understanding, and that computers will never 'understand' text the way humans do. So what are we doing when testing learners? Understanding requires at least an affective dimension as well as the cognitive and the behavioural.

Both the Turing test and the Chinese room have similarities with assessment, especially in mathematics. As a teacher trying to assess what learners know, the problem is very similar: you set them some questions and then from their responses you want to judge the depth of their understanding. But all you have is their answers. So you grade their answer against a prepared answer sheet, and where the candidate deviates, you assess the correctness of their argument. Might they have simply memorised sufficient problem-types so as to recognise the type and then reproduce the technique but with no real understanding of what they were doing or why the technique works? The more sophisticated the questions set, the less well candidates do, so most examiners are content to set questions which are similar to ones previously encountered. Where they differ from familiar ones, fewer candidates do well, so teachers train the next year's candidates in the 'new type' of question. Put another way, how might you test for *relational understanding* (see p. 295), for *educated awareness* (see p. 61), for *transfer* (see p. 291) or flexibility in *situatedness* of learning (see p. 86)?

One of the extra features of assessment is that as soon as an examination is taken, teachers have additional information from which to plan their teaching for the following year. Within a few years it becomes possible to teach to any test which has a relatively invariant standard format. But expecting learners to be creative and to tackle novel problems within a limited examination period seems most unreasonable, since so many minor things can go wrong, obscuring what candidates could do in other circumstances. Furthermore, you want to enable everyone to show what they can do, and be rewarded, not depress people by making them expose what they cannot (yet) do. And how do you take into account the observation that learning is a maturation process which happens over time, since what is currently obscure can become clear even when no further attention is devoted to it?

SOLO taxonomy: John Biggs and Kevin Collis

Inspired by Piaget's research and insight into how people come to know, but dissatisfied with a stage-theory approach to development, John Biggs and Kevin Collis (1982) turned their attention to responses that learners make to tasks, in an attempt to distinguish different forms of understanding. They developed this in the SOLO taxonomy (Structure of the Observed Learning Outcome), and illustrated it with examples drawn from across the school curriculum and over the whole age-span. They distinguished, for example, between *prestructural, unistructural, multistructural, relational,* and *extended abstract* responses, as follows:

> *pre-structural*: a reaction which is often a denial of the problem, a tautology, or a transduction; bound to specifics, with no apparent concern for consistency and often no evidence of appreciating the problem.
>
> *uni-structural*: an instant reaction to a question stressing one particular feature which might or might not be relevant; generalises one aspect only, no evidence of need for consistency, jumps to conclusions on one aspect; tends to close on first idea.
>
> *multi-structural*: a response which mentions several disparate factors or aspects; aware of consistency but tends to close on a few isolated fixations on data, and so can reach different conclusions on same data according to what is stressed.
>
> *relational*: a response which mentions several factors and weaves them into some sort of related 'story' or account; generalises within given or experienced context using related aspects.
>
> *extended abstract*: a response which reasons logically using the stressed features as data or as justification; uses deduction and induction, generalises to situations not experienced; attempts to resolve inconsistencies; satisfied not to close but to leave conclusions open.
>
> (summarised from Biggs and Collis, 1982, pp. 24–5 and pp. 61–93)

For example, a unistructural response to tasks involving the use of algebraic symbols sees each letter as identified with a particular value (such as the position in the alphabet). Multistructural responses were satisfied on having tried a few cases, whereas a relational response appreciates the notion of generalised number, and extended abstract responses showed appreciation of the notion of variable beyond that of generalised number (Biggs and Collis, 1982, pp. 68–70). The research on which this and other examples in the book were based was carried out in the late 1970s, and since then these issues have been researched and described in other ways. Nevertheless, the structural essence of the SOLO levels remain valid and useful for making distinctions.

Apparent or explicit desire for closure was a major feature in the elucidation of the taxonomy in mathematics (ibid., p. 67): instant closure on the first idea (*unistructural*); being triggered by operations to complete them (*multistructural*); a sense that questions have single correct answers (*relational*); or are not always required (*extended abstract*). Each form of response (rather than stage or level) seems to be specified by absence of limitations of less sophisticated responses, but the essence of the forms corresponds quite closely with a holistic reaction, recognising distinctions, appreciating relationships, and property use, corresponding to the *structure of attention* (see p. 60) and van Hiele *phases* (see p. 59 and p. 163).

Understanding is difficult to capture in words, but has to do with the sensitisation and enriching of awareness, including connections and images, access to language, and extension of powers to make sense of phenomena; and training of behaviour in significant procedures and techniques.

Attention is structured, and learning can be seen in terms of shifts in the way we attend to phenomena, indeed the way we select and identify the phenomena to which we attend.

Learners encounter different kinds of obstacles, inherent in the content, arising from the teaching, and stemming from their own propensities and dispositions.

Testing for understanding is essentially the Turing test. The Chinese room shows that behaviour alone is not sufficient to determine understanding. Nevertheless it is possible to develop sophisticated instruments such as the SOLO taxonomy for gauging possible or probable understanding from responses to test items. Getting learners to make up their own questions often reveals a good deal about what learners are attending to and what they are aware of.

Epilogue

The issue of understanding closes a cycle, for deciding what it means to understand is very close to deciding what it means to learn. Teaching involves stimulating learners to take initiative, to act and to make use of their natural powers in order to make sense of phenomena which attract their attention. They do this by acting on objects (previously reified) and restructuring what they attend to, and what they are sensitised to notice, as well as through gaining facility in the use of techniques. Awareness is educated and behaviour is trained through the harnessing of emotions arising from becoming aware of a disturbance, of something unexpected. It is the unexpected which strikes the learners' attention, and activates the sense-making apparatus.

The constructs highlighted in this collection are ones which have struck us as editors and practitioners. We hope that at least some of the extracts have prompted you to want to read more of the authors' original works, to hear their voices in a more extended form. Above all, we hope that by using various constructs to make sense of your own experience, you find yourself stimulated to act in fresh ways, and to find new means of interpreting what you notice.

Bibliography

Ahmed, A. 1987. *Better Mathematics: A Curriculum Development Study based on the Low Attainers in Mathematics Project (LAMP)*. HSMO, London.

Ainley, J. 1982. *ME234 Using Mathematical Thinking, Unit 9 Mathematical Thinking in the Primary Curriculum*. Open University, Milton Keynes.

Ainley, J. 1987. Telling questions. *Mathematics Teaching*, **118**, pp. 24–6.

Anthony, G. 1994. *The Role of the Worked Example in Learning Mathematics: SAME Papers 1994*. University of Waikato, Hamilton, pp. 129–43.

Armstrong, M. 1980. *Closely Observed Children: The Diary of a Primary Classroom*. Writers and Readers, Richmond.

Artigue, M. 1993. Didactical engineering as a framework for the conception of teaching products. In Biehler, R., Scholz, R., Straßer R. and Winkelman, B. (eds), *Didactics of Mathematics as a Scientific Discipline*. Kluwer, Dordrecht, pp. 27–39.

Atherton, J. webref. *Learning and Teaching: Learning from Experience*. www.dmu.ac.uk/~jamesa/learning/experien.htm.

Atkinson, R., Derry, S., Renkl, A. and Wortham, D. 2000. Learning from examples: Instructional principles from the worked examples research. *Review of Educational Research*, **70** (2), pp. 181–214.

Ausubel, D. 1963. *The Psychology of Meaningful Verbal Learning*. Grune and Stratton, New York.

Ausubel, D. 1978. In defense of advance organizers: A reply to the critics. *Review of Educational Research*, **48**, pp. 251–7.

Ausubel, D. and Robinson, F. 1969. *School Learning: An Introduction to Educational Psychology*. Holt, Rhinehart and Winston, New York.

Bachelard, G. 1938 (reprinted 1980). *La Formation de l'Esprit Scientifique*, J. Vrin, Paris.

Bachelard, G. 1958. *The Poetics of Space*. (Maria, J. trans. 1969). Beacon Press, Boston.

Bachelard, G. 1968. *The Philosophy of No: A Philosophy of the New Scientific Mind*. (Waterston, G. trans.) Orion Press, New York.

Bachelard, G. webref, for example www.creativequotations.com.

Balacheff, N. 1986. Cognitive versus situational analysis of problem solving behaviours. *For the Learning of Mathematics*, **6** (3), pp. 10–12.

Balacheff, N. 1990. Towards a problématique for research on mathematics teaching. *Journal for Research in Mathematics Education*, **21** (4), pp. 258–72.

Ball, D. 1992. Magical hopes: Manipulatives and the reform of math education. *American Educator*, **16** (2), pp. 14–18, pp. 46–7.

Ballard, P. 1928. *Teaching the Essentials of Arithmetic*. University of London Press, London.

Banwell, C., Saunders, K. and Tahta, D. 1972 (updated 1986). *Starting Points: For Teaching Mathematics in Middle and Secondary Schools.* Tarquin, Diss.

Bartlett, F. 1932. *Remembering: A Study in Experimental and Social Psychology.* Cambridge University Press, London.

Baruk, S. 1985. *L'âge du Capitaine: De l'Erreur en Mathématiques.* Éditions du seuil, Paris, p. 23.

Bauersfeld, H. 1980. Hidden dimensions in the so-called reality of a mathematics classroom. *Educational Studies in Mathematics,* **11** (February), pp. 23–41.

Bauersfeld, H. 1988. Interaction, construction and knowledge: Alternative perspectives for mathematics education. In Grouws, D., Cooney, T. and Jones, D. (eds), *Perspectives on Research on Mathematics Education.* NCTM and Erlbaum, Mahwah, NJ, pp. 27–46.

Bauersfeld, H. 1992. Integrating theories for mathematics education. *For the Learning of Mathematics,* **12** (2), pp. 19–28.

Bauersfeld, H. 1993. Theoretical perspectives on interaction in the mathematics classroom. In Biehler, R., Scholz, R., Straser, R. and Winkelmann, B. (eds), *Didactics of Mathematics as a Scientific Discipline.* Dordrecht, Kluwer, pp. 133–46.

Bauersfeld, H. 1995. 'Language games' in the mathematics classroom: Their function and their effects. In Cobb, P. and Bauersfeld, H. (eds), *The Emergence of Mathematical Meaning: Interaction in Classroom Cultures.* Erlbaum, Mahwah, NJ, pp. 271–89.

Bell, A. 1986. Diagnostic teaching 2: Developing conflict: Discussion lesson. *Mathematics Teaching,* **116**, pp. 26–9.

Bell, A. 1987. Diagnostic teaching 3: Provoking discussion. *Mathematics Teaching,* **118**, pp. 21–3.

Bell, A. 1993. Principles for the design of teaching. *Educational Studies in Mathematics,* **24**, pp. 5–34.

Benbachir, A. and Zaki, M. 2001. Production d'exemples et de contre-examples en analyse: étude de cas en première d'université. *Educational Studies in Mathematics,* **47**, pp. 273–95.

Bennett, J. 1956–1966. *The Dramatic Universe* (four volumes). Hodder and Stoughton, London.

Bennett, J. 1993. *Elementary Systematics: A Tool for Understanding Wholes.* Bennett Books, Santa Fe.

Beth, E. W. and Piaget, J. 1966. *Mathematical Epistemology and Psychology.* Reidel, Dordrecht.

Biggs J. and Collis K. 1982. *Evaluating the Quality of Learning: The SOLO Taxonomy.* Academic Press, New York.

Bills, L. 1996. The use of examples in the teaching and learning of mathematics. In Puig, L. and Gutierrez, A. (eds), *Proceedings of PME XX, Vol. 2.* Valencia, Spain, pp. 81–8.

Bills, L. and Rowland, T. 1999. Examples, generalisation and proof. In Brown, L. (ed.), *Making Meaning in Mathematics: A Collection of Extended and Refereed Papers from the British Society for Research into Learning Mathematics,* Visions of Mathematics 2, Advances in Mathematics Education 1. QED, York, pp. 103–16.

Black, P. and Wiliam, D. 1998. *Inside the Black Box: Raising Standards through Classroom Assessment.* School of Education, Kings College, London.

Black, P., Harrison, C., Lee, C., Marshall, B. and Wiliam, D. 2002. *Working Inside the Black Box.* Department of Education and Professional Studies, Kings College, London.

Boaler, J. 1997. *Experiencing School Mathematics: Teaching Styles, Sex and Setting.* Open University Press, Buckingham.

Boaler, J. 2000. Exploring situated insights into research and learning. *Journal for Research in Mathematics Education*, **31** (1), pp. 113–19.

Boaler, J. (ed.) 2000a. *Multiple Perspectives on Mathematics Teaching and Learning, International Perspectives on Mathematics Education*. Ablex, London.

Boero, P., Rossella, G. and Mariotti, M. webref. *Some Dynamic Mental Processes Underlying Producing and Proving Conjectures*. www-didactique.imag.fr/preuve/ Resumes/Boero/Boero96.html.

Boero P., Rossella G. and Mariotti M. 1996. Some dynamic mental processes underlying producing and proving conjectures. In Puig, L. and Gutiérrez, A. (eds), *Proceedings of PME XX, Vol. 2*, pp. 121–8.

Boole, M. 1901. Indian thought and Western science in the nineteenth century. In Boole, M., (1931), Cobham, E. (ed.), *Collected Works, Vol. 3*. C. W. Daniel Co., London, pp. 947–67.

Boulton-Lewis, G. 1998. Children's strategy use and interpretations of mathematical representations. *Journal of Mathematical Behavior*, **17** (2), pp. 219–37.

Bouvier, A. 1987. The right to make mistakes. *For the Learning of Mathematics*, **7** (3), pp. 17–25.

Brousseau, G. and Otte, M. 1991. The fragility of knowledge. In Bishop, A., Mellin-Olsen, S. and Van Dormolen, J. (eds), *Mathematical Knowledge: Its Growth through Teaching*. Kluwer, Dordrecht, pp. 13–36.

Brousseau, G. 1984. The crucial role of the didactical contract in the analysis and construction of situations in teaching and learning mathematics. In Steiner, H. (ed.), *Theory of Mathematics Education, Paper 54*. Institut fur Didaktik der Mathematik der Universitat Bielefeld, pp. 110–19.

Brousseau, G. 1986. Fondemonts et méthodes de la didactique des mathématiques, *Recherches en Didactique des Mathématiques*, **7** (2), p. 33–115.

Brousseau, G. 1997. Theory of didactical situations in mathematics: Didactiques des mathématiques, 1970–1990. (Balacheff, N., Cooper, M., Sutherland, R. and Warfield, V. trans.) Kluwer, Dordrecht.

Brown J. S., Collins, A. and Duguid, P. 1989. Situated cognition and the culture of learning. *Educational Researcher*, **18** (1), pp. 32–41.

Brown L. and Coles, A. 1999. Needing to use algebra: A case study. In Zaslavsky, O. (ed.), *Proceedings of PME–XXIII, Vol. 2*, Haifa, pp. 153–60.

Brown, L. and Coles, A. 2000. Same/different: A 'natural' way of learning mathematics. In Nakahara, T. and Koyama, M. (eds.), *Proceedings of the 24th Conference of the International Group for the Psychology of Mathematics Education, Vol 2*. Hiroshima, Japan, pp. 153–60.

Brown, M. 2001. Influences on the teaching of number in England. In Anghileri, J. (ed.), *Principles and Practices in Arithmetic Teaching: Innovative Approaches for the Primary Classroom*. Open University Press, Buckingham, pp. 35–48.

Brown, M. and Küchemann, D. 1976. Is it an 'add', Miss?: Part 1. *Mathematics in School*, **5** (5), pp. 15–17.

Brown, M. and Küchemann, D. 1977. Is it an 'add', Miss?: Part 2. *Mathematics in School*, **6** (1), pp. 9–10.

Brown, M. and Küchemann, D. 1981. Is it an 'add', Miss?: Part 3. *Mathematics in School*, **10** (1), pp. 26–8.

Brown, S. and Walter, M. 1993. *Problem Posing: Reflections and Applications*. Lawrence Elbaum Associates, Hillsdale, NJ.

Bruner, J. 1965 (reprint from 1962). *On Knowing: Essays for the Left Hand*. Atheneum, New York.

Bruner, J. 1966. *Towards a Theory of Instruction*. Harvard University Press, Cambridge, MA.

Bruner, J. 1986. *Actual Minds, Possible Worlds*. Harvard University Press, Cambridge, MA.

Bruner, J. 1996. *The Culture of Education*. Harvard University Press, Cambridge, MA.

Bruner, J., Goodnow, J. and Austin, G. 1956. *A Study of Thinking*. Wiley, New York.

Bryant, P. 1982. The role of conflict and of agreement between intellectual strategies in children's ideas about measurement. *British Journal of Psychology*, **73**, pp. 243–51.

Burger, W. and Shaughnessy, J. 1986. Characterizing the Van Hiele levels of development in geometry. *Journal for Research in Mathematics Education*, **17** (1), pp. 31–48.

Burkhardt, H. 1981. *The Real World of Mathematics*. Blackie, Glasgow.

Bussi, M. webref. *Italian Research in Innovation: Towards a New Paradigm?* elib.zib.de/IMU/ICMI/bulletin/45/ItalianResearch.html.

Butler, R. 1988. Enhancing and undermining intrinsic motivation: The effects of task-involving and ego-involving evaluation on interest and performance. *British Journal of Educacational Psychology*, **58**, pp. 1–14.

Byers, V. and Herscovics, N. 1977. Understanding school mathematics. *Mathematics Teaching*, **81**, pp. 24–7.

Caillot, M. 2002. French Didactiques. *Canadian Journal of Science, Mathematics and Technology Education*, **2** (3), pp. 397–403.

Calkin, J. 1910. *Notes on Education: A Practical Work on Method and School Management*. Mackinlay, Halifax.

Campbell, S. and Dawson, S. 1995. Learning as embodied action. In Sutherland, R. and Mason, J. (eds), *Exploiting Mental Imagery with Computers in Mathematics Education*. Springer, New York.

Chi, M. and Bassok, M. 1989. Learning from examples via self-explanation. In Resnick, L. (ed.), *Knowing, Learning and Instruction: Essays in Honor of Robert Glaser*. Erlbaum, Mahwah, NJ.

Christiansen, B. and Walther, G. 1986. Task and activity. In Christiansen, B., Howson, G. and Otte, M. (eds), *Perspectives in Mathematics Education*. Dordrecht, Reidel, pp. 243–307.

Clarke, D. webref. *Assessment for Teaching and Learning*. http://mcs.open.ac.uk/cme/Clarke_on_tasks1.htm.

Cobb, P. 1991. Reconstructing elementary school mathematics. *Focus on Learning Problems in Mathematics*, **13** (2), pp. 3–22.

Cobb, P. 1995. Learning and small-group interaction. In Cobb, P. and Bauersfeld, H. (eds), *The Emergence of Mathematical Meaning: Interaction in Classroom Cultures*. Erlbaum, Mahwah, NJ.

Cobb, P. and Merkel, G. 1989. Thinking strategies: Teaching arithmetic through problem solving. In Trafton, P. and Shulte, A. (eds), *New Directions for Elementary School Mathematics: 1989 Yearbook*. National Council of Teachers of Mathematics, Reston, pp. 70–81.

Cobb, P., McClain, K. and Whitenack, J. 1997. Reflective discourse and collective reflection. *Journal for Research in Mathematics Education*, **28** (3), pp. 258–77.

Cobb, P., Wood, T. and Yackel, E. 1991. A constructivist approach to second grade mathematics. In Von Glasersfeld, E. (ed.), *Radical Constructivism In Mathematics Education*. Reidel, Dordrecht, p. 157–76.

Cobb, P., Yackel, E. and Wood, T. 1992. A constructivist alternative to the representational view of mind in mathematics education. *Journal for Research in Mathematics Education, 23* (1), pp. 2–33.

Colburn, W. 1863. *Intellectual Arithmetic: Upon the Inductive Method of Instruction.* Houghton, Cambridge.

Cole, M. 1985. The zone of proximal development: Where culture and cognition create each other. In Wertsch, J. (ed.), *Culture, Communication and Cognition: Vygotskian perspectives.* Cambridge University Press, Cambridge, pp. 141–61.

Coles, A. and Brown, L. 1999. Meta-commenting: Developing algebraic activity in a 'community of inquirers'. In Bills, L. (ed.), *Proceedings of the British Society for Research into Learning Mathematics MERC.* Warwick University, pp. 1–6.

Confrey, J. 1990. What constructivism implies for teaching. In Davis, R., Maher, C. and Noddings, N. (eds), *Constructivist Views on the Teaching of and Learning of Mathematics.* NCTM, Reston, pp. 107–22.

Confrey, J. 1991. Steering a course between Vygotsky and Piaget. *Educational Researcher, 20* (2), pp. 29–32.

Confrey, J. 1994. A theory of intellectual development, Part III. *For the Learning of Mathematics, 15* (2), pp. 36–45.

Confrey, J. 1994a. A theory of intellectual development, Part I. *For the Learning of Mathematics, 14* (3), pp. 2–8.

Confrey, J. 1994b. A theory of intellectual development, Part II. *For the Learning of Mathematics, 15* (1), pp. 38–48.

Confrey, J. 1995. How compatible are radical constructivism, sociocultural approaches, and social constructivism? In Steffe, L. and Gale, J. (eds), *Constructivism in Education.* Erlbaum, Mahwah, NJ.

Cook, T. 1979. *The Curves of Life* (reprint of 1914 edition). Dover, New York.

Courant, R. 1981. Reminiscences from Hilbert's Göttingen. *Math Intelligencer, 3* (4), pp. 154–64.

Cremin, L. 1961. *The Transformation of the School: Progressivism in American Education, 1876–1957.* Knopf, New York.

Crowley, M. 1987. The van Hiele model of the development of geometric thought. In Lindquist, M. and Shulte, A. (eds), *Learning and Teaching Geometry K–12: 1987 Year Book.* NCTM, Reston, pp. 1–16.

Cuoco, A., Goldenberg, P. and Mark, J. 1996. Habits of mind: An organizing principle for mathematics curricula. *Journal of Mathematical Behavior, 15*, pp. 375–402.

Da Vinci, L. webref. www-history.mcs.st-andrews.ac.uk/history/Quotations/Leonardo.html.

Dahlberg, R. and Housman, D. 1997. Facilitating learning events through example generation. *Educational Studies in Mathematics, 33*, pp. 283–99.

Davies, H. B. 1978. A seven-year-old's subtraction technique. *Mathematics Teaching, 83*, pp. 15–16.

Davis, B. 1996. *Teaching Mathematics: Toward a Sound Alternative.* Garland, London.

Davis, B., Summara, D. and Kieren, T. 1996. Cognition, co-emergence, curriculum. *Jouranl for Curriculum Studies, 28*, (2), pp. 151–69.

Davis, G., Tall, D. and Thomas, M. webref. *What is the Object of the Encapsulation of a Process?* www.davidtall.com.

Davis, P. and Hersh, R. 1981. *The Mathematical Experience.* Harvester, Boston and London.

Davis, R. 1966. Discovery in the teaching of mathematics. In Shulman, L. and Keislar, E. (eds), *Learning by Discovery: A Reappraisal.* Rand McNally, Chicago.

Davis, R. 1984. *Learning Mathematics: The Cognitive Science Approach*. Croom Helm, London.

De Morgan, A. 1865. A speech of Professor De Morgan, President, at the first meeting of the London Mathematical Society. *Proceedings of the London Mathematical Society, Vol. 1* (1866), pp. 1–9.

De Morgan, A. 1898. *Of the Study and Difficulty of Mathematics*. Open Court, London.

Dearden R. 1967. Instruction and learning by discovery. In Peters, R. (ed.), *The Concept of Education*. Routledge and Kegan Paul, London, p. xx.

Denvir, B. and Brown, M. 1986. Understanding number concepts in low attaining 7–9 year-olds. *Educational Studies in Mathematics*, **17** (1), pp. 15–36.

Denvir, B. and Brown, M. 1986a. Understanding number concepts in low attaining 7–9 year-olds: Part II. *Educational Studies in Mathematics*, **17** (2), pp. 143–64.

Detterman, D. and Sternberg, R. (eds). 1993. *Transfer on trial: Intelligence, Cognition, and Instruction*. Abbex, Norwood, NJ, pp. 99–167.

Dewey, J. webref. '*My Pedagogic Creed' by John Dewey*. www.rjgeib.com/biography/credo/dewey.html.

Dewey, J. 1902. *The Child and The Curriculum, (reprinted 1971), The Child and The Curriculum and The School and Society*. University of Chicago Press, Chicago, pp. 19–31.

Dewey, J. 1933. *How We Think: A Restatement of the Relation of Reflective Thinking to the Educative Process*. D.C. Heath and Co., London.

Dewey, J. 1938. *Experience and Nature*. Dover, New York.

Dienes, Z. 1960. *Building Up Mathematics*. Hutchison, London.

Dienes, Z. P. 1963. *An Experimental Study of Mathematics-learning*. Hutchinson Educational, London.

Donaldson, M. 1963. *A Study of Children's Thinking*. Tavistock Publications, London.

Dörfler, W, 1991. Meaning: Image schemata and protocols: Plenary lecture. In Furinghetti, F. (ed.), *Proceedings of PME XV, Vol. I*. Assisi, Italy, pp. 17–33.

Dörfler, W. 2002. Formation of mathematical objects as decision making. *Mathematical Thinking and Learning*, **4** (4), pp. 337–50.

Dubinsky, E. 1991. Reflective abstraction in mathematical thinking. In Tall, D. (ed.), *Advanced Mathematical Thinking*. Kluwer, Dordrecht, pp. 95–126.

Dubinsky, E. webref. trident.mcs.kent.edu/~edd/.

Duffin, J. 1996. *Calculators in the Classroom*. Manutius Press, Liverpool.

Duffin, J. and Simpson, A. 2000. A search for understanding. *The Journal of Mathematical Behaviour*, **18** (4), pp. 415–28.

Duroux, A. webref. 1982. (Warfield, V. trans.) *Calculus By Scientific Debate as an Application of Didactique*. www.math.washington.edu/~warfield/articles/Calc&Didactique.html.

Dweck, C. 1999. *Self-theories: Their Role in Motivation, Personality and Development*. Psychology Press, Philadelphia.

Edwards, D. and Mercer, N. 1987. *Common Knowledge: The Development of Understanding in the Classroom*. Routledge, London.

Egan, K. webref. *Kieran Egan's Home Page*, www.educ.sfu.ca/kegan/TaSTintro.html.

Egan, K. webref a. *Getting it Wrong from the Beginning: The Mismatch between School and Children's Minds*. www.educ.sfu.ca/kegan/Wrong-article.html.

Egan, K. 1986. *Teaching as Story Telling: An Alternative Approach to Teaching and Curriculum in the Elementary School*. University of Chicago Press, Chicago.

Elbaz, F. 1983. *Teacher's Thinking: A Study of Practical Knowledge*. Nichols, New York.

Enright, M. and Cox, D. webref. *Foundations Study Guide: Montessori Education.* http://www.objectivistcenter.org/articles/foundations_montessori-education.asp

Erlwanger, S. 1973. Benny's conception of rules and answers in IPI mathematics. *Journal of Children's Mathematical Behavior,* 1 (2), pp. 7–26.

Festinger, L. 1957. *A Theory of Cognitive Dissonance.* Stanford University Press, Stanford.

Fischbein, E. 1987. *Intuition in Science and Mathematics: An Educational Approach.* Reidel, Dordecht.

Floyd, A. (ed.) 1981. *Developing Mathematical Thinking.* Addison Wesley, London.

Floyd, A., *et al.*. 1982. *EM235 Developing Mathematical Thinking.* Open University, Milton Keynes.

Fox, D. 1983. Personal theories of teaching. *Studies in Higher Education,* **8** (2), pp. 151–163.

Frankenstein, M. 1989. *Relearning Mathematics: A Different R – Radical Math(s).* Free Association, London.

Freudenthal, H. 1973. *Mathematics as an Educational Task.* Reidel, Dordrecht.

Freudenthal, H. 1978. *Weeding and Sowing: Preface to a Science of Mathematical Education.* Reidel, Dordrecht.

Freudenthal, H. 1983. *Didactical Phenomenology of Mathematical Structures.* Reidel, Dordrecht.

Freudenthal, H. 1991. *Revisiting Mathematics Education: China Lectures.* Kluwer, Dordrecht.

Gagné, R. 1985. *The Conditions of Learning* (4th edn). Holt, Rinehart and Winston, New York.

Gagné, R., Briggs, L. and Wager, W. 1992. *Principles of Instructional Design* (4th edn). HBJ College Publishers, Fort Worth.

Gattegno, C. 1963. *For the Teaching of Mathematics.* Educational Explorers, Reading.

Gattegno, C. 1970. *What We Owe Children: The Subordination of Teaching to Learning.* Routledge and Kegan Paul, London.

Gattegno, C. 1970a. The human element in mathematics. In *Mathematical Reflections: contributions to mathematical thought and teaching* (written in memory of A. G. Sillito). Association of Teachers of Mathematics, Cambridge University Press, Cambridge, MA, pp. 131–8.

Gattegno, C. 1974. *The Common Sense of Teaching Mathematics.* Educational Solutions, New York.

Gattegno, C. 1981. Children and mathematics: A new appraisal. *Mathematics Teaching,* **94**, pp. 5–7.

Gattegno, C. 1983. On algebra. *Mathematics Teaching,* **105**, pp. 34–5.

Gattegno, C. 1987 *The Science of Education, Part 1: Theoretical Considerations.* Educational Solutions, New York.

Gattegno, C. 1988. *The Science of Education, Part 2B: The Awareness of Mathematization.* Educational Solutions, New York.

Gibson, J. 1977. The theory of affordances. In Shaw, R. E. and Bransford, J. (eds), *Perceiving, Acting, and Knowing.* Erlbaum, Mahwah, NJ.

Gibson, J. 1979. *The Ecological Approach to Visual Perception.* Houghton Mifflin, London.

Gibson, J. webref. http://www.alamut.com/notebooks/a/affordances.html.

Giles, G. 1966. Notes on mathematical activity. In Atkin, B., *et al.* (eds), *The Development of Mathematical Ability in Children: The Place of the Problem in this Development.* Association of Teachers of Mathematics, Nelson, pp.8–12.

Goldenberg, P., Lewis, P. and O'Keefe, J. 1992. Dynamic representation and the development of a process understanding of function. In Dubinsky, E. and Harel, G. (eds), *The Concept of Function: Aspects of Epistemology and Pedagogy*. MAA Monograph series, Washington, pp. 235–60.

Goodman, N. 1978. *Ways of World Making*. Harvester, Boston and London.

Gravemeijer, K. 1990. Context problems and realistic mathematics education. In Gravemeijer, K., Van den Heuvel, M. and Streefland, L. (eds), *Contexts, Productions Tests and Geometry in Realistic Mathematics Education*, Technipress, Culemborg.

Gravemeijer, K. 1994. *Developing Realistic Mathematics Education*. Freudenthal Institute, Utrecht.

Gray, E. and Tall, D. 1994. Duality, ambiguity and flexibility: A proceptual view of simple arithmetic. *Journal for Research in Mathematics Education*, **25** (2), pp. 116–140.

Green, D. 1989. School pupils' understanding of randomness. In Morris, R. (ed.), *Studies In Mathematics Education: The Teaching of Statistics, Vol. 7*. Unesco, Paris, pp. 27–39.

Greeno, J. 1991. Number sense as situated knowing in a conceptual domain. *Journal for Research in Mathematics Education*. **22** (3), pp. 170–218.

Greeno, J. 1994. Gibson's affordances. *Psychological Review*, **101** (2), pp. 336–42.

Greeno, J., Smith, D. and Moore, J. 1993. Transfer of situated learning. In Detterman, D. and Sternberg, R. (eds), *Transfer on Trial: Intelligence, Cognition and Instruction*. Abbex, Norwood, pp. 99–167.

Griffin, P. 1989. Teaching takes place in time, learning takes place over time. *Mathematics Teaching*, **126**, pp. 12–13.

Griffin, P. and Gates, P. 1989. *Project Mathematics UPDATE: PM753A, B ,C, D, Preparing To Teach Angle, Equations, Ratio and Probability*. Open University, Milton Keynes.

Hall, E. 1981. *The Silent Language*. Anchor Press, Doubleday, New York.

Halmos, P. 1975. The problem of learning to teach. *American Mathematical Monthly*, **82** (5), pp. 466–76.

Halmos, P. 1980. The heart of mathematics. *American Mathematical Monthly*, **87** (7), pp. 519–24.

Halmos, P. 1985. *I Want to be a Mathematician: An Automathography*. Springer-Verlag, New York.

Halmos, P. 1994. What is teaching? *American Mathematical Monthly*, **101** (9), pp. 848–854.

Hamilton, E. and Cairns, H. 1961. *The Collected Dialogues of Plato, Bollingen Series LXXI*. Princeton University Press, Princeton.

Hamming, R. webref. *The Unreasonable Effectiveness of Mathematics*. www. lecb.ncifcrf. gov/~toms/Hamming.unreasonable.html.

Hamming, R. 1980. The unreasonable effectiveness of mathematics. *American Mathematical Monthly*, **87** (2), pp. 81–90.

Hanson, N. 1958. *Patterns of Discovery: An Inquiry into the Conceptual Foundations of Science*. Cambridge University Press.

Harel, G. and Kaput, J. 1992. The role of conceptual entities and their symbols in building advanced mathematical concepts. In Tall, D. (ed.), *Advanced Mathematical Thinking*. Kluwer, Dordrecht, pp. 82–94.

Harré, R. and van Langenhove, L. (eds). 1999. *Positioning Theory: Moral Contexts of Intentional Action*. Blackwell, Oxford.

Harré, R. and van Langenhove, L. 1992. Varieties of positioning. *Journal for the Theory of Social Behaviour*, **20**, pp. 393–407.

Hart, K. 1993. Confidence in success. In Hirabayashi, I., Nohda, N., Shigematsu, K. and Lin, F-L. (eds). *Psychology of Mathematics Education, PME XVII, Vol. 1*, University of Tsukuba, Tsukuba, pp. 17–31.

Hart, K, 1981. Ratio and proportion. In Hart, K. (ed.), *Children's Understanding of Mathematics: 11–16*. John Murray, London.

Hart, K. 1984. *Ratio: Children's Strategies and Errors*. NFER-Nelson, Windsor.

Hart, K., Brown, M., Küchemann, D., Kerlsake, D., Ruddock, G. and McCartney, M. 1981. *Children's Understanding of Mathematics*. John Murray, London.

Healy, L. and Hoyles, C. 2000. Study of proof conceptions in algebra. *Journal for Research in Mathematics Education*, **31** (4), pp. 396–428.

Hewitt, D. 1994. *The Principle of Economy in the Learning and Teaching of Mathematics*. Unpublished Ph.D dissertation, Open University, Milton Keynes.

Hewitt, D. 1999. Arbitrary and necessary, Part 1: A way of viewing the mathematics curriculum. *For the learning of Mathematics*, **19** (3), pp. 2–9.

Hiebert, J. and Carpenter, T. 1992. Learning and teaching with understanding. In Grouws, D. (ed.), *Handbook of Research on Mathematics Teaching and Learning*. MacMillan, New York, pp. 65–93.

Hiebert, J. and Wearne, D. 1992. Links between teaching and learning place value with understanding in first grade. *Journal for Research in Mathematics Education*, **23** pp. 98–122.

Higgins, K. webref. *Introduction to Performance Assessment*. oregonstate.edu/instruct/ed527/module2/527A2.htm.

Hogben, L. 1938. Clarity is not enough: An address on the needs and difficulties of the average pupil. *Mathematical Gazette*, **XXII** (249), pp. 105–23.

Holt, J. 1964. *How Children Fail*. Pitman, London.

Holt, J. 1967. *How Children Learn*. Pitman, New York.

Holt, J. 1970. *What Do I Do Monday?* Dutton, New York.

Holton, D. webref. *Personal Thoughts on an ICMI Study*. Department of Mathematics and Statistics, University of Otago, New Zealand. www.maths.otago.ac.nz/ICMI_Study.doc.

Houssart, J. 2001. Rival classroom discourses and inquiry mathematics: 'The whisperers'. *For the Learning of Mathematics*, **21** (3), pp. 2–8.

Hughes, M. 1986. *Children and Number: Difficulties in Learning Mathematics*. Blackwell, Oxford.

Jackson, P. 1992. *Untaught Lessons*. Teachers College Press, Columbia University, New York.

James, W. 1899 (reprinted Dover 1961). *Talks to Teachers on Psychology and to Students on Some of Life's Ideals*. Henry Holt, New York.

Johnson-Laird, P. and Wason, P. 1977. A theoretical analysis of insight into a reasoning task. In Johnson-Laird, P. and Wason, P. (eds), *Thinking: Readings in Cognitive Science*. Cambridge University Press, Cambridge, pp. 143–51.

Jong, T. and Ferguson-Hessler, M. 1996. Types and qualities of knowledge. *Educational Psychologist*, **31** (2), pp. 105–13.

Jowett, B. 1871. *The Dialogues of Plato, Vol. II*. Oxford University Press, Oxford.

Kahneman, D. and Tversky, A. 1982. Subjective probability: A judgement of representativeness. In Kahneman, D., Slovic, P. and Tversky, A. (eds), *Judgement Under Uncertainty: Heuristics and Biases*. Cambridge University Press, Cambridge, pp. 32–47.

Kant, I. 1781. (Meiklejohn, J. M. D., trans.) *Critique of Pure Reason*. MacMillan, London.

Kilpatrick, J., Swafford, J. and Findell, B. (eds) 2001. Adding it up: Helping children learn mathematics. *Mathematics Learning Study Committee*, National Academy Press, Washington.

King, A. 1993. From sage on the stage to guide on the side. *College Teaching*, **41** (1), pp. 30–5.

Kitcher, P. 1983. *The Nature of Mathematical Knowledge*. Oxford University Press, Oxford.

Kline, M. 1980. *Mathematics: The Loss of Certainty*. Oxford University Press, New York.

Kolb, D. A. 1984. *Experiential Learning: Experience as the Source of Learning and Development*. Prentice-Hall, Englewood Cliffs.

Krainer, K. 1993. Powerful tasks: A contribution to a high level of acting and reflecting in mathematics instruction. *Educational Studies in Mathematics*, **24**, pp. 65–93.

Krutetskii, V. 1976. *The Psychology of Mathematical Abilities in Schoolchildren*. University of Chicago Press, Chicago.

Küchemann, D. 1981. Algebra. In Hart, K., Brown, M., Küchemann, D., Kerlsake, D., Ruddock, G. and McCartney, M. (eds), *Children's Understanding of Mathematics*. John Murray, London, pp. 102–19.

Laborde, C. 1989. Audacity and reason: French research in mathematics education. *For the Learning of Mathematics*, **9** (3), pp. 31–6.

Lakatos, I. 1976. Proofs and refutations. In Worral, J. and Zahar, E. (eds), *The Logic of Mathematics Discovery*. Cambridge University Press, Cambridge.

Lakoff, G. and Johnson, M. 1980. *Metaphors We Live By*. University of Chicago Press, Chicago.

Lampert, M. 1986. Knowing, doing and teaching multiplication. *Cognition and Instruction*, **3**, pp. 305–42.

Lampert, M. 1990. When the problem is not the question and the solution is not the answer: Mathematical knowing and teaching. *American Educational Research Journal*, **27** (1), pp. 29–63.

Lampert, M. 2001. *Teaching Problems and the Problems of Teaching*. Yale University Press, New Haven.

Lave, J. 1988. *Cognition in Practice: Mind, Mathematics and Culture in Everyday Life*. Cambridge University Press, Cambridge.

Lave, J. 1993. The practice of learning. In Chalkin, S. and Lave, J. (eds), *Understanding Practice: Perspectives on Activity and Context*. Cambridge University Press, Cambridge, pp. 3–32.

Lave, J. 1993a. Situated learning in communities of practice. In Resnick, L., Levine, J. and Teasley, T. (eds), *Perspectives on socially shared cognition*. American Psychological Association, Washington DC, pp. 63–85.

Lave, J. 1996. Teaching as learning. *Practice, Mind, Culture and Activity*, **3** (3), pp. 149–64.

Lave, J. and Wenger, E. 1991. *Situated Learning: Legitimate Peripheral Participation*. Cambridge University Press, Cambridge.

Lawler, R. 1981. The progressive construction of mind. *Cognitive Science*, **5**, pp. 1–30.

Leapfrogs, 1982. *Geometric Images*. Association of Teachers of Mathematics, Derby.

Legrand, M. 1993. *Débate Scientifique en Cour de Mathématiques*. Repères IREM, no 10, Topiques Edition.

Legrand, M. 1995. Mathématiques, mythe ou réalité, un point de vue éthique sur l'enseignement scientifique, *Repères IREM*, **20** and **21**. Topiques Editions.

Leont'ev, A. 1979. The problem of activity in psychology. In Wertsch, J. (trans., ed.), *The Concept of Activity in Soviet Psychology*. Sharpe, New York, pp 37–71.

Leont'ev, A. 1981. *Psychology and the Language Learning Process*. Pergamon, Oxford.

Lerman, S. 2000. The social turn in mathematics education. In Boaler, J. (ed.), *Multiple Perspectives on Mathematics Teaching and Learning, International Perspectives on Mathematics Education*. Ablex, London, pp. 20–44.

Li, S. 1999. Does practice make perfect? *For the Learning of Mathematics*, **19** (3), pp. 33–5.

Li, Y. and Dù, S. 1987. (Crossley, J. and Lun, A., trans.) *Chinese Mathematics: A Concise History*. Clarendon Press, Oxford.

Locke, J. 1693. *Conduct of Understanding*. Quick Edition.

Love, E. and Mason, J. 1992. *Teaching Mathematics: Action and Awareness*. Open University, Milton Keynes.

MacGregor, M. 1991. *Making Sense of Algebra: Cognitive Processes Influencing Comprehension*. Deakin University, Geelong.

MacGregor, M. and Stacey, K. 1993. Cognitive models underlying students' formulation of simple linear equations. *Journal for Research in Mathematics Education*, **24** (3), pp. 217–32.

McIntosh, A. 1977. When will they ever learn? *Forum*, **19** (3), pp. 92–5.

Martino, A. and Maher, C. 1999. Teacher questioning to stimulate justification and generalization in mathematics: What research practice has taught us. *Journal of Mathematical Behavior*, **18** (1), pp. 53–78.

Marton, F. 1981. Phenomenography: Describing conceptions of the world around us. *Instructional Science*, **10**, pp. 177–200.

Marton, F. and Booth, S. 1997. *Learning and Awareness*. Erlbaum, Mahwah, NJ.

Marton, F. and Saljo, R. 1976. On qualitative differences in learning. *British Journal of Educational Psychology*, **46**, pp. 4–11.

Mason, J. 1979. Which medium, which message? *Visual Education*, Feb., pp. 29–33.

Mason, J. 1980. When is a symbol symbolic? *For the Learning of Mathematics*, **1** (2), pp. 8–12.

Mason, J. 1988. *ME234 Unit 3*. Open University, Milton Keynes.

Mason, J. 1989. Mathematical abstraction seen as a delicate shift of attention. *For the Learning of Mathematics*, **9** (2), pp. 2–8.

Mason, J. 1990. *Supporting Primary Mathematics: Space and Shape*. Open University, Milton Keynes.

Mason, J. 1992. Doing and construing mathematics in screen space. In Southwell, B., Perry, B. and Owens, K. (eds), *Space – The First and Final Frontier: Proceedings of the 15th Annual Conference of the Mathematics Education Research Group of Australasia* (MERGA-15), pp. 1–17.

Mason, J. 1996. Expressing generality and roots of algebra. In Berdnarz, N., Kieran, C. and Lee, L. (eds), *Approaches to Algebra: Perspectives for Research and Teaching*. Kluwer, Dordrecht, pp. 65–86.

Mason J. 1998. Enabling teachers to be real teachers: Necessary levels of awareness and structure of attention. *Journal of Mathematics Teacher Education*, **1** (3), pp. 243–67.

Mason, J. 2001. Modelling modelling: Where is the centre of gravity of-for-when modelling? In Matos, J., Blum, W., Houston, S. and Carreira, S. (eds), *Modelling and Mathematics Education: ICTMA 9 Applications in Science and Technology*. Horwood Publishing, Chichester, pp. 39–61.

Mason, J. 2001a. *Workshop notes*. Johor Baru.

Mason, J. 2002. *Mathematics Teaching Practice: A Guide for University and College Lecturers*. Horwood Publishing, Chichester.

Mason, J. 2002a. Generalisation and algebra: Exploiting children's powers. In Haggerty, L. (ed.), *Aspects of Teaching Secondary Mathematics: Perspectives on Practice*. RoutledgeFalmer, London, pp. 105–20.

Mason, J. 2002b. Minding your Qs and Rs: Effective Questioning and Responding in the Mathematics Classroom. In Haggerty, L. (ed.), *Aspects of Teaching Secondary Mathematics: Perspectives on Practice*. RoutledgeFalmer, London, pp. 248–58.

Mason, J. 2002c. *Researching Your Own Practice: The Discipline of Noticing*. RoutledgeFalmer, London.

Mason J., Burton, L. and Stacey, K. 1982. *Thinking Mathematically*. Addison Wesley, London.

Maturana, H. 1978. Biology of language: The epistemology of reality. In Miller, G. and Lenneberg, E. (eds), *Psychology and Biology of Language and Thought: Essays in Honor of Eric Lunneberg*. Academic Press, New York, pp. 27–63.

Maturana, H. webref. www.hum.auc.dk/~rasand/Artikler/M78BoL.html.

Maturana, H. and Varela, F. 1988. *The Tree of Knowledge: The Biological Roots of Human Understanding*. Shambala, Boston.

Meira, L. 1998. Making sense of instructional devices: The emergence of transparency in mathematical activity. *Journal for Research in Mathematics Education*, **29** (2), pp. 121–42.

Mellin-Olsen, S. 1987. *The Politics of Mathematics Education*. Reidel, Dordrecht.

Merseth, K. webref. *How Old Is the Shepherd?: An Essay About Mathematics Education*. lsc-net.terc.edu/do.cfm/paper/8198/show/use_set-papers_pres.

Merseth, K. 1993. How old is the shepherd?: An essay about mathematics education. *Phi Delta Kappan*, **74** (March 1993), pp. 548–54.

Michener, E. 1978. Understanding understanding mathematics. *Cognitive Science*, **2,** pp. 361–83.

Monroe, P. 1909. *A Textbook in the History of Education*. MacMillan, New York.

Montaigne, M. de 1588. (Screech, M. (trans.) 1987). *Michel de Montaigne: The Complete Essays*. Penguin, London.

Montessori, M. 1912. (George, A. (trans.) reprinted 1964). *The Montessori Method*. Schocken Books, New York.

Morris, R. (ed.) 1989. *Studies in Mathematics Education: The Teaching of Statistics, Vol. 7*. UNESCO, Paris.

Movshovits-Hadar, N. 1988. School mathematics theorems – An endless source of surprise. *For the Learning of Mathematics*, **8** (3), pp. 34–40.

Moyer, P. S. 2001. Are we having fun yet?: How teachers use manipulatives to teach mathematics. *Educational Studies in Mathematics*, **47**, pp. 175–97.

NCTM. webref. http://standards.nctm.org/document/chapter2/learn.htm.

Nesher, P. and Winograd, T. 1992. What fifth graders learn when they write their own math problems. *Educational Leadership*, **49** (7), pp. 64–7.

Nesher, P. 1987. Towards an instructional theory: The role of students' misconceptions. *For the Learning of Mathematics*, **7** (3), pp. 33–40.

Nesher, P. webref. *Towards an Instructional Theory: The Role of Students' Misconceptions*. construct.haifa.ac.il/~nesherp/Public.ht.

Newman, J. 1956. *The World of Mathematics: A Small Library of the Literature of Mathematics from A'h-mosé the Scribe to Albert Einstein, presented with commentaries and notes* (four vols.) Simon and Schuster, New York.

Nietz, J. A. 1966. *The Evolution of American Secondary School Textbooks*. Charles E. Tuttle, Rutland, VT.

Northfield, J. and Baird, J. 1992. *Learning from the PEEL Experience*. Monash University Printing Service, Melbourne.

Nunes, T. webref. *How Mathematics Teaching Develops Pupils' Reasoning Systems*. Inaugural Lecture, www.brookes.ac.uk/schools/social/psych/staff/tnicme2000/sld060.htm.

Nunes, T. 1999. Mathematics learning as the socialization of the mind. *Mind, Culture and Activity*, **6** (1), pp. 33–52.

Nunes, T., Schliemann, A. and Carraher, D. 1993. *Street Mathematics and School Mathematics*. Cambridge University Press, Cambridge.

Ollerton, M. 2002. *Learning and Teaching Mathematics without a Textbook*. Association of Teachers of Mathematics, Derby.

Ollerton, M. and Watson, A. 2001. *Inclusive Mathematics: 11–18*. Sage, London.

Open University. 1978. *M101 Mathematics Foundation Course, Block V Unit 1*. Open University, Milton Keynes, p. 31.

Orage, A. 1966 (4th edn). *On Love: With Some Aphorisms and Other Essays*. Samuel Weiser, New York.

Pasteur, L. 1979. *Oxford Dictionary of Quotations* (3rd edn). Oxford University Press, Oxford.

Papert, S. 1980. *Mind Storms*. Basic Books, New York.

Papert, S. 1993. *The Children's Machine: Rethinking School in the Age of the Computer*. Basic Books, New York. Reproduced at www.stemnet.nf.ca/~elmurphy/emurphy/papert.html.

Papy, G. 1963. *Modern Mathematics, Vol. 1*. Collier-Macmillan, London.

Peirce, C. S. 1902. The essence of mathematics (reprinted 1956). In Newman, J. R. (ed.), *The World of Mathematics*. Simon and Schuster, New York, p. 1779.

Piaget, J. 1937. *La Construction du Réal chez L'enfant*. De la Chaux et Niestlé, Neuchâtel, Switzerland.

Piaget, J. and Garcia, R. 1983. *Psychogenesis and the History of Science* (Feider, H. trans.) Columbia University Press, New York.

Piaget, J. 1970. *Genetic Epistemology*. Norton, New York.

Piaget, J. 1971. *Biology and Knowledge: An Essay on the Relations between Organic Regulations and Cognitive Processes*. University of Chicago Press, Chicago. (Originally published in French, 1963.)

Piaget, J. 1972. *The Principles of Genetic Epistemology* (Mays, W. trans.) Routledge and Kegan Paul, London.

Piaget, J. 1973. *To Understand Is To Invent: The Future of Education*. Grossman, New York. (Originally published in French, 1948.)

Piaget, J. 1980. *Adaptation and Intelligence: Organic Selection and Phenocopy*. University of Chicago Press, Chicago. (Originally published in French, 1974.)

Piaget, J. 1985. *The Equilibration of Cognitive Structures* (Brown, T. and Thampy, K. J. trans.) Harvard University Press, Cambridge, MA. (Original published 1975.)

Pirie, S. and Kieren, T. 1989. A recursive theory of mathematical understanding. *For the Learning of Mathematics*, **9** (3), pp. 7–11.

Pirie, S. and Kieren, T. 1994. Growth in mathematical understanding: How can we characterise it and how can we represent it? *Educational Studies in Mathematics*, **26** (2–3) pp. 165–90.

Plowden, B. 1967. *The Plowden Report: Children and Their Primary Schools*. HMSO, London.

Polanyi, M. 1958. *Personal Knowledge*. Routledge and Kegan Paul, London.

Polya, G. 1954. *Induction and Analogy in Mathematics*. Princeton University Press, Princeton.

Polya, G. 1957. *How to Solve it*. Anchor, New York.

Polya, G. 1962. *Mathematical Discovery: On Understanding, Learning and Teaching Problem Solving*. Combined edition, Wiley, New York.

Pramling, I. 1994. *Becoming Able: Testing a Phenomenographic Approach to Develop Children's Ways of Conceiving the World Around Us*. www.ped.gu.se/biorn/phgraph/civil/graphica/oth.su/praml94.html.

Renkl, A., Mandl, H. and Gruber, H. 1996. Inert knowledge: Analyses and remedies. *Educational Psychologist*, **31** (2), pp. 115–21.

Rig Veda, Samhita 1.164.20.

Rosnick, P. and Clement, R. 1980. Learning without understanding: The effect of tutoring strategies on algebra misconceptions. *Journal of Mathematical Behaviour*, **3** (1), pp. 3–27.

Runesson, U. 1999. The pedagogy of variation: Different ways of handling a mathematical topic. *Acta Univertsitatis Gothoburgensis*, Göteborg, University of Göteborg.

Runesson, U. 2001. What matters in the mathematics classroom?: Exploring critical differences in the space of learning. In Bergsten, C. (ed.), *Proceedings of NORMA01*, Kristianstad.

Russell, B. 1926. *On Education: Especially in Early Childhood*. George Allen and Unwin, London.

Ryle, G. 1949. *The Concept of Mind*. Hutchinson, London.

Schoenfeld, A. 1985. *Mathematical Problem Solving*. Academic Press, New York.

Schoenfeld, A. 1987. Confessions of an accidental theorist. *For the Learning of Mathematics*, **7** (1), pp. 30–8.

Schools Council 1965. *Mathematics in Primary Schools, Curriculum Bulletin No. 1*. HMSO, London.

Searle, J. 1987. Minds and brains without programs. In Blakemore, C. and Greenfield, S. (eds), *Mindwaves: Thoughts on Intelligence, Identity and Consciousness*. Blackwell, Oxford, pp. 209–33.

Selden, A. and Selden, J. webref. *Constructivism*. www.maa.org/t_and_l/sampler/construct.html.

Sfard, A. 1991. On the dual nature of mathematical conceptions: Reflections on processes and objects as different sides of the same coin. *Educational Studies in Mathematics*, **22**, pp. 1–36.

Sfard, A. 1992. Operational origins of mathematical notions and the quandary of reification: The case of function. In Dubinsky, E. and Harel, G. (eds), *The Concept of Function: Aspects of Epistemology and Pedagogy*. Mathematical Association of America, Washington.

Sfard, A. 1994. The gains and pitfalls of reification: The case of algebra. *Educational Studies in Mathematics*, **26**, pp. 191–228.

Sfard, A. 1994a. Reification as the birth of metaphor. *For the Learning of Mathematics*, **14** (1), pp. 44–55.

Shiu, C. 1978. *The Development of Some Mathematical Concepts in School Children*. Unpublished Ph.D thesis, University of Nottingham.

Shuard, H., Walsh, A., Goodwin, J. and Worcester, V. 1991. *Calculators, Children and Mathematics*. Simon and Shuster, London.

Shulman, L. 1987. Knowledge and teaching: Foundations of the new reform. *Harvard Educational Review*, **57** (1), pp. 1–14.

Shulman, L. webref. *President of the Foundation: Lee Shulman.* www.carnegie foundation.org/president/biography.htm.

Sierpinska, A. 1987. Humanities students and epistemological obstacles related to limits. *Educational Studies in Mathematics,* **18**, pp. 371–97.

Sierpinska, A. 1994. *Understanding in Mathematics.* Falmer Press, London. pp. 78–9.

Sigel, I. 1981. Social experience in the development of representational thought: Distancing theory. In Sigel, I., Brodzinsky, D. M. and Golinkoff, R. M. (eds), *New directions in Piagetian Theory and Practice.* Lawrence Erlbaum, Hillsdale, NJ.

Skemp, R. 1966. The development of mathematical activity in schoolchildren. In Brookes, W. (ed.), *The Development of Mathematical Activity in Children: The Place of the Problem in this Development.* ATM, Nelson, pp. 76–8.

Skemp, R. 1971. *The Psychology of Learning Mathematics.* Penguin, Harmondsworth.

Skemp, R. 1976. Relational understanding and instrumental understanding. *Mathematics Teaching,* **77**, pp. 20–6.

Skemp, R. 1979. *Intelligence, Learning and Action: A Foundation for Theory and Practice in Education.* Wiley, Chichester.

Smith, M. K. 1997. webref. www.infed.org/thinkers/et-mont.htm.

Smith, T. 1954. *Number: An Account of Work in Number with Children Throughout the Primary School Stage.* Basil Blackwell, Oxford.

Snyder, B. 1971. *The Hidden Curriculum.* Alfred-Knopff, New York.

Spencer, H. 1878. *Education: Intellectual, Moral and Physical.* Williams and Norgate, London.

Spencer, H. 1911. *Essays on Education, etc.* (Charles W. Eliot, intro.) Dent, London. (The constituent essays of this collection were first published in the 1850s.)

Steffe, L. and Gale, J. 1995. *Constructivism in Education.* Erlbaum, Mahwah, NJ.

Steffe, L., Nesher, P., Cobb, P., Goldin, G. and Greer, B. 1996. *Theories of Mathematical Learning.* Erlbaum, Mahwah, NJ.

Stein, S. 1987. Gresham's law: Algorithm drives out thought. *For the Learning of Mathematics,* **7** (2), pp. 2–4.

Stenmark, J. K. (ed.) 1991. *Mathematics Assessment: Myth, Models, Good Questions and Practical Suggestions.* NCTM, Reston, VA.

Stigler, J. and Hiebert, J. 1998. Teaching is a cultural activity. *American Educator,* Winter 1998, pp. 4–11.

Stigler J. and Hiebert, J. 1999. *The Teaching Gap: Best Ideas from the World's Teachers for Improving Education in the Classroom.* Free Press, New York.

Streefland, L. (ed.) 1991. *Realistic Mathematics Education in Primary School.* CD-B Press/Freudenthal Institute, Utrecht, p. 63.

Streefland, L. 1991. *Fractions in Realistic Mathematics Education.* Kluwer, Dordrecht, p. 50 and p. 63.

Tahta, D. 1972. *A Boolean Anthology: Selected Writings of Mary Boole on Mathematics Education.* Association of Teachers of Mathematics, Derby.

Tahta, D. 1980. About geometry, *For the Learning of Mathematics,* **1** (1), pp. 2–9.

Tahta, D. 1981. Some thoughts arising from the new Nicolet Films, *Mathematics Teaching,* **94**, pp. 25–9. Reprinted in Beeney, R., Jarvis, M., Tahta, D., Warwick, J. and White, D. (1982) *Geometric Images,* Leapfrogs, Association of Teachers of Mathematics, Derby, pp. 117-18.

Tahta, D. 1991. Understanding and desire. In Pimm, D. and Love, E. (eds), *Teaching and Learning School Mathematics.* Hodder and Stoughton, London, pp. 220–46.

Tahta, D. and Brookes, W. 1966. The genesis of mathematical activity. In Brookes,

W. (ed.), *The Development of Mathematical Activity in Children: The Place of the Problem in this Development*. ATM, Nelson, pp. 3–8.

Tall, D. and Vinner, S. 1981. Concept image and concept definition in mathematics with particular reference to limits and continuity. *Educational Studies in Mathematics*, **12** (2), pp. 151–69. Also www.warwick.ac.uk/staff/David.Tall/pdfs/dot1988e-concept-image-icme.pdf.

Taylor, C. 1991. The dialogical self. In Hiley, D., Bohman, J. and Shusterman, R. (eds), *The Interpretive Turn: Philosophy, Science, Culture*. Cornell University Press, Ithaca.

Teplow, D. webref. *Fresh Approaches: Promoting Teaching Excellence*. www.acme_assn.org/almanac/jan97.htm.

Thompson, P. and Thompson, A. 1990. Salient aspects of experience with concrete manipulatives. In Booker, G., Cobb, P. and de Menduciti, T. (eds), *Proceedings of PME XIV*. Oaxtepec, Mexico, pp. 46–52.

Thorndike, E. 1914. *Educational Psychology: Briefer Cause*. New York: Teachers College, Columbia University.

Thorndike, E. 1922. *The Psychology of Arithmetic*. Macmillan, New York.

Thurston, W. 1990. Mathematical education. *Notices of the American Mathematical Society*, **37**, pp. 844–850. Reprinted in *For the Learning of Mathematics*, **15** (1) (February 1995), pp. 29–37.

Tizard, B. and Hughes, M. 1984. *Young Children Learning: Talking and Thinking at Home and at School*. Fontana, London.

Treffers, A. 1986. *Three Dimensions: A Model of Goal and Theory Description in Mathematics Instruction – The Wiskobas Project*. Kluwer, Dordrecht.

Turing, A. 1950. Computing machinery and intelligence. *Mind: A Quarterly Review of Philosophy and Psychology*, **59** (236), pp. 433–60.

Turing, A. webref. http://cogprints.ecs.soton.ac.uk/archive/00000499/.

Tversky, A. and Kahneman, D. 1982. Judgement under uncertainty: Heuristics and biases. In Kahneman, D., Slovic, P. and Tversky, A. (eds), *Judgement Under Uncertainty: Heuristics and Biases*. Cambridge University Press, Cambridge, pp. 3–20.

Ulich, R. (ed.) 1999. *Three Thousand Years of Educational Wisdom: Selections from the Great Documents*. Harvard University Press, London.

Van den Brink, J. 1993. Different aspects in designing mathematics education: Three examples from the Freudenthal Institute. *Educational Studies in Mathematics*, **24** (1), pp. 35–64.

Van Hiele, P. 1986. *Structure and Insight: A Theory of Mathematics Education*. Academic Press, Orlando, FL.

Van Hiele-Geldof, D. 1957. The didactiques of geometry in the lowest class of secondary school. Reprinted in Fuys, D., Geddes, D. and Tichler, R. (eds) (1984) *English Translation of Selected Writings of Dina van Hiele-Geldof and Pierre M. van Hiele*. National Science Foundation, Brooklyn College.

Van Lehn, K. 1990. *Mind Bugs: The Origins of Procedural Misconceptions*. Bradford Book, MIT Press, Cambridge, MA.

Van Maanen, J. (ed.) 1977. *Organizational Careers: Some New Perspectives*. Wiley, London.

Vergnaud, G. 1981. Quelques orientations théoriques et méthodologiques des recherches françaises en didactique des mathématiques. *Actes du Vième Coilloque de PME, Vol. 2*. Edition IMAG, Genoble, pp. 7–17.

Vergnaud, G. 1982. A classification of cognitive tasks and operations of thought involved in addition and subtraction problems. In Carpenter, T., Moser, J. and

Romberg, T. (eds), *Addition and Subtraction: A Cognitive Perspective*. Erlbaum, Mahwah, NJ, pp. 39–59.

Vergnaud, G. 1982a. Cognitive developmental psychology and research in mathematics education: Some theoretical and methodological issues. *For the Learning of Mathematics*, **3** (2), pp. 31–41.

Vergnaud, G. 1983. Multiplicative structures. In Lesh, R. and Landau, M. (eds), *Acquisition of Mathematics Concepts and Structures*. Academic Press, New York, pp. 127–74.

Vico, G.-B. 1744. *The New Science*. (Bergin, T. and Fisch, M. trans. 1961). Anchor Books, New York.

Voight, J. 1985. Patterns and routines in classroom interaction. *Recherches en Didactiques des Mathématiques*, **6** (9), pp. 69–118.

Von Glasersfeld, E. 1983. Learning as a constructive activity. *PME-NA Proceedings*. Montreal, 1983, pp. 41–69.

Von Glasersfeld, E. 1984. An introduction to radical constructivism. In Watzlawick, P. (ed.), *The Invented Reality*. Norton, London, pp. 17–40.

Von Glasersfeld, E. 1985. Reconstructing the concept of knowledge. *Archives de Psychologie*, **53**, pp. 91–101.

Von Glasersfeld, E. 1991. Abstraction, re-presentation and reflection. In Steffe, L. (ed.), *Epistemological Foundations of Mathematical Experience*. Springer, New York, pp. 45–67.

Von Glasersfeld, E. 1996. Learning and adaptation in constructivism. In Smith, L. (ed.), *Critical Readings on Piaget*. Routledge, London, pp. 22–7.

Vygotsky, L. 1962. *Thought and Language*, MIT Press, Cambridge, MA.

Vygotsky, L. 1965. (Hanfmann, E. and Vakar, G. trans.) *Thought and Language*. MIT Press, Cambridge, MA.

Vygotsky, L. 1978. *Mind in Society: the Development of the Higher Psychological Processes*. Harvard University Press, London.

Vygotsky, L. 1979. The genesis of higher mental functions. In Wertsch, J. (trans., ed.), *The Concept of Activity in Soviet Psychology*. Sharpe, New York, pp. 144–88.

Warden, J. 1981. Making space for doing and talking with groups in a primary classroom. In Floyd, A. (ed.), *Developing Mathematical Thinking*. Addison Wesley, London, pp. 248–57.

Warfield, V. webref. *Calculus By Scientific Debate As An Application Of Didactique*. Department of Mathematics, University of Washington. www.math.washington.edu/~warfield/articles/Calc&Didactique.html.

Watson, A. 2001. Low attainers exhibiting higher-order mathematical thinking. *Support for Learning*, **16** (4), Nov., pp. 179–83.

Watson, A. 2002. Working with students on questioning to promote mathematical thinking. *Mathematics Education Review*, **15**, pp. 32–42.

Watson, A. 2002a. Teaching for understanding. In Haggerty, L. (ed.), *Aspects of Teaching Secondary Mathematics: Perspectives on Practice*. RoutledgeFalmer, London.

Watson, A. and Mason, J. 2002. Extending example spaces as a learning/teaching strategy in mathematics. In Cockburn, A. and Nardi, E. (eds), *Proceedings of PME 26*. University of East Anglia, Vol. 4, p. 377.

Watson A. and Mason, J. 2002a. Student-generated examples in the learning of mathematics. *Canadian Journal of Science, Mathematics and Technology Education*, **2** (2), pp. 237–49.

Watson, A. and Mason, J. (in press). *Mathematics as a Constructive Activity: The Role of Learner-generated Examples*. Erlbaum, Mahwah, NJ.

Waywood, A. 1992. Journal writing and learning mathematics. *For the Learning of Mathematics*, **12** (2), pp. 34–43.

Waywood, A. 1994. Informal writing-to-learn as a dimension of a student profile. *Educational Studies in Mathematics*, **27**, pp. 321–40.

Wertheimer, M. 1961. *Productive Thinking* (enlarged edition, Wertheimer, E. ed.) Social Science Paperbacks with Tavistock Publications, London.

Wertsch, J. 1991. *Voices of the Mind: A Sociocultural Approach to Meditated Action*. Harvard University Press, Cambridge, MA.

Wheatley, G. webref. *Quick Draw: A Simple Warm-up Exercise Helps Students Develop Mental Imagery of Mathematics*. www.learnnc.org/index.nsf/doc/quickdraw.

Wheatley, G. 1992. The role of reflection in mathematics learning. *Educational Studies in Mathematics*, **23** (5), pp. 529–41.

Wheeler, D. 1965. Teaching for understanding. *Mathematics Teaching*, **33**, pp. 47–50.

Wheeler, D. 1982. Mathematization matters. *For the Learning of Mathematics*, **3** (1), pp. 45–7.

Whitehead, A. 1911 (reset 1948). *An Introduction to Mathematics*. Oxford University Press, London.

Whitehead, A. 1932. *The Aims of Education and Other Essays*. Williams and Norgate, London.

Whiteside, D. 1968. *The Mathematical Papers of Isaac Newton, Vol. II, 1667–1670*. Cambridge University Press, Cambridge.

Wigner E. webref. *The Unreasonable Effectiveness of Mathematics in the Natural Sciences*. www.dartmouth.edu/~matc/MathDrama/reading/Wigner.html.

Wigner, E. 1960. The unreasonable effectiveness of mathematics in the natural sciences. *Communications in Pure and Applied Mathematics,* **13** (1), pp. 1–14.

Winograd, T. and Flores, F. 1986. *Understanding Computers and Cognition: A New Foundation for Design*. Ablex, Norwood.

Wood, T. 1998. Funneling or focusing? Alternative patterns of communication in mathematics class. In Steinbring, H., Bartolini-Bussi, M. G. and Sierpinska, A. (eds), *Language and Communication in the Mathematics Classroom*. National Council of Teachers of Mathematics, Reston, VA, pp. 167–78.

Wood, D. and Middleton, D. 1975. A study of assisted problem-solving. *British Journal of Psychology*, **66** (2), pp. 181–91.

Wood, D., Bruner, J. and Ross, G. 1976. The role of tutoring in problem solving. *Journal of Child Psychology*, **17**, pp. 89–100.

Yackel, E. 2001. Perspectives on arithmetic from classroom-based research in the USA. In Anghileri, J. (ed.), *Principles and Practices in Arithmetic Teaching*. Open University Press, Buckingham, pp. 15–31.

Zaehner, R. (trans.) 1966. *Hindu Scriptures*. Dent and Sons, New York.

Zammattio, C., Marinoni, A. and Brizio, A. 1980. *Leonardo the Scientist*. McGraw-Hill, New York.

Zeichner, K. and Liston, D. 1987. Teaching student teachers to reflect. *Harvard Educational Review*, **57** (1), pp. 23–48.

Zeichner, K. and Liston, D. 1996. *Reflective Teaching*. Erlbaum, Mahwah, NJ.

Index

abilities: learning 119–20

abstraction 59, 60, 154; and classification 134–5, 154; education 45; empirical 171; learning 59, 60, 154; mathematics education 253, 256–7; nature of 133, 134; pseudo-empirical 171; reflective 171–2

accommodation: learning 149–51

actions: APOS theory 172; formulated 290; for learning 153–61; unformulated 290–1

activity: and learning 235–7; mathematical 228–59, 260–79, 280–7

activity theory 84–92; activity levels 85–6; attention 90–1; community of practice 95–6; consciousness for two 88–9; internalisation 85; labelling distinctions 91–2; mediation 85; psychological processes 87, 95; realm of developmental possibilities 89–90; zone of proximal development 85, 88, 89, 90

adaptation: learning 149–50

affordances: mathematics education 246–7, 259

Ainley, Janet: questioning 270–1; using situations 250–1

algebra: and mental imagery 130; middle years 19; necessity for survival 134; use by children 134

America see USA

analysis: and learning 59, 118

angles: triangles 22–3, 102, 252

APOS theory 172–3

apparatus: enactive mode of interaction 3; mathematics teaching 2, 3, 253–9

arbitrariness: mathematics 159–60

arithmetic: early years 7–9; fractions 18; horizontal 14–15; middle years 16–17;

Plato's views 99; street 16–17; vertical 14–15

arithmetic teaching: Philip Ballard 50–1; England 50–1; USA 51, see also mathematics teaching

assessment: understanding 305–10

assimilation: in learning 147, 149–51

attention: activity theory 90–1; structure of see structure of attention

Ausubel, David: advance organisers 258–9; types of learning 152–3

authentic activity: learning motivation 108–10; and zone of proximal relevance 110

awareness: in articulation 63; educating 61–3, 161, 204; in-action 62; and knowing 290; and learning 63; mathematisation 189; nature of 188–9; and reflection 283; of sense 62; structuring 58; and understanding 300

awareness of awareness 189, 290

babies: discernment 125–6

Bachelard, Gaston: epistemological obstacles 302–3

BACOMET group: intended curriculum 106–8

Balacheff, Nicolas: problématique 83–4, 252

Ballard, Philip: arithmetic teaching 50–1

Banwell, Colin: children's learning abilities 123; invariance amidst change 194–5; using situations 249–50

Bartlett, Frederick: memory 31

Bauersfeld, Heinrich: activity theory 87; funnelling 274–5; integrated teaching 224; interactionism 76–7

Bell, Alan: activity and learning 235–7; diagnostic teaching 233–5

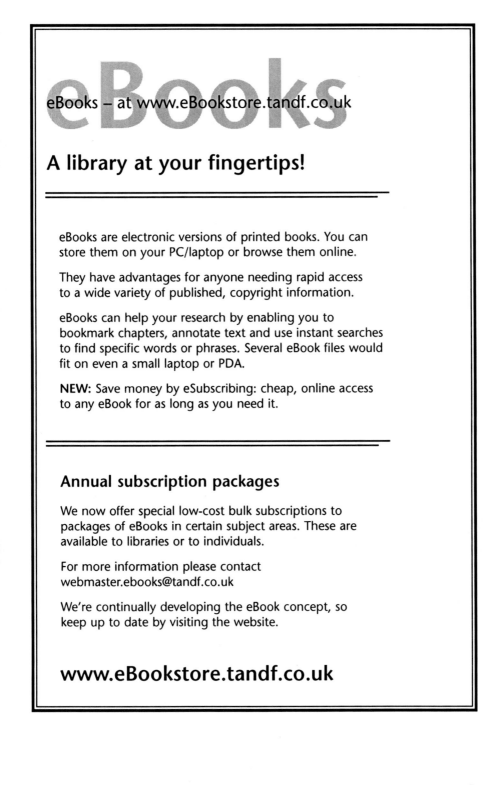